Kaplan Publishing are constantly fi
ways to make a difference to your s
exciting online resources really do
different to students looking for ex

This book comes with free MyKaplan online resources so that you can study anytime, anywhere. This free online resource is not sold separately and is included in the price of the book.

Having purchased this book, you have access to the following online study materials:

CONTENT	ACCA (including FFA,FAB,FMA)		FIA (excluding FFA,FAB,FMA)	
	Text	Kit	Text	Kit
Eletronic version of the book	✓	✓	✓	✓
Check Your Understanding Test with instant answers	✓			
Material updates	✓	✓	✓	✓
Latest official ACCA exam questions*		✓		
Extra question assistance using the signpost icon**		✓		
Timed questions with an online tutor debrief using clock icon***		✓		
Interim assessment including questions and answers	✓		✓	
Technical answers	✓	✓	✓	✓

* Excludes F1, F2, F3, F4, FAB, FMA and FFA; for all other papers includes a selection of questions, as released by ACCA

** For ACCA P1-P7 only

*** Excludes F1, F2, F3, F4, FAB, FMA and FFA

How to access your online resources

Kaplan Financial students will already have a MyKaplan account and these extra resources will be available to you online. You do not need to register again, as this process was completed when you enrolled. If you are having problems accessing online materials, please ask your course administrator.

If you are not studying with Kaplan and did not purchase your book via a Kaplan website, to unlock your extra online resources please go to www.mykaplan.co.uk/addabook (even if you have set up an account and registered books previously). You will then need to enter the ISBN number (on the title page and back cover) and the unique pass key number contained in the scratch panel below to gain access.

You will also be required to enter additional information during this process to set up or confirm your account details.

If you purchased through Kaplan Flexible Learning or via the Kaplan Publishing website you will automatically receive an e-mail invitation to MyKaplan. Please register your details using this email to gain access to your content. If you do not receive the e-mail or book content, please contact Kaplan Publishing.

Your Code and Information

This code can only be used once for the registration of one book online. This registration and your online content will expire when the final sittings for the examinations covered by this book have taken place. Please allow one hour from the time you submit your book details for us to process your request.

Please scratch the film to access your MyKaplan code.

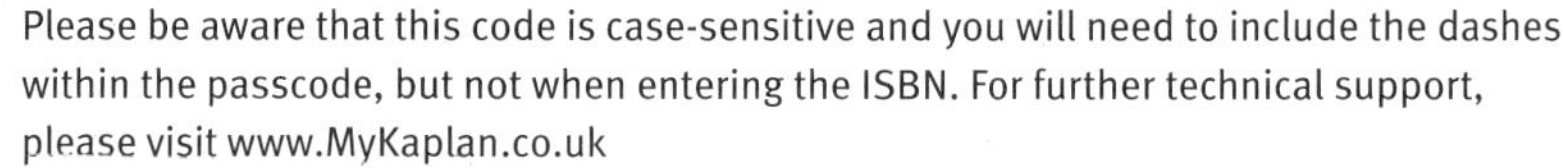

Please be aware that this code is case-sensitive and you will need to include the dashes within the passcode, but not when entering the ISBN. For further technical support, please visit www.MyKaplan.co.uk

ACCA

Paper P7 (INT/UK)

Advanced Audit and Assurance

Study Text

British Library Cataloguing-in-Publication Data

A catalogue record for this book is available from the British Library.

Published by:
Kaplan Publishing UK
Unit 2 The Business Centre
Molly Millars Lane
Wokingham
Berkshire
RG41 2QZ

ISBN: 978-1-78415-821-7

Acknowledgements

This product includes content from the International Auditing and Assurance Standards Board (IAASB) and the International Ethics Standards Board of Accountants (IESBA), published by the International Federation of Accountants (IFAC) in 2015 and is used with permission of IFAC.

This product contains material that is ©Financial Reporting Council Ltd (FRC). Adapted and reproduced with the kind permission of the Financial Reporting Council. All rights reserved. For further information, please visit www.frc.org.uk or call +44 (0)20 7492 2300.

This Product includes propriety content of the International Accounting Standards Board which is overseen by the IFRS Foundation, and is used with the express permission of the IFRS Foundation under licence. All rights reserved. No part of this publication may be reproduced, stored in a retrieval system, or transmitted in any form or by any means, electronic, mechanical, photocopying, recording, or otherwise, without prior written permission of Kaplan Publishing and the IFRS Foundation.

IFRS

Chapter 23	Additional practice questions	603
Chapter 24	References	669

Contents

		Page
Chapter 1	Regulation in a global economy	1
Chapter 2	Code of ethics and conduct	31
Chapter 3	Professional appointments	77
Chapter 4	Quality control	89
Chapter 5	Advertising, publicity, obtaining professional work and fees	117
Chapter 6	Tendering	133
Chapter 7	Money laundering	143
Chapter 8	Professional responsibilities and liability	155
Chapter 9	Planning, materiality and assessing the risk of misstatement	199
Chapter 10	Group and transnational audits	257
Chapter 11	Evidence	289
Chapter 12	Completion	335
Chapter 13	Auditors' reports	367
Chapter 14	Reports to those charged with governance	421
Chapter 15	Other assignments	431
Chapter 16	Prospective financial information	463
Chapter 17	Audit of social, environmental and integrated reporting	483
Chapter 18	Forensic audits	507
Chapter 19	Outsourcing and internal audit	521
Chapter 20	UK syllabus only: Auditing aspects of insolvency	531
Chapter 21	INT syllabus only: Audit of performance information in the public sector	549
Chapter 22	P7 Financial reporting revision	561

chapter

ntroduction

Paper Introduction

This document references IFRS® Standards and IAS® Standards, which are authored by the International Accounting Standards Board (the Board), and published in the 2016 IFRS Standards Red Book.

How to Use the Materials

These Kaplan Publishing learning materials have been carefully designed to make your learning experience as easy as possible and to give you the best chances of success in your examinations.

The product range contains a number of features to help you in the study process. They include:

(1) Detailed study guide and syllabus objectives

(2) Description of the examination

(3) Study skills and revision guidance

(4) Study text

(5) Question practice

The sections on the study guide, the syllabus objectives, the examination and study skills should all be read before you commence your studies. They are designed to familiarise you with the nature and content of the examination and give you tips on how to best to approach your learning.

The **study text** comprises the main learning materials and gives guidance as to the importance of topics and where other related resources can be found. Each chapter includes:

- The **learning objectives** contained in each chapter, which have been carefully mapped to the examining body's own syllabus learning objectives or outcomes. You should use these to check you have a clear understanding of all the topics on which you might be assessed in the examination.
- The **chapter diagram** provides a visual reference for the content in the chapter, giving an overview of the topics and how they link together.
- The **content** for each topic area commences with a brief explanation or definition to put the topic into context before covering the topic in detail. You should follow your studying of the content with a review of the illustration/s. These are worked examples which will help you to understand better how to apply the content for the topic.
- **Test your understanding** sections provide an opportunity to assess your understanding of the key topics by applying what you have learned to short questions. Answers can be found at the back of each chapter.

- **Summary diagrams** complete each chapter to show the important links between topics and the overall content of the paper. These diagrams should be used to check that you have covered and understood the core topics before moving on.
- **Question practice** is provided at the back of each text.

Quality and accuracy are of the utmost importance to us so if you spot an error in any of our products, please send an email to mykaplanreporting@kaplan.com with full details, or follow the link to the feedback form in MyKaplan.

Our Quality Coordinator will work with our technical team to verify the error and take action to ensure it is corrected in future editions.

Icon Explanations

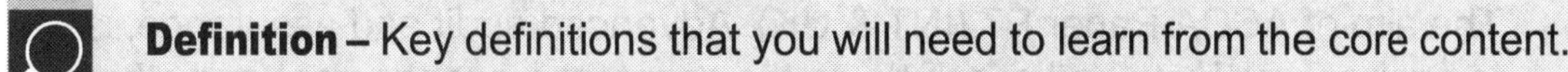

Definition – Key definitions that you will need to learn from the core content.

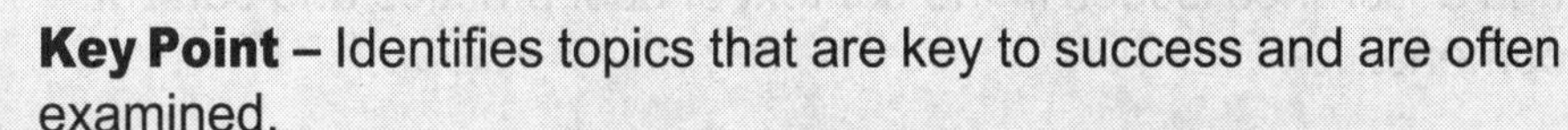

Key Point – Identifies topics that are key to success and are often examined.

New – Identifies topics that are brand new in papers that build on, and therefore also contain, learning covered in earlier papers.

Test Your Understanding – Exercises for you to complete to ensure that you have understood the topics just learned.

Illustration – Worked examples help you understand the core content better.

Tricky topic – When reviewing these areas care should be taken and all illustrations and test your understanding exercises should be completed to ensure that the topic is understood.

Tutorial note – Included to explain some of the technical points in more detail.

Footsteps – Helpful tutor tips.

Online subscribers

Our online resources are designed to increase the flexibility of your learning materials and provide you with immediate feedback on how your studies are progressing. Ask your local customer services staff if you are not already a subscriber and wish to join.

If you are subscribed to our online resources you will find:

(1) Online reference ware: reproduces your Study Text online, giving you anytime, anywhere access.

(2) Online testing: provides you with additional online objective testing so you can practice what you have learned further.

(3) Online performance management: immediate access to your online testing results. Review your performance by key topics and chart your achievement through the course relative to your peer group.

Paper introduction

Paper background

The aim of ACCA Paper P7 (INT & UK), Advanced audit and assurance, is to analyse, evaluate and conclude on the assurance engagement and other audit and assurance issues in the context of best practice and current developments.

Objectives of the syllabus

- Recognise the legal and regulatory environment and its impact on audit and assurance practice.
- Demonstrate the ability to work effectively on an assurance or other service engagement within a professional and ethical framework.
- Assess and recommend appropriate quality control policies and procedures in practice management and recognise the auditor's position in relation to the acceptance and retention of professional appointments.
- Identify and formulate the work required to meet the objectives of audit assignments and apply the International Standards on Auditing.
- Identify and formulate the work required to meet the objectives of non-audit assignments.
- Evaluate findings and the results of work performed and draft suitable reports on assignments.
- Understand the current issues and developments relating to the provision of audit-related and assurance services.

Core areas of the syllabus

- Regulatory environment
- Professional and ethical considerations
- Practice management
- Audit of historical financial information
- Other assignments
- Reporting
- Current issues and developments.

Approach to INT and UK syllabus elements

Due to the alignment of the INT and UK syllabus elements one text has been produced to address both variants. Both streams apply the principles of International Standards on Auditing (ISAs) and International Financial Reporting Standards (IFRS® Standards).

The International variant has been used as the basis of the text. Any variances relevant only to the UK syllabus (such as compliance with the Companies Act 2006) have been included at the end of each chapter (or section) in expandable text boxes headed "UK syllabus". All test your understandings have also been appended to reflect any UK specific variations.

Syllabus objectives

We have reproduced the ACCA's syllabus below, showing where the objectives are explored within this book. Within the chapters, we have broken down the extensive information found in the syllabus into easily digestible and relevant sections, called Content Objectives. These correspond to the objectives at the beginning of each chapter.

Syllabus learning objective	Chapter reference
A REGULATORY ENVIRONMENT	
1 International regulatory frameworks for audit and assurance services	
(a) Explain the need for laws, regulations, standards and other guidance relating to audit, assurance and related services.[2]	1

(b) Outline and explain the need for the legal and professional framework including: [2] 1

(i) public oversight of audit and assurance practice

(ii) the impact of corporate governance principles on audit and assurance practice

(iii) the role of audit committees and impact on audit and assurance practice (UK: discuss the provision of the UK Corporate Governance Code and its impact on audit and assurance practice).

2 Money laundering

(a) Define 'money laundering' and discuss international methods for combatting money laundering.[2] 7

(b) Explain the scope of criminal offences of money laundering and how professional accountants may be protected from criminal and civil liability.[2] 7

(c) Explain the need for ethical guidance in this area.[2] 7

(d) Describe how accountants meet their obligations to help prevent and detect money laundering including record keeping and reporting of suspicion to the appropriate regulatory body.[2] 7

(e) Explain the importance of customer due diligence (CDD) (*UK: 'know your customer' information (KYC)*) and recommend the information that should be gathered as part of CDD/KYC.[2] 7

(f) Recognise potentially suspicious transactions and assess their impact on reporting duties.[2] 7

(g) Describe, with reasons, the basic elements of an anti-money laundering program.[2] 7

3 Laws and regulations

(a) Compare and contrast the respective responsibilities of management and auditors concerning compliance with laws and regulations in an audit of financial statements.[2] 8

(b) Describe the auditors' considerations of compliance with laws and regulations and plan audit procedures when possible non-compliance is discovered.[2] 8

(c) Discuss how and to whom non-compliance should be reported.[2] 8

(d) Recognise when withdrawal from an engagement is necessary.[2] 8

B PROFESSIONAL AND ETHICAL CONSIDERATIONS

1 Code of ethics for professional accountants (UK: Code of ethics and conduct)

(a)	Explain the fundamental principles and the conceptual framework approach.[1]	2
(b)	Identify, evaluate and respond to threats to compliance with the fundamental principles.[3]	2
(c)	Discuss and evaluate the effectiveness of available safeguards.[3]	2
(d)	Recognise and advise on conflicts in the application of fundamental principles.[3]	2
(e)	Discuss the importance of professional scepticism in planning and performing an audit.[2]	9
(f)	Consider the ethical implications of the external auditor providing non-audit services to a client including an internal audit service.[2]	2
(g)	Assess whether an engagement has been planned and performed with an attitude of professional scepticism, and evaluate the implications.[3]	9

2 Fraud and error

(a)	Identify and develop an appropriate response to circumstances which indicate a high risk of error, irregularity, fraud or misstatement in the financial statements or a given situation.[2]	8
(b)	Compare and contrast the respective responsibilities of management and auditors for fraud and error.[2]	8
(c)	Describe the matters to be considered and procedures to be carried out to investigate actual and/or potential misstatements in a given situation.[2]	8
(d)	Explain how, why, when and to whom fraud and error should be reported and the circumstances in which an auditor should withdraw from an engagement.[2]	8
(e)	Discuss the current and possible future role of auditors in preventing, detecting and reporting error and fraud.[2]	8

3 Professional liability

(a)	Recognise circumstances in which professional accountants may have legal liability and the criteria that need to be satisfied for legal liability to be recognised.[2]	8

(b) Describe the factors to determine whether or not an auditor is negligent and discuss the auditor's potential liability in given situations.[2] 8

(c) Compare and contrast liability to client with liability owed to third parties (i.e. contract vs establishing a duty of care).[3] 8

(d) Evaluate the practicability and effectiveness of ways in which liability may be restricted including the use of liability limitation agreements.[3] 8

(e) Discuss and appraise the principal causes of audit failure and other factors that contribute to the 'expectation gap' (e.g. responsibilities for fraud and error) and recommend ways in which the expectation gap may be bridged.[3] 8

C PRACTICE MANAGEMENT

1 Quality control

(a) Explain the principles and purpose of quality control of audit and other assurance engagements.[1] 4

(b) Describe the elements of a system of quality control relevant to a given firm.[2] 4

(c) Select and justify quality control procedures that are applicable to a given audit engagement.[3] 4

(d) Assess whether an engagement has been planned and performed in accordance with professional standards and whether reports issued are appropriate in the circumstances.[3] 4

2 Advertising, publicity, obtaining professional work and fees

(a) Recognise situations in which specified advertisements are acceptable.[2] 5

(b) Discuss the restrictions on practice descriptions, the use of the ACCA logo and the names of practising firms.[2] 5

(c) Discuss the extent to which reference to fees may be made in promotional material.[2] 5

(d) Outline the determinants of fee-setting and justify the bases on which fees and commissions may and may not be charged for services.[3] 5

(e) Discuss the ethical and other professional problems, for example, lowballing, involved in establishing and negotiating fees for a specified assignment.[3] 5

3 Tendering

(a) Discuss the reasons why entities change their auditors/professional accountants.[2] 6

(b) Recognise and explain the matters to be considered when a firm is invited to submit a proposal or fee quote for an audit or other professional engagement.[2] 6

(c) Identify the information to be included in a proposal.[2] 6

4 Professional appointments

(a) Explain the matters to be considered and the procedures that an audit firm/professional accountant should carry out before accepting a specified new client/engagement or continuing with an existing engagement, including: [3] 3

(i) client acceptance

(ii) engagement acceptance

(iii) establish whether the preconditions for an audit are present

(iv) agreeing the terms of engagement.

(b) Recognise the key issues that underlie the agreement of the scope and terms of an engagement with a client.[2]

D AUDIT OF HISTORICAL FINANCIAL INFORMATION

1 Planning, materiality and assessing the risk of misstatement

(a) Define materiality and performance materiality and demonstrate how it should be applied in financial reporting and auditing.[2] 9

(b) Identify and explain business risks for a given assignment.[3] 9

(c) Identify and explain audit risks for a given assignment.[3] 9

(d) Identify and explain risks of material misstatement for a given assignment.[3] 9

(e) Discuss and demonstrate the use of analytical procedures in the planning of an assignment.[3] 9

(f) Explain how the result of planning procedures determines the relevant audit strategy.[2] 9

(g) Explain the planning procedures specific to an initial audit engagement.[2] 9

(h) Identify additional information that may be required to assist the auditor in obtaining an understanding of the entity.[2] 9

(i) Recognise matters that are not relevant to the planning of an assignment.[2] 9

2 Evidence

(a) Identify and describe audit procedures (including substantive and tests of control) to obtain sufficient, appropriate audit evidence from identified sources. [2] 11

(b) Assess and describe how IT can be used to assist the auditor and recommend the use of Computer-assisted audit techniques (CAATs) where appropriate.[2] 9

(c) Identify additional information that may be required to effectively carry out a planned assignment.[2] 9

(d) Identify and evaluate the audit evidence expected to be available to: [3] 11

(i) support financial statement assertions and accounting treatments (including fair values)

(ii) support disclosures made in the notes to the financial statements.

(e) Apply analytical procedures to financial and non-financial data.[2] 11

(f) Explain the specific audit problems and procedures concerning related parties and related party transactions.[2] 11

(g) Recognise circumstances that may indicate the existence of unidentified related parties and select appropriate audit procedures.[2] 11

(h) Evaluate the use of written management representations to support other audit evidence.[2] 11

(i) Recognise when it is justifiable to place reliance on the work of an expert (e.g. a surveyor employed by the audit client).[2] 11

(j) Assess the appropriateness and sufficiency of the work of internal auditors and the extent to which reliance can be placed on it.[2] 11

3 Evaluation and review

(a) Evaluate the matters (e.g. materiality, risk, relevant accounting standards, audit evidence) relating to:[3] 12

(i) inventory

(ii) standard costing systems

(iii) statement of cash flows

(iv) changes in accounting policy

(v) taxation (including deferred tax)

(vi) segmental reporting

(vii) non-current assets

(viii) fair values

(ix) leases

(x) revenue from contracts with customers

(xi) employee benefits

(xii) government grants

(xiii) related parties

(xiv) earnings per share

(xv) impairment

(xvi) provisions, contingent liabilities and contingent assets

(xvii) intangible assets

(xviii) financial instruments

(xix) investment properties

(xx) share-based payment transactions

(xxi) business combinations

(xxii) assets held for sale and discontinued operations

(xxiii) events after the end of the reporting period

(xxiv) the effects of foreign exchange rates

(xxv) borrowing costs

(b) Explain the use of analytical procedures in evaluation and review.[3] 12

(c) Explain how the auditor's responsibilities for corresponding figures, comparative financial statements, and 'other information' are discharged.[3] 12

(d) Apply the further considerations and audit procedures relevant to initial engagements.[2] 12

(e) Specify audit procedures designed to identify subsequent events that may require adjustment to, or disclosure in, the financial statements of a given entity.[2] 12

(f) Identify and explain indicators that the going concern basis may be in doubt and recognise mitigating factors.[2] 12

(g) Recommend audit procedures, or evaluate the evidence that might be expected to be available and assess the appropriateness of the going concern basis in given situations.[3] 12

(h) Assess the adequacy of disclosures in financial statements relating to going concern and explain the implications for the auditor's report with regard to the going concern basis.[3] 12

4 Group audits

(a) Recognise the specific matters to be considered before accepting appointment as group auditor to a group in a given situation.[3] 10

(b) Explain the responsibilities of the component auditor before accepting appointment, and the procedures to be performed in a group situation.[2]

(c) Identify and explain the matters specific to planning an audit of group financial statements including assessment of group and component materiality, the impact of non-coterminous year ends within a group, and changes in group structure.[2] 10

(d) Recognise the audit problems and describe audit procedures specific to: a business combination including the classification of investments, the determination of goodwill and its impairment, group accounting policies, inter-company trading, equity accounting for associates and joint ventures, changes in group structure including acquisitions and disposals, and accounting for a foreign subsidiary.[3] 10

(e) Identify and explain the audit risks, and necessary audit procedures relevant to the consolidation process.[3] 10

(f) Identify and describe the matters to be considered and the procedures to be performed at the planning stage, when a group auditor considers the use of the work of component auditors.[3] 10

(g) Consider how the group auditor should evaluate the audit work performed by a component auditor.[2] 10

(h) Justify the situations where a joint audit would be appropriate.[2] 10

(i) Explain the implications for the auditor's report on the financial statements of an entity where the opinion on a component is modified in a given situation.[2] 10

E OTHER ASSIGNMENTS

1 Audit-related and assurance services

(a) Describe the nature of audit-related services and the comparative levels of assurance provided by professional accountants and distinguish between: [2] 15

(i) audit-related services and an audit of historical financial statements

(ii) an attestation engagement and a direct engagement.

(b) Plan review engagements, for example:[2] 15

(i) a review of interim financial information

(ii) a 'due diligence' assignment (when acquiring a company, business or other assets).

(c) Explain the importance of enquiry and analytical procedures in review engagements and apply these procedures.[2] 15

(d) Describe the main categories of assurance services that audit firms can provide and assess the benefits of providing these services to management and external users.[3]

(e) Describe the level of assurance (reasonable, high, moderate, limited, negative) for an engagement depending on the subject matter evaluated, the criteria used, the procedures applied and the quality and quantity of evidence obtained.[3] 15

2 Prospective financial information

(a) Define 'prospective financial information' (PFI) and distinguish between a 'forecast', a 'projection', a 'hypothetical illustration' and a 'target'.[1] 16

(b) Explain the principles of useful PFI.[1] 16

(c) Identify and describe the matters to be considered before accepting a specified engagement to report on PFI.[2] 16

(d) Discuss the level of assurance that the auditor may provide and explain the other factors to be considered in determining the nature, timing and extent of examination procedures.[1] 16

(e) Describe examination procedures to verify forecasts and projections.[2] 16

(f) Compare the content of a report on an examination of PFI with reports made in providing audit-related services.[2] 16

3 Forensic audits

(a) Define the terms 'forensic accounting', 'forensic investigation' and 'forensic audit'.[1] 18

(b) Describe the major applications of forensic auditing (e.g. fraud, negligence, insurance claims) and analyse the role of the forensic auditor as an expert witness.[2] 18

(c) Apply the fundamental ethical principles to professional accountants engaged in forensic audit assignments.[2] 18

(d) Plan a forensic audit engagement.[2] 18

(e) Select investigative procedures and evaluate evidence appropriate to determining the loss in a given situation.[3] 18

4 Internal audit

(a) Evaluate the potential impact of an internal audit department on the planning and performance of the external audit.[2] 9

(b) Explain the benefits and potential drawbacks of outsourcing internal audit.[2] 19

(c) Consider the ethical implications of the external auditor providing an internal audit service to a client.[2] 19

5 Outsourcing

(a) Explain the different approaches to 'outsourcing' and compare with 'insourcing'.[2] 19

(b) Discuss and conclude on the advantages and disadvantages of outsourcing finance and accounting functions.[3] 19

(c) Recognise and evaluate the impact of outsourced functions on the conduct of an audit.[3] 19

6 INT Syllabus Only: The audit of performance information (pre-determined objectives) in public sector

(a) Describe the audit of performance information (pre-determined objectives) and differentiate from performance auditing.[2] 21

(b) Plan the audit of performance information (pre-determined objectives), and describe examination procedures to be used in the audit of performance information.[3] 21

(c) Discuss the audit criteria of reported performance information, namely compliance with reporting requirements, usefulness, measurability and reliability.[3] 21

(d) Discuss the form and content of a report on the audit of performance information.[2] 21

(e) Discuss the content of an audit conclusion on an integrated report of performance against predetermined objectives.[3] 21

6 UK Syllabus Only: Auditing aspects of insolvency (and similar procedures)

(a) Explain the meaning of, and describe the procedures involved in placing a company into voluntary or compulsory liquidation or administration.[2] 20

(b) Explain the consequences of liquidation or administration for a company and its stakeholders.[2] 20

(c) Advise on the differences between fraudulent and wrongful trading and the consequences for the company directors.[2] 20

(d) Examine the financial position of a company and determine whether it is insolvent.[2] 20

(e) Identify the circumstances where administration could be adopted as an alternative to liquidation, and explain the benefits of administration compared to liquidation.[2] 20

(f) Explain and apply the priority for the allocation of company assets.[2] 20

F REPORTING

1 Auditor's reports

(a) Determine the form and content of an unmodified audit report and assess the appropriateness of the contents of an unmodified auditor's report.[3] 13

(b) Recognise and evaluate the factors to be taken into account when forming an audit opinion in a given situation and justify audit opinions that are consistent with the results of audit procedures.[3] 13

(c) Critically appraise the form and content of an auditor's report in a given situation.[3] 13

(d) Assess whether or not a proposed audit opinion is appropriate.[3] 13

(e) Advise on the actions which may be taken by the auditor in the event that a modified auditor's report is issued.[3] 13

(f) Recognise when the use of an emphasis of matter paragraph, other matter paragraph and KAM disclosure would be appropriate.[3] 13

(g) Discuss the courses of action available to an auditor if a material inconsistency or material misstatement exists in relation to other information such as contained in the integrated report.[2] 13

2 Reports to those charged with governance

(a) Critically assess the quality of a report to those charged with governance and management.[3] 14

(b) Advise on the content of reports to those charged with governance and management in a given situation.[3] 14

3 Other reports

(a) Analyse the form and content of the professional accountant's report for an assurance engagement as compared with an auditor's report.[2] 15

(b) Discuss the content of a report for an examination of prospective financial information.[2] 16

(c) Discuss the effectiveness of the 'negative assurance' form of reporting and evaluate situations in which it may be appropriate to modify a conclusion.[3] 15

G CURRENT ISSUES AND DEVELOPMENTS

1 Professional and ethical developments

(a) Discuss emerging ethical issues and evaluate the potential impact on the profession, firms and auditors.[3] 2

(b) Discuss the content and impact of exposure drafts, consultations and other pronouncements issued by IFAC and its supporting bodies (including IAASB, IESBA and TAC).[3] 2

2 Transnational audits

(a) Define 'transnational audits' and explain the role of the Transnational Audit Committee (TAC) of IFAC.[1] 10

(b) Discuss how transnational audits may differ from other audits of historical financial information (e.g. in terms of applicable financial reporting and auditing standards, listing requirements and corporate governance requirements).[2] 10

3 The audit of social, environmental and integrated reporting

(a) Plan an engagement to provide assurance on integrated reporting (performance measures and sustainability indicators). [2] 16

(b) Describe the difficulties in measuring and reporting on economic, environmental and social performance and give examples of performance measures and sustainability indicators.[2] 16

(c) Explain the auditor's main considerations in respect of social and environmental matters and how they impact on entities and their financial statements (e.g. impairment of assets, provisions and contingent liabilities).[2] 16

(d)	Describe substantive procedures to detect potential misstatements in respect of socio-environmental matters.[2]	16
(e)	Discuss the form and content of an independent verification statement of an integrated report.[2]	16

4 Other current issues

(a)	Discuss current developments in auditing standards including the need for new and revised standards and evaluate their impact on the conduct of audits.[3]	1
(b)	Discuss current developments in business practices, practice management and audit methodology and evaluate the potential impact on the conduct of an audit and audit quality.[3]	7,8
(c)	Discuss current developments in emerging technologies, including big data and the use of data analytics and the potential impact on the conduct of an audit and audit quality.[3]	9

The superscript numbers in square brackets indicate the intellectual depth at which the subject area could be assessed within the examination. Level 1 (knowledge and comprehension) broadly equates with the Knowledge module, Level 2 (application and analysis) with the Skills module and Level 3 (synthesis and evaluation) to the Professional level. However, lower level skills can continue to be assessed as you progress through each module and level.

The examination

Examination format

The examination is constructed in two sections. Questions in both sections will be almost entirely discursive. However, candidates will be expected, for example, to be able to assess materiality and calculate relevant ratios where appropriate.

Section A questions will be based on 'case study' type questions. That is not to say that they will be particularly long, rather that they will provide a setting within which a range of topics, issues and requirements can be addressed. Different types of question will be encountered in Section B and will tend to be more focused on specific topics, for example 'auditor's reports', 'quality control' etc. (This does not preclude these topics from appearing in Section A.) Current issues will be examined across a number of questions.

	Number of marks
Section A	
Two compulsory questions:	
Question 1	35
Question 2	25
Section B	
Answer two questions from a choice of three, 20 marks each	40
	100

Total time allowed: 3 hours 15 minutes

Paper-based examination tips

Spend the first few minutes of the examination reading the paper.

Where you have a choice of questions, decide which ones you will do.

Unless you know exactly how to answer the question, spend some time **planning** your answer. Stick to the question and **tailor your answer** to what you are asked. Pay particular attention to the verbs in the question.

Spend the last five minutes reading through your answers and making any additions or corrections.

If you **get completely stuck** with a question, leave space in your answer book and return to it later.

If you do not understand what a question is asking, state your assumptions. Even if you do not answer in precisely the way the examiner hoped, you may be given some credit, if your assumptions are reasonable.

You should do everything you can to make things easy for the marker. The marker will find it easier to identify the points you have made if your answers are legible and well spaced out.

Computations: It is essential to include all your workings in your answers. Many computational questions require the use of a standard format. Be sure you know these formats thoroughly before the exam and use the layouts that you see in the answers given in this book and in model answers.

Scenario-based questions: Most questions will contain a hypothetical scenario. To write a good answer, first identify the area in which there is a problem, outline the main principles/theories you are going to use to answer the question, and then apply the principles/theories to the case. It is vital that you relate your answer to the specific circumstances given.

Reports, memos and other documents: some questions ask you to present your answer in the form of a report or a memo or other document. So use the correct format, there will be professional marks to gain here.

Study skills and revision guidance

This section aims to give guidance on how to study for your ACCA exams and to give ideas on how to improve your existing study techniques.

Preparing to study

Set your objectives

Before starting to study decide what you want to achieve – the type of pass you wish to obtain. This will decide the level of commitment and time you need to dedicate to your studies.

Devise a study plan

Determine which times of the week you will study.

Split these times into sessions of at least one hour for study of new material. Any shorter periods could be used for revision or practice.

Put the times you plan to study onto a study plan for the weeks from now until the exam and set yourself targets for each period of study – in your sessions make sure you cover the course, course assignments and revision.

If you are studying for more than one paper at a time, try to vary your subjects as this can help you to keep interested and see subjects as part of wider knowledge.

When working through your course, compare your progress with your plan and, if necessary, re-plan your work (perhaps including extra sessions) or, if you are ahead, do some extra revision/practice questions.

Effective studying

Active reading

You are not expected to learn the text by rote, rather, you must understand what you are reading and be able to use it to pass the exam and develop good practice. A good technique to use is SQ3Rs – Survey, Question, Read, Recall, Review:

(1) **Survey the chapter** – look at the headings and read the introduction, summary and objectives, so as to get an overview of what the chapter deals with.

(2) **Question** – whilst undertaking the survey, ask yourself the questions that you hope the chapter will answer for you.

(3) **Read** through the chapter thoroughly, answering the questions and making sure you can meet the objectives. Attempt the exercises and activities in the text, and work through all the examples.

(4) **Recall** – at the end of each section and at the end of the chapter, try to recall the main ideas of the section/chapter without referring to the text. This is best done after a short break of a couple of minutes after the reading stage.

(5) **Review** – check that your recall notes are correct.

You may also find it helpful to re-read the chapter to try to see the topic(s) it deals with as a whole.

Note-taking

Taking notes is a useful way of learning, but do not simply copy out the text. The notes must:

- be in your own words
- be concise
- cover the key points
- be well-organised
- be modified as you study further chapters in this text or in related ones.

Trying to summarise a chapter without referring to the text can be a useful way of determining which areas you know and which you don't.

Three ways of taking notes:

Summarise the key points of a chapter.

Make linear notes – a list of headings, divided up with subheadings listing the key points. If you use linear notes, you can use different colours to highlight key points and keep topic areas together. Use plenty of space to make your notes easy to use.

Try a diagrammatic form – the most common of which is a mind-map. To make a mind-map, put the main heading in the centre of the paper and put a circle around it. Then draw short lines radiating from this to the main sub-headings, which again have circles around them. Then continue the process from the sub-headings to sub-sub-headings, advantages, disadvantages, etc.

Highlighting and underlining

You may find it useful to underline or highlight key points in your study text – but do be selective. You may also wish to make notes in the margins.

Revision

The best approach to revision is to revise the course as you work through it. Also try to leave four to six weeks before the exam for final revision. Make sure you cover the whole syllabus and pay special attention to those areas where your knowledge is weak. Here are some recommendations:

Read through the text and your notes again and condense your notes into key phrases. It may help to put key revision points onto index cards to look at when you have a few minutes to spare.

Review any assignments you have completed and look at where you lost marks – put more work into those areas where you were weak.

Practise exam standard questions under timed conditions. If you are short of time, list the points that you would cover in your answer and then read the model answer, but do try to complete at least a few questions under exam conditions.

Also practise producing answer plans and comparing them to the model answer.

If you are stuck on a topic find somebody (a tutor) to explain it to you.

Read good newspapers and professional journals, especially ACCA's **Student Accountant,** this can give you an advantage in the exam.

Ensure you **know the structure of the exam** – how many questions and of what type you will be expected to answer. During your revision attempt all the different styles of questions you may be asked.

Further reading

You can find further reading and technical articles under the student section of ACCA's website.

chapter

1

Regulation in a global economy

Chapter learning objectives

This chapter covers syllabus areas:

- A1 – International regulatory frameworks for audit and assurance services
- G4a – Discuss current developments in auditing standards including the need for new and revised standards and evaluate their impact on the conduct of audits

Detailed syllabus objectives are provided in the introduction section of the text book.

Exam focus

This chapter considers the reasons behind the mechanisms for regulating assurance services and how standards of corporate governance are maintained, including much of the background to developments in the profession. You need to have an awareness of recent developments in the profession, which will require you to read around the topic to develop your understanding and develop an ability to form your own opinion and reach your own conclusions.

1 The need for assurance services

Assurance professionals provide reports that give an independent opinion as to whether subject matter complies with pre-determined criteria. This enables the end user of that information to place more or less reliance on that information when making decisions.

Decision makers within financial markets need to have the confidence to make **informed decisions**. In order to make these decisions they need information that they can trust. The main investment decisions that take place concern the buying and selling of shares. Without credible, reliable information at their disposal investors cannot make those decisions.

It is not just shareholders who rely on this information, there are a range of other stakeholders who also rely on assurance services. For example, it is common for banks to seek audited financial statements and independently examined forecasts before making lending decisions. Many companies request audited financial statements before buying from or supplying a company in case that company is nearing insolvency.

As well as investments in businesses, other stakeholders must make decisions about how to deploy resources: suppliers, customers, employees and prospective lenders all need information before making significant decisions that could have damaging financial repercussions.

2 Regulation of the profession

As a result of financial scandals, and the public concern that followed, many changes were implemented in the global auditing and accountancy profession.

Examples of developments include:

- The IAASB's International Standards on Auditing have been adopted or are being used as a basis for national standards in over 100 countries worldwide.
- The World Federation of Exchanges endorsed the IAASB's standard setting process and ISAs.

- The Code of Ethics for Professional Accountants has been adopted by many member institutions.
- The largest accountancy firms have all committed to auditing in accordance with ISAs and to apply relevant sections of the Code of Ethics.
- Legislative changes have been established to introduce new corporate governance requirements. The most famous of these, The Sarbanes Oxley Act (SOX) in the US, led to the creation of the Public Company Accounting Oversight Board, who create standards for listed entities and conduct inspections of audit firms' work.
- The Public Interest Oversight Board (in conjunction with the International Organisation of Securities Commissions, the Basel Committee on Banking Supervision, the Financial Stability Forum and the World Bank) was set up in 2005 to oversee IFAC's auditing and assurance, ethics, and education standard setting activities and its membership compliance programme.

Global regulation

The main problem is that harmonisation requires national regimes to adopt International Standards on Auditing. IFAC cannot impose them on a global scale. Many countries have adopted ISAs but they have been adapted to suit local customs/laws and as a result many differences still exist in the quality of audits worldwide.

The need for regulation

Business failures, particularly large, high-profile businesses, cause loss of confidence within global financial markets. Confidence in the reliability of financial information is essential to the functioning of these markets. Whilst it is not the only factor in helping to achieve that confidence, good quality, independent audit and assurance has a key role to play. A series of recent and high profile corporate failures has eroded trust in the assurance market and as a result mechanisms for increased regulation of the auditing profession have been introduced.

The requirement for audited financial statements was seen as a way to reduce this risk and to protect:

- the owners of a business from unscrupulous management
- the world at large from abuse of limited liability status.

Self-regulation

Initially the system relied on self-regulation. In the 1970s the accountancy profession began to introduce standards to regulate financial reporting and shortly afterwards auditing standards were introduced.

Standards were set **by** the accounting profession **for** the accounting profession to follow.

Self-regulation seemed to make sense because:

- the accountancy organisations usually had a 'public interest' remit written into their constitutions
- they understood the business of financial reporting and auditing better than anyone.

However, two factors have led to the questioning of self-regulation as a satisfactory mechanism, which are:

- globalisation
- high profile corporate failures, such as Enron.

Globalisation

The globalisation of business, professions and investment markets has been rapid.

Once businesses started to cross national borders it soon became clear that the variation of laws and regulations in different countries made life rather difficult, both for the multinationals and the professions trying to provide services to them.

Global Regulation

This realisation led to the foundation of **IFAC** – the International Federation of Accountants in 1977.

IFAC is structured to operate through a network of boards and committees.

IFAC COUNCIL

IFAC BOARD

INTERNATIONAL AUDIT AND ASSURANCE STANDARDS BOARD

COMPLIANCE ADVISORY PANEL

PROFESSIONAL ACCOUNTING ORGANISATION DEVELOPMENT COMMITTEE

INTERNATIONAL ACCOUNTING EDUCATION STANDARDS BOARD

INTERNATIONAL ETHICS STANDARDS BOARD FOR ACCOUNTANTS

PROFESSIONAL ACCOUNTANTS IN BUSINESS COMMITTEE

INTERNATIONAL PUBLIC SECTOR ACCOUNTING STANDARDS BOARD

SMALL AND MEDIUM PRACTICES COMMITTEE

TRANSNATIONAL AUDIT COMMITTEE

Detailed explanation of IFAC structure

International Federation of Accountants

The International Federation of Accountants (IFAC) is the global organisation for the accountancy profession. It was formed in 1977 and is based in New York. As at 1 January 2017, IFAC has more than 175 member bodies of accountants (including the ACCA), representing 3 million accountants from 130 separate countries.

IFAC's overall mission is to serve the public interest, strengthen the worldwide accountancy profession, and contribute to the development of strong international economies by establishing and promoting adherence to high quality professional standards.

The structure of IFAC is as follows:

The **IFAC Council** comprises one representative from each member body. It meets once a year and elects the board.

The **IFAC Board** is responsible for setting policy and overseeing the work of the various committees.

The **IFAC Nominating Committee** makes recommendations regarding the composition of IFAC boards, committees and task forces.

The main bodies to be aware of are:

- The **International Auditing and Assurance Standards Board (IAASB):** develops and promotes ISAs and other assurance standards to improve the uniformity of auditing practices and related services throughout the world.
- The **International Ethics Standards Board for Accountants:** promotes the Code of Ethics. Significantly, the committee continually monitors and stimulates debate on a wide range of ethical issues to ensure that its guidance is responsive to the expectations and challenges of individuals, businesses, financial institutions and others relying on accountants' work.
- The **Transnational Auditors Committee (TAC):** deals with issues arising due to cross-border auditing. It is the executive committee of the Forum of Firms (FoF), open to all firms performing or wishing to perform transnational audits. The TAC is discussed in more detail in chapter 10.

Other constituent bodies include:

- The **Compliance Advisory Panel (CAP)**
- The **Professional Accountancy Organisation Development Committee**
- The **International Accounting Education Standards Board**
- The **Professional Accountants in Business Committee (PAIB)**
- The **International Public Sector Accounting Standards Board**
- The **Small and Medium Practices Committee**

The trouble with IFAC

IFAC has encountered a number of difficulties in carrying out its role:

- It was set up by, and continues to be financed by, the accountancy profession worldwide. It therefore represents a self regulatory body. It is suggested that this is an inappropriate mechanism for regulating the audit profession.
- National interests still apply leading to the implementation of international standards being bogged down in arguments between different national approaches.
- Its members are the professional accountancy bodies, whose authority has been eclipsed to some extent by the power of the largest accountancy firms.

The need for Global Accounting Networks

Although companies have had their securities listed in both the European and US markets for a number of years, the ability to be based virtually anywhere in the world, and to manufacture, sell and manage businesses on a truly global basis is a more recent phenomenon. Global businesses need global professional firms to support, advise and audit them. The emergence of the 'Big 4' global practices has been an accelerating process that has its origins in the 1970s. Similar globalisation has happened in the banking and assurance industries and the introduction of external shareholders into the securities markets has led to, e.g. Nasdaq from the US investing in the London Stock Exchange.

3 Corporate governance

Corporate governance is the system of rules, practices and processes by which a company is directed and controlled.

It is about ensuring that public companies are managed effectively for the benefit of the company and its shareholders.

Corporate governance pronouncements tend to respond to corporate scandals that arise because unscrupulous management has:

- manipulated the share price for personal gain
- disguised poor results/mismanagement
- extracted funds from the company
- raised finance fraudulently.

The UK Corporate Governance Code

The UK Corporate Governance Code is seen as best practice and the principles form the basis of corporate governance guidance and regulation around the world.

The Code consists of principles (main and supporting) and provisions. The Listing Rules require companies to apply the Main Principles and report to shareholders on how they have done so. If an alternative to a provision is justified and good governance can be achieved, the reasons should be explained to the shareholders ('comply or explain').

The main provisions of the UK Corporate Governance Code are:

Leadership

- Every company should be headed by an effective board with collective responsibility.
- There should be a clear division of responsibilities between the Chairman and the Chief Executive.
- No one individual should have unfettered powers of decision.
- The chairman is responsible for leadership of the board and ensuring its effectiveness on all aspects of its role.
- Non-executive directors should constructively challenge and help develop proposals on strategy.

Effectiveness

- The board should have the appropriate balance of skills, experience, independence and knowledge.
- There should be a formal, rigorous and transparent procedure for the appointment of new directors.
- All directors should be able to allocate sufficient time to the company to discharge their responsibilities effectively.
- All directors should receive an induction and should regularly update and refresh their skills and knowledge.
- The board should be supplied with quality and timely information to enable it to discharge its duties.
- The board and individuals should be subject to a formal and rigorous annual evaluation of performance.
- All directors should be submitted for re-election at regular intervals.

Accountability

- The board should present a balanced and understandable assessment of the company's position and prospects.
- The board is responsible for determining the nature and extent of the principal risks it is willing to take in achieving its strategic objectives.
- The board should maintain sound risk management and internal control systems.
- The board should establish formal and transparent arrangements for corporate reporting and risk management and internal control principles and for maintaining an appropriate relationship with the company's auditors.

Remuneration

- Executive directors' remuneration should be designed to promote the long-term success of the company.
- Performance-related elements should be transparent, stretching and rigorously applied.
- There should be a formal and transparent procedure for developing policy on executive remuneration and for fixing the remuneration packages of individual directors.
- No director should be involved in deciding his or her own remuneration.

Relations with shareholders

- There should be a dialogue with shareholders based on the mutual understanding of objectives.
- The board as a whole has responsibility for ensuring that a satisfactory dialogue with shareholders takes place.
- The board should use the general meetings to communicate with investors and to encourage their participation.

Relevance of corporate governance to external auditors

If a company complies with corporate governance best practice, the control environment of the company is likely to be stronger. There will be a greater focus on financial reporting and internal controls which should reduce control risk and inherent risk which together reduce the risk of material misstatements in the financial statements.

In addition, external auditors may be required to report on whether companies are compliant with the Code. For example, in the UK, external auditors of listed entities are required to report on whether the company is compliant with the UK Corporate Governance Code.

Corporate governance

There are two models of board structure adopted around the world:

- the 'unitary board' structure, as used in the UK and Ireland and jurisdictions whose company law systems have a similar basis.
- the 2 tier, 'supervisory board' structure, as used in the US and similar jurisdictions.

Features of a unitary board include:

- collective board responsibility
- no distinction in law between the responsibilities of executive and non-executive directors
- the need to distinguish between the function of executive and non-executive directors
- the need to establish board committees to monitor and act on different functions – nomination committee, remuneration committee, audit committee, etc.

Features of a 2 tier system include:

- Lower level management (operating) board
  - Comprises executive management – CEO, CFO, Vice presidents, etc.
  - Operational responsibility for running the business.
  - Coordinated by the CEO.
- Upper level supervisory board
  - Comprises non-executives, employee representatives, environmental groups and other stakeholders.
  - Appoints, supervises and advises the management board.
  - Strategic oversight of the organisation.
  - Members elected by shareholders at the AGM.
  - Receives information and reports from the management board.
  - Coordinated by the chairman.

Sarbanes Oxley

In the **US** corporate governance is enshrined in law, namely the Sarbanes Oxley Act. As well as dealing with the oversight of auditors, the act enforces certain governance responsibilities, such as:

- sound systems of controls.
- clear documentation of financial processes, procedures, risks, and controls.
- evidence that management has evaluated the adequacy of the design and the effectiveness of operation of procedures and controls.
- evidence that the auditor has adequately evaluated the design and operation of financial controls.
- evidence that the audit committee has taken a keen interest in the effectiveness of controls
- explicit sign off procedures by the chief executive and chief financial officer (see 'Sarbanes Oxley').

Overview of the Act

'The primary benefit is to provide the company, its management, its board and audit committee, and its owners and other stakeholders with a reasonable basis to rely on the company's financial reporting.

The integrity of financial reporting represents the foundation upon which this country's public markets are built.'

The key characteristics of Section 302

CEO and CFO need to certify that:

- the SEC report being filed has been reviewed.
- the report does not contain any untrue statements or omit any material facts.
- the financial statements fairly present the financial position, results of operations and cash flows of the registrant.
- they are responsible for, and have designed, established, and maintained disclosure controls and procedures as well as evaluated and reported on the effectiveness of those controls and procedures within 90 days of the report filing date.
- deficiencies and material weaknesses in disclosure controls and procedures have been disclosed to the registrant's audit committee and external auditors.

- significant changes in internal control affecting transactions in the period have been reported.

The key characteristics of Section 404

With the filing of their accounts, companies are required to include an annual internal control report of management over financial reporting which includes:

- responsibilities for establishing and maintaining adequate internal controls and procedures.
- conclusions about the effectiveness of the company's internal controls and procedures.
- an attestation by the company's registered public accounting firm on management's evaluation.

Enron

The Sarbanes Oxley Act came into force as a result of the Enron corporate failure.

The fraudulent financial reporting at the heart of the Enron collapse has had major repercussions for the accountancy profession worldwide. It was one of the largest and most complex bankruptcy cases the world has ever witnessed. Consequent investigations identified numerous creative accounting techniques designed to improve reported profits and hide significant debts from investors.

Ultimately the scandal that followed in the wake Enron's bankruptcy led to the collapse of one of the 'Big 5' accountancy firms, Arthur Andersen. The role of Arthur Andersen in the financial fraud came under close public scrutiny and much of the already fragile trust in the auditing profession, due to other high profile frauds, was lost.

Before its bankruptcy, Enron employed approximately 22,000 people and was one of the world's leading electricity, natural gas, and communications companies. In 2001 its revenue peaked at nearly $101 billion. Much of the reported profit and position was sustained by institutionalised and systematic accounting fraud.

The scandal also caused the dissolution of Arthur Andersen. The firm was found guilty of obstruction of justice for destroying documents related to the Enron audit and was forced to stop auditing public companies (although the conviction was later thrown out by the US Supreme Court).

The story can be briefly summarised as follows:

- A significant portion of Enron's profits were the result of deals with special purpose entities (SPEs), which it controlled.
- Many of the entities were offshore, which allowed Enron to avoid taxes, move currency and hide overall company losses.
- Enron used an accounting technique known as marking to market (MTM), which effectively meant that Enron could recognise revenue and earnings on deals a long time before the actual revenue was realised.
- The huge profits Enron reported drove up its share price. This allowed executives (who knew about the offshore accounts and hidden losses!) to trade millions of dollars worth of Enron stock to their own benefit.
- Share prices began to fall and Enron's massive liabilities started to exert pressure on its liquidity. This eventual led to problems with its debt agreements and credit downgrades.
- The lower credit rating increased the cost of Enron's borrowing to unsustainable limits.
- Wall Street analyst queries exposed a number of inconsistencies and problems with Enron's accounts until finally the veil was lifted and the extent of earnings management was exposed.

Weak ethical leadership was partly to blame. However there was a deep flaw running right the way through Enron's corporate culture. Were these failures in ethical and business judgment caused by a few people at the top or was the flaw endemic within the whole business?

4 Audit committees

Audit committees form part of the governance structure of an organisation.

The broad objectives of an audit committee are threefold:

- To increase public confidence in the credibility and objectivity of published financial information.
- To assist directors in meeting their responsibilities in respect of financial reporting.
- To strengthen the independent position of a company's external auditor.

The following requirements are taken from the FRC Guidance on Audit Committees. The guidance is designed to assist company boards when implementing the Corporate Governance Code.

- Companies with a premium listing are required to comply with the Code or explain why they have not done so.
- Audit committee arrangements should be proportionate to the task and will vary according to size and complexity of the company.
- All directors have a duty to act in the interests of the company, however, the audit committee must act independently from the executive to ensure that the interests of the shareholders are properly protected in respect of financial reporting and internal control.
- There should be a frank, open working relationship and a high level of mutual respect between audit committee chairman and board chairman, the chief executive and the finance director.
- Management is under an obligation to ensure the audit committee is kept properly informed. All directors must cooperate with the audit committee.
- The core functions of audit committees are oversight, assessment and review. It is not the duty of the audit committee to carry out functions that belong to others. For example, they should make sure there is a proper system in place for monitoring of internal controls but should not do the monitoring themselves.
- The board should review the audit committee's effectiveness annually.

Membership, appointment and skills

- The committee should comprise of independent, non-executive directors.
- The committee should have at least 3 members (2 for smaller companies).
- The committee as a whole should have competence relevant to the sector in which the company operates.
- At least one member should have recent and relevant financial experience with an appropriate professional accountancy qualification.
- Committee members should be independent of operational management.
- Appointments to the audit committee should be made by the board on the recommendation of the nomination committee taking into consideration the skills, experience and qualifications to meet corporate governance requirements.
- Appointments should be for a period of up to 3 years, extendable by no more than two additional 3 year periods.
- New members should receive induction and training should be provided to all members on a continuing basis as required.

Meetings

- The audit committee should hold as many meetings as the roles and responsibilities require and it is recommended that no fewer than three meetings are held.
- No one other than the audit committee chairman and members is entitled to be present at a meeting of the audit committee. The audit committee will decide if non-members, such as the finance director, head of internal audit or external audit partner, should attend a particular meeting.
- The audit committee should meet the external and internal auditors without management at least annually to discuss any issues arising from the audit.
- In addition to the formal committee meetings, the audit committee should keep in touch on a continuing basis with the key people involved in the company's governance.

Resources

- The audit committee should be provided with sufficient resources to undertake its duties.
- The company secretary should ensure information is provided to the audit committee on a timely basis.
- Funds should be provided to enable it to take independent legal, accounting or other advice when required.

Remuneration

- The remuneration should take into account the level of fees paid to the other members of the board.
- The chairman will be paid more than the other members to reflect the additional responsibilities and demands on their time.

Relationship with the board

- The audit committee should report to the board on how it has discharged its responsibilities.
- Where there is disagreement between the audit committee and the board, adequate time should be allowed to resolve the disagreement and the audit committee should have the right to report the issue to the shareholders.
- The audit committee should not just rely on the external auditor to raise issues but should consider matters using their own initiative.

Annual reports

The audit committee should:

- Review and report to the board on the significant financial reporting issues and judgments made in connection with the preparation of the financial statements.

- Consider the appropriateness of significant accounting policies, significant estimates and judgments.
- Review the annual report and accounts and advise the board on whether they are fair, balanced and understandable.

Internal control and risk management

The board has ultimate responsibility for risk management and internal control but may delegate some functions to the audit committee such as:

- Reviewing the systems established by management to identify, assess, manage and monitor financial risks.
- Receiving reports from management on the effectiveness of systems and the conclusions of any testing carried out by internal and external auditors.
- Reviewing and recommending disclosures to be included in the annual report in relation to internal control and risk management.

Internal audit process

- The audit committee should regularly review the need for establishing an internal audit function,
- Where there is an internal audit function the audit committee should review and approve the internal audit plan. The plan should be aligned with the key risks of the business.
- The audit committee should ensure the function has unrestricted scope, the necessary resources and access to information to be able to perform its work in accordance with professional standards for internal auditors.
- The audit committee will approve the appointment or termination of the head of internal audit.
- The internal audit function should have a reporting line independent of the executive so it can exercise independent judgment.
- The audit committee should monitor and review the effectiveness of the internal audit function's work. This includes:
  - Confirming that the quality, experience and expertise of the function is appropriate for the business.
  - Meeting with the head of internal audit without the presence of management to discuss effectiveness.
  - Receive a report on the results of the internal auditors' work.
- The audit committee may consider an independent, third party review of the internal audit function's effectiveness.

External audit process

- FTSE 350 companies should put the audit out to tender at least once every ten years to enable the audit committee to compare the quality and effectiveness of the services provided by the incumbent auditor with those of other firms.
- The audit committee has primary responsibility for the appointment of the auditor including the tendering process and selection procedures.
- An annual assessment should be made of the qualifications, expertise, resources and independence of the external auditor.
- If the external auditor resigns the audit committee should investigate the issues giving rise to the resignation.
- The audit committee should approve the remuneration and terms of engagement.
- The audit committee should monitor compliance with the Ethical Standards including the level of fees, former employees of the audit firm who now work for the company, partner rotation and non-audit services.
- The audit committee should set and apply a formal policy specifying the types of non-audit services which are approved.
- At the start of the audit, the audit committee should ensure that appropriate plans are in place for the audit including whether the planned materiality level and the resources are consistent with the scope of the work to be performed.
- The audit committee should discuss with the external auditor any matters which could affect audit quality.
- The audit committee should review and monitor management's responsiveness to the external auditor's findings and recommendations and should also review the written representation letter before it is signed.
- The audit committee should assess the effectiveness of the external audit process including:
  - asking the auditor to explain the risks to audit quality
  - whether the auditor has met the agreed audit plan
  - obtaining feedback from key people involved such as the finance director about the conduct of the audit
  - reviewing the content of the management letter and whether recommendations have been acted upon.

Communication with shareholders

A separate section of the annual report should describe the work of the committee. Specifically:

- A summary of the role of the audit committee.
- The names and qualifications of all members of the audit committee during the period.
- The number of audit committee meetings.
- The significant issues that the committee considered in relation to the financial statements and how these issues were addressed.
- An explanation of how it has assessed the effectiveness of the external audit process and the approach taken to the appointment or reappointment of the external auditor.
- The chairman of the audit committee should be present at the AGM to answer questions.

Benefits and drawbacks of audit committees

Benefits

- Improved credibility of the financial statements, through an impartial review of the financial statements, monitoring of the independence of the external auditors, and discussion of significant issues with the external auditors.
- The quality of management accounting will be improved as the audit committee is better placed to criticise internal functions.
- The control environment may be strengthened as the internal audit function will report to the audit committee increasing their independence and adding weight to their recommendations.
- Communication between the directors, external auditors and management may be improved.
- Conflicts between management and auditors may be reduced/avoided.
- The skills, knowledge and experience (and independence) of the audit committee members can be an invaluable resource for a business.
- It may be easier and cheaper to arrange finance as the presence of an audit committee can give a perception of good corporate governance.
- It would be less burdensome to meet listing requirements if an audit committee (which is usually a listing requirement) is already established.

Drawbacks:

- Difficulties recruiting the right non-executive directors who have relevant skills, experience and sufficient time to become effective members of the committee.
- A fear that their purpose is to police executive management.
- Non-executive directors may be overburdened with detail.
- Additional cost. Non-executive directors are normally remunerated, and their fees can be quite expensive.

FRC Audit Quality – Practice aid for audit committees

The Corporate Governance Code requires audit committees to assess the quality and effectiveness of the external auditor. To help fulfil this requirement, the FRC has issued guidance to audit committees. Assessment of the external auditor should cover three main areas:

(1) **Inputs**

The audit committee should obtain evidence from a variety of sources including:

- Management
- Internal auditors
- Other company personnel
- External auditors
- Regulators
- Audit committee

(2) **Evaluation**

4 key elements of audit quality should be evaluated:

- Mindset and culture – adherence to high professional and ethical principles.
- Skills, character and knowledge – strong auditing skills developed through effective training and relevant experience.
- Quality control – identifying the risks to audit quality and establishing adequate controls to address these.
- Judgment – professional judgment is applied at all stages of the audit.

(3) **Concluding and reporting**

Before concluding and reporting, the audit committee should consider if they have sufficient evidence to conclude on the quality of the audit and the effectiveness of external audit. This includes whether:

- The auditor has communicated key accounting and audit judgments to the audit committee.
- The management letter demonstrates a good understanding of the business.
- Any changes made to materiality have been reported to the audit committee.

UK syllabus

Regulation of auditing

Audit and Assurance in the United Kingdom is regulated by the **Financial Reporting Council** (FRC).

The FRC has two divisions, one of which is the **Codes and Standards** division. The Codes and Standards division is responsible for maintaining an effective framework of UK codes and standards for Corporate Governance, Stewardship, Accounting, Auditing and Assurance, and Actuarial technical standards.

The codes and standards division has three councils:

- the Auditing and Assurance Council
- the Accounting Council
- the Actuarial Council.

The Auditing and Assurance Council considers and advises the FRC Board and the Codes and Standards Committee on audit and assurance matters. The FRC issues International Standards on Auditing for use within the United Kingdom. The standards are supplemented and revised before issuing them, mainly in order to ensure that they remain compliant with national laws, such as the Companies Act 2006.

In addition the FRC:

- Develops and maintains ethical guidance for auditors' and reporting accountants' in the UK.
- Has statutory responsibility for the oversight and regulations of the accountancy profession and of statutory auditors, which is managed by the Professional Oversight team, part of the Conduct division.
- Monitors the quality of the audits of listed and other major public interest entities. This is the responsibility of the Audit Quality Review team.
- Ensures that appropriate standards are maintained by members and member firms, by operating an independent professional disciplinary scheme for accountants, overseen by the Conduct division.

Scope and authority of Audit and Assurance Pronouncements March 2013

Audit and Assurance regulations include

- Quality control standards.
- The Auditor's Code.
- Ethical and engagement standards.
- Guidance for auditors, reporting accountants and auditors involved with other assurance engagements.

These regulations are applicable to:

- Statutory audits of companies in accordance with the Companies Acts.
- Audits of entities in accordance with other legislation e.g banks, charities, pension funds.
- Public sector audits.
- Other audits that are required to comply with UK standards.

Practice notes and bulletins are further forms of guidance but are less prescriptive than ISAs.

Failure by auditors to apply the FRC regulations are liable to regulatory action which may include the withdrawal of registration and therefore eligibility to perform company audits.

Audit exemption

In accordance with the Companies Act 2006 those companies falling below the small company threshold are not required, in law, to have an annual audit. Companies may still choose to have one voluntarily.

The main criteria for audit exemption which apply from 1 January 2016 are:

- Turnover not exceeding £10.2m
- Gross assets not exceeding £5.1m and
- The number of employees must not exceed 50.

In order to qualify, the company must meet two out of the three criteria.

UK syllabus: Developments in audit

Developments in Audit 2015/16 An Overview (FRC)

Confidence in audit

Audit quality in the UK is improving.

- Audit firms are seen as more independent as a result of regulatory changes.
- Mandatory rotation was implemented in 2016 and rules regarding provision of non-audit services are being tightened.
- Large firms are improving audit efficiency and effectiveness through the use of technology.

However, there are still improvements to be made

- There is still an expectation gap and people would like to see the remit of audit being expanded to address this.
- The relationship between the auditor and client is still an area of concern.
- The future use of technology and data analytics raises concerns for how smaller firms will compete and for larger companies and public interest entities, the Big Four are expected to continue to dominate.

Audit tendering, rotation and audit fees

A survey of audit committee chairs was performed and out of over 200 responses, 17% of companies had conducted an audit tender with 75% of those resulting in a change of auditor.

The selection process for tenders focused on independence, the judgment and scepticism of key audit partners and evidence of internal and external quality reviews. Price was not a deciding factor.

However, audit tendering has had no impact on the dominance of the Big Four and further concentration of the audit market may arise. Such concentration means that failure of any one of these firms would have a disproportionate impact on the functioning of the capital markets. The FRC is encouraging enhanced contingency planning to respond to the potential failure of one of these firms.

Audit committees

Audit committees are feeling positive in respect of audit quality. Investors are valuing the extended audit committee reporting as well as extended auditor reporting.

Extended auditor reporting

Investors welcomed the information included in the extended auditor's reports. The best reports tend to be well structured, signpost key information and make innovative use of graphics, diagrams and colour.

Auditor independence and ethics

The FRC has recently issued revised auditing standards and UK Corporate Governance Code. The changes are designed to address the perception of auditors being too close to their clients by introducing requirements on retendering, rotation and provision of non-audit services.

Audit quality monitoring

During 2015, 1402 monitoring visits were carried out. 76% of audits were assessed as good or only requiring limited improvements compared with 67% in the prior year. Only two audits required significant improvements compared with ten in the previous year.

The five most common areas of concern were:

- Fair value and value in use measurements including impairment testing and property valuations.
- Revenue recognition
- Audit committee communication
- Internal controls testing
- Independence and ethics

Enforcement

There are currently 15 ongoing audit investigations. There is a continuing trend of closing more cases than cases being opened.

Technology in support of quality

Audit firms are making significant investment in audit methodologies which use technology to improve effectiveness and/or efficiency. The FRC is currently carrying out a thematic review on the use of data analytics and considering whether audit standards remain fit for purpose in their approach to audit evidence gained through the use of technology.

FRC future activity

- Working with auditors, audit committees and investors to communicate good practice and promote continuous improvement.
- Improving confidence with effective enforcement.
- Continuing to promote audit quality internationally.
- Keeping pace with and facilitating changes in audit and its use of technology in improving the effectiveness and quality of audit.

Test your understanding 1

Becher is an independent construction company, dealing with large scale contracts throughout the UK and with some international interest in Europe, particularly in Spain. Becher has recently established an Audit Committee, the members of which are very concerned about meeting corporate governance 'best practice', particularly since they are currently looking at the possibility of obtaining a stock exchange listing.

You are an internal auditor with the company and have been asked to conduct a review of how well the company is meeting relevant corporate governance requirements.

You are required to prepare a report that addresses the following.

(a) What is meant by 'corporate governance' and why is it important that companies should comply with relevant corporate governance requirements?

(4 marks)

(b) What are the key issues for Becher to address to achieve effective corporate governance?

(5 marks)

(c) What is the role of the audit committee in relation to corporate governance?

(4 marks)

(d) List the types of regular reporting that would be useful for Becher in the context of establishing sound corporate governance.

(3 marks)

5 Chapter summary

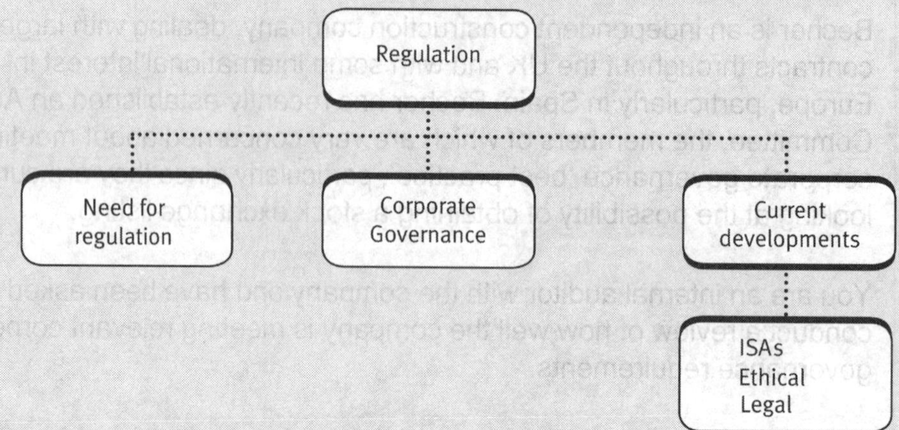

Test your understanding answers

Test your understanding 1

(a) **Corporate governance**

Corporate governance concerns the way that a company is directed and controlled. It encompasses the following key aspects:

- The role of the board and audit committee.
- Overall control and risk management framework.

Corporate Governance has become increasingly important in the wake of high profile accounting frauds. These frauds have had a damaging impact on the effective operation of world stock markets due to reductions in investor (and public) confidence in the roles of directors and company auditors.

Management and control is often more difficult to achieve in larger, more complex organisations. In addition, shareholders (the owners) tend to be more remote from the directors who manage the company on their behalf. Having an agreed set of corporate governance standards therefore facilitates the adoption of good corporate governance practices and improves accountability to investor groups.

Failure to comply with these agreed standards of corporate governance could lead to significant penalties, namely:

- fines and penalties, where corporate governance is enforced through law, the US for example. This could, in the most extreme cases, lead to imprisonment of directors.
- penalties imposed by stock market regulators, such as removal from the listing.
- replacement of board members.

(b) **Requirements of corporate governance**

The nature of issues to address depend upon the legal or listing requirements in place in the country of operation. However the following basic principles may be universally applied:

- The board should be responsible for the assessment of and response to risk.

- The board should be responsible for designing, implementing and monitoring the effectiveness of the system of internal control.
- An independent system (including the use of committees) should be established to enable the effective recruitment and retention of directors.
- Communication with, and independence of auditors, should be facilitated by the use of an audit committee.
- There should be explicit and transparent reporting of compliance with corporate governance requirements/principles.

UK Syllabus Focus

In the UK listed companies need to report upon how, and whether, they have complied with the UK Corporate Governance Code.

(c) **Role of the audit committee**

The role and importance of the audit committee has increased as corporate governance requirements have been strengthened. The audit committee should have at least three non-executive directors who should be independent of the company, i.e. have no direct involvement in the day to day running of its affairs.

The audit committee should:

- assess the framework for complying with corporate governance guidelines within the company, including the risk assessment procedures.
- review the major risks identified including their chances of occurring and their likely impact.
- require regular reporting from internal and external auditors and any other review bodies, showing how the risks are being managed.
- receive and review internal audit assignment reports and follow up information.
- discuss and consider any concerns of directors and internal audit staff.
- review annual financial statements and the results of the external auditors' examination to ensure that the auditors have performed an effective, efficient and independent audit.
- receive and deal with external auditors' comments on management and ensure that recommendations of internal and external auditors have been implemented.

(d) **Types of regular reporting**

Types of regular reporting that could be produced include:

- analysis of current operational risks, including assessment of likelihood and potential impact.
- report on strategy for current management of risks identified.
- details of any issues arising that had not previously been identified and, therefore, were not being managed.
- independent expert analysis of technical matters, for example: the structural condition of oil rigs, risk assessment for operating in politically unstable economies.

chapter

2

Code of ethics and conduct

Chapter learning objectives

This chapter covers syllabus areas:

- B1 – Code of Ethics for Professional Accountants
- G1 – Professional and ethical developments

Detailed syllabus objectives are provided in the introduction section of the text book.

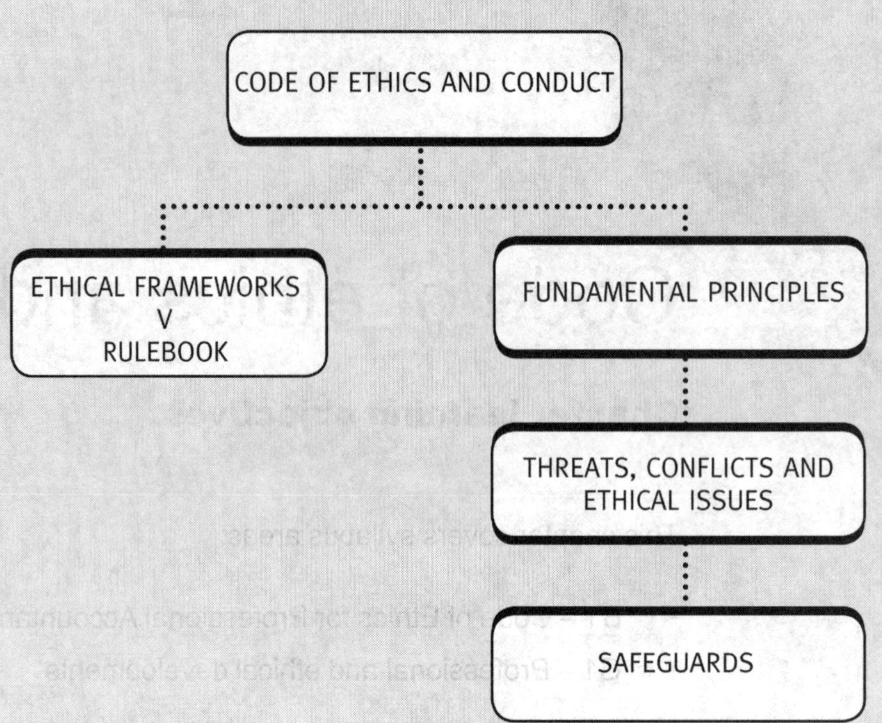

Exam focus

- Professional and ethical considerations are a key element of the P7 paper. The examiner has commented that ethical and professional issues are likely to feature in every sitting.
- A typical requirement will ask you to evaluate the ethical and professional issues in a scenario. Note that this incorporates all of the fundamental principles, not just objectivity, as well as professional issues discussed later in this text.
- Evaluation requires more than just identification and explanation of the threats. You will also need to consider the **significance** of the threat.
- You should consider any safeguards available to reduce the threat to an acceptable level as part of your evaluation.
- A question on ethics will require you to state the rules and principles and apply them to a scenario.

1 Conceptual framework

Ethical guidance can either be a conceptual framework approach (principles-based) or rules-based.

Advantages of a 'conceptual framework' approach

With a conceptual framework approach, the onus is placed on the auditor to demonstrate that all matters are considered within the principles of the framework.

The auditor should consider whether their behaviour would be considered appropriate by a reasonable and informed third party, irrespective of whether there is specific guidance issued by the profession.

A conceptual framework approach has advantages over rule-based systems.

- A framework is more appropriate to changing circumstances in a dynamic profession.
- Principles may be applied across national boundaries, where laws may not.
- A framework approach may include some specific prohibitions or deal with specific matters that are likely to affect many accountancy firms.

Both IFAC and the ACCA adopt a principles-based approach.

The 'rulebook' approach

A rulebook can be useful as it provides clarity regarding what is and is not permitted.

However, it is virtually impossible for rule-based systems to be able to deal with every situation that may arise, particularly across various national boundaries and in a dynamic industry.

Rules can also be interpreted narrowly in order to circumvent the intention of the rule.

The fundamental principles

IESBA develops and promotes the IFAC Code of Ethics for Professional Accountants, which applies to all professional accountants, whether in public practice or not. The IFAC Code serves as the foundation for codes of ethics developed and enforced by member bodies of IFAC. All ACCA members and students are obliged to follow the fundamental principles.

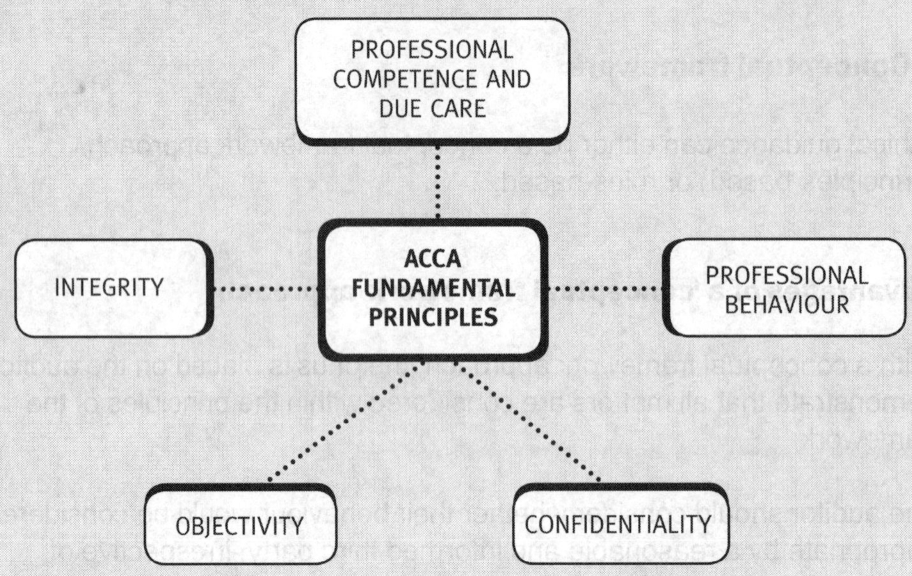

Conflicts within the fundamental principles

An auditor or accountant may find themselves being asked to breach the fundamental principles by an employer e.g. if being asked to misrepresent the financial statements or being asked to lie to the auditor.

The professional accountant should always apply the conceptual framework, which requires assessment of the significance of the threat and the application of an appropriate safeguard.

Appropriate safeguards include:

- Seeking advice from within the employer (e.g. Human Resources department).
- Seeking advice from the ACCA or other independent professional advisor.
- Using the organisation's formal dispute resolution process.
- Seeking legal advice.

Fundamental principles definitions

- **Integrity:** Members should be straightforward and honest in all professional and business relationships.
- **Objectivity:** Members should not allow bias, conflicts of interest or undue influence of others to override professional or business judgments.

- **Professional competence and due care:** Members have a continuing duty to maintain professional knowledge and skill at a level required to ensure that a client or employer receives competent professional service based on current developments in practice, legislation and techniques. Members should act diligently and in accordance with applicable technical and professional standards when providing professional services.
- **Confidentiality:** Members should respect the confidentiality of information acquired as a result of professional and business relationships and should not disclose any such information to third parties without proper and specific authority or unless there is a legal or professional right or duty to disclose. Confidential information acquired as a result of professional and business relationships should not be used for the personal advantage of members or third parties.
- **Professional behaviour:** Members should comply with relevant laws and regulations and should avoid any action that discredits the profession.

2 Ethical threats

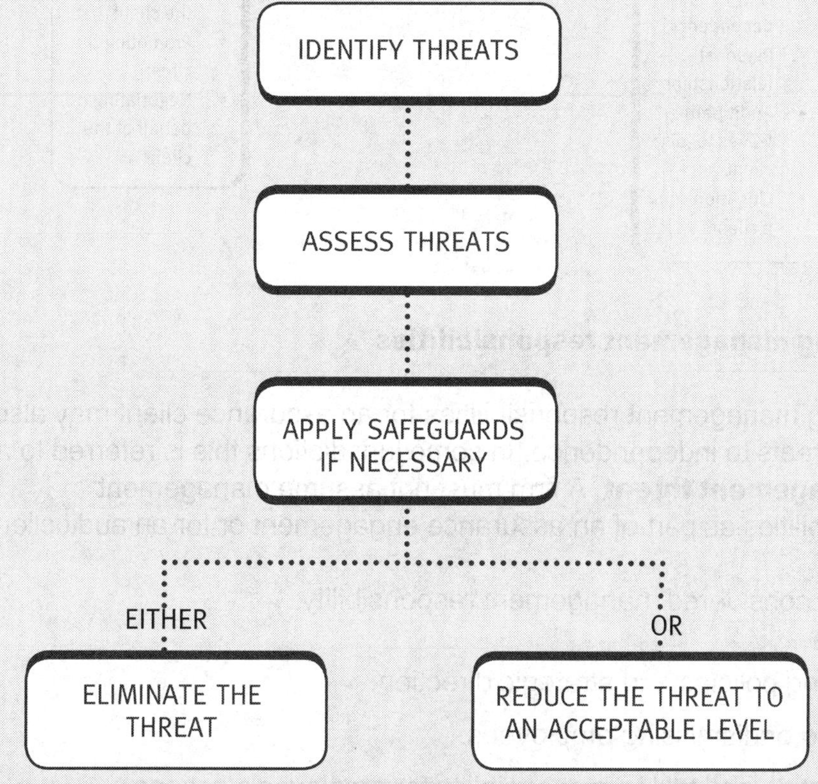

Identifying threats

Self Interest

- Own shares
- Fee dependency
- Gifts & hospitality
- Loans
- Business and personal relationships
- Employment with client
- Overdue fees
- Contingency fees
- Litigation with a client

Self Review

- Accounts preparation
- Internal audit
- Tax computations
- Valuation services
- Client staff joins the audit firm

Familiarity

- Long association
- Personal relationships
- Movement of staff between the firm and client
- Gifts & hospitality

Threats to objectivity

Intimidation

- Fee dependency
- Personal relationships
- Audit partner leaves to join client
- Litigation with a client

Advocacy

- Representing the client
- Promoting the client
- Negotiating on behalf of the client

Assuming management responsibilities

Assuming management responsibilities for an assurance client may also create threats to independence. In some jurisdictions this is referred to as the **management threat**. A firm must not assume management responsibilities as part of an assurance engagement or for an audit client.

Activities considered management responsibility:

- Setting policies and strategic direction.
- Hiring or dismissing employees.
- Directing and taking responsibility for employee's actions.
- Authorising transactions.
- Deciding which recommendations to implement.
- Taking responsibility for the preparation and fair presentation of the financial statements.

- Taking responsibility for designing, implementing and maintaining internal controls.

The firm should take steps to ensure that client management make all judgments and decisions.

Administrative services which are routine and do not involve professional judgment are generally not considered a threat. However, the significance of any threat created should be evaluated and safeguards applied if necessary.

The auditor must ensure **informed management** is in place. This means the auditor believes management is capable of making decisions for the company based on the information available (rather than based solely on the auditor's advice).

Ethical implications for non-audit services

When a practitioner provides non-audit services, ethical implications must still be considered before accepting the work.

A practitioner must always be competent to provide the service being requested.

In addition, if assurance is being provided, the practitioner must be objective as a conclusion is being provided on a subject matter which will be relied upon by an intended user. For example, if a practitioner prepared a forecast for a client and then gave assurance on that forecast, a self-review threat would arise in the same way as a self-review threat would arise if the auditor prepared the financial statements they were auditing.

Therefore the threats listed above must still be assessed and safeguards implemented to reduce the threat to an acceptable level.

Assessing the significance of threats

The assessment of and response to ethical threats is a key element of the P7 exam. It is therefore critical that you can discuss the significance of a threat and recommend an appropriate safeguard.

Factors affecting the significance of the threat include:

- Value – e.g. when considering gifts and hospitality.
- Seniority of staff – e.g. when considering rotation of staff.
- Impact to the audit firm – e.g. when considering fee dependency.
- Materiality to the financial statements – e.g. when considering whether a non-audit service can be provided.

Safeguards

The ACCA Code of Ethics divides safeguards into two broad categories:

- **Safeguards created by the profession, legislation or regulation:** These include: requirements for entry into the profession, continuing professional development, corporate governance, professional standards, monitoring and disciplinary procedures.
- **Safeguards created by the work environment:** These are discussed below, but include, rotation/removal of relevant staff from the engagement team, independent quality control reviews, using separate teams, etc.

Definitions and examples of threats

Self-interest threats

Where the auditor has a financial or other interest that will inappropriately influence their judgment or behaviour.

Threat	Safeguards
Fee dependency Over-dependence on an audit client could lead the auditor to ignore adjustments required in the financial statements for fear of losing the client.	Non-listed clients If fees from an audit client represent a large proportion of the firm's total fees, the firm should implement safeguards such as: • reducing dependency on the client • consulting with a third party on key audit judgments • having an external quality control review.

	Listed clients A firm's independence is threatened, and should be reviewed if total fees from a listed audit client exceed 15% of the firm's total fees for two consecutive years. • The firm should disclose the issue to those charged with governance at the client. • An independent engagement quality control review should be performed by a person not a member of the audit firm expressing the opinion or by the professional regulatory body.
Gifts and hospitality Acceptance of goods, services or hospitality from an audit client can create self-interest and familiarity threats as the auditor may feel indebted to the client.	Only gifts which are trivial and inconsequential should be accepted and even these should be approved by a partner. The offer of gifts and hospitality must be documented in the audit file even if refused.
Owning shares/financial interests The auditor will want to maximise return from the investment and overlook audit adjustments which would affect the value of their investment.	Any member of the audit team or their immediate family must not have a financial interest in the audit client therefore they must dispose of the shares immediately or be removed from the team. Any member of the audit team who has a close family member who owns shares should be removed from the audit team or the family member should dispose of their shares. A partner of the firm in the office connected with the audit engagement, or any partner providing non-audit services to the audit client should not have a financial interest in the client.

Loans and guarantees A loan or guarantee from (or deposit with) an assurance client will not create a threat to independence provided that: • it is on commercial terms, and • made in the normal course of business.	If the loan is made to the firm (rather than a member of the audit team), it must be immaterial to both the firm and the client. If it is material, a self-interest threat may arise and appropriate safeguards should be put into place, e.g. an external review of the work performed. Loans and guarantees between audit clients and audit team members and their immediate family that are not in the normal course of business or not on commercial terms are not permitted.
Business relationships If audit firms (or members) enter into business relationships with clients (e.g. joint ventures, marketing arrangements), this leads to self-interest because the auditor would have an interest in the successful operation of the client. The purchase of goods and services from an assurance client would not normally give rise to a threat to independence, provided the transaction is in the normal course of business and on commercial terms.	In the case of audit firms, or partners of those firms, unless immaterial, no safeguard can reduce this threat to an acceptable level. In the case of audit team members, the individual with the connection to the audit client should be removed from the audit team. If the purchase of goods and services by an audit team member represents a material amount, that person should be removed from the audit team or they should reduce the magnitude of the transactions.
Potential employment with an audit client If a member of the engagement team has reason to believe they may become an employee of the client they will not wish to do anything to affect their potential future employment.	The policies and procedures of the firm should require such individuals to notify the firm of the possibility of employment with the client. Remove the individual from the assurance engagement. Perform an independent review of any significant judgments made by that individual.

Overdue fees The overdue fees may be regarded as a loan (loans are not permitted to an audit client).	Do not perform any further work for, or issue any reports to, the client until the outstanding fees are paid or arrangements have been agreed with the client for payment. An independent review of the work should be performed.
Contingent fees The auditor would have incentive to ensure a particular outcome is achieved in order to maximise the audit fee. E.g. overlook audit adjustments that would reduce profit if the fee is a percentage of the profit.	Fees based on a particular outcome, e.g. level of profits of the company, are not permitted for assurance services.
Actual or threatened litigation Litigation could represent a breakdown of trust in the relationship between auditor and client. This may affect the impartiality of the auditor, and lead to a reluctance of management to disclose relevant information to the auditor. The significance of the threat depends on the materiality of the litigation and whether the litigation relates to a prior assurance engagement.	It may be possible to continue other assurance engagements, depending on the significance of the threat by: • Discussing the matter with the client's audit committee. • If the litigation involves an individual, removing that individual from the engagement team. • Obtaining an external review of the work done. If adequate safeguards cannot be implemented the firm must withdraw from or decline the engagement.

Familiarity threats

When the auditor becomes too sympathetic or too trusting of a client and loses professional scepticism, or where the relationship between the auditor and client goes beyond professional boundaries.

Threat	Safeguards
Long association of senior personnel Using the same senior personnel in an engagement team over a long period may cause the auditor to become too trusting/less sceptical of the client resulting in material misstatements going undetected. The firm should consider: • The length of time on the audit team. • The structure of the firm. • Whether the client's management team has changed. • Whether the complexity of the subject matter has changed.	Non-listed clients • Rotate senior personnel. • Independent partner/quality control reviews. Listed clients • Key audit partners must be rotated after no more than seven years with a minimum break of two years. If the client becomes listed, the length of time the partner has served before becoming listed is taken into account. • In exceptional circumstances, a maximum one year extension is permitted where necessary to maintain audit quality. **Tutorial note:** Large listed companies must put the audit out to tender at least every every ten years. However, this is the responsibility of the company not the audit firm.
Family and other personal relationships A familiarity threat (and self-interest threat or intimidation threat) may occur when a member of the engagement team has a family or personal relationship with someone at the client who is able to exert significant influence over the financial statements (or subject matter of another assurance engagement).	Remove the individual from the engagement team. Structure the engagement team so that the individual does not deal with matters that are the responsibility of the close family member.

Consideration should be given to the possibility that such a threat may also arise when a partner (or employee) of the firm has a family or personal relationship with someone at the client who is able to exert significant influence over the subject matter, even when the individual is not a member of the engagement team.	
Recruitment services Familiarity, self-interest and intimidation threats may occur if the firm is involved in recruiting senior personnel for the client. The firm may also be considered to be assuming management responsibilities. Reviewing qualifications and interviewing applicants to advise on financial competence is allowed.	Listed clients The firm cannot provide recruitment services in respect of directors or senior management who would be in a position to exert significant influence over the financial statements.
Audit staff leave the firm to join the client A self-interest, familiarity or intimidation threat may arise where an employee of the firm becomes a director or employee of an assurance client (in a position to exert significant influence over the financial statements or subject matter of another assurance engagement). The threat is significant if significant connection remains between the employee and the firm such as entitlement to benefits or payments from the firm, or participation in the firm's business and professional activities.	Assign individuals to the audit team who have sufficient experience in relation to the individual who has joined the client. Perform a quality control review of the engagement. For partners joining public interest entities, independence would be deemed to be compromised unless, subsequent to the partner ceasing to be a key audit partner or senior partner, the public interest entity had issued audited financial statements covering a period of not less than twelve months and the partner was not a member of the audit team with respect to the audit of those financial statements.

The firm should consider: • The position taken at the client. • The involvement the person is likely to have with the audit team. • The length of time since the individual was a member of the audit team.	

Self-review threats

Where non-audit work is provided to an audit client and is then subject to audit, the auditor will be unlikely to admit to errors in their own work, or may not identify the errors in their own work.

Threat	Safeguards
Accounting and bookkeeping services	Non-listed clients • A firm can provide a non-listed audit client with accounting and bookkeeping services, including payroll services, of a routine or mechanical nature. • Separate teams must be used. • Managerial decisions must not be made by the firm, and the source data, underlying assumptions, and subsequent adjustments must be originated or approved by the client. Listed clients • A firm cannot provide a listed audit client with accounting and bookkeeping services. • A firm can provide accounting services for divisions or related entities of a listed client if separate teams are used and the service relates to matters immaterial to the division/related entity.

Internal audit services In addition to the self-review threat, the auditor needs to be careful not to assume management responsibilities.	A firm cannot provide internal audit services for a listed audit client, where the service relates to internal controls over financial reporting, financial accounting systems, or in relation to amounts or disclosures that are material to the financial statements. Where services are provided, separate teams must be used.
Taxation services Tax calculations for inclusion in the financial statements and tax planning advice create a self-review threat. Completion of tax returns is **not** deemed to create a self-review threat.	Non-listed clients • Advice should be obtained from an external tax professional. • Where an audit team member performs the tax calculation the work should be reviewed by a senior person with appropriate expertise that has not been involved with the audit. Listed clients • A firm cannot prepare tax calculations for a listed audit client.
Tax advice	The firm should not provide tax advice that depends on a particular accounting treatment and is material to the financial statements. Other tax advice is allowable with safeguards.
IT services IT services may create a self-review threat and also be considered to be assuming management responsibilities.	The firm can only provide IT services which involve: • Design or implementation of IT systems unrelated to internal controls or financial reporting. • Implementation of off-the-shelf accounting software. • Evaluating and making recommendations on a system designed or operated by another service provider or by the entity.

Valuation services	Non-listed clients • Valuation of matters that are material to the financial statements and involve a significant degree of subjectivity should not be provided. • Where the threat is not deemed significant, different personnel should be used. • A professional should review the valuation work performed. Listed clients • Valuation services that are material to the financial statements (regardless of subjectivity) should not be provided to listed audit clients.
Temporary staff assignments A self-review threat will be created if staff are loaned from the audit firm to the client. If the person was assigned to the audit they would be evaluating work for which they had been responsible during the temporary assignment and may not detect errors in their work.	Staff may be loaned to the client provided: • The loan period is short. • The person does not assume management responsibilities. • The client is responsible for directing and supervising the person. • The loaned staff member is not a member of the audit team.

Client staff joins audit firm A self-interest, self-review, or familiarity threat may arise where a director or employee of an assurance client (in a position to exert significant influence over the financial statements or subject matter of another assurance engagement) becomes an employee of the firm.	Such individuals should not be assigned to the audit if that person would be evaluating elements of the financial statements for which they had prepared accounting records. An employee or partner of a firm cannot also be an employee or director of an assurance client, as the self-interest and self-review threats created would be so significant that no safeguard could reduce the threats to an acceptable level.

Advocacy threats

Promoting the position of a client or representing them in some way would mean the audit firm is seen to be 'taking sides' with the client.

Examples include:

- Promoting a share issue for an audit client.
- Representing the client in court or in any dispute where the matter is material to the financial statements.
- Negotiating on the client's behalf for finance.

The audit firm must not act for the audit client in this way. Any request for such services must be politely declined.

Intimidation threats

Actual or perceived pressures from the client, or attempts to exercise undue influence over the assurance provider create an intimidation threat, e.g. actual or threatened litigation between the auditor and audit client (in which case it may be necessary to resign from the engagement).

Intimidation can arise from some of the same situations mentioned above, for example:

- Fee dependency
- Personal relationships
- Audit partner joining the client
- Litigation between the audit firm and client.

The safeguards to address these threats are the same as to address the other threats.

Public interest entities

A public interest entity is one which is:

- Listed
- Defined by regulation or legislation as public interest
- Audited under the same independence requirements as a listed entity.

Audit firms are also encouraged to treat entities where there are a wide range, or significant number of stakeholders, as public interest entities e.g. banks, insurance companies and credit institutions.

UK syllabus – Safeguards from the FRC Ethical Standard

The FRC has issued a UK specific ethical standard designed to ensure practitioners comply with ethical requirements. The standard refers to 'covered persons', 'persons closely associated' and 'other close family relationships'.

Covered persons include the partners and staff involved in the engagement, but could also be:

- any other person placed at the disposal of the audit team e.g. an expert.
- anyone in the audit firm with supervisory, management or other oversight responsibility for the partners involved in the engagement.
- any other person in the firm who is in a position to influence the conduct or outcome of the audit.

Persons closely associated include immediate family members i.e. spouse and dependents.

Other close family relationships comprise parents, non-dependent children and siblings.

An individual can usually be presumed to be aware of matters concerning persons closely associated with them and to be able to influence their behaviour.

Many of the requirements extend to affiliated companies (i.e. subsidiaries).

Section 1 – General requirements and guidance

- The audit firm shall establish policies and procedures to ensure that the firm, and all those involved in the audit, act with integrity, objectivity and independence.
- The leadership of the audit firm shall take responsibility for establishing a control environment that places adherence to ethical principles above commercial considerations.
- The audit firm shall designate an ethics partner.
- The audit firm shall establish policies and procedures to prevent employees from taking decisions that are the responsibility of management of the audited entity.
- The audit firm shall establish policies and procedures to assess the significance of threats to the auditor's objectivity:
  - (i) when considering whether to accept or retain an audit or non-audit service
  - (ii) when planning the audit
  - (iii) when forming an opinion on the financial statements
  - (iv) when considering whether to provide non-audit services
  - (v) when potential threats are reported.
- The audit engagement partner shall not accept or shall not continue an audit engagement if he or she concludes that any threats to the auditor's objectivity and independence cannot be reduced to an acceptable level.
- In the case of listed companies, an Engagement Quality Control Reviewer must be appointed who must:
  - (i) reach an overall conclusion on independence
  - (ii) communicate to those charged with governance at the client all significant matters that bear upon the auditor's objectivity.

Section 2 – Financial, business, employment and personal relationships

- The audit firm, partners, or persons closely associated with them shall not hold any financial interest in an audited entity.
- Audit firms, covered persons and persons closely associated with them shall not make loans to, or guarantee the borrowings of, an audited entity (and vice versa).
- Audit firms, covered persons and persons closely associated with them shall not enter into business relationships with an audited entity.
- An audit firm shall not second partners or employees to an audit client unless:
  - the secondment is for a short period of time, and
  - the audited entity agrees that the individual concerned will not hold a management position.
- Where a partner or employee returns to a firm on completion of a secondment to an audit client, that individual shall not be given any role on the audit involving any function or activity that they performed or supervised during that assignment.
- Where a partner joins an audited entity, the audit firm shall take action to ensure that no connections remain between the firm and the individual.
- Where a partner leaves a firm and is appointed as a director or to a key management position with an audited entity, having acted as audit engagement partner at any time in the two years prior to this appointment, the firm shall resign as auditor.
- A partner, or employee of the audit firm who undertakes audit work, shall not accept appointment:
  - to the board of directors of the audited entity, or
  - to any subcommittee of that board.

Section 3 – Long association with engagements and with entities relevant to engagements

- The audit firm shall establish policies and procedures to monitor the length of time that senior staff serve as members of the engagement team for each audit.
- Where senior staff have a long association with the audit, the audit firm shall assess the threats to the auditor's objectivity and independence and shall apply safeguards to reduce the threats to an acceptable level. Such safeguards include partner rotation or appointment of an EQCR. Where appropriate safeguards cannot be applied, the audit firm shall either resign as auditor or not stand for reappointment, as appropriate.
- Once an audit engagement partner on a non-listed client has held this role for ten years, careful consideration must be given as to whether their objectivity would be perceived to be impaired and rotation of the partner should be considered. If the partner is not rotated, other safeguards must be applied and the reason for not rotating must be communicated to those charged with governance.
- In the case of listed companies, the audit firm shall establish policies and procedures to ensure that no one shall act as audit engagement partner for more than five years, and should not return within five years. The audit committee may approve an extension of two years in certain circumstances.
- When the audit client becomes listed, if the audit engagement partner has already served four or more years they may continue for a maximum of two years.
- In the case of listed companies, the audit engagement partner shall review the safeguards put in place to address the threats arising where senior staff have been involved in the audit for a period longer than seven years.

Note: Listed companies are required to put the audit out to tender every ten years in accordance with EU regulations. This is an action that the company must take rather than the auditor.

Section 4 – Fees, remuneration and evaluation policies, gifts and hospitality, litigation

- Sufficient partners and staff with time and skill to complete the audit should be assigned, regardless of the audit fee charged.
- Audit fees should not be influenced by the provision of non-audit services to the clients.
- An audit shall not be undertaken on a contingent fee basis.
- The audit fee for the previous audit and the arrangements for its payment shall be agreed with the audited entity before the audit firm formally accepts appointment as auditor in respect of the following period.
- Listed client: fees for providing non-audit services shall be limited to 70% of the average audit fee for the last 3 years. Where the fees charged for non-audit services for a financial year exceed the audit fee for that year, disclose to the Ethics Partner and consider the need for safeguards.
- Where it is expected that the total fees receivable from a listed audited entity will regularly exceed 10% of the annual fee income (15% if non-listed) of the audit firm, the firm shall not act as the auditor of that entity.
- Where regular fee income is expected to exceed 5% (listed) / 10% (non-listed) of the firm's fee income – disclose to the Ethics Partner and those charged with governance and consider whether safeguards need to be applied.
- New firms may find the economic dependence requirements difficult to comply with so should consider the use of an external quality control reviewer.
- The audit firm shall establish policies and procedures to ensure that the objectives and appraisal of members of the audit team do not include selling non-audit services.
- Where litigation with a client is already in progress, or where it is probable, the audit firm shall either not continue with or not accept the audit engagement.
- The audit firm, including employees, shall not accept gifts from the audited entity, unless the value is trivial.
- Audit firm employees shall not accept hospitality from the audited entity, unless it is reasonable in terms of its frequency, nature and cost.

Section 5 – Non-audit/additional services

- Anyone in the audit firm considering providing a non-audit service to one of the firm's audit clients must communicate the details to the audit engagement partner.
- Before accepting non-audit work, consider whether a reasonable and informed third party would regard the non-audit work as impairing the firm's objectivity and independence.
- Where safeguards are insufficient to mitigate the threats to independence, the non-audit work should not be accepted.
- General safeguards for non-audit services include separate teams for the audit and non-audit work and engagement quality control review of the work and conclusions of the audit team in relation to the non-audit service.
- Consider whether there is informed management i.e.
  - Objective and transparent information provided to the client
  - The client has a genuine opportunity to decide between alternative courses of action
  - A member of management has been designated to receive the result of non-audit services – this individual must have the capability to make judgments and decisions on the basis of the information provided.

  Without informed management it is unlikely that any safeguards could be effective against the management threat.
- Communicate matters that have a bearing on the auditor's objectivity and independence related to the provision of non-audit services to those charged with governance.

Prohibited non-audit services for listed clients:

- Tax services
- Taking part in management or decision-making
- Bookkeeping and preparing accounting records or financial statements
- Payroll services
- Design and implementation of internal controls, risk management procedures or information technology systems relating to financial information
- Valuation services (including actuarial valuation) where the valuation would have a material effect on the financial statements
- Legal services
- Internal audit

- Corporate finance services (including financing, investment strategy and promoting/dealing in or underwriting shares)
- Human resources services

Section 6 – Provisions available for audits of small entities

When auditing the financial statements of a small entity the audit firm is **not required** to:

- Comply with the requirement that an external independent quality control review is performed.
- Comply with Section 5, relating to providing non-audit services. The firm is not required to apply safeguards to address the self-review threat provided there is informed management, more regular 'cold review' of audits where non-audit services have been provided and disclosure of the non-audit services in the auditor's report.
- Comply with the requirement that where an audit partner joins the client the firm should resign and cannot accept appointment as auditor until 2 years have passed. The firm can continue as auditor provided there is no significant threat to the audit team's integrity, objectivity and independence and disclosure of the partner joining the client is made in the auditor's report.
- Comply with the requirement for an external independent quality control review if fees from a client are expected to exceed 10% but not exceed 15%. There is no requirement for the independent quality control review, but the issue must be disclosed to the Ethics Partner and those charged with governance at the client.

3 Confidentiality

Members acquiring information in the course of their professional work should not disclose such information to third parties without first obtaining permission from the client, unless there is a legal right or duty to disclose, or it is in the public interest to do so.

Circumstances in which disclosure is permitted or required

The general rule is that disclosure should only be made if:

- disclosure is permitted by law and the client's permission has been given.
- disclosure is required by law e.g. to provide evidence in legal proceedings or disclosure is required to a regulatory authority. This would include money laundering reporting.
- there is a professional right or duty to disclose e.g.

– to comply with a quality review
– to respond to an enquiry by a regulatory authority
– to protect the member's interests
– to comply with technical or ethical requirements.

Disclosure of confidential information – specific examples

Permitted or required by law

The most common offences members are likely to encounter in their professional work are in relation to:

- fraud or theft including fraudulent financial reporting, falsification or alteration of accounting records or other documents and misappropriation of assets
- taxation law
- money laundering
- insider dealing, market abuse, and bribery
- health and safety law
- employment law
- environmental offences.

Public interest

An auditor may disclose information if they consider it to be in the public interest. There is no official definition of 'public interest'. The auditor must employ a combination of judgment and legal advice. A good rule of thumb is that if a member of the public could incur physical or financial damage that the auditor could knowingly have prevented it is likely that the auditor has failed in their public duty.

In determining the need to disclose matters in the public interest the auditor should consider:

- whether those charged with governance have rectified the matter or are taking effective corrective action
- whether members of the public are likely to be affected
- the gravity of the matter
- the likelihood of repetition
- the reasons for the client's unwillingness to make the disclosures
- relevant legislation, accounting standards and auditing standards
- legal advice obtained.

The auditor will be protected from the risk of liability for breach of confidence provided that disclosure is made in the public interest, disclosure is made to an appropriate body or person, and there is no malice motivating the disclosure.

Conflicts of interest

Professional accountants should always act in the best interests of the client. However, where conflicts of interest exist, such as when a firm acts for competing clients, the firm's work should be arranged to **avoid the interests of one being adversely affected** by those of another and to prevent a breach of **confidentiality**.

In order to ensure this, the firm must notify all affected clients of the conflict and **obtain their consent to act.** The following additional safeguards should be considered:

- Separate engagement teams (with different engagement partners and team members).
- Procedures to prevent access to information, e.g. physical separation of the team members and confidential/secure data filing.
- Signed confidentiality agreements by the engagement team members.
- Regular review of the application of safeguards by an independent person of appropriate seniority.
- Advise the clients to seek independent advice.

If adequate safeguards cannot be implemented (i.e. where the acceptance/continuance of an engagement would, despite safeguards, materially prejudice the interests of any clients) the firm must decline or resign from one or more conflicting engagements.

Current issue: Revisions pertaining to safeguards

Exposure Draft: Proposed Revisions Pertaining to Safeguards in the Code – Phase 1

The exposure draft has been written to address concerns that safeguards in the Code of Ethics may be inappropriate or ineffective. The aim of the revisions is to improve clarity, appropriateness and effectiveness of the safeguards by improving the application material included in the Code. The following proposals have been suggested.

Requiring the accountant to :

- Apply the conceptual framework which involves identifying, evaluating and addressing threats to compliance with the fundamental principles.
- Exercise professional judgment, remain alert to changing circumstances, and take into account whether a reasonable and informed third party would likely conclude that the accountant has complied with the fundamental principles.

  The definition of the reasonable and informed third party test is given as 'evaluation by a hypothetical person who possesses skills, knowledge and experience to objectively evaluate the appropriateness of the professional accountant's judgments and conclusions'.

When evaluating threats the accountant must evaluate whether the threat is at an acceptable level. The definition of acceptable is given as 'a level which a reasonable and informed third party would likely conclude that the professional accountant complies with the fundamental principles'.

When addressing threats, the professional accountant can

- Eliminate the circumstances, including interests or relationships, that are creating the threats.
- Apply safeguards, where available and capable of being applied.
- Decline or discontinue with the specific professional activity or service involved.

The definition of a safeguard is given as 'actions, individually or in combination, that the professional accountant takes that effectively eliminate threats to compliance with the fundamental principles or reduce them to an acceptable level'.

If the accountant becomes aware of new information or changes in facts and circumstances that might impact whether a threat has been eliminated or reduced to an acceptable level, they shall re-evaluate and address the threat accordingly.

The accountant shall review judgments made and overall conclusions reached to determine that threats are eliminated or reduced to an acceptable level, and that no further action is needed.

Other proposals include

- Deleting examples of safeguards that no longer meet the proposed revised description of safeguards for example discussing ethical issues with those charged with governance.
- Removing the terms 'safeguards created by the profession or legislation', 'safeguards in the work environment', and 'safeguards implemented by the entity'.

Current issue: Long association

Exposure Draft: Limited Re-exposure of Proposed Changes to the Code Addressing Long Association of Personnel With an Audit Client

An Exposure Draft (ED) was issued in 2014 containing proposed revisions to the Code of Ethics in respect of long association. Responses to the ED have resulted in some requirements being re-drafted and put out for re-exposure. If approved, the new provisions will become effective for audits of financial statements beginning on or after 15 December 2018.

The ED covers:

- Rotation periods for engagement partners (EP), key audit partners (KAP), engagement quality control reviewers (EQCRs) and engagement team members.
- Length of cooling-off periods for EPs, KAPs and EQCRs.
- Restrictions on activities that can be performed during the cooling-off period
- Whether the provisions should apply to listed public interest entities or all public interest entities.

Students are reminded that exposure drafts are examinable to the extent that relevant articles are published by the examining team.

Exam-style question: Ethical and professional issues

You are an audit manager in Fox & Steeple, a firm of Chartered Certified Accountants, responsible for allocating staff to the following three audits of financial statements for the year ending 31 December 20X3:

Blythe Co is a new audit client. This private company is a local manufacturer and distributor of sportswear. The company's finance director, Peter, sees little value in the audit and put it out to tender last year as a cost-cutting exercise. In accordance with the requirements of the invitation to tender your firm indicated that there would not be an interim audit.

Huggins Co, a long-standing client, operates a national supermarket chain. Your firm provided Huggins Co with corporate financial advice on obtaining a listing on a recognised stock exchange in 20X2. Senior management expects a thorough examination of the company's computerised systems, and are also seeking assurance that the annual report will not attract adverse criticism.

Gray Co has been an audit client for seven years after your firm advised management on a successful buyout. Gray provides communication services and software solutions. Your firm provides Gray with technical advice on financial reporting and tax services. Most recently you have been asked to conduct due diligence reviews on potential acquisitions.

Required:

Identify and discuss the ethical and other professional issues raised, and recommend any actions that should be taken in respect of:

(a) Blythe Co

(b) Huggins Co

(c) Gray Co

Test your understanding 1 – Aventura

Aventura International, a listed company, manufactures and wholesales a wide variety of products including fashion clothes and audio-video equipment. The company is audited by Voest, a firm of Chartered Certified Accountants, and the audit manager is Darius Harken. The following matters have arisen during the audit of the group's financial statements for the year to 31 March 20X4 which is nearing completion:

(i) During the annual physical count of fashion clothes at the company's principal warehouse, the audit staff attending the count were invited to purchase any items of clothing or equipment at 30% of their recommended retail prices.

(ii) The chief executive of Aventura International, Armando Thyolo, owns a private jet. Armando invoices the company, on a monthly basis, for that proportion of the operating costs which reflects business use. One of these invoices shows that Darius Harken was flown to Florida in September 20X3 and flown back two weeks later. Neither Aventura nor Voest have any offices or associates in Florida.

(iii) Last week Armando announced his engagement to be married to his personal assistant, Kirsten Fennimore. Before joining Aventura in January 20X4, Kirsten had been Voest's accountant in charge of the audit of Aventura.

Required:

Identify and discuss the ethical issues raised in each of the scenarios and the responses required by the auditor in relation to these matters.

(15 marks)

Test your understanding 2 – Audit partner rotation

In order to comply with the ethical code of conduct it is widely recognised that senior audit personnel should be removed from engagements after a certain period (between five and ten years, depending upon the status of the client and national customs). To strengthen the ethical code of conduct further, professional accountancy bodies are currently debating whether to impose mandatory "rotation" periods for senior personnel as low as every two years.

Required:

(a) Discuss why audit partner rotation is important in an ethical code of conduct.

(4 marks)

(b) Identify and explain **TWO** problems a small or medium sized firm of chartered certified accountants might face if the threshold is lowered and identify a possible solution to each problem.

(4 marks)

Test your understanding 3 – Blake Seven

(a) Explain the importance of the role of confidentiality to the auditor-client relationship.

(5 marks)

(b) Your firm acts as auditor and adviser to Blake Seven and to its four directors. The company is owned 50% by Brad Capella, 25% by his wife Minerva and 10% by Janus Trebbiano. Brad is the chief executive and Janus the finance director. Janus's sister, Rosella Trebbiano, has recently resigned from the executive board, following a disagreement with the Capellas. Rosella has now formed her own company, Blakes Heaven, in competition with Blake Seven.

Rosella is currently negotiating with her former co-executives the profit-related remuneration due to her and the sale of her 15% holding of shares in Blake Seven to one or all of them.

Rosella has contacted you to find out Brad's current remuneration package since he refuses to disclose this to her.

She has also requested that your firm should continue to act as her personal adviser and become auditor and adviser to Blakes Heaven.

Required:

Comment on the matters that you should consider in deciding whether or not your audit firm can comply with Rosella's requests.

(10 marks)

(Total: 15 marks)

Test your understanding 4 – UK syllabus only

Weller & Co is facing competition from other audit firms, and the partners have been considering how the firm's revenue could be increased. A proposal has been made that all audit managers should suggest to their audit clients that, as well as providing the external audit service, Weller & Co can provide the internal audit service as part of an 'extended audit' service.

Required:

Comment on the ethical and professional issues raised by the proposal to increase the firm's revenue, and explain how the Auditing Practices Board has responded to the ethical issues raised by audit firms offering an 'extended audit' service.

(8 marks)

4 Chapter summary

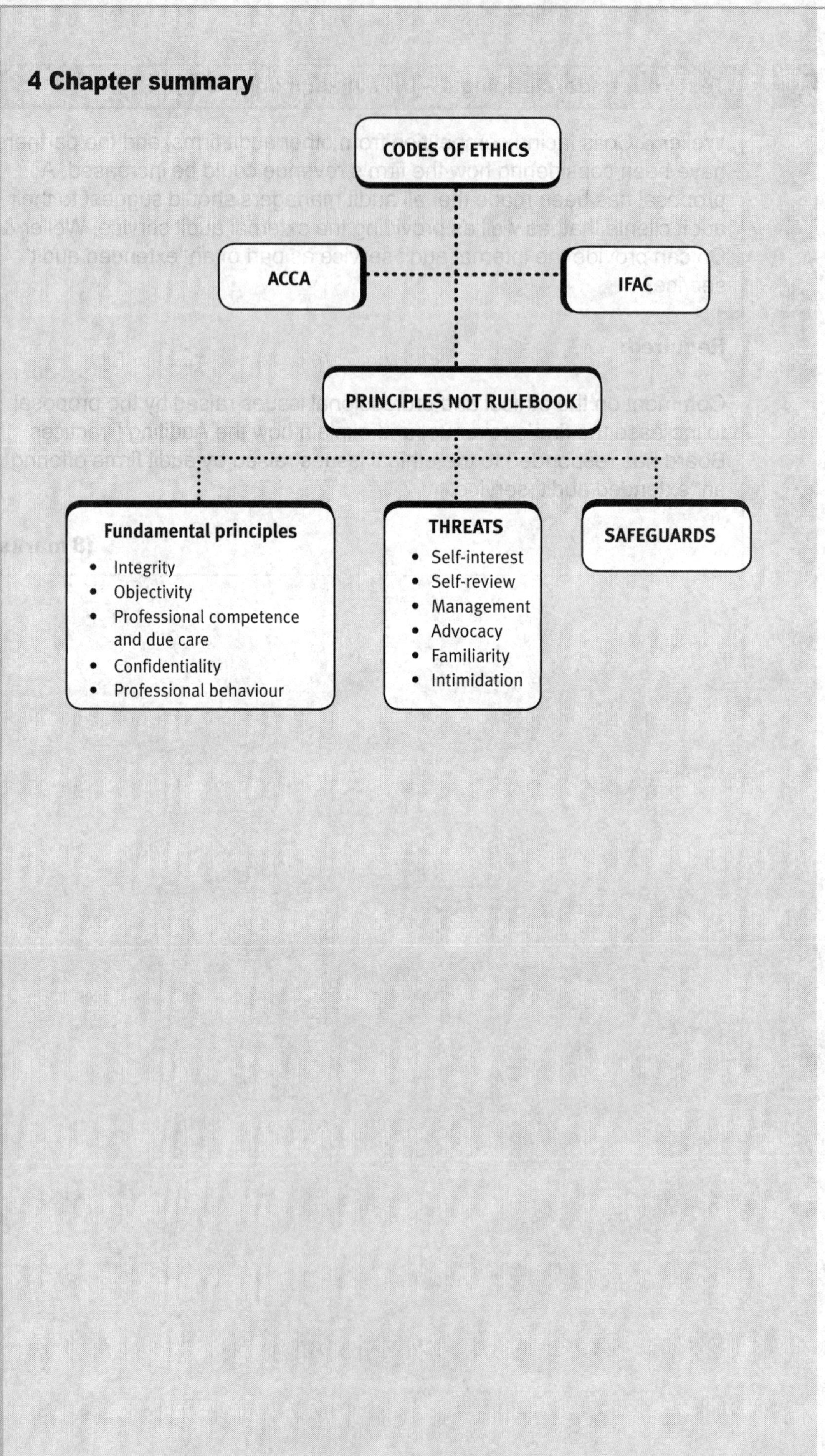

Test your understanding answers

Exam-style question: Ethical and professional issues

(a) **Blythe Co**

Intimidation and self-interest threats to objectivity may be created as the audit was put out to tender as a cost-cutting exercise. A threat to the fundamental principle of professional competence and due care also arises.

Peter may have applied pressure by stipulating that there should not be an interim audit in order to reduce fees.

This could mean the audit firm does not obtain sufficient appropriate evidence to form an appropriate opinion.

Senior staff assigned to Blythe should be alert to the need to exercise a high degree of professional scepticism in light of Peter's attitude towards the audit. The audit senior allocated to Blythe will need to be experienced in standing up to client management such as Peter.

As Blythe is a new client, detection risk will be higher and an engagement quality control review partner should be assigned.

(b) **Huggins Co**

Self-interest

The self-interest threat may be great for Huggins as the company is listed on a recognised stock exchange which may give prestige and credibility to Fox & Steeple.

Fox & Steeple could be pressured into overlooking material misstatements to avoid the loss of a listed client.

The engagement fee may be significant and Fox & Steeple may not wish to do anything to risk losing this client. This may include issuing an inappropriate opinion on the financial statements.

The fee level should be monitored to ensure that recurring fees from Huggins do not exceed the level set out by the profession for more than two consecutive years [INT: 15% of the firm's total fee income, UK: 10% of the firm's total fee income].

Familiarity

The familiarity threat of using the same lead engagement partner on an audit over a prolonged period is particularly relevant to Huggins, which is now a listed entity.

The audit firm may lack professional scepticism when performing the audit and fail to detect material misstatements.

The engagement partner should be rotated after a predefined period [INT: 7 years, UK: 5 years].

Self-review

A self-review threat is created when the audit firm provides non-audit services which affect the financial statements such as providing assurance over the computerised systems relevant to financial reporting.

The auditor may be unlikely to identify errors in their own work. If errors are found, they may be unlikely to admit to them.

The threat is significant as Huggins is a national chain and a listed client therefore significant reliance may be placed on the systems by the auditor.

As Huggins is listed, the examination of the computerised systems should not be undertaken if the systems relate to financial reporting or internal controls as the threat would be too significant.

If the systems do not relate to financial reporting or internal controls, separate teams should be used for each service. The team assigned to the systems examination should have appropriate skills.

Intimidation

As Huggins are seeking assurance the annual report will not attract adverse criticism, an intimidation threat may be created.

Huggins may put pressure on the auditors to allow them to omit disclosures which would generate adverse criticism.

The team must be aware of this risk and apply sufficient professional scepticism when performing the audit.

(c) **Gray Co**

Familiarity

Gray has been a client for seven years therefore a familiarity threat may be created if the same partner has been assigned for that time. The partner may become complacent and lack professional scepticism, possibly failing to challenge the client to the extent they would if it was a new client.

The threat is not significant at this time. Partner rotation will only be required if Gray becomes listed but the firm may wish to consider appointing an engagement quality control review partner in the future to ensure the audit is being performed with sufficient professional scepticism.

Self-review

Fox & Steeple provide technical advice on financial reporting as well as tax services. A due diligence engagement has also been requested. These additional services create a self-review threat.

The auditor will be auditing financial statements that have been prepared based on the advice of the firm and may therefore be reluctant to criticise the accounting treatment of certain elements as it would be seen to be criticising their own firm.

The threat may be considered significant depending on the nature of the advice and tax services provided. However, as Gray is not listed, the firm can still provide these services with safeguards applied.

Separate teams must be used and each team must have the relevant skills and competence for the service provided. Gray will require senior audit staff to be experienced in financial reporting matters specific to communications and software solutions e.g. in revenue recognition issues and accounting for internally generated intangible assets.

Assuming management responsibilities/Management threat

The provision of advice may be seen to be acting in the capacity of management if the advice provided is acted on without any consideration of Gray's management.

Activities such as authorising transactions, taking responsibility for the preparation and fair presentation of the financial statements, taking responsibility for designing, implementing and maintaining internal controls relevant to financial reporting or determining or changing journal entries, should not be performed without obtaining Gray's approval and acknowledgement that they are ultimately responsible.

Tutorial Note: General matters affecting Fox & Steeple

- All three assignments have the same financial year-end, therefore resourcing of each engagement will need to be carefully planned.
- As a listed company, Huggins is likely to have the tightest reporting deadline.
- Time budgets will need to be prepared for each assignment to determine manpower requirements and to schedule audit work.

Test your understanding 1 – Aventura

(i) **Goods**

The acceptance of gifts or hospitality, particularly during the inventory count, may be perceived to be a self-interest threat to objectivity. The count should be performed in an entirely neutral way but staff may ignore this in order to ensure they get their 'perk' of the engagement.

From an external perspective, this may be considered to be a bribe for a more relaxed inventory count check.

Inventory counts should be performed with the least disruption possible. Movements in inventory during the count vastly increase the risk of incorrect procedures being performed. If staff are purchasing items during the day this constitutes inventory movement.

The offer should not have been accepted during the physical count and all offers of goods should be discussed with senior audit management.

The value of the goods in question should be considered. 30% of manufacturer's recommended price amounts to a 70% discount. This is unlikely to be material to the client but may be significant enough to the audit team to be considered more than a 'trivial' gift.

The offer should be compared to any current staff discount schemes which Aventura offers to its employees. If Aventura does not offer staff discounts, the offer of discounted goods should have been declined.

In general it is prudent to avoid accepting gifts. If it later transpired that there was a problem with the count or the subsequent inventory valuation there would be increased risk of negligence claims (i.e. the audit team were not sufficiently diligent or that they accepted bribes).

(ii) **Services/hospitality**

Darius Harken has received a substantial benefit from his association with the audit client creating a self-interest threat. Darius may feel indebted to the client because of the gift and therefore overlook issues identified during the audit.

In addition it could be argued that Darius Harken is over-familiar with the chief executive Armando Thyolo. Darius may lack professional scepticism when auditing Aventura.

The value of this gift is likely to be significant and could be perceived to be outside the boundaries of a normal, professional relationship.

Darius Harken should not have accepted the use of the jet without the express permission of the audit engagement partner. It is possible that Darius may have paid for the use of the jet. However, the question of over-familiarity would still be relevant, as he could have used a commercial airline.

The fact that this arrangement only came to light during the audit of certain invoices suggests that Darius was intentionally withholding information about this beneficial transaction. Whilst there is no evidence that he tried to conceal it, a manager should understand his ethical position and concerns should be raised about his conduct.

Darius Harken should be removed from the audit immediately and potentially disciplined.

The requirement to have all gifts approved by a senior member of the audit team should be communicated to all staff to ensure this does not happen again.

All Darius' previous work on the client should now be reviewed again before the auditor's report is signed to ensure that appropriate procedures have been carried out and that he has remained objective. Particular attention should be paid to all matters of the audit manager's judgment.

Darius should be asked whether he has used the jet on other occasions and this should be confirmed with Armando.

(iii) **Ex-audit staff employed by client**

As Kirsten was the accountant in charge (AIC), not the audit manager or partner, it is unlikely that a significant lack of objectivity could have impaired the audit opinion for the year ended 31 March 20X3 or for any interim work done in 20X4.

However, her work may have been influenced given that she has developed a personal relationship with Armando Thyolo.

Upon beginning the relationship with Armando, Kirsten should have been immediately removed from the audit engagement. Either the senior management team are responsible for a lack of professional due care when assigning team members, or Kirsten has acted with a lack of professional behaviour and not informed the firm of the relationship.

Kirsten is now a member of staff at Aventura. There is likely to be a strong familiarity threat between her and the current audit team. The audit team may be less sceptical when auditing the client because they trust Kirsten having worked with her in the past.

The audit files for 20X3 and 20X4, in particular the work of Kristen, should be reviewed again. This should be done by an independent engagement partner.

The members of the audit team assigned to Aventura may need to be rotated in order to reduce the familiarity threat. A team from a different office could be used.

Test your understanding 2 – Audit partner rotation

Importance of rotation

Rotation of senior audit staff is important because it reduces the risk of **familiarity threat**. This arises when relationships between members of the audit team and the client develop beyond normal professional boundaries. This raises a number of concerns with regard to the professional completion of audit assignments.

Familiarity increases the risk of collusion between the directors of the client and senior audit personnel to bring about mutually beneficial ends, rather than performing the objective services required by shareholders. In the worst case scenario this could lead to fraud. Rotation of key staff reduces the likelihood of such undesirable relationships developing.

Familiarity could encourage the development of personal or business relationships between the auditor and their client. This would then create a self-interest threat to objectivity, where the audit firm may benefit financially from the client. Rotating the partner reduces the likelihood of this occurring.

Rotation reduces potential threats to professional competence and due care. This is due to the fact that an over-reliance on historical knowledge of a business and trust of directors can cause senior audit staff to overlook key issues. It is vital that auditors maintain professional scepticism at all times. Rotation freshens up perspectives and ideas, which should ensure consistently high quality services and professional due care.

Problems faced by small/medium sized firms

In some legislative authorities there are limits that restrict the requirement for small companies to have a statutory audit. For example, in the UK, companies with revenue of less than £10.2m and a statement of financial position total of less than £5.1m are exempt. Therefore many small accountancy firms have few, if any, remaining audit clients. The impact on these firms will be minimal.

In many firms, partners specialise in certain industries, meaning there would only be a small pool of partners to rotate between. This could be overcome by allowing partners to return to a previous client after a cooling off period. It could also be overcome by firms pooling their audit teams to reduce specialist departments, replacing them with staff able to adapt to a broad range of industries.

Each time a new partner takes over a client there will be a necessary handover of knowledge. It could potentially take a significant amount of time for a partner to understand the key issues and risks relating to a client that the previous partner would have been aware of. To overcome this successor partners could be identified well in advance. They could then review the audit file each year prior to taking over the client to build an awareness of the key issues. Another solution might be the creation of a 'knowledge bank' by the incumbent partner that they could give to their successor.

Test your understanding 3 – Blake Seven

(a) **The importance of confidentiality to the auditor-client relationship**

Confidentiality and security of information is one of the fundamental ethical principles. It applies to all professional accountants.

In particular:

- Confidential information is only disclosed to those entitled to receive it.
- Information obtained in the course of professional work is not used for purposes other than the client's benefit.
- Any decision to override the duty of confidentiality (e.g. if required by a court order) is taken after due consideration and discussion with professional colleagues.
- The duty of confidentiality continues even after an auditor-client engagement ceases.
- An accountant who moves into new employment must distinguish previously gained experience from confidential information acquired from their former employment.
- Prospective accountants must treat any information given by existing accountants in the strictest confidence.

As well as being a fundamental principal of the Code of Ethics, confidentiality will also undoubtedly be an implied contractual term.

In order to fulfil their duties, auditors require full disclosure of all information they consider necessary. A duty of confidentiality is therefore essential to ensuring that the scope of the audit is not limited as a result of information being withheld.

(b) **Matters to consider**

Rosella has made three requests:

(1) disclosure of a former co-executive's level of remuneration

(2) continuing to act as personal adviser

(3) accepting an appointment as auditor and adviser to Blakes Heaven.

(1) **Disclosure of remuneration package**

In an audit appointment, the auditor owes a duty of confidentiality to the client (i.e. the company not individual shareholders or executives). There is no legal or professional right or duty to disclose client information on an ad hoc basis merely because it is available to the auditor.

It would be a breach of the audit firm's duty of confidentiality to Blake Seven (in acting as auditor) and Brad (in acting as adviser) to disclose the information requested when clearly there is no process of law or public interest involved.

The audit firm could only disclose the information to Rosella with Brad's consent. This is highly unlikely since Brad has refused to do so.

In general, the audit firm's working papers are its own property and any request for them (e.g. if Rosella requested a schedule of emoluments, etc) should be refused.

The latest audited financial statements (which are available to Rosella in her capacity as a shareholder) may disclose Brad's remuneration for the previous year (e.g. as chairman and/or highest paid executive). Rosella will need to wait for this information to be publicly available.

As a member of the company (i.e. shareholder), Rosella would also be entitled to inspect any relevant documents required to be held at Blake Seven's registered office (e.g. if Brad has a service contract with the company).

(2) **Continuing as personal adviser**

A conflict between the interests of Blake Seven (and its continuing directors) and Rosella Trebbiano (in a personal capacity) is likely to arise (e.g. over the valuation of Rosella's shareholding).

It would be inappropriate for one adviser to act for both parties in certain matters, such as negotiating a share price, without appropriate safeguards.

Valuing Rosella's shareholding and negotiating her profit-related remuneration may appear to threaten the objectivity of the audit of Blake Seven. Rosella may try to exert influence to overstate profits (e.g. over Janus, as her brother and finance director, as well as the auditor).

However, the interests of these clients may not be materially prejudiced in all matters if:

- adequate disclosure is possible (i.e. of all relevant matters to all parties), and
- appropriate safeguards are implemented (e.g. advising one or all clients to seek additional independent advice).

In particular it may be possible to advise Rosella on personal tax matters.

(3) **Appointment as auditor**

A conflict between the interests of Rosella's new company, Blakes Heaven, and Blake Seven is likely to arise as the former has been set up in competition with the latter.

There is nothing improper in having both companies as audit clients if there are appropriate safeguards (e.g. different reporting partners and teams of staff for each audit engagement).

However, even with safeguards, the directors of Blake Seven (the Capellas in particular) may perceive that the involvement of the company's auditor with a competitor (in the capacity of auditor and adviser) could materially prejudice their interests. Also, that the new company has been set up with so similar a name suggests that Rosella may be quite aggressive in targeting Blake Seven's business.

In view of the adversarial relationship between Rosella and Blake Seven it would be prudent to include in their respective engagement letters a clause reserving the right to act for other clients subject to confidential information being kept secure.

The provision of other services (as adviser) could threaten the objectivity of the audit assignment. In particular, it would be inappropriate for the personal adviser to be the reporting partner or otherwise involved in the audit.

Conclusion

The request to disclose Brad's remuneration must be declined. However, Rosella may be directed to alternative sources of information, which may be of use (though not strictly current).

The firm may continue to act as Rosella's personal adviser subject to appropriate conditions and safeguards being put in place in respect of matters which may materially prejudice either client. For example:

- the agreement of Blake Seven (and the remaining directors)
- Rosella being advised to seek additional independent advice.

However, given the apparent acrimony between Rosella and her former associates, it seems unlikely that Blake Seven would agree to such an arrangement.

The audit appointment could only be accepted with appropriate safeguards (e.g. reporting partner and audit staff not involved in the audit of Blake Seven or the provision of other services). However, even with safeguards, if Rosella's appointments are accepted, Blake Seven may decide not to re-appoint the firm in future.

Test your understanding 4 – UK syllabus only

Weller & Co must ensure that any efforts to increase the firm's revenue do not create any threats to objectivity and independence. Offering an 'extended audit' service to clients such as providing an internal audit service to an audit client creates a self-review threat if the firm uses the internal audit work in the course of a subsequent external audit.

The self-review threat arises because of the possibility that the audit team will use the results of the internal audit service, without appropriately evaluating those results or exercising the same level of professional scepticism as would be exercised when the internal audit work is performed by individuals who are not members of the firm.

Performing a significant part of the client's internal audit activities increases the possibility that firm personnel providing internal audit services will assume a management responsibility. This threat cannot be reduced to an acceptable level.

Audit personnel should not assume a management responsibility when providing internal audit services to an audit client. Management responsibility may include, for example, performing procedures that are part of the internal control and taking responsibility for designing, implementing and maintaining internal control.

Section 5 of the FRC Ethical Standard states that the greatest threats to objectivity created by performing an internal audit service to an audit client are those of self-review and the management threat. It also acknowledges that the range of internal audit services is wide, and may not always be termed as such by the audited entity.

Audit firms are prohibited from undertaking an engagement to provide internal audit services to an audited entity where it is reasonably foreseeable that:

- For the purpose of the audit of the financial statements, the auditor would place significant reliance on the internal audit work performed by the audit firm, or
- For the purposes of the internal audit services, the audit firm would undertake part of the role of management.

Safeguards may be used to reduce the threat to an acceptable level, for example, by ensuring that external audit work and internal audit work are performed by separate teams. In addition, the audit work should be reviewed by a partner who is not involved with the audit.

Where internal audit services are supplied to an audit client, they should be the subject of a separate engagement letter and billing arrangement, and should also be pre-approved by those charged with governance of the audited entity.

chapter

3

Professional appointments

Chapter learning objectives

This chapter covers syllabus areas:

- C4 – Professional appointments

Detailed syllabus objectives are provided in the introduction section of the text book.

Exam focus

A common requirement in the P7 exam is to explain the matters to consider and the procedures that should be performed before acceptance of an engagement. This is not confined to audit engagements, it could be in relation to a different type of assurance engagement. The principles are the same for most engagements.

1 Prior to acceptance

An audit firm should only take on clients and work of an appropriate level of risk. For this reason, the firm will perform 'client screening'. The firm will consider the following matters before accepting a new engagement or client:

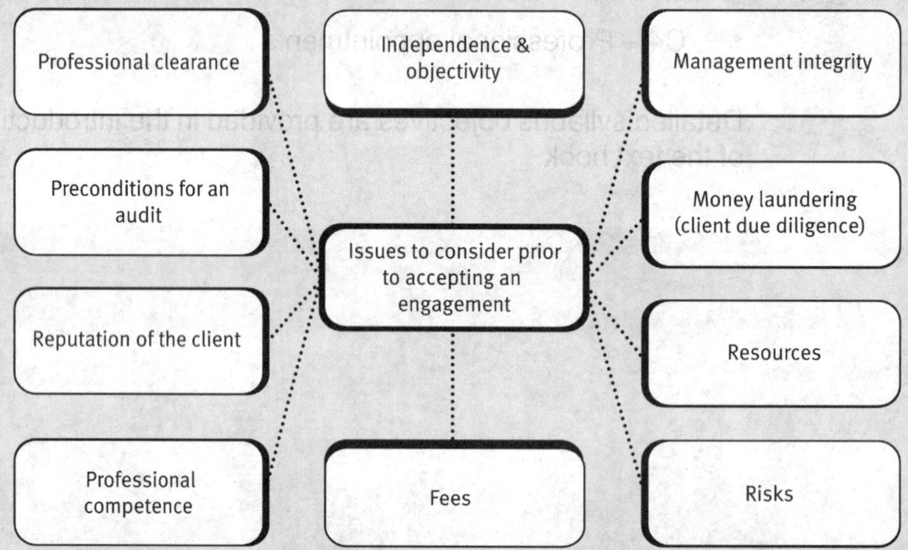

The main consideration is that the firm should only take on engagements and clients of acceptable risk. If there are any reasons why the firm believes they may not be able to issue an appropriate opinion, they should not accept the engagement.

Preconditions for an audit

ISA 210 *Agreeing the Terms of Audit Engagements* and the Code of Ethics and Conduct provide guidance to the professional accountant when accepting new work.

Before accepting (or continuing with) an engagement the auditor must establish whether the preconditions for an audit are present and that there is a common understanding between the auditor and management and, where appropriate, those charged with governance.

The preconditions for an audit are:

- That an acceptable financial reporting framework is to be applied to the preparation of the financial statements.
- That management understands and acknowledges its responsibilities for preparing the financial statements and providing the auditor with access to all relevant information and explanations.

If the client imposes a limitation on the scope of the auditor's work to the extent that the auditor believes it likely that a disclaimer of opinion will ultimately be issued then the auditor shall not accept the engagement, unless required to do so by law.

Continuance

Once the audit is complete, the audit firm must revisit the acceptance considerations again to ensure it is appropriate to continue with the engagement for the following year. If any significant issues have arisen during the year such as disagreements with management or doubts over management integrity, the auditor may consider resigning.

Acceptance considerations

Professional clearance

If offered an audit role, the prospective audit firm must contact the existing accountant to obtain professional clearance and determine whether there are any reasons that would preclude the accountant from taking on this engagement. The prospective firm should:

- Ask the client for permission to contact the existing auditor (and refuse the engagement if the client refuses).
- Contact the outgoing auditor, asking for all information relevant to the decision whether or not to accept appointment (e.g. overdue fees, disagreements with management, breaches of laws & regulations). This is also referred to as a professional etiquette letter.
- If a reply is not received, the prospective auditor should try and contact the outgoing auditor by other means e.g. by telephone.
- If a reply is still not received the prospective auditor may still choose to accept but must proceed with care.
- Consider the outgoing auditor's response and assess if there are any ethical or professional reasons why they should not accept appointment.
- The existing auditor must ask the client for permission to respond to the prospective auditor.

- If the client refuses permission, the existing auditor should notify the prospective auditor of this fact.

Independence and objectivity

If the auditor is aware, prior to accepting an engagement, that the threats to objectivity cannot be managed to an acceptable level, the audit should not be accepted.

Management integrity

If the audit firm has reason to believe the client lacks integrity there is a greater risk of fraud and intimidation.

Money laundering (client due diligence)

The audit firm must comply with Money Laundering Regulations which requires client due diligence to be carried out. If there is any suspicion of money laundering, or actual money laundering committed by the prospective client, the audit firm cannot accept the engagement.

Resources

The firm should consider whether there are adequate resources available at the time the audit is likely to take place to perform the work properly. If there is insufficient time to conduct the work with the resources available the quality of the audit could be impacted.

Risks

Any risks identified with the prospective client (e.g. poor performance, poor controls, unusual transactions) should be considered. These risks can increase the level of audit risk, i.e. the risk the auditor issues an inappropriate opinion. The auditor should only take on clients of acceptable risk.

Fees

The audit firm should consider the acceptability of the fee. The fee should be commensurate with the level of risk.

In addition, the creditworthiness of the prospective client should be considered as non-payment of fees can create a self-interest threat.

Professional competence

An engagement should only be accepted if the audit firm has the necessary skill and experience to perform the work competently.

Reputation of the client

The audit firm should consider the reputation of the client and whether its own reputation could be damaged by association.

Additional professional work

- Accountants may be asked to undertake work that is complementary or additional to the work of existing accountants, who are not being replaced.
- Before accepting such work, the accountant should communicate with the existing accountants to inform them of the general nature of the work being done.
- If permission is not given to communicate with the existing accountants, the engagement should be declined.

2 Agreeing the terms of engagement

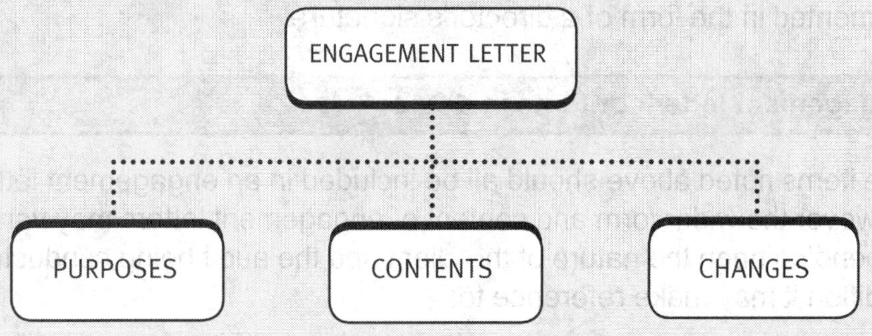

Purpose

The engagement letter specifies the nature of the contract between the audit firm and client.

Its purpose is to:

- minimise the risk of any misunderstanding between the auditor and client
- confirm acceptance of the engagement
- set out the terms and conditions of the engagement.

Contents

ISA 210 states that the auditor shall agree the terms of the audit engagement with management or those charged with governance, as appropriate. The terms are recorded in a written audit engagement letter and should include:

- The objective and scope of the audit of the financial statements
- The responsibilities of the auditor
- The responsibilities of management
- Identification of the applicable financial reporting framework for the preparation of the financial statements
- Reference to the expected form and content of any reports to be issued by the auditor.

The content of the engagement letter should be agreed with the client before any engagement related work commences.

The client's acknowledgement of the terms of the letter should be formally documented in the form of a director's signature.

Engagement letter contents in detail

The items noted above should all be included in an engagement letter. However the wider form and content of engagement letters may vary depending upon the nature of the client and the audit being conducted. In addition it may make reference to:

- Applicable regulations, legislation, ISAs and ethical pronouncements.
- The form of any other communications as a result of the engagement.
- The inherent limitations of audit procedures.
- Arrangements regarding the planning and performance of the audit.
- The expectation that management will provide written representations.
- The agreement of management to make available to the auditor draft financial statements and any accompanying information in time to allow the auditor to complete the audit in accordance with the timetable.
- The agreement of management to make available to the auditor facts pertinent to the preparation of the financial statements, which management may become aware of during the period from the date of the auditor's report to the date the financial statements are issued.
- The basis upon which fees are computed and billed.

- A request for management to acknowledge receipt of the engagement letter and to agree to the terms of engagement outlined therein.
- Arrangements concerning the involvement of other auditors and experts (where relevant).
- Arrangements concerning the involvement of internal auditors (where relevant).
- Any restriction on the auditor's liability, when such possibility exists.
- Any obligations to provide audit working papers to other parties.

Changes to the engagement letter

The engagement letter specifies the nature of the contract between the audit firm and the client. The auditor should issue a new engagement letter if the scope or context of the assignment changes after initial appointment.

Reasons for changes would include:

- changes to statutory duties due to new legislation
- changes to professional duties, for example, due to new or updated ISAs
- changes to 'other services' as requested by the client.

Audit of components of a group

- Where the auditor of a parent company is also the auditor of a subsidiary, branch or division of the group, the audit firm must decide whether to issue a single engagement letter covering all the components, or a separate letter to each component.
- If the audit firm sends one letter relating to the group as a whole, it is recommended that the firm should identify in the letter the components of the group for which the firm is being appointed as auditor.

3 After acceptance

Appointment as auditor

Where an accountant is being appointed as the new auditor of a company they should confirm that:

- the outgoing auditor has vacated office in a correct manner
- they have been properly appointed as the incoming auditor in accordance with relevant local legislation. This is usually achieved through a majority vote at the AGM, which should be documented in a formal minute.

Test your understanding 1

Your firm has been approached by Tomlin Co to provide the annual external audit following the resignation of the previous auditor. The company's year-end is 31 December which is the same as the majority of your firm's other audit clients. Tomlin Co supplies goods to major retailers. Your firm does not audit any other retailers. The company is currently recruiting a new finance director after the previous finance director was found guilty of bribing customers in order to win major contracts.

Required:

Explain the matters to be considered in deciding whether to accept the appointment as auditor of Tomlin Co.

Test your understanding 2

AB Accountants has been invited to become the auditors of XY Co, a company with a poor reputation since several senior managers were convicted of corruption recently. The company is adamant that it has now changed its culture, and is hoping that AB Accountants will become its auditors as part of this new ethical outlook.

Identify possible safeguards AB Accountants might consider using.

4 Chapter summary

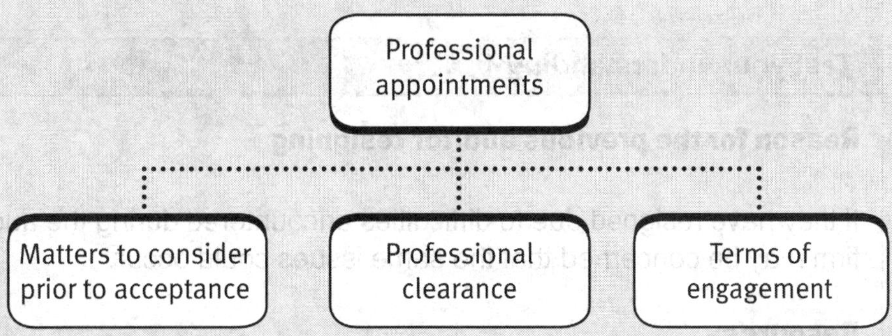

Test your understanding answers

Test your understanding 1

Reason for the previous auditor resigning

If they have resigned due to difficulties encountered during the audit, the firm may be concerned that the same issues could occur.

Resources

As Tomlin's year-end is the same as most other audit clients, the firm may not have sufficient audit staff available to assign to the audit.

Competence

As the firm does not audit any other retailers the company may not be sufficiently experienced to deal with such an audit. The firm may not understand the industry laws and regulations and the risks associated with that industry which increases audit risk.

Absence of a finance director

Without a finance director, the financial reporting processes are not being overseen by anyone. The financial statements may not be prepared on time and difficulties could be encountered by the audit team obtaining audit evidence.

Bribery

The previous FD was found guilty of bribing customers. This also indicates high control risk and may cast doubt over the integrity of management if other directors were aware of the bribery. The audit firm may decide the engagement is too risky to accept.

Independence

The firm would need to confirm independence from the client. Ethical threats such as self-interest and familiarity should be considered, and whether effective safeguards could be applied.

Fees

The level of the fee should be considered and whether the fee is acceptable for the amount of work involved and the level of risk associated with the engagement.

Test your understanding 2

AB Accountants must weigh up the possible costs and benefits of accepting nomination. The firm may wish to apply safeguards such as:

- Performing client due diligence in accordance with money laundering regulations.
- Obtaining a detailed knowledge of the client before accepting nomination.
- Securing the client's commitment to implement strong internal controls and the highest standards of corporate governance.
- Allocating the senior partner of the firm to be the engagement partner rather than a more junior partner.

If the firm does not believe that any such safeguards could reduce the threats to an acceptable level, then the firm should decline nomination.

chapter

4

Quality control

Chapter learning objectives

This chapter covers syllabus areas:

- C1 – Quality control

Detailed syllabus objectives are provided in the introduction section of the text book.

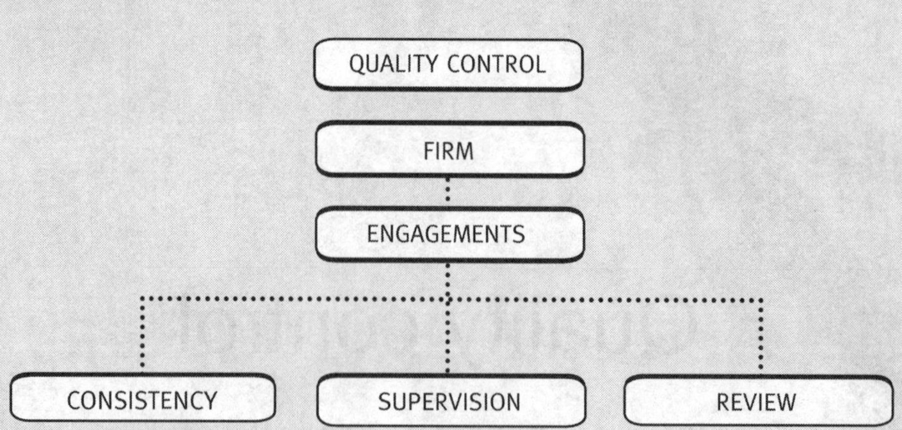

Exam focus

A common requirement in the P7 exam is to critically evaluate the audit work already performed on an engagement and identify if the audit has been carried out to the required standard of quality. If the firm does not perform work to a high quality it increases the risk of issuing an inappropriate report which could damage the reputation of the firm and the profession.

In order to assess the quality of the audit you should consider factors such as:

- Is there any evidence that ISAs have not been complied with?
- Has the work been allocated to the appropriate level of staff?
- Has the audit been time pressured and potentially rushed resulting in insufficient work being performed?
- Has the appropriate type of evidence been obtained?
- Has the audit been performed in accordance with the audit plan?
- Has the audit been properly supervised and reviewed?

1 The principles and purpose of quality control

The purpose of assurance services is to enhance the intended user's confidence in the subject matter they are using to make decisions.

In order for there to be confidence in the assurance process, engagements must be performed that are of satisfactory quality.

Failure to do so would not only mean a loss of confidence in the profession as a whole but could lead to professional negligence claims against the assurance provider.

Therefore firms must:

- perform work that complies with professional standards and regulatory and legal requirements, and
- issue reports that are appropriate in the circumstances.

If a professional negligence claim is made, and the firm has followed suitable quality control procedures, they should be able to defend the claim.

There are two standards that set out the responsibilities of auditors regarding quality control:

ISQC 1 *Quality Control for Firms that Perform Audits and Reviews of Financial Statements, and Other Assurance and Related Services Engagements*

Sets out an accountancy firm's responsibilities with regard to their systems of quality control for audits, reviews and other assurance engagements.

ISA 220 *Quality Control for an Audit of Financial Statements*

Applies to audit engagements only. It establishes the responsibilities of the auditor (mainly the engagement partner and engagement quality reviewer) regarding their quality control procedures during audits.

Most of the requirements of ISA 220 are covered by ISQC 1. This chapter therefore focuses on ISQC 1 requirements.

2 ISQC 1

ISQC 1 identifies six key principles:

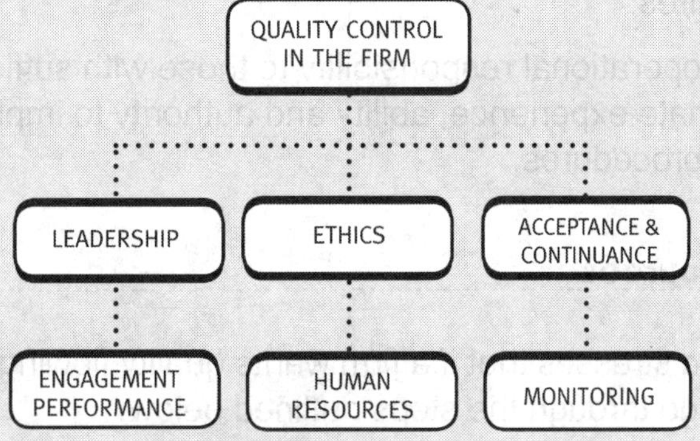

- **Leadership:** Strong and ethical leadership demonstrated by the managing partners.
- **Ethics:** Firms comply with ethical requirements such as the Code of Ethics.
- **Acceptance and continuance:** Only suitable clients and engagements are accepted and retained.
- **Human resources:** A firm and its employees have the necessary knowledge, technical competence, and experience.
- **Engagement performance:** Engagements are performed in an effective manner.
- **Monitoring:** Evaluating the quality control procedures to ensure they are effective.

Chapter 2 dealt with ethical considerations. Chapter 3 dealt with arrangements for the acceptance and continuance of client relationships and specific engagements.

In this chapter we will focus on the remaining four key principles.

Leadership

Firms must establish policies and procedures to **promote an internal culture that recognises the importance of quality** in performing engagements. This requires the firm's management team (i.e. managing partners) to:

- Establish policies and procedures to address performance evaluation, compensation and promotion to demonstrate commitment to quality.
- Ensure commercial consideration does not override quality.
- Ensure resources are sufficient to support the quality control procedures.
- Assign operational responsibility to those with sufficient and appropriate experience, ability and authority to implement those quality control procedures.

Human resources

The standard stresses that if a firm wants quality flowing through all levels of staff it must go through the steps outlined below.

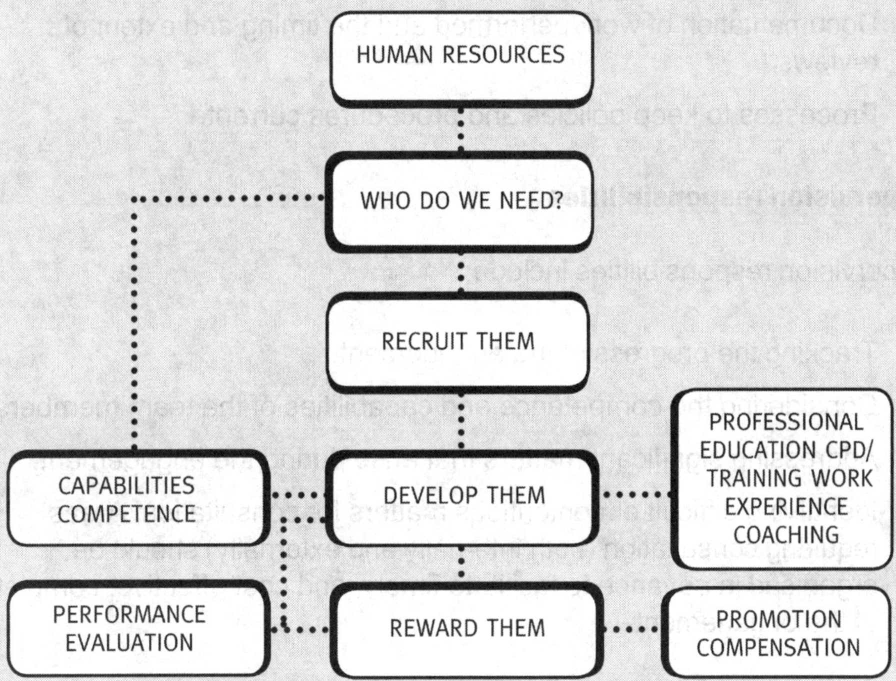

A firm must have policies and procedures in place to ensure an appropriate engagement partner is assigned to an engagement, i.e. one who has the competence, capability and time to perform the role. The engagement partner should then ensure the right people are allocated to the engagement team, i.e. staff with the relevant knowledge, experience, and training.

Engagement performance

Firms must design policies and procedures to ensure engagements are performed to a satisfactory standard. Policies and procedures should cover:

- Matters relevant to promoting **consistency** in the quality of engagements.
- **Supervision** responsibilities.
- **Review** responsibilities.

Consistency in the quality of engagement performance

Firms promote consistency through their policies and procedures. This is often accomplished through written manuals, software tools and standardised documentation. Particular matters that can be addressed include:

- How engagement teams are briefed to obtain an understanding of the engagement and their objectives.
- Processes for complying with engagement standards.
- Processes of engagement supervision, training and coaching.
- Methods of reviewing work, judgments and reports issued.

- Documentation of work performed and the timing and extent of reviews.
- Processes to keep policies and procedures current.

Supervision responsibilities

Supervision responsibilities include:

- Tracking the progress of the engagement.
- Considering the competence and capabilities of the team members.
- Addressing significant matters that arise during the engagement.
- Identifying difficult or contentious matters for consultation. Areas requiring consultation (both internally and externally) should be organised in advance to facilitate timely, and cost effective, completion of the engagement.

Review responsibilities

Work of less experienced team members should be reviewed by more experienced team members to identify whether:

- The work has been performed in accordance with professional standards.
- Significant matters have been raised for further consideration.
- Appropriate consultations have taken place and resulting conclusions have been documented.
- The work performed supports the conclusions reached and is appropriately documented.
- The evidence obtained is sufficient and appropriate to support the report.
- The objectives of the engagement procedures have been achieved.

Engagement quality control review

Listed entities and other high risk clients should be subject to an engagement quality control review (EQCR). This is also referred to as a pre-issuance review or 'Hot' review.

High risk clients include those which are in the public interest, those with unusual circumstances and risks, and those where laws or regulations require an EQCR.

The EQCR should include:

- Discussion of significant matters with the engagement partner.
- Review of the financial statements and the proposed report.
- Review of selected engagement documentation relating to significant judgments the engagement team made and the conclusions reached. This includes:
  - Significant risks and responses to those risks
  - Judgments with respect to materiality and significant risks
  - Significance of uncorrected misstatements
  - Matters to be communicated to management and those charged with governance, and where applicable, other parties such as regulatory bodies.
- Evaluation of conclusions reached in formulating the report and consideration of whether the proposed report is appropriate.
- The engagement team's evaluation of the firm's independence.
- Whether appropriate consultation has taken place on matters involving differences of opinion and the conclusions of those consultations.
- Whether documentation selected for review reflects work performed in relation to significant judgments and supports the conclusions reached.

Eligibility criteria

The engagement quality control reviewer:

- should have the technical qualifications to perform the role, including the necessary experience and authority, and
- should be objective. To be objective the reviewer should not be selected by the engagement partner and should not participate in the engagement.

Monitoring

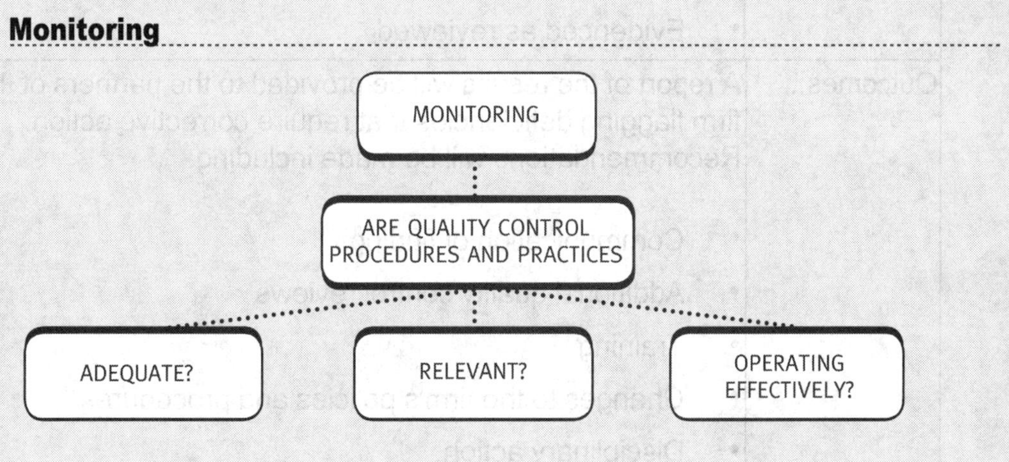

Quality control policies alone do not ensure good quality work. They must be implemented effectively. Therefore the firm must evaluate:

- Adherence to professional standards and regulatory/legal requirements.
- Whether quality controls have been implemented on a day-to-day basis.
- Whether the firm's quality control policies and procedures are effective so that reports issued by the firm are appropriate in the circumstances.

Firms should carry out post-issuance or 'cold' reviews to ensure that quality control procedures are adequate, relevant, and are operating effectively.

	Post-issuance (Cold) review
Purpose...	To assess whether the firm's policies and procedures were implemented during an engagement and to identify any deficiencies therein.
When...	After an engagement has been completed.
Which files...	A selection of completed engagements.
Who by...	A dedicated compliance or quality department/a qualified external consultant/an independent partner.
What considered...	Working papers should demonstrate that: • Sufficient appropriate evidence has been obtained • All matters were resolved before issuing the auditor's report All working papers should be: • On file • Completed • Signed as completed • Evidenced as reviewed
Outcomes...	A report of the results will be provided to the partners of the firm flagging deficiencies that require corrective action. Recommendations will be made including: • Communication of findings • Additional quality control reviews • Training • Changes to the firm's policies and procedures • Disciplinary action.

Summary of pre and post-issuance reviews

	Pre-issuance (Hot) review	**Post-issuance (Cold) review**
Purpose...	To enhance the quality of assurance work.	Monitoring – to identify any deficiencies in the firm's processes.
When...	Before the auditor's report is issued.	After the auditor's report has been issued.
Which files...	• Listed clients • Public interest engagements • Engagements where there are particular risks. • Each partner should have some of their engagements reviewed.	A selection of completed engagements.
Who by...	An independent partner of suitable experience and authority.	A dedicated compliance or quality department/a qualified external consultant/an independent partner.
What considered...	Processes underpinning judgments made.	Wholesale review of all working papers on an audit file.
Specifically...	Processes underpinning judgments about: • Significant risks and responses to them • Matters requiring consultation • Materiality • Independence • Conclusions • Misstatements • The audit opinion • Matters to be communicated to management and those charged with governance.	To ensure that all working papers are: • On file • Complete • Signed as completed • Evidenced as reviewed • The work undertaken is sufficient and has been documented appropriately.

Outcomes...	A reduction in audit risk, i.e. the risk that the auditor expresses an inappropriate audit opinion when the financial statements are materially misstated.	Identify corrective action that should be taken. Recommendations will be made including: • Communication of findings • Additional quality control reviews • Training • Changes to the firm's policies and procedures • Disciplinary action.

Audit quality monitoring

In the UK, 1402 monitoring visits were carried out during 2015 by the national regulatory body. 76% of audits were assessed as good or only requiring limited improvements compared with 67% in the prior year. Only two audits required significant improvements compared with ten in the previous year.

The five most common areas of concern were:

- Fair value and value in use measurements including impairment testing and property valuations.
- Revenue recognition
- Audit committee communication
- Internal controls testing
- Independence and ethics

FRC Audit Quality Thematic Review

Engagement Quality Control Reviews (EQCR)

Thematic reviews are inspections performed by the FRC which look at specific aspects of the audit process. In February 2016 the FRC published the results of its thematic review into EQCR.

One tenth of the audits reviewed identified weaknesses in the audit work that the EQCR did not identify which could directly impact audit quality. The FRC has recommended that audit firms evaluate the effectiveness of the EQCR to prevent these weaknesses recurring.

When ensuring the EQCR is effective firms must consider:

- The eligibility of the person to perform the EQCR taking into consideration the qualifications and experience of the reviewer.
- Objectivity of the EQCR throughout the whole audit, not just at the start of the audit.
- The EQCR should be performed in a timely and effective manner to ensure there is sufficient time to resolve issues and perform more audit work if necessary.
- There must be evidence of the EQCR.

In order to ensure effectiveness of the EQCR firms should:

- Complete checklists confirming completion of procedures required by standards.
- Copies of financial statements and reports to the audit committee should be annotated by the EQCR and kept as evidence of review.
- Key audit working papers should be signed off by the EQCR to indicate that they have read them.
- EQCR notes should be kept as evidence.
- Audit file notes of significant matters discussed with the audit team and how they were resolved should be kept as evidence.
- The time recorded by the EQCR on the audit should be recorded.
- Firms should ensure the ECQR has sufficient industry experience.
- The EQCR should be required to re-confirm their objectivity at the completion stage to ensure any issues arising during the audit have been appropriately dealt with.

Principal findings

- Some EQCRs did not have sufficient specialist experience, limiting their ability to evaluate key judgments specific to the industry.
- The need to be objective is not always adhered to. For example, on one audit the EQCR was to become the audit partner following the audit and had attended audit committee meetings as an observer. In several audits the name of the EQCR was included in the tender document and could therefore have been contacted by the audit committee which would threaten their objectivity.
- In several audits there was insufficient evidence that the EQCR had been performed.
- In several audits the EQCR had been performed too late to provide meaningful input.
- In several audits the EQCR had not identified deficiencies in the work performed by the audit team that should have been identified and raised by the EQCR.

Good quality monitoring

Monitoring should be performed on an ongoing, cyclical basis, including an inspection of at least one completed engagement for each engagement partner. The responsibility for this monitoring process should be assigned to a partner and those performing the inspections should not have had any involvement in the engagements under review.

The monitoring process goes beyond the simple enforcement of policies and procedures. It has to consider:

- How the firm responds to new developments in professional standards and regulatory and legal requirements.
- How the firm ensures compliance with independence rules by all its partners and staff. (Usually achieved through the use of independence or 'fit and proper' forms, which will need checking for completeness).
- How the firm ensures all partners and staff comply with continuing professional development requirements. (Often achieved by controlling course bookings centrally, or by maintaining training logs).
- How the firm ensures that appropriate decisions are made about the acceptance of new appointments or the continuance of client relationships. (Should be covered as part of the independent review of assignments).

Arrangements then need to be made for follow up where breaches of policy or ineffective procedures are revealed.

3 Documentation

In addition to the main elements of quality control identified in the previous sections, ISA 220 *Quality Control for an Audit of Financial Statements* also requires auditors to document certain matters:

- Issues with respect to ethical requirements and how they were resolved.
- Conclusions on compliance with independence requirements.
- Conclusions reached regarding the acceptance and continuance of engagements.
- The nature, scope and conclusions resulting from consultations undertaken during the course of the audit.

During completion of the audit the engagement quality reviewer has to document:

- The procedures required by the firm's engagement quality review procedures.
- That the engagement quality review has been completed (on or before the date of the auditor's report).
- That the reviewer is not aware of any unresolved matters that would cause the reviewer to believe that the significant judgments of the team were not appropriate.

Applying ISQC 1 proportionately with the size and nature of a firm

- The IAASB allows proportionate application of the requirements of ISQC 1 for smaller firms.
- Firms need only comply with those requirements that are relevant to the services provided.
- Firms can exercise appropriate judgment in implementing a system of quality control.
- Firms can draw on external resources to meet some of the requirements.

- ISQC 1 does not suggest a specific approach to implementation in order to allow smaller firms the flexibility to apply the provisions proportionately.
- Smaller firms may have less formal processes, procedures and communication than larger firms.
- Smaller firms can use advisory services provided by other firms, professional and regulatory bodies and commercial organisations that provide quality control services.
- Monitoring of quality control procedures must still be performed by smaller firms. These may be performed by individuals who are responsible for the design and implementation of the policies and procedures, or who may be involved with the quality control review.
- The firm can also choose a qualified external person to carry out inspections.
- The existence of an audit regulator inspection program is not a substitute for the firm's own monitoring program.
- ISQC 1 requires inspection of at least one completed engagement for each engagement partner on a cyclical basis. This must not be conducted by personnel involved in performing the engagement. Smaller firms may make arrangements with other smaller firms to perform inspections of each other's files.

A framework for audit quality

The objectives of the Framework of Audit Quality include:

- Raising awareness of the key elements of audit quality.
- Encouraging key stakeholders to explore ways to improve audit quality.
- Facilitating greater dialogue between key stakeholders on the topic.

The IAASB expects that the Framework will generate discussion, and positive actions to achieve a continuous improvement to audit quality.

The IAASB believes that such a Framework is in the public interest as it will:

- Encourage firms and professional accountancy organisations to reflect on how to improve audit quality and better communicate information about audit quality.
- Raise the level of awareness and understanding among stakeholders of the elements of audit quality.

- Enable stakeholders to recognise factors which require priority to enhance audit quality.
- Assist standard setting, both nationally and internationally.
- Facilitate dialogue between the IAASB and key stakeholders.
- Stimulate academic research.
- Assist auditing students to understand the fundamentals of the profession.

A quality audit is likely to have been achieved by an engagement team that has:

- Exhibited appropriate values, ethics and attitudes.
- Was sufficiently knowledgeable, skilled and experienced and had sufficient time allocated.
- Applied a rigorous audit process and audit quality control procedures compliant with law, regulation and applicable standards.
- Provided useful and timely reports.
- Interacted appropriately with relevant stakeholders.

The Framework contains the following elements:

(1) **Inputs**

The values, ethics and attitudes of auditors.

(2) **Process**

The rigor of the audit process and quality control procedures that impact audit quality. The firm's audit methodology should evolve with changes in professional standards. Whilst methodologies enable an efficient and effective audit to take place, there is a risk that insufficient emphasis will be given to tailoring the audit procedures to the specific circumstances of the client. Therefore a firm's methodologies should be flexible and adapted to each client to ensure a quality audit is performed.

(3) **Outputs**

The reports and information that are formally prepared and presented by one party to another. The outputs from the audit are often determined by the context, including legislative requirements.

(4) **Key interactions within the financial reporting supply chain**

The formal and informal communications between stakeholders groups. Audit quality will be affected by the frequency of communication and the nature of the information communicated. Expectations can be managed through effective communication.

(5) **Contextual factors**

These are environmental factors such as laws and regulations and corporate governance which have the potential to impact the nature and quality of financial reporting and therefore audit quality.

Test your understanding 1 – Agnesal

(a) 'The objective of the auditor is to implement quality control procedures at the engagement level that provide the auditor with reasonable assurance that:

– The audit complies with professional standards and applicable legal and regulatory requirements; and

– The auditor's report issued is appropriate in the circumstances.'

(**ISA 220** *Quality Control for an Audit of Financial Statements*)

Required:

Describe the nature and explain the purpose of quality control procedures appropriate to the individual audit.

(7 marks)

(b) You are the manager responsible for the quality of the audits of new clients of Signet, a firm of Chartered Certified Accountants. You are visiting the audit team at the head office of Agnesal, a limited liability company, the date is 5 June 20X4. The audit team comprises Artur Bois (audit supervisor), Carla Davini (audit senior) and Errol Flyte and Gavin Holst (trainees). The company provides food hygiene services which include the evaluation of risks of contamination, carrying out bacteriological tests and providing advice on health regulations and waste disposal.

Agnesal's principal customers include food processing companies, wholesale fresh food markets (meat, fish and dairy products) and bottling plants. The draft accounts for the year ended 31 March 20X4 show revenue $19.8 million (20X3: $13.8 million) and total assets $6.1 million (20X3: $4.2 million).

You have summarised the findings of your visit and review of the audit working papers relating to the audit of the financial statements for the year to 31 March 20X4 as follows:

(i) Against the analytical procedures section of the audit planning checklist, Carla has written 'not applicable – new client'. The audit planning checklist has not been signed off as having been reviewed by Artur.

(ii) Artur is currently assigned to three other jobs and is working from Signet's office. He last visited Agnesal's office when the final audit commenced two weeks ago. In the meantime, Carla has completed the audit of non-current assets (including property and service equipment) which amount to $1.1 million as at 31 March 20X4 (20X3: $1.1 million).

(iii) Errol has just finished sending out requests for confirmation of trade receivable balances as at 31 March 20X4 when trade receivables amounted to $3.5 million (20X3: $1.6 million).

(iv) Agnesal's purchase clerk, Jules Java, keeps $2,500 cash to meet sundry expenses. The audit program shows that counting it is 'outstanding'. Carla has explained that when Gavin was sent to count it he reported back, two hours later, that he had not done it because it had not been convenient for Jules. Gavin had, instead, been explaining to Errol how to extract samples using value-weighted selection. Although Jules had later announced that he was ready to have his cash counted, Carla decided to postpone it until later in the audit. This is not documented in the audit working papers.

(v) Errol has been assigned to the audit of inventory (comprising consumable supplies) which amounts to $150,000 (20X3: $90,000). Signet was not appointed as auditor until after the year-end physical count. Errol has therefore carried out tests of controls over purchases and issues to confirm the 'roll-back' of a sample of current quantities to quantities as at the year-end count.

(vi) Agnesal has drafted its first 'Report to Society' which contains health, safety and environmental performance data for the year to 31 March 20X4. Carla has filed it with the comment that it is 'to be dealt with when all other information for inclusion in the company's annual report is available'.

Required:

Identify and comment on the implications of these findings for Signet's quality control policies and procedures.

(18 marks)

(Total: 25 marks)

Test your understanding 2 – Cello

You are a senior manager with Flute and Co and are a member of the team conducting cold reviews. You are currently reviewing the audit file of Cello Co, a subsidiary of a listed overseas parent, which imports and distributes office furniture, usually manufactured by other group companies.

During your review you notice the following.

- Minutes of the planning meeting are on file but were not signed by the partner.
- The company's year-end is 31 December. Fieldwork was completed by 15 February and the financial statements together with the auditor's report were signed on 15 April. The subsequent events checklist was completed on 15 February.
- The company has very little headroom in its overdraft and apparently no other borrowing facilities.
- There is a letter of support on file from the holding company dated 15 April.
- Materiality is calculated at $60,000, which is in line with the firm's recommended procedures.

- Non-current assets consist of office furniture, office equipment and racking and forklifts for the rented warehouse. Carrying value is $250,000 and additions in the year were $40,000. Copy invoices for all the additions are on file but you find it difficult to see precisely what work was done and the working papers other than the pre-printed audit programme and lead schedule were neither initialled nor dated.
- The receivables circularisation was successful except for one non-reply for $40,000.

Required:

- What conclusions are you able to draw about the quality of the audit of Cello Co?
- What recommendations would you make to the firm's audit quality committee?

4 Chapter summary

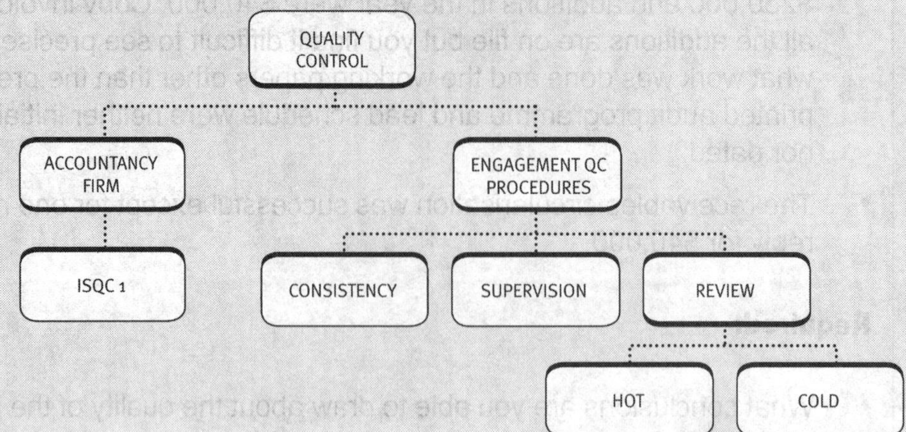

Test your understanding answers

Test your understanding 1 – Agnesal

(a) **Quality control procedures**

Quality controls are the policies and procedures adopted by a firm to provide reasonable assurance that all audits done by a firm are being carried out in accordance with the objective and general principles governing an audit.

Individual audit level

Work delegated to assistants should be directed, supervised and reviewed to ensure the audit is conducted in compliance with ISAs.

Assistants should be professionally competent to perform the work delegated to them with due care.

Direction (i.e. informing assistants about their responsibilities and the nature, timing and extent of audit procedures they are to perform) may be communicated through:

- briefing meetings and on-the-job coaching
- the overall audit plan and audit programs
- audit manuals and checklists
- time budgets.

Supervisory responsibilities include monitoring the progress of the audit to ensure that assistants are competent, understand their task and are carrying them out as directed. Supervisors must also address accounting and auditing issues arising during the audit (e.g. by modifying the overall audit plan and audit program).

The work of assistants must be reviewed to assess whether:

- it is in accordance with the audit program
- it is adequately documented
- significant matters have been resolved
- objectives have been achieved
- conclusions are appropriate (i.e. consistent with results).

Documentation which needs to be reviewed on a timely basis includes:

- the overall audit plan and any modifications thereto
- results from tests of control and substantive procedures
- conclusions drawn
- audit adjustments
- financial statements
- proposed audit opinion.

An independent review (i.e. by personnel not otherwise involved in the audit), to assess the quality of the audit (before issuing the auditor's report) should be undertaken for listed and other public interest or high risk audit clients.

Additional point

Quality control procedures reduce the risk of litigation claims thereby reducing the risk of reputational damage.

(b) **Implications of findings for QC policies and procedures**

(i) **Analytical procedures**

Analytical procedures should have been performed at the planning stage, to assist in understanding the business and in identifying areas of potential risk, in accordance with ISA 315 (Revised) *Identifying and Assessing the Risks of Material Misstatement through Understanding the Entity and Its Environment*. The audit senior should know this.

Audit staff may have insufficient knowledge to assess the risks of the highly specialised service industry in which this new client operates. In particular, Agnesal may be exposed to risks resulting in unrecorded liabilities (both actual and contingent) if claims are made against the company in respect of outbreaks of contamination.

The audit has been inadequately planned and audit work has commenced before the audit plan has been reviewed by the audit supervisor. The audit may not be carried out effectively and efficiently.

(ii) **Supervisor's assignments**

The senior has performed work on non-current assets which is a less material (18% of total assets) audit area than trade receivables (57% of total assets) which has been assigned to an audit trainee. Non-current assets also appears to be a lower risk audit area than trade receivables because the carrying amount of non-current assets is comparable with the prior year ($1.1m at both year-ends), whereas trade receivables have more than doubled (from $1.6m to $3.5m). This corroborates the implications of (i).

The audit is being inadequately supervised as work has been delegated inappropriately. It appears that the firm does not have sufficient audit staff with relevant competencies to meet its supervisory needs.

(iii) **Direct confirmation**

It is usual for direct confirmation of trade receivables to be obtained where trade receivables are material and it is reasonable to expect customers to respond. However, it is already more than two months after the statement of financial position date and, although trade receivables are clearly material (57% of total assets), an alternative approach may be more efficient (and cost effective). For example, testing of after-date cash will provide evidence about the collectability of trade receivables as well as corroborate their existence.

This may be a further consequence of the audit having been inadequately planned.

Supervision of the audit may be inadequate. For example, if the audit trainee did not understand the alternative approach but mechanically followed circularisation procedures.

Depending on the reporting deadline, there may still be time to perform a circularisation. However, consideration should be given to circularising the most recent month-end balances (i.e. May) rather than the year-end balances which customers may be unable or reluctant to confirm retrospectively.

(iv) **Cash count**

Although $2,500 is very immaterial, the client's management may expect the auditor to count it to confirm that it has not been misappropriated.

The briefing given to the trainee may have been inadequate. For example, Gavin may not have understood the need to count the cash at the time the request was made of the client. However, the behaviour of Gavin also needs to be investigated in that he failed to report back to the audit senior on a timely basis and allowed himself to be unsupervised.

The trainees do not appear to have been given appropriate direction. Gavin may not be sufficiently competent to be explaining sample selection methods to another trainee.

Although it is not practical to document every matter, details should have been recorded to support Carla's decision to change the timing of a planned procedure. Carla's decision appears justified as it is inappropriate to perform a cash count when the client is 'ready' for it. Also, if some irregularity is discovered by the client at a later date (e.g. if Jules is found to be 'borrowing' the cash), documentation must support why this was not detected sooner by the auditor.

(v) **Inventory**

Whilst material, (2.5% of total assets), inventory is relatively low risk given the company has no inventory-in-trade, only consumables used in the supply of service. Therefore it seems appropriate that a trainee should be auditing it. However, the audit approach appears highly inefficient. Such in-depth testing (of controls and details) on a relatively low risk area may be due to a lack of monitoring or a mechanical approach being adopted by a trainee. This provides further evidence that the audit has been inadequately planned, and demonstrates a lack of knowledge and understanding about Agnesal's business.

(vi) **'Report to society'**

The audit senior appears to have assumed that this is other information to be included in a document containing audited financial statements (the annual report). To be dealt with presumably means to be read with a view to identifying significant misstatements or inconsistencies. The comment indicates that Carla possibly does not know what needs to be done with the report. By leaving it until the end of the audit, it could cause problems, for instance if the audit firm is actually required to provide assurance on the Report to Society there may not be sufficient time to perform the work required to be able to issue the report by the required deadline.

As the preceding analysis casts doubts on Signet's ability to deliver a quality audit to Agnesal, it seems unlikely that Signet has the resources and expertise necessary to provide such assurance services.

Conclusions

The audit is not being conducted in accordance with ISAs e.g. ISA 315 *Identifying and Assessing the Risks of Material Misstatement Through Understanding the Entity and Its Environment* and ISA 520 *Analytical Procedures* which indicates Signet's quality control policies and procedures are not established and/or not being communicated to personnel.

Audit work is being assigned to personnel with insufficient technical training and proficiency which indicates weaknesses in procedures for hiring and/or training of personnel.

Insufficient direction, supervision and review of work at all levels suggests a lack of resources.

In deciding whether or not to accept the audit of Agnesal, Signet should have considered whether it had the ability to serve the client properly. The partner responsible for accepting the engagement does not appear to have evaluated the firm's (lack of) knowledge of the industry.

Test your understanding 2 – Cello

Planning meeting

The planning should be documented fully and approved by the partner before the start of fieldwork. It is possible that evidence of this approval is to be found elsewhere on the file, but it would have been better if the partner had signed off the meeting minutes as soon as they were available.

Going concern and subsequent events

- The subsequent events review should be updated to the date of signing the auditor's report. The review should arguably be more rigorous and comprehensively documented because of the lack of financial facilities and the raised risk of going concern issues.
- The fact that the parent is listed overseas does not mean that the comfort letter is valid evidence that Cello Co is a going concern.
- It may be that the letter of comfort from the holding company is sufficient to eliminate this risk, but this should be made clear on the file, and the checklist still needs updating.

Non-current assets

- Non-current assets might be considered low risk, but the total is material, even if the current year's additions may not be material.
- This section of the file demonstrates a lack of clarity in the approach to the audit and the firm's basic procedures for initialling and dating working papers have not been observed, albeit in what may be a relatively low-risk area.

Receivables

- The uncleared item may not be material as such, but it may be in excess of the tolerable error threshold.
- The item should have been followed up and other evidence obtained and, if this was not possible, the potential misstatement should have been calculated in theoretical terms to see if the misstatement in the financial statements as a whole might have been material.

Conclusions/recommendations

- There is a risk that the auditor's report (on the assumption that an unmodified opinion was given) is wrong because of the going concern and receivables issues.
- Planned audit procedures need to be followed for the planning meeting, subsequent events review, non-current assets working papers and receivables sample.
- Training implications need to be considered.

chapter

5

Advertising, publicity, obtaining professional work and fees

Chapter learning objectives

This chapter covers syllabus areas:

- C2 – Advertising, publicity, obtaining professional work and fees

Detailed syllabus objectives are provided in the introduction section of the text book.

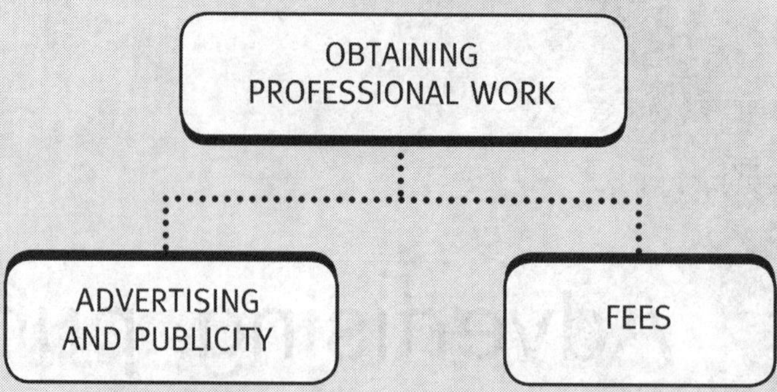

Exam focus

You should always be prepared for any syllabus area to be tested. Fees are an important part of this chapter as one of the ethical and professional issues that should be considered during the acceptance phase of an engagement. This includes consideration of the factors to be considered when setting the fee and the issues of lowballing and contingency fees. Exam questions may also examine the appropriateness of advertisements.

1 Advertising

The ACCA Rulebook states that it is acceptable in principle for ACCA members to advertise their services, but there is a general proviso that the advertising must not reflect adversely on:

- the member
- the ACCA, or
- the accountancy profession as a whole.

The aim of adverts should be 'to inform, rather than impress'.

The rules state that advertisements and promotional material should not:

- bring the ACCA into disrepute or bring discredit to the member, firm or the accountancy profession.
- discredit the services offered by others whether by claiming superiority for the member's own services or otherwise.
- be misleading, either directly or by implication.
- fall short of the requirements of any relevant national Advertising Standards Authority's Code of Advertising Practice, notably as to legality, decency, clarity, honesty, and truthfulness.

2 Restrictions on practice names and descriptions

There are restrictions on practice names and descriptions and the use of the ACCA logo.

Members' descriptions

- Members of the ACCA are entitled to call themselves Chartered Certified Accountants or just Certified Accountants, and may use the letters ACCA (as members) or FCCA (if they are fellows).
- These descriptions may **not** be used in the registered names of companies. For example you may not set up a company called John Smith Certified Accountant Ltd.

Practice descriptions

- An accountancy firm may describe itself as a 'firm of Chartered Certified Accountants', or a 'firm of Certified Accountants', or an 'ACCA practice' provided that:
  - at least half of the partners (or directors) are ACCA members, and
  - these partners (or directors) control at least 51% of the voting rights under the firm's partnership agreement (or constitution).
- A firm in which all partners are ACCA members may use the description 'Members of the Association of Chartered Certified Accountants' on its professional stationery .
- In the case of a mixed firm (e.g. some partners are ACCA members and others are members of other Chartered Accountancy bodies), the firm should not use the description 'Certified Accountants and Chartered Accountants' or similar, since this could be misleading.
- Instead they may print the following statement on their stationery: 'The partners of this firm are members of either the Association of Chartered Certified Accountants or (e.g.) the Institute of Chartered Accountants in England and Wales'.

Use of the ACCA logo

- A firm that has at least one ACCA member as a partner (or director) may use the ACCA logo (also called the ACCA 'mark') on its professional stationery and on its website.
- The ACCA logo should be separate from the logo of the firm.
- The positioning, size and colour of the ACCA logo should be chosen so that it is clearly recognisable.
- The logo can be downloaded by members from the ACCA website in electronic format.

Names of practising firms

Generally, members may practice under whatever name they want, but:

- a practice name should be consistent with the dignity of the profession.
- a practice name should not be misleading (e.g. a firm could not trade as 'PQ International Accountants' if all its offices were in one country).
- a practice name should not run the risk of being confused with the name of another firm.
- a sole practitioner should not add 'and partners' to the name under which he practices.

3 Fees

The need for guidance

The setting of fees is a sensitive subject, so the ACCA Rulebook contains a number of important provisions to:

- Minimise the possibility of a dispute between a member and their clients.
- Ensure that the member behaves at all times in accordance with the fundamental principles.

Determinants for fee-setting

- Members are entitled to charge a fair and reasonable fee for their services. This amount will be:
  - the fee considered appropriate for the work undertaken
  - the fee in accordance with the basis agreed with the client
  - the fee by reference to custom in certain specialised areas.
- Members will usually consider the following matters in setting a fee:
  - the seniority of the persons necessarily engaged on the work
  - the time spent by each person
  - the degree of risk and responsibility that the work entails
  - the urgency of the work to the client
  - the importance of the work to the client
  - the overhead expenses of the firm.
- The fee charged should include the recovery of any expenses properly incurred by the audit staff in the course of the engagement.
- The general basis on which fees are normally computed should be communicated to clients or potential clients in the letter of engagement, in order to reduce the risk of misunderstandings.

Lowballing

Lowballing is the setting of a low price at the start of an arrangement in order to secure the business, with the intention of later raising it or recovering the losses made on that engagement with other, more lucrative, services.

This could lead to a self-interest threat as the auditor may try and keep their client happy simply in order to win other contracts with them.

Professional competence and due care may be affected if the low fee leads the firm to cut corners on the audit to try and minimise losses.

If a member is investigated following allegations of unsatisfactory work, an inappropriate fee quote may be taken into account during the disciplinary process. A reasonable and informed third party may perceive that insufficient time has been taken to do the audit and quality has been affected because of the low fee.

However, it should be noted that there is no evidence that lowballing has actually led to negligent auditing. The regulatory system and the desire of audit firms to maintain their reputation should be sufficient to maintain audit quality regardless of the fee. The cost of litigation and the fear of high profile public scandals is a significant deterrent.

Bases on which fees and commissions may be charged

Contingency fees

A contingency fee is an arrangement made at the outset of an engagement under which a predetermined amount or percentage is payable to the accountant upon the completion of a specified event, or the achievement of a particular outcome.

Contingency fees could lead to practitioners forcing a specific outcome that would not normally have been obtained to try and achieve higher fees. For example, tax fees may be agreed based upon the tax savings the practitioners create or an auditor may be paid for unusually rapid completion of an audit. This could lead to the engagement being conducted without necessary due care and objectivity.

The ACCA's position is that **fees should not be charged on a percentage, contingency or similar basis**, except where that course of action is generally accepted practice e.g. insolvency work.

Fixed fee quotations

Most firms agree a fixed fee as clients prefer the certainty of a known cost. When determining the fee, the above factors will be taken into consideration. This arrangement can raise issues such as setting the fee at a low figure to secure the work or setting the fee at a level that is not profitable for the audit firm because of poor budgeting.

If a fee quoted is so low that it becomes difficult to perform the engagement in accordance with applicable professional standards for that price, then an ethical threat to professional competence and due care may be created.

Safeguards may be applied to eliminate this threat or to reduce it to an acceptable level, for example:

- making it clear to the client which services are covered by the quoted fees and the basis upon which fees are to be charged.
- performing a rigorous budgeting process to ensure that costs can be recovered.
- assigning sufficient time and appropriate staff to the assignment to ensure it is performed effectively.

Hourly rates

Alternatively, the accountancy firm can set an hourly rate for each grade of staff and invoice the client for the number of hours involved in the assignment. The final fee will only be known at the end of the engagement which may not be an acceptable arrangement for the client as they will not know how much to budget for the audit fee.

Introductions

Members may pay a referral fee to a third party, in return for the introduction of a client. The payment of such a fee may create a self-interest threat, therefore safeguards should be established to eliminate the threat or reduce it to an acceptable level. This is usually achieved by disclosing any such arrangements to the client.

References to fees in promotional material

- Where reference is made in promotional material to fees, the basis on which those fees are calculated, hourly or other charging rates, etc. should be clearly stated.
- Members may make comparisons in their promotional material between their fees and the fees of other accounting practices, whether members or not, provided that any such comparison complies with relevant codes of conduct and does not give a misleading impression.
- Promotional material that is based on the offer of percentage discounts on existing fees is permitted but must not detract from the professional image of the firm and the profession as a whole.
- Members may offer a free consultation to potential clients, at which levels of fees will be discussed.

Current issue: Downward fee pressure

Ethical considerations relating to audit fee setting in the context of downward fee pressure

Pressure on an audit firm to reduce audit fees arises for several reasons:

- Entities trying to reduce costs
- Increased competition in the audit market
- Mandatory audit firm rotation
- Increased audit threshold

Reductions in fees can threaten the fundamental ethical principles of professional competence and due care, and objectivity.

A firm may quote whatever fee is deemed appropriate however, the firm must always ensure that the work is performed in accordance with professional standards and that the audit team have the appropriate expertise and experience taking into consideration the nature, size and complexity of the audit engagement. The firm should also recognise that some audits may be more challenging than others which will require an increase in the level of time and expertise needed.

Other stakeholders have an important role to play in ensuring that fee levels do not impair audit quality. In particular, those charged with governance (TCWG) should consider whether adequate time and resources are planned for the audit when negotiating audit fees. Management and TCWG should recognise that high quality audits are part of good corporate governance and therefore audits should not be viewed as a cost to be minimised.

Test your understanding 1

Possible advertisement

Comment on whether the following advertisement is acceptable?

Deidre Jones ACCA

www.djonesacca.co.uk

Advice for small businesses

Friendly and professional service

Business start-up specialist

'The best and friendliest service in this town'

Test your understanding 2 – Hawk

You are a training manager in Hawk Associates, a firm of Chartered Certified Accountants. The firm has suffered a reduction in fee income due to increasing restrictions on the provision of non-audit services to audit clients. The following proposals for obtaining professional work are to be discussed at a forthcoming in-house seminar:

(a) 'Cold calling' (i.e. approaching directly to seek new business) the chief executive officers of local businesses and offering them free second opinions.

(5 marks)

(b) Placing an advertisement in a national accountancy magazine that includes the following:

'If you have an asset on which a large chargeable gain is expected to arise when you dispose of it, you should be interested in the best tax planning advice. However your gains might arise, there are techniques you can apply. Hawk Associates can ensure that you consider all the alternative fact presentations so that you minimise the amount of tax you might have to pay. No tax saving – no fee!'

(6 marks)

(c) Displaying business cards alongside those of local tradesmen and service providers in supermarkets and libraries. The cards would read:

Hawk ACCA Associates
For PROFESSIONAL Accountancy, Audit,
Business Consultancy and Taxation Services
Competitive rates. Money back guarantees.

(4 marks)

Required:

Comment on the suitability of each of the above proposals in terms of the ethical and other professional issues that they raise.

(Total: 15 marks)

Test your understanding 3

Ethical aspects of auditing

The provision of audit services to clients (as opposed to other assurance services or non-assurance services) brings with it specific ethical issues in relation to fees. What do you believe are the appropriate responses to the following ethical problems?

(a) The assignment of audit staff to a low audit fee engagement.

(b) The acceptability of contingency fees.

(c) Overdue fees from the previous audit.

Test your understanding 4

Explain, with reasons, how a member of The Association of Chartered Certified Accountants should respond to a request to provide a 'second opinion'.

(5 marks)

4 Chapter summary

OBTAINING PROFESSIONAL WORK

Professional guidance is needed on obtaining professional work in order to ensure that ACCA members apply the Fundamental Principles of the ACCA Code of Ethics in their daily conduct

ADVERTISING AND PUBLICITY

Material must not:

- Bring disrepute to the ACCA
- Discredit the services offered by others
- Be misleading
- Fall short of any advertising codes

FEES

Fees should be:

- Fair and reasonable
- Based on factors such as staff seniority, time spent, urgency of the work, etc.
- Contingency fees should be avoided except where customary (e.g. in merger and acquisition work)

TENDERING FOR ENGAGEMENTS

See next chapter

Test your understanding answers

Test your understanding 1

- Deidre Jones is entitled to inform the public of her skills (e.g. advice for small businesses, business start-ups, etc.) but claiming that she offers the best service in the area discredits the services offered by other accountants.
- The smiley symbols are not consistent with an image of professionalism and should be replaced.
- She should state a business telephone number or physical address in the advertisement, not just a web address.
- Nowhere in the advertisement does Deidre Jones state that she is an accountant (although the ACCA designation states this for those who know what it means). If this advertisement is to be included in a directory of accountants, there is no need to include this point. However, if the advertisement is to go into a general publication, it is probably best to clearly state the fact that Deidre Jones is a certified accountant or chartered certified accountant (as well as including the ACCA designation after her name).
- Deidre is also not permitted to use the term 'ACCA' in her web address as this indicates that she works for them, when in fact she is simply a professional member of the ACCA.

Test your understanding 2 – Hawk

A good working knowledge of the professional codes is required here and an ability to apply them. However, it should be helpful to identify issues which common sense would indicate do not sit comfortably with a professional approach.

(a) **Cold calling**

Tutorial note: Recognising that there are three issues to address (i.e. 'cold calling', 'free' and 'second opinions') is likely to earn more marks than focusing on just one.

- Cold calling is prohibited in certain countries, therefore the direct approach may not be suitable. Where cold-calling is allowed, it may still only be permitted for existing business clients (i.e. to offer them additional services). The direct approach to non-business clients may still be prohibited.
- The fundamental ethical principles must be adhered to. Whilst solicitation which is decent, honest and truthful may be acceptable, cold calling which amounts to harassment is not.
- Offering a service for free is not prohibited provided that the client is not misled about future levels of fees.
- There are strict ethical codes regarding second opinions (on accounting treatments). Practitioners are advised NOT to provide second opinions, when requested, without following a procedure of contacting the incumbent auditor/accountant.

Tutorial note: Second opinions should only be given where the auditor has been given permission to speak to the original auditor to ascertain the information available to them at the time of their report. The second auditor should not consider any information that became available subsequently.

(b) **Tax planning**

- Advertising is generally allowed subject to the observance of the fundamental principles of ethical codes (e.g. IFAC's Code of Ethics for Professional Accountants, ACCA's Code of Ethics and Conduct).
- Direct advertising (i.e. on television, radio, cinema) is prohibited in some jurisdictions, but advertisements in a national accountancy magazine are generally permitted.
- Where advertising is permitted, the minimum requirements are that it be decent, honest, truthful and in good taste. These criteria may not be met in this proposal.
- 'The best tax planning advice' is likely to be a self-laudatory statement and not based on verifiable facts. This may be an unjustifiable claim of expertise or specialism in the field of tax. This may also be making an unjustifiable comparison with other professional accountants in public practice.
- 'Can ensure …' and the assertion of 'all' may not be a supportable claim, therefore the advertisement is not honest in this respect.
- There is a fine line between tax avoidance and tax evasion and 'techniques you can apply' and 'alternative fact presentations' may lean toward the latter and so not be in keeping with the integrity of the profession. This statement may imply an ability to influence taxation authorities.
- The assertion of being able to 'minimise the amount of tax' may expose Hawk Associates to litigation. The engagement risk associated with taking on this work would be high and so should carry commensurately high fees. Expectations of favourable results (lower tax liabilities) may be unjustifiable or created deceptively.
- The 'no tax saving – no fee' offer does not compensate for the risk associated with undertaking the work advertised. Contingency fees, whereby no fee will be charged unless a specific result is obtained, are prohibited by IFAC except for certain services such as insolvency.

(c) **Business cards**

- Business cards may be considered a form of stationery and should be of an acceptable professional standard and comply with legal and member body requirements concerning names of partners, principals, professional descriptions, designatory letters, etc.
- Whilst placing such an advertisement where a target audience might reasonably be expected to exist (e.g. in an Institute of Directors), displaying it alongside local tradesmen may appear to belittle the status of professional accountants.
- An advertisement the size of a business card would be sufficient to provide a name and contact details and in this respect is suitable. However, the danger of giving a misleading impression is pronounced when there is such limited space for information.
- The tone of the advertisement may discredit the ACCA name. It is also unsuitable that it seeks to take unfair advantage of the ACCA name. Although the ACCA mark can be used by Hawk Associates on letterheads and stationery (for example) it cannot be used in any way which confuses it with the firm.
- The emphasis on 'professional' may be unsuitable as it could suggest that other firms are not professional.
- Offering a range of non-audit services in the same sentence as audit may mislead interested persons picking up the card into thinking that Hawk can provide them together. This conflicts with the fact that Hawk is restricted in providing non-audit services to audit clients.
- It is unlikely that any professional would offer money back. In the event of dispute (e.g. over fees), the matter would be taken to arbitration (with their member body) if a satisfactory arrangement could not be reached with the client.
- A tradesman may guarantee the quality of his work and that it can be made good in the event that the customer is not satisfied. However, an auditor cannot guarantee a particular outcome for the work undertaken (e.g. reported profit or tax payable). Most certainly an auditor cannot guarantee the truth and fairness of the financial statements in giving an audit opinion.

Test your understanding 3

(a) Every audit must have sufficient staff and sufficient time to carry out the audit properly, regardless of the audit fee to be charged. There are no circumstances in which a low audit fee can justify any lack of appropriate resource or time taken to perform a proper audit in compliance with auditing and ethical standards.

(b) No audit can be carried out on a contingency fee basis. The threat to objectivity from such an arrangement would be too great.

(c) Arrangements to pay such overdue fees must be agreed with the client before an auditor can accept appointment as auditor for the following period. If the amounts overdue are significant, the engagement partner should consider whether the firm can continue as auditor, or whether it is necessary to resign.

Test your understanding 4

Responding to a request

When asked to provide a second opinion a member should seek to minimise the risk of giving inappropriate guidance, by ensuring that they have access to all relevant information.

The member should therefore:

- Ascertain why their opinion is being sought.
- Contact the auditor to provide any relevant facts.
- With the entity's permission, provide the auditor with a copy of their opinion.

If asked to give an opinion in a hypothetical situation the member should make it clear that their response is not based on specific facts or circumstances relating to a particular organisation.

The member who is not the entity's auditor must be alert to the possibility that their opinion, if it differs from that of the auditor, may create undue pressure on the auditor's judgment and so threaten the objectivity of the audit.

The member's opinion is more likely to differ if it is based on information which is different (or incomplete) as compared with that available to the auditor. The member should decline to act if permission to communicate with the auditor is not given.

chapter

6

Tendering

Chapter learning objectives

This chapter covers syllabus areas:

- C3 – Tendering

Detailed syllabus objectives are provided in the introduction section of the text book.

Exam focus

Tendering does not feature in every exam in P7, but is examined periodically. It is a crucial part of the audit process as it is the main method by which audit/accounting firms obtain work. The purpose of tendering is to sell the firm's services to the client. If asked to explain what is included in a tender proposal, think of it as a sales pitch to the prospective client. What makes your firm stand out above the others?

Tendering is the process of quoting a fee for work before the work is carried out.

1 Changing auditors/professional accountants

Why change auditors?

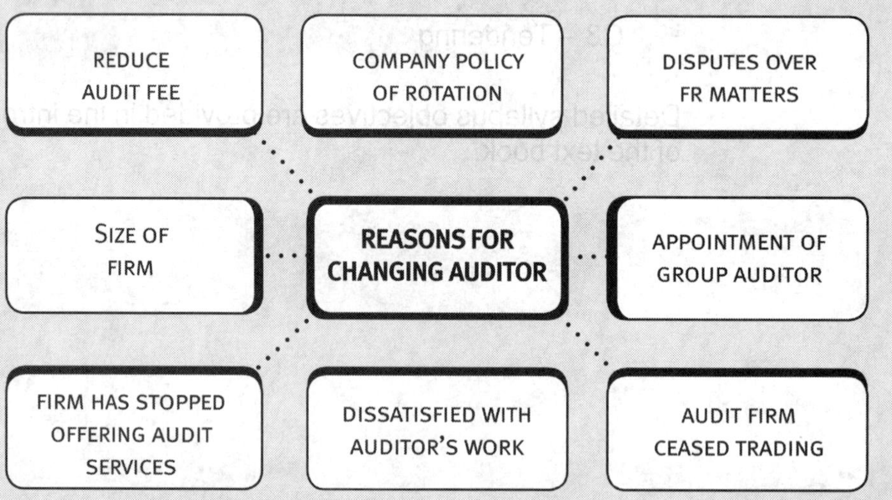

Why step down?

Audit firms may not seek re-appointment for many reasons. Examples include:

- independence issues which cannot be safeguarded.
- doubts regarding the integrity of the company's management.
- strategic decision such as concentrating on other services or markets.

2 Matters to be considered when a firm is invited to tender

When invited to tender, a firm must decide whether it wishes to take part in the tendering process.

In addition to the risk associated with any new client as covered in chapter 3, the specific risks of being involved with the tender include:

- Wasted time if the audit tender is not accepted. The firm will not be paid for the time spent putting the tender proposal together.
- Setting an uncommercially low fee in order to win the contract (see 'lowballing' in the previous chapter).
- Making unrealistic claims or promises in order to win the contract.

3 The engagement proposal document

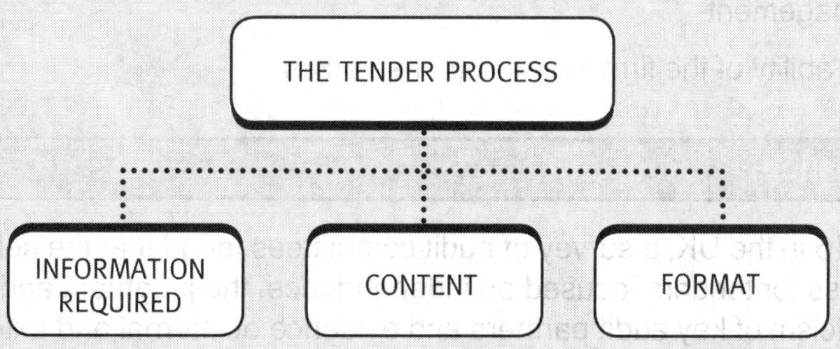

The preparation of an engagement proposal document is an important step in obtaining new work.

Information required for the proposal

Prior to drafting any proposals an audit firm should consider the following:

- What does the potential client expect from its auditors?
- What timetable does the client expect: an interim audit followed by a final audit or a longer final audit after the year-end?
- By what date are the audited financial statements required?
- What are the company's future plans, e.g. public flotation, expansion, contraction, concentration on certain markets?
- Are there any perceived problems with the potential client's current auditors?

The content of the proposal

The content of the proposal should include:

- the fee and how it has been calculated
- the nature, purpose and legal requirements of an audit (clients are often not clear about this)
- an assessment of the requirements of the client
- an outline of how the audit firm proposes to satisfy those requirements
- the assumptions made, e.g. on geographical coverage, deadlines, work done by client, availability of information, etc.
- the proposed approach to the audit or audit methodology
- an outline of the firm and its personnel
- quality control procedures of the firm including those relevant to the engagement
- the ability of the firm to offer other services.

Illustration

In 2015 in the UK, a survey of audit committees found that the selection process for tenders focused on independence, the judgment and scepticism of key audit partners and evidence of internal and external quality reviews. Price was not the deciding factor.

The format of the proposal

The tender should be made in the format required by the prospective client. However most tenders include a formal written document supported by an oral presentation. All presentations should be dynamic, professional and within the limits of the ethical framework.

UK syllabus

The UK Corporate Governance Code states:

- The audit committee should have primary responsibility for making a recommendation on the appointment, reappointment and removal of the external auditors.
- **FTSE 350 companies should put the external audit contract out to tender at least every ten years** (but can retain the current auditor if they provide the best quality and most effective audit), or explain in the annual report why they have not.
- If the board does not accept the audit committee's recommendation, it should include in the annual report, and in any papers recommending appointment or reappointment, a statement from the audit committee explaining the recommendation and should set out reasons why the board has taken a different position.

Benefits and drawbacks of tendering process

The benefits and drawbacks to the process of tendering and possible practice of constantly changing auditors include the following:

Benefits

- Audit firms are forced to look at ways of doing the audit more efficiently to keep the fee down.
- A tendency by companies to boost their internal audit departments so as to reduce external audit costs.
- Companies have also tended to simplify their group structures to reduce audit costs (among other reasons).
- Less risk of a familiarity threat if tendering results in a change of audit firm.

Drawbacks

- Greater market concentration, which has in fact reduced market choice.
- Loss of long-term relationships with auditors.
- Focus on cost of the audit not quality. Lowballing issues.
- The costs involved to the company and the audit firm to go through the tendering process, more so now with compulsory tendering being introduced.

Test your understanding 1

You are an audit manager in Weller & Co, an audit firm which operates as part of an international network of firms. This morning you received a note from a partner regarding a potential new audit client:

'I have been approached by the audit committee of the Plant Group, which operates in the mobile telecommunications sector. Our firm has been invited to tender for the audit of the individual and group financial statements for the year ending 31 March 20X3, and I would like your help in preparing the tender document. This would be a major new client for our firm's telecoms audit department.

The Plant Group comprises a parent company and six subsidiaries, one of which is located overseas. The audit committee is looking for a cost effective audit, and hopes that the strength of the Plant Group's governance and internal control mean that the audit can be conducted quickly, with a proposed deadline of 31 May 20X3. The Plant Group has expanded rapidly in the last few years and significant finance was raised in July 20X2 through a stock exchange listing.'

Required:

Identify and explain the specific matters to be included in the tender document for the audit of the Plant Group.

Test your understanding 2

How can small and medium sized audit firms win the audits of large companies if those companies don't even invite them to tender for the audit?

4 Chapter summary

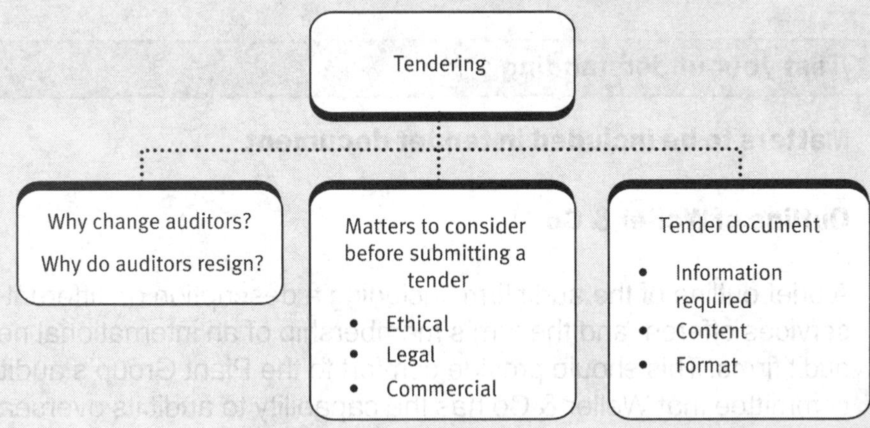

Test your understanding answers

Test your understanding 1

Matters to be included in tender document

Outline of Weller & Co

A brief outline of the audit firm, including a description of different services offered, and the firm's membership of an international network of audit firms. This should provide comfort to the Plant Group's audit committee that Weller & Co has the capability to audit its overseas subsidiary, and that the audit firm has sufficient resources to conduct the Plant Group audit now and in the future, given the Plant Group's rapid expansion.

Specialisms of Weller & Co

A description of areas of particular audit expertise, focusing on those areas of relevance to the Plant Group, namely the audit firm's telecoms audit department. The tender document should emphasise the audit firm's specialism in auditing this industry sector, which highlights that an experienced audit team can be assembled to provide a high quality audit.

Identify the audit requirements of the Plant Group

An outline of the requirements of the client, including confirmation that Weller & Co would be providing the audit service to each subsidiary, as well as to the parent company, and to the Plant Group. Weller & Co may also wish to include a clarification of the purpose and legal requirements of an audit in the jurisdictions of the components of the Plant Group, as requirements may differ according to geographical location.

Identify any audit-related services that may be required

Due to the Plant Group's listed status, there may be additional work to be performed. For example, depending on the regulatory requirements of the stock exchange on which the Plant Group is listed, there may be additional reporting requirements relevant to corporate governance and internal controls. This should be clarified and included in the tender document to ensure that the audit committee understands any such requirements, and that Weller & Co can provide an all-encompassing service.

Audit approach

A description of the proposed audit approach, outlining the stages of the audit process and the audit methodology used by the firm. Weller & Co may wish to emphasise any aspects of the proposed audit methodology which would be likely to meet the audit committee's requirement of a cost effective audit. The proposed audit approach could involve reliance to some extent on the Plant Group's controls, which are suggested to be good, and the tender document should explain that the audit firm will have to gauge the strength of controls before deciding whether to place any reliance on them.

Deadlines

The audit firm should clarify the timescale to be used for the audit. This is very important, given the audit committee's hope for a quick audit. It would be time pressured for the audit of all components of the Plant Group and of the consolidated financial statements to be completed in two months, especially given the geographical spread of the Plant Group. The audit firm may wish to propose a later deadline, emphasising that it may be impossible to conduct a quality audit in such a short timeframe.

Quality control and ethics

Weller & Co should clarify its adherence to the Code of Ethics and to International Standards on Quality Control. This should provide assurance that the audit firm will provide an unbiased and credible auditor's report. This may be particularly important, given the recent listing obtained by the Plant Group, and consequential scrutiny of the financial statements and auditor's report by investors and potential investors.

Fees

The proposed audit fee should be stated, with a breakdown of the main components of the fee. The audit firm may wish to explain that the audit fee is likely to be higher in the first year of auditing the Plant Group, as the firm will need to spend time obtaining business understanding and ensuring there is appropriate documentation of systems and controls. The tender document could explain that the audit is likely to become more cost effective in subsequent years, when the audit firm has gone through a learning curve.

Additional non-audit services

The audit firm should describe any non-audit services that it may be able to provide, such as tax services or restructuring services, which may be relevant given the rapid expansion of the Plant Group. The provision of such services would have to be considered carefully by the audit firm due to the threat to objectivity that may be created, so the tender document should outline any safeguards that may be used to reduce risks to an acceptable level. This is particularly important, given the listed status of the Plant Group. This part of the tender document may remind the audit committee members that corporate governance requirements may prohibit the audit firm from offering certain non-audit services.

Test your understanding 2

In countries like the UK, the audit market is becoming increasingly concentrated. Every FTSE 100 company is audited by a 'Big 4' audit firm.

Small and medium sized firms find it difficult to enter the market for auditing large companies. Less than 10% of FTSE 350 companies surveyed said that they would consider using a mid-tier firm. Even if they are invited to tender, the costs of assembling a credible bid are high, so there is a real risk of high wasted costs if the bid is unsuccessful.

Until mid-tier firms can acquire a credible reputation among large company finance directors and audit committees, and can establish a coordinated international presence, this situation is unlikely to change.

chapter

7

Money laundering

Chapter learning objectives

This chapter covers syllabus areas:

- A2 – Money laundering

Detailed syllabus objectives are provided in the introduction section of the text book.

Exam focus

Money laundering can be examined as part of professional issues to be considered when deciding whether or not to accept an engagement, or as a distinct requirement. Money laundering requirements may be knowledge based, in which you are required to explain the basic elements of an anti-money laundering program or define and give examples of money laundering offences. You may also need to identify a potentially suspicious transaction and explain the requirement to report knowledge or suspicion of money laundering.

1 Definition of money laundering

Money laundering is the process by which criminals attempt to conceal the true origin and ownership of the proceeds generated by illegal means, allowing them to maintain control over the proceeds and, ultimately, providing a legitimate cover for their sources of income.

Money laundering involves 3 main stages:

(1) Placement – where cash obtained through criminal activity is first placed into the financial system.

(2) Layering – where the illegal cash is disguised by passing it through complex transactions making it difficult to trace.

(3) Integration – where the illegally obtained funds are moved back into the legitimate economy and is now 'clean'.

Money laundering offences

There are five basic money laundering offences:

- Acquiring, possession or use of criminal property.
- Concealing or disguising or transferring criminal property, or removing it from the country.
- Failure to disclose knowledge or suspicion of money laundering.
- Tipping off.
- Failure by a financial services business to meet their obligations under money laundering regulations.

'Tipping off' means to carry out any action that may make suspected money launderers aware that they are under investigation, or prejudicing the outcome of an investigation.

Failure to disclose knowledge or suspicion of money laundering may include:

- Failure by an individual in the regulated sector to inform the Financial Intelligence Unit (FIU) or the firm's Money Laundering Reporting Officer (MLRO), as soon as practicable, of knowledge or suspicion that another person is engaged in money laundering, or
- Failure by MLROs in the regulated sector to make the required report to the FIU as soon as practicable if an internal report leads them to know or suspect that a person is engaged in money laundering.

Criminal property and criminal conduct

Criminal property is property that has arisen from criminal conduct. Examples include:

- Property acquired by theft
- The proceeds of tax evasion
- Bribery or corruption
- Saved costs arising from a criminal failure to comply with a regulatory requirement

Examples

Consider the following scenarios.

- Whilst preparing or auditing accounts you realise that a client has incorrectly reclaimed value added tax (or other national recoverable taxes) on the purchase of a motor car. You point this out to the client and propose an adjustment to the financial statements to provide for the additional tax that is due. You also advise the client that they must rectify this with the tax authorities. However, the client tells you that they have just had an inspection by the tax authorities that did not reveal the error and they do not wish to do anything further.
- An auditor knowingly receives payment for one invoice twice (i.e. payment has been duplicated). The sole director has told the accounts department to ignore negative balances when they issue statements of account to customers hoping that they fail to notice.

Errors and mistakes of the type illustrated above may not constitute criminal conduct, provided that they are corrected. However, in both cases there appears to be an intention to gain a permanent benefit from another's mistake or to avoid a legal liability. As such, each of these cases would result in the accountant knowing or suspecting that a client is involved in money laundering.

2 Anti-money laundering program: basic elements

The main legislation and requirements below relate to the money laundering regulatory regime as it stands in the UK. The principles, however, are appropriate on an international basis.

Money Laundering Regulations impose certain obligations on financial services businesses, which are designed to assist in detecting money laundering and preventing the financial services organisations being used for money laundering purposes.

At a minimum, an anti-money laundering program should incorporate:

- Customer identification procedures.
- Enhanced record keeping for:
  - all transactions
  - the verification of clients' identities.
- Appointment of a Money Laundering Reporting Officer (MLRO).
- Establishing internal reporting procedures to the MLRO.
- Procedures for the reporting of suspicious transactions to the Financial Intelligence Unit (FIU).
- Communication and training of all staff in the main requirements of the legislation.
- Systems and controls that effectively manage the risk that the firm is exposed to in relation to money laundering activities and ensure compliance with the legislation.

In the UK, for example, these measures are covered by the Money Laundering Regulations 2007 (MLR 2007) with reporting to the National Crime Agency (NCA).

Customer identification procedures/Know your customer

Accountants are required to establish that new clients are who they claim to be by obtaining satisfactory evidence of identity from the client. This is often referred to as 'customer due diligence' or 'know your customer' procedures.

Customer due diligence is an essential part of the anti-money laundering requirements. It ensures that accountants:

- know who their clients are, and
- do not unknowingly accept clients which are too high risk.

It may be helpful for the auditor to explain to the client the reason for requiring evidence of identity and this can be achieved by including this matter in the engagement letter.

It may also be helpful to inform clients of the auditor's responsibilities to report knowledge or suspicion that a money laundering offence has been committed and the restrictions created by the 'tipping off' rules on the auditor's ability to discuss such matters with their clients.

Customer due diligence must be performed as soon as is reasonably practicable after contact is first made between the two parties. Where satisfactory evidence of identity is not obtained by the accountant, the business relationship or one-off transaction must not proceed any further.

Basic identification procedures include:

- **For individuals (including key management personnel where the client is an entity):** inspection of evidence to establish the full name and permanent address of the client, e.g:
  - driving licence
  - passport
  - recent utility bill to confirm the address.
- **For businesses:**
  - the certificate of incorporation
  - lists of registered members and directors
  - certificate of registered address.
- **For trusts:** inspection of evidence to establish and confirm:
  - the nature and purpose of the trust
  - its original source of funding
  - the identities of the trustees, controllers and beneficiaries.

Example engagement letter money laundering clauses

'In accordance with the *Proceeds of Crime Act 2002* and *Money Laundering Regulations 2007* you agree to waive your right to confidentiality to the extent of any report made, document provided or information disclosed to the *National Crime Agency (NCA*).

You also acknowledge that we are required to report directly to the N*CA* without prior reference to you or your representatives if during the course of undertaking any assignment the person undertaking the role of Money Laundering Reporting Officer becomes suspicious of money laundering.

As a specific requirement of the Money Laundering Regulations we may require you to produce evidence of identity of the company and its owners and managers. This will include for the business, proof of registration and address, and for the individuals, proof of identity and address. Copies of such records will be maintained by us for a period of at least five years after we cease to act for the business.'

Note: The above clauses include references to the relevant legislation and regulatory bodies in the United Kingdom. The references would be amended for the specific jurisdiction(s).

Enhanced record keeping

It is very important that accountants keep comprehensive records to show that they have complied with money laundering regulations, and protect themselves if there is an investigation into one of their clients.

Records must be kept of:

- All customer due diligence completed, including copies of the evidence inspected.
- Transactions with each client.
- Internal and external money laundering/suspicious activity reports.

Records must be held for five years after a relationship with a client has ended or the date a transaction is completed.

The MLRO

The MLRO should be an individual of suitable seniority and experience. Alternative arrangements must be made when the MLRO is unavailable (on holiday, sick, jury service, etc). Sole practitioners with no employees or associates are exempt from the requirement to appoint an MLRO, since clearly they would be reporting to themselves.

Reporting procedures

It is a criminal offence not to report knowledge or suspicion of money laundering. Money laundering regulations require that:

- A person in the organisation is nominated to receive disclosures (usually an MLRO).
- Anyone in the organisation, to whom information comes in the course of the relevant business as a result of which he suspects that a person is engaged in money laundering, must disclose it to the MLRO.
- Where a disclosure is made to the MLRO, they must consider it in the light of any relevant information which is available to the organisation and determine whether it gives rise to suspicion.
- Where the MLRO does so determine, the information must be disclosed to a regulatory body authorised for the purposes of these regulations (the FIU), such as the NCA in the UK.
- The MLRO completes a standard form that identifies:
  - the suspect's name, address, date of birth and nationality
  - any identification or references seen
  - the nature of the activities giving rise to suspicion
  - any other information that may be relevant.

Note that in the UK the obligation to report does not depend on the amount involved or the seriousness of the offence. There are no de minimis concessions.

Potentially suspicious transactions

There is no formal definition of suspicious. A suspicious transaction will often be inconsistent with the client's known or usual legitimate activities. Examples include:

- Unusually large cash deposits.
- Frequent exchanges of cash into other currencies.
- Overseas business arrangements with no clear business purpose.

Communication and training

Financial services firms in the conduct of relevant business must take appropriate measures to ensure that employees are:

- made aware of the provisions of anti-money laundering regulations, and
- are given training in how to recognise and deal with transactions which may be related to money laundering.

Systems and controls

The systems and controls described above (client due diligence, record keeping, reporting and communication and training of employees) should be tested periodically to ensure that they comply with the relevant money laundering laws and regulations.

This would include checking that employees are completing available training, and testing their understanding of it.

3 The need for ethical guidance on money laundering

ACCA provides guidance in its Code of Ethics and Conduct in the area of money laundering.

This is needed because there is a clear conflict between:

(1) the accountant's professional duty of confidentiality in relation to his client's business, and

(2) the duty to report suspicions of money laundering to the appropriate authorities is required by law.

Professional accountants are not in breach of their professional duty of confidentiality if they report in good faith their knowledge or suspicions of money laundering to the appropriate authority.

Disclosure in bad faith or without reasonable grounds would possibly lead to the accountant being sued.

Financial Action Task Force

International efforts to combat money laundering

The Financial Action Task Force (FATF) is an international body that promotes policies globally to combat money laundering and terrorist financing. FATF issued recommendations to combat money laundering.

The recommendations included:

- International cooperation including extradition of suspects.
- Implement relevant international conventions on money laundering.
- Criminalise money laundering and enable authorities to confiscate the proceeds of money laundering.
- Implement customer due diligence, record keeping and suspicious transaction reporting requirements for financial institutions and designated non-financial businesses and professions.
- Establish a financial intelligence unit to receive suspicious transaction reports.

As an example, the UK Financial Intelligence Unit is run by the National Crime Agency (NCA).The NCA became operational in October 2013 and replaced the Serious Organised Crime Agency (SOCA).

FATF focuses on three principal areas:

- Setting standards aimed at combating money laundering and terrorist financing.
- Evaluating the degree to which countries have implemented measures that meet those standards.
- Identifying and studying money laundering and terrorist financing techniques.

In 1990, FATF drew up a document entitled "The Forty Recommendations" as an initiative to combat the misuse of financial systems to launder drug money. These recommendations (including the ones noted above) were endorsed by over 130 countries worldwide and now form the benchmark against which national anti-money laundering systems are assessed. Although different countries have moved forward in different ways.

In addition, 9 further special recommendations on terrorism financing have been introduced since the 2001 September 11 attacks.

The UK has adopted the recommendations of FATF.

The USA has a number of similar Acts:

- the Bank Secrecy Act 1970: this requires all cash deposits, withdrawals and transfers above $10,000 to be reported to the Inland Revenue Service
- the Money Laundering Control Act 1986
- the Uniting and Strengthening America by Providing Appropriate Tools Required to Intercept and Obstruct Terrorism (USA PATRIOT) Act 2001: this requires all financial institutions to establish an anti-money laundering program, including the development of internal policies and the designation of a compliance officer.

UK legislative background

Following the 1993 Criminal Justice Act, four further laws have tightened up the regulations in the UK:

- Terrorism Act 2000
- Proceeds of Crime Act 2002 (POCA)
- Money Laundering Regulations 2007 (the Regulations)
- Serious Organised Crime Police Act (SOCPA) 2005

In December 2007 the ACCA issued Technical Fact Sheet 145 'Anti-money Laundering Guidance for the accountancy sector.

4 Chapter summary

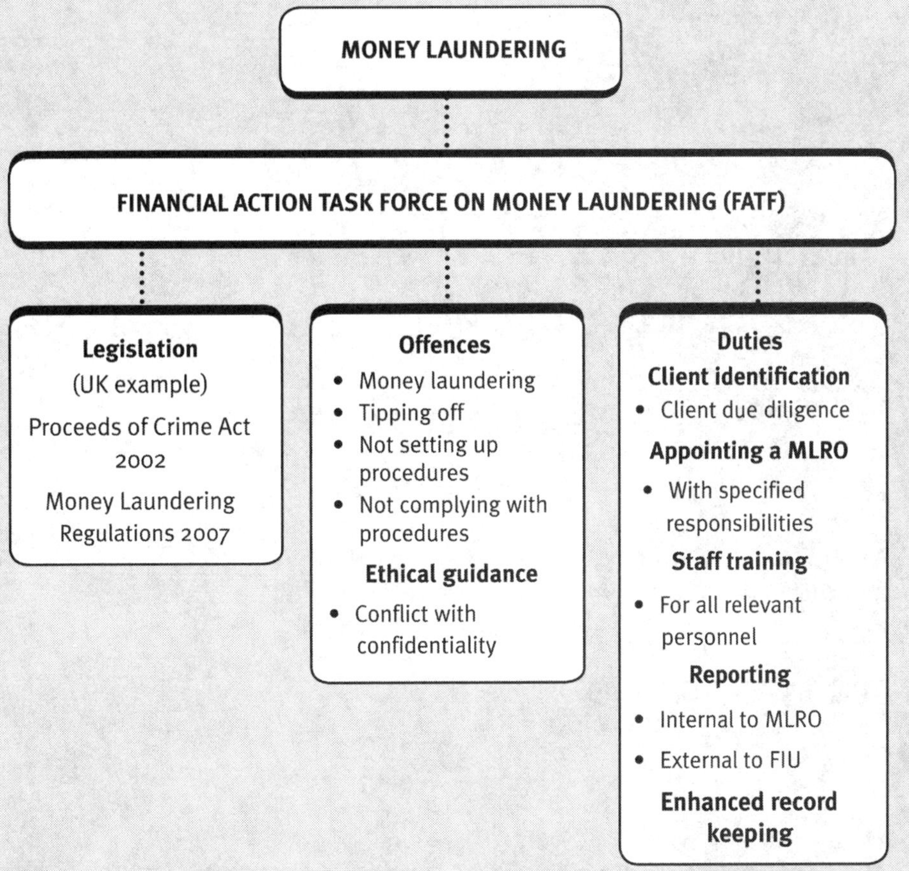

MONEY LAUNDERING

FINANCIAL ACTION TASK FORCE ON MONEY LAUNDERING (FATF)

Legislation
(UK example)
Proceeds of Crime Act 2002
Money Laundering Regulations 2007

Offences
- Money laundering
- Tipping off
- Not setting up procedures
- Not complying with procedures

Ethical guidance
- Conflict with confidentiality

Duties

Client identification
- Client due diligence

Appointing a MLRO
- With specified responsibilities

Staff training
- For all relevant personnel

Reporting
- Internal to MLRO
- External to FIU

Enhanced record keeping

chapter

8

Professional responsibilities and liability

Chapter learning objectives

This chapter covers syllabus areas:

- A3 – Laws and regulations
- B2 – Fraud and error
- B3 – Professional liability

Detailed syllabus objectives are provided in the introduction section of the text book.

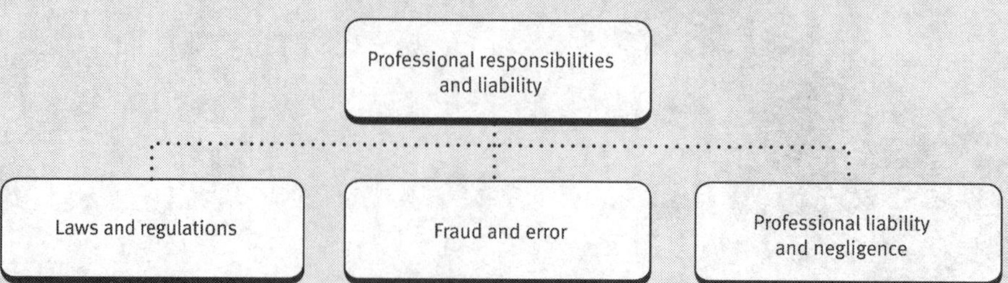

Exam focus

Professional issues are usually examined alongside ethical issues but can be examined in their own right. In addition, professional liability can be examined in conjunction with quality control as an audit which hasn't complied with quality control standards would generally mean that the auditor is liable. Typical exam questions may ask for respective responsibilities in respect of fraud & error or laws & regulations, or could ask whether an auditor is liable in a given situation.

1 Laws and regulations

Guidance regarding responsibility to consider laws and regulations in an audit of financial statements is provided in ISA 250 *Consideration of Laws and Regulations in an Audit of Financial Statements.*

Non compliance with laws and regulations may lead to material misstatement if liabilities for non-compliance are not recorded, contingent liabilities are not disclosed, or if they lead to going concern issues which would require disclosure or affect the basis of preparation of the financial statements.

'Non-compliance' means acts of omission or commission by the entity, either intentional or unintentional, which are contrary to the prevailing laws or regulations. Non-compliance must specifically relate to the business activities i.e. transactions entered into on behalf of the company. It does not include personal misconduct.

Responsibilities are considered from the perspective of both auditors and management.

Responsibilities of management

ISA 250 states that it is the responsibility of management, with the oversight of those charged with governance, to ensure that the entity's operations are conducted in accordance with relevant laws and regulations, particularly those that determine the reported amounts and disclosures in the financial statements.

Management responsibilities

In order to help prevent and detect non-compliance, management can implement the following policies and procedures:

- Monitoring legal requirements applicable to the company and ensuring that operating procedures are designed to meet these requirements.
- Instituting and operating appropriate systems of internal control.
- Developing, publicising and following a code of conduct.
- Ensuring employees are properly trained and understand the code of conduct.
- Monitoring compliance with the code of conduct and acting appropriately to discipline employees who fail to comply with it.
- Engaging legal advisors to assist in monitoring legal requirements.
- Maintaining a register of significant laws and regulations with which the entity has to comply.

In larger entities, these policies and procedures may be supplemented by assigning appropriate responsibilities to:

- An internal audit function
- An audit committee
- A compliance function.

Responsibilities of the auditor

The auditor is responsible for obtaining reasonable assurance that the financial statements taken as a whole, are free from material misstatement, whether caused by fraud or error (ISA 200 *Overall Objectives of the Independent Auditor and the Conduct of an Audit in Accordance with International Standards on Auditing*). Therefore, in conducting an audit of financial statements the auditor must perform audit procedures to help identify non-compliance with laws and regulations that may have a material impact on the financial statements.

The auditor must obtain sufficient, appropriate evidence regarding compliance with:

- laws and regulations generally recognised to have a **direct effect** on the determination of material amounts and disclosures in the financial statements (e.g. company law, tax law, applicable financial reporting framework).
- other laws and regulations that may have a material impact on the financial statements (e.g. environmental legislation, employment laws).

Further discussion of auditor responsibility

IFAC recognises that the auditors have a role in relation to non-compliance with laws and regulations. Auditors plan, perform and evaluate their audit work with the aim of providing reasonable, though not absolute, assurance of detecting any material misstatement in the financial statements which arises from non-compliance with laws or regulations.

However, auditors cannot be expected to be experts in all the many different laws and regulations where non-compliance might have such an effect. There is also an unavoidable risk that some material misstatements may not be detected due to the inherent limitations in auditing.

Audit procedures to identify instances of non-compliance

- **Obtaining a general understanding** of the legal and regulatory framework applicable to the entity and the industry, and of how the entity is complying with that framework.
- **Inspecting correspondence** with relevant licensing or regulatory authorities.
- **Enquiring of the management and those charged with governance** as to whether the entity is in compliance with such laws and regulations.
- **Remaining alert** to the possibility that other audit procedures applied may bring instances of non-compliance to the auditor's attention.
- **Obtaining written representation** from the directors that they have disclosed to the auditors all those events of which they are aware which involve possible non-compliance, together with the actual or contingent consequences which may arise from such non-compliance.

How to obtain a general understanding

- Using the auditor's existing understanding of the industry.
- Updating the auditor's understanding of laws and regulations that directly determine reported amounts and disclosures in the financial statements.
- Enquiry of management as to other laws and regulations that may be expected to have a fundamental effect on the operations of the entity.
- Enquiry of management concerning the entity's policies and procedures regarding compliance.
- Enquiry of management regarding the policies or procedures adopted for identifying, evaluating and accounting for litigation claims.

Investigations of possible non-compliance

When the auditor becomes aware of information concerning a possible instance of **non-compliance** with laws or regulations, they should:

- understand the **nature of the act and circumstances** in which it has occurred
- obtain sufficient other information to **evaluate** the possible effect on the financial statements.

Audit procedures when non-compliance is identified

- Enquire of management of the penalties to be imposed.
- Inspect correspondence with the regulatory authority to identify the consequences.
- Inspect board minutes for management's discussion on actions to be taken regarding the non-compliance.
- Enquire of the company's legal department as to the possible impact of the non-compliance.

Reporting non-compliance

- The auditor should report non-compliance to management and those charged with governance.
- If the auditor suspects management or those charged with governance are involved in the non-compliance, the matter should be reported to the audit committee or supervisory board.

- If the non-compliance has a material impact on the financial statements, a modified opinion should be issued.
- The auditor should also consider whether they have any responsibility to report non-compliance to third parties e.g. to a regulatory authority.

Engagement withdrawal

The auditor may decide that the non-compliance with laws and regulations is so serious that they need to withdraw from the engagement (i.e. resign as auditor).

In addition, if there has been a breakdown of trust between the auditor and management, or the auditor has doubts about the competence of management, the auditor may consider resignation.

The auditor should seek legal advice before taking this course of action.

Responding to Non-Compliance with Laws and Regulations

Final Pronouncement: Responding to Non-Compliance with Laws and Regulations

This publication sets out the professional accountant's responsibilities when non-compliance with laws and regulations (NOCLAR) is identified or suspected.

The accountancy profession is expected to act in the public interest. This means considering matters that could cause harm to investors, creditors, employees or the general public.

Examples of laws and regulations covered by this publication:

- Fraud, corruption and bribery
- Money laundering, terrorist financing and proceeds of crime
- Securities markets and trading
- Banking and financial products and services
- Data protection
- Tax and pension liabilities and payments
- Environmental protection
- Public health and safety

Matters which are not covered by this publication are:

- Matters which are clearly inconsequential
- Personal misconduct unrelated to the business activities of the client

Responsibilities of the professional accountant

Obtain an understanding of the matter

- Apply knowledge, professional judgment and expertise. The accountant may consult on a confidential basis with others within the firm, a network firm or a professional body, or with legal counsel.
- Discuss the matter with management and those charged with governance. This may help to obtain an understanding of the matter and may prompt management to investigate the matter.

Address the matter

Discuss the matter with management and advise them to take appropriate action such as

- Rectify, remediate or mitigate the consequences of the non-compliance
- Deter the commission of non-compliance where it has not yet occurred
- Disclose the matter to an appropriate authority where required by law or regulation or where considered necessary in the public interest.

Determine what further action is needed

Assess the appropriateness of management's response including whether:

- The response is timely
- The non-compliance has been adequately investigated
- Action has been, or is being, taken to rectify, remediate or mitigate the consequences of non-compliance
- Action has been or is being taken to deter the commission of any non-compliance where it has not yet occurred
- Appropriate steps have been taken to reduce the risk of re-occurrence.
- The non-compliance has been disclosed to an appropriate authority where appropriate.

The professional accountant should consider whether management integrity is in doubt e.g. if the accountant suspects management are involved in the non-compliance or if management are aware of the non-compliance but have not reported it to an appropriate authority within a reasonable period.

Further action may include

- Disclose the matter to a regulatory authority even when there is no legal or regulatory requirement to do so.
- Withdraw from the engagement and the professional relationship where permitted by law or regulation.

The professional accountant should provide the successor accountant with all such facts about the non-compliance that they need to be aware of before deciding whether to accept the audit.

Professional accountants who are not the external auditor of the entity

If the professional accountant is performing non-audit services for an audit client of the firm, the matter should be communicated within the firm.

If the professional accountant is performing non-audit services for an audit client of a network firm, the matter should be communicated in accordance with the network's procedures or directly to the engagement partner.

If the professional accountant is performing non-audit services to a client that is not an audit client of the firm or a network firm, the matter should be communicated to the client's external auditor unless this would be contrary to law or regulation.

A professional accountant in business should discuss non-compliance identified or suspected with their immediate superior or the next higher level if they suspect the superior is involved in the matter.

2 Fraud and error, misstatements and irregularities

Guidance regarding responsibility to consider fraud and error in an audit of financial statements is provided in ISA 240 *The Auditor's Responsibilities Relating to Fraud in an Audit of Financial Statements.*

Definitions

Irregularity

Irregularity is the collective term for fraud, error, breaches of laws and regulations, and deficiencies in the design or operating effectiveness of controls. An irregularity may or may not result in a misstatement in the financial statements.

Misstatement

A misstatement is defined by ISA 450 *Evaluation of Misstatements Identified During the Audit* as "A difference between the amount, classification, presentation, or disclosure of a reported financial statement item and the amount, classification, presentation, or disclosure that is required for the item to be in accordance with the applicable financial reporting framework."

Misstatements can arise from fraud or error. The distinguishing factor between fraud and error is whether the underlying action that results in the misstatement of the financial statements is intentional or unintentional."

Fraud

Fraud is an intentional act involving the use of deception to obtain an unjust or illegal advantage. It may be perpetrated by one or more individuals among management, employees or third parties.

ISA 240 identifies two categories of fraud that are of concern to auditors:

- Fraudulent financial reporting, and
- Misappropriation of assets.

Misappropriation of assets means theft e.g. the creation of dummy suppliers or ghost employees to divert company funds into a personal bank account.

Fraudulent financial reporting in particular may be viewed as more prevalent nowadays for the following reasons:

- Increased pressure on companies to publish improved results to shareholders and the markets.
- Greater emphasis on performance related remuneration to comply with corporate governance best practise incentivises directors to inflate profits to achieve bigger bonuses.
- When trading conditions are difficult as has been seen over recent years, additional finance may be required. Finance providers are likely to want to rely on the financial statements when making lending decisions. Directors may make the financial statements look more attractive in order to secure the finance.
- If existing borrowings are in place with covenants attached, directors may manipulate the financial statements to ensure the covenants are met.

Error

An error can be defined as an unintentional misstatement in financial statements, including the omission of amounts or disclosures, such as the following:

- A mistake in gathering and processing data from which financial statements are prepared.
- An incorrect accounting estimate arising from oversight or a misinterpretation of facts.
- A mistake in the application of accounting principles relating to measurement, recognition, classification, presentation or disclosure.

Errors are normally corrected by clients when they are identified. If a material error has been identified but has not been corrected, it will require the audit opinion to be modified.

Management responsibilities

ISA 240 explains that the primary responsibility for the prevention and detection of fraud rests with both those charged with governance of an entity and with management.

This should be achieved by the design and implementation of an effective system of internal control.

Management should:

- Place a strong emphasis on fraud prevention and error reduction.
- Reduce opportunities for fraud to take place.
- Ensure the likelihood of detection and punishment for fraud is sufficient to act as a deterrent.
- Ensure controls are in place to provide reasonable assurance that errors will be identified.
- Foster, communicate and demonstrate a culture of honesty & ethical behaviour.
- Consider potential for override of controls or manipulation of financial reporting.
- Implement and operate adequate accounting and internal control systems.

Auditor responsibilities

- Provide reasonable assurance that the financial statements are free from material misstatement, whether caused by fraud or error.
- Plan, perform and review audits in light of the risk of misstatement due to fraud.
- Apply professional scepticism and remain alert to the possibility that fraud could take place.
- Consider the potential for management override of controls and recognise that audit procedures that are effective for detecting error may not be effective for detecting fraud.

This can be achieved by performing the following procedures:

- Discuss the susceptibility of the client's financial statements to material misstatement due to fraud with the engagement team.
- Enquire of management regarding their assessment of fraud risk, the procedures they conduct and whether they are aware of any actual or suspected instances of fraud.
- Enquire of the internal audit function to establish if they are aware of any actual or suspected instances of fraud.
- Enquire of those charged with governance with regard to how they exercise oversight of management processes for identifying the risk of fraud and whether they are aware of any actual or suspected fraud.
- Consideration of relationships identified during analytical procedures.

Due to the inherent limitations of an audit, there is an unavoidable risk that some material misstatements may not be detected, even though the audit is properly planned and performed in accordance with ISAs. This risk is greater in relation to misstatement due to fraud, rather than error, because of the potentially sophisticated nature of organised criminal schemes.

Investigations of possible misstatements

When an actual or potential misstatement is identified by an auditor, a number of matters must be considered, and procedures carried out, to determine the impact (if any) on the audit.

- The nature of the event and the circumstances in which it has occurred should be understood.
- Sufficient information should be gathered to allow evaluation of the possible effect on the financial statements.
- If the auditors believe that the indicated fraud or error could have a material effect on the financial statements, they should perform appropriate modified or additional procedures.

Audit procedures when fraud is suspected or discovered

- Review journal entries made to identify manipulation of figures recorded or unauthorised journal adjustments:
  - Enquire of those involved in financial reporting about unusual activity relating to adjustments.
  - Select journal entries and adjustments made at the end of the reporting period.
  - Consider the need to test journal entries throughout the period.
- Review management estimates for evidence of bias:
  - Evaluate the reasonableness of judgments and whether they indicate any bias on behalf of management.
  - Perform a retrospective review of management judgments reflected in the prior year.
- Review transactions outside the normal course of business, or transactions which appear unusual and assess whether they are indicative of fraudulent financial reporting.
- Use unpredictable procedures to obtain evidence.

Reporting of fraud and error

- If the auditor identifies a fraud they must communicate the matter on a timely basis to the appropriate level of management (i.e. those with the primary responsibility for prevention and detection of fraud).
- If the suspected fraud involves management the auditor must communicate the matter to those charged with governance. If the auditor has doubts about the integrity of those charged with governance they should seek legal advice regarding an appropriate course of action.
- If the fraud has a material impact on the financial statements the auditor's report will be modified. When the auditor's report is modified, the auditor will explain why it has been modified and this will make the shareholders aware of the fraud.
- In addition to these responsibilities the auditor must also consider whether they have a responsibility to report the occurrence of a suspicion to a party outside the entity. Whilst the auditor does have an ethical duty to maintain confidentiality, it is likely that any legal responsibility will take precedence. In these circumstances it is advisable to seek legal advice.

Withdrawal from the engagement

In exceptional circumstances the auditor may consider it necessary to withdraw from the engagement. This may be if fraud is being committed by management or those charged with governance and therefore casts doubt over the integrity of the client and reliability of representations from management.

The auditor should seek legal advice first as withdrawal may also require a report to be made to the shareholders, regulators or others.

Implications for the audit

Modified or additional procedures

Procedures will depend on the nature of the fraud indicated, the likelihood of its occurrence and the likely effect on the financial statements. Auditors cannot assume that frauds are isolated. Where such additional procedures do not dispel the suspicion of fraud or error, the auditor should discuss the matter with management and consider whether it has been properly reflected in the financial statements.

Implications for the audit

Auditors should consider the effect of the fraud or error on their preliminary risk assessment and on the reliability of representations from management. This is particularly important where senior management is involved.

Discuss with management

Regardless of the materiality of the actual or suspected fraud or error, the auditor will need to communicate factual findings with management and those charged with governance in order to:

(i) Keep them informed and to ensure that they understand the position correctly.

(ii) Discover what action they have taken or intend to take to rectify the position, e.g. management may consider amending the system of internal control in order to reduce or eliminate the risk of such irregularities in the future.

(iii) Evaluate the likelihood that the irregularity will recur.

(iv) Discover what, if any, legal advice has been taken.

Article focus

The examiner classifies fraud into three distinct areas: corruption, misappropriation of assets, and financial statement fraud.

The article 'Forensic Auditing' (Sep 2008) provides further detail and provides a link between fraud and forensic accounting, a topic covered later in these notes. It can be found on the ACCA website under P7 resources.

A subsequent article 'Massaging the Figures' (April 2009) picks up on this topic and explores how creative accounting techniques, when intentionally misleading, can lead to fraudulently prepared financial statements.

The future of fraud and the audit

Fraud is a controversial area for auditors, and the extent of auditor responsibility for the prevention and detection of fraud continues to be debated by those in the profession, governments and other users of financial statements.

The Kingston Cotton Mill case (1896) emphasised that the reader of the auditor's report should have a realistic viewpoint of what the auditor's role should actually be.

The judge in the case set the benchmark for auditor responsibility when he said "An auditor is not bound to be a detective, or… to approach his work with suspicion, or with a foregone conclusion that there is something wrong. He is a watchdog, not a bloodhound."

Auditors do have a recognised responsibility for considering fraud when conducting an audit of financial statements, but the primary responsibility for fraud and error continues to rest with management, and those charged with governance. However, the auditor's responsibility with respect to fraud could change.

Auditors are currently responsible for detecting material misstatements whether caused by fraud or error. However, misstatements due to fraud are, by their very nature, extremely difficult to detect. Auditors are not trained as, nor expected to be, forensic investigators and even the most experienced auditor may have failed to detect a material misstatement caused by fraud. The auditor's responsibility for detecting material misstatements could be limited to exclude those caused by fraud.

Conversely, many users would like to see auditors' responsibility for fraud extended. In order to achieve this, auditors would have to be given the training necessary to identify fraud. In addition, the extent of auditor's responsibilities would have to be defined. It would not be possible to expect the auditor to detect all fraud. Some frauds (especially where collusion is involved) are almost impossible to identify. However, auditors could be given responsibility for performing audit procedures specifically to detect fraud, possibly in those areas that are more susceptible to fraud (e.g. payroll).

The audit profession is dynamic and subject to much debate at the current time. It is not possible to know what the future holds, but perhaps auditors will be required to move towards the role of a bloodhound in the not too distant future.

Not absolute assurance

An auditor **cannot provide absolute assurance** over the accuracy of the financial statements because of such factors as:

- the use of judgment
- the use of sampling
- the inherent limitations of internal control, and
- the fact that much of the audit evidence available to the auditor is persuasive rather than conclusive in nature.

3 Legal liability

Liability to the client and liability to third parties

Liability to the client

- Liability to the client arises from contract law. The company has a contract with the auditor, the engagement letter, and hence can sue the auditor for breach of contract if the auditor delivers a negligently prepared auditor's report.
  - When carrying out their duties the auditor must exercise due care and skill.
  - Generally, if auditors can show that they have complied with generally accepted auditing standards, they will not have been negligent.

Liability to third parties

A third party (i.e. a person who has no contractual relationship with the auditor) may sue the auditor for damages, i.e. a financial award.

In the ***tort of negligence***, the plaintiff (i.e. the third party) must prove that:

(1) the defendant (i.e. the auditor) owes a duty of care, and

(2) the defendant has breached the appropriate standard of care as discussed above, and

(3) the plaintiff has suffered loss as a direct result of the defendant's breach.

The critical matter in most negligence scenarios is whether a duty of care is owed in the first place.

When is a duty of care owed?

A duty of care exists when there is a special relationship between the parties, i.e. where the auditors knew, or ought to have known, that the audited financial statements would be made available to, and would be relied upon by, a particular person (or class of person).

The injured party must therefore prove:

- The auditor knew, or should have known, that the injured party was likely to rely on the financial statements.
- The injured party has sufficient 'proximity', i.e. belongs to a class likely to rely on the financial statements.

- The injured party did in fact so rely.
- The injured party would have acted differently if the financial statements had shown a different picture.

Has the auditor exercised due professional care?

The auditor will have exercised due professional care if they have:

- Applied the most up-to-date accounting and auditing standards.
- Adhered to all standards of ethical behaviour laid down by the relevant professional bodies.
- Complied with the terms and conditions of appointment as set out in the letter of engagement and as implied by law.
- Employed competent staff who are adequately trained and supervised in carrying out instructions.

Has the injured party suffered a loss?

This is normally a matter of fact. For example, if X relies on the audited financial statements of Company A and pays $5m to buy the company, but it soon becomes clear that the company is worth only $1m, then a loss of $4m has been incurred.

Criminal vs. civil

Auditors' liability can be categorised under the following headings:

- civil or criminal liability arising under legislation
- liability arising from negligence.

Civil liability

Auditors may be liable in the following circumstances.

- To third parties suffering loss as a result of relying on a negligently prepared audit report – see below.
- Under insolvency legislation to creditors – auditors must be careful not to be implicated in causing losses to creditors alongside directors.
- Under tax legislation – particularly where the auditor is aware of tax frauds perpetrated by his client.
- Under financial services legislation to investors.
- Under stock exchange legislation and/or rules.

The only possible penalty for a civil offence is payment of damages.

Criminal liability

Criminal liability can arise in the following circumstances:

- Acting as auditor when ineligible.
- Fraud, such as: theft, bribery and other forms of corruption, falsifying accounting records, and knowingly or recklessly including misleading matters in an auditor's report.
- Insider dealing.
- Knowingly or recklessly making false statements in connection with the issue of securities.

Penalties for criminal liability include fines and/or imprisonment.

In addition to the various civil and criminal liabilities the professional bodies that regulate accountants and auditors have various sanctions, such as warnings, fines, reprimands, severe reprimands and exclusion from membership for misconduct by members. Conviction of a criminal offence involving financial misconduct is normally sufficient to warrant exclusion from membership of a professional body.

Case Study: Caparo

The Caparo case (Caparo Industries v Dickman and others (1984))

Caparo Industries took over Fidelity plc in 1984 and alleged that it increased its shareholding on the basis of Fidelity's accounts, audited by Touche Ross. Caparo sued Touche Ross for alleged negligence in the audit, claiming that the stated $1.3m profit for the year to 31 March 1984 should have been reported as a loss of $460,000.

It was held in this case that the auditors owed no duty of care in carrying out the audit to individual shareholders or to members of the public who relied on the accounts in deciding to buy shares in the company.

The House of Lords looked at the purpose of statutory accounts. They concluded that such accounts, on which the auditor must report, are published with the principal purpose of providing shareholders as a class with information relevant to exercising their proprietary interests in the company. They are not published to assist individuals (whether existing shareholders or not) to speculate with a view to profits.

Case Study: Bannerman

The Bannerman case (Royal Bank of Scotland (RBS) v Bannerman Johnstone Maclay (2002))

RBS provided overdraft facilities to APC Limited and Bannerman were APC's auditors. The relevant facility letters between RBS and APC contained a clause requiring APC to send RBS, each year, a copy of the annual audited financial statements.

In 1998 APC was put into receivership with approximately $13.25m owing to RBS. RBS claimed that, due to a fraud, APC's financial statements for the previous years had misstated the financial position of APC and Bannerman had been negligent in not detecting the fraud. RBS contended that it had continued to provide the overdraft facilities in reliance on Bannerman's unmodified opinions.

Bannerman applied to the court for an order striking out the claim on the grounds that, even if all the facts alleged by RBS were true, the claim could not succeed in law because Bannerman owed no duty of care to RBS.

The judge held that the facts pleaded by RBS were sufficient in law to give rise to a duty of care and so the case could proceed to trial. The judge held that, although there was no direct contact between Bannerman and RBS, knowledge gained by Bannerman in the course of their ordinary audit work was sufficient, in the absence of any disclaimer, to create a duty of care owed by Bannerman to RBS. In order to consider APC's ability to continue as a going concern, Bannerman would have reviewed the facilities letters and so would have become aware that the audited financial statements would be provided to RBS for the purpose of RBS making lending decisions. Having acquired this knowledge, Bannerman could have disclaimed liability to RBS but did not do so. The absence of such a disclaimer was an important circumstance supporting the finding of a duty of care.

Case Study: ADT Ltd v BDO Binder Hamlyn

ADT Ltd v BDO Binder Hamlyn (1995)

BDO BH were the joint auditors of the Britannia Security Systems Group. Before the 1989 audit was finished, ADT were considering bidding for Britannia, so an ADT representative met the BDO BH audit partner and asked him to confirm that the audited accounts gave a true and fair view and that he had learnt nothing subsequently which cast doubt on the accounts. The partner said that BDO BH stood by the accounts and there was nothing else that ADT should be told. ADT then bought Britannia for $105m, but it was found to be worth only $40m.

It was held that BDO BH owed ADT a duty of care when the partner made his statements, and the accounts had been negligently audited, so ADT were awarded $65m plus interest. The shortfall in BH's insurance cover was $34m. The partners were individually liable for that amount.

BH appealed, and ADT agreed an out-of-court settlement.

Case Study: Lloyd Cheyham v Littlejohn de Paula

Lloyd Cheyham v Littlejohn de Paula (1985)

Littlejohn de Paula successfully defended themselves against a negligence claim in this case by showing:

- That they had followed the standard expected of the normal auditor, i.e. auditing standards.
- That their working papers were good enough to show consideration of the problems raised by the plaintiff and reasonable decisions made after consideration.
- That the plaintiff had not made all the reasonable enquiries one could expect when purchasing a company. For example a review of the business was not undertaken upon investigating the purchase but only after purchase.

The judge, therefore, held that far too much reliance was placed on the accounts by the plaintiff and he awarded costs against the plaintiff to the defendant.

Restricting auditors' liability

Audit firms may take the following steps to minimise their exposure to negligence claims:

- **R**estrict the use of the auditor's report and assurance reports to their specific, intended purpose.
- **E**ngagement letter clause to limit liability to third parties.
- **S**creening potential audit clients to accept only clients where the risk can be managed.
- **T**ake specialist legal advice where appropriate.
- **R**espective responsibilities and duties of directors and auditors communicated in the engagement letter and auditor's report to minimise misunderstandings.
- **I**nsurance – professional indemnity insurance (PII).
- **C**arry out high quality audit work.
- **T**ake on LLP status.
- **S**et a liability cap with clients.

The impact of limiting audit liability

Some commentators have argued that limiting audit liability is contrary to the public interest, since auditors will be less motivated to do a first class job if they know that they won't have to pay for their mistakes.

Other commentators say that this ignores the professional nature of the audit discipline. People choose to be audit partners because they want to do a high quality job for themselves and for society.

The expectation gap

The **expectation gap** is the gap between what the public believe that auditors do (or ought to do) and what they actually do.

This expectation gap can be categorised into:

- **Standards and performance gap** – where users believe auditing standards to be more comprehensive than they actually are and therefore the auditor does not perform the level of work the user expects.
- **Liability gap** – where users do not understand to whom the auditor is legally responsible.

Bridging the expectation gap

Recent developments and proposals include:

- Educating users to reduce the standards gap e.g.
  - auditor's reports now include greater detail of the auditor's responsibilities and key audit matters, detail that was not included in the shorter wording used previously.
  - written representation letters require management to sign to acknowledge their responsibilities in respect of the financial statements.
- Increasing communication between the auditor and those charged with governance regarding respective responsibilities of the company and the audit firm.
- Increasing the scope of the work of the auditor e.g. to require greater detection of fraud and error.

Expectation gap: Examples

- Users believe that auditors are responsible for preventing and detecting fraud and error, while ISAs require auditors to only have a reasonable expectation of detecting material fraud and error.
- Users believe that they can sue the auditors if a company fails, while auditors maintain that it is the directors' responsibility to run their business as a going concern, and following Caparo it is not the auditor's function to protect individual shareholders if they make a poor investment decision.
- Users believe the audit firm will report externally all 'wrong doing' e.g. non-compliance with laws and regulations. The auditor will only report externally where there is a duty to do so. If the non-compliance does not lead to material misstatement in the financial statements, there is nothing to mention in the auditor's report.
- Users believe the audit firm will highlight poor decisions / performance by management. The objective of the auditor is to express an opinion on the financial statements about whether or not they give a true and fair view. If poor decisions have been made by management but the financial effects of these decisions have been properly reflected in the financial statements, there is nothing to mention in the auditor's report. Only issues which have a material impact on the financial statements will be mentioned in the auditor's report.

Disclaimer statements

Reaction to the Bannerman decision – disclaimer statements

In the Bannerman case the judge commented that, if the auditors had inserted a disclaimer statement in their report, then they would have had no legal liability to RBS who was suing them.

Following this case, the ICAEW recommended additional wording to be routinely included in all auditor's reports by ICAEW members:

> 'This report is made solely to the company's members as a body. Our audit work has been carried out so that we might state to the company's members those matters we are required to state to them in an audit report and for no other purpose. We do not accept responsibility to anyone other than the company and the company's members as a body, for our audit work or for the opinions we have formed.'

The ACCA's view (in Technical Factsheet 84) is that standard disclaimer clauses should be discouraged since they could have the effect of devaluing the auditor's report. Disclaimers of responsibility should be made in appropriate, defined circumstances (e.g. where the auditor knows that a bank may rely on a company's financial statements) but the ACCA does not believe that, where an audit is properly carried out, such clauses are always necessary to protect auditors' interests.

In practice, the difference of opinion between the ICAEW and the ACCA may not be so great. If an ACCA auditor is not aware that a bank is going to place reliance on an audit report (so no disclaimer is given), then it seems likely under Caparo or Bannerman that no duty of care would be owed to the bank in any event.

Possible methods of limiting audit liability

(a) **A financial cap on liability**

This could be a fixed amount (as in Germany) or a multiple of the audit fee. A possible adverse effect of the latter would be to either reduce the quality of work done, or to reduce the fee, as the lower the fee, the lower the liability.

In the UK such agreements were illegal until the Companies Act 2006, which now permits liability limitation agreements between auditors and companies, subject to shareholders' approval. The Act does not specify what sort of limit can be agreed, so a fixed cap, or a multiple of fees, or any other type are all now possible.

(b) **Incorporating audit firms as limited liability partnerships (now permitted in the UK under the Limited Liability Partnerships Act 2000).**

(c) **Modification of the 'joint and several liability' principle.**

Auditors are jointly and severally liable with directors where negligence claims are made, either under legislation, or under case law. This means that directors and auditors are held responsible together for the issue of negligently prepared and audited financial statements. If, say, the auditors and directors share the blame for falsifying records (i.e. the auditors did not detect it), the auditor may bear all of the costs if the directors have no resources to pay. The objective is to protect the plaintiff and maximise their chances of recovery of losses. The effect in practice is to pass all of the costs onto auditors who have to be insured!

An associated problem is the fact that all partners and directors are responsible for the misconduct of other partners and directors in audit firms, regardless of whether they were directly involved in a particular audit. In the US, and now the UK, this problem is partly dealt with by limited liability partnerships.

(d) **Compulsory insurance for directors – for the reasons noted above.**

Insurance for accountancy firms

One of the obligations of practising as a professional accountant is to ensure that, if an accountant's negligence has caused loss to a client, the accountant has an insurance policy to ensure that he can pay any damages awarded.

- **Professional indemnity insurance (PII)** is insurance taken out by an accountant against claims made by clients and third parties arising from work that the accountant has carried out.
- **Fidelity guarantee insurance (FGI)** is insurance taken out by an accountant against any liability arising through acts of fraud or dishonesty by any partner or employee in respect of money or goods held in trust by the accountancy firm.

Settlements out of court

Legal cases may be settled out of court due to negotiation between the plaintiff and the dependent.

Benefits

- Cost saving (i.e. lower fees).
- Time saving.
- Less risk of damage to reputation.

Drawbacks

- Does not address the importance of the practitioner's legal responsibilities.
- May be due to pressure from insurers, who are willing to risk a court settlement.
- Insurance premiums may still rise.

Exam style question: Ethical, professional and legal issues

Study note: this question is typical of the current P7 exam. It is one of the core topics identified in the 'Examiner's Approach to Paper P7' article. Therefore a question of this nature should be expected in each sitting of P7.

You are an audit manager in Ebony, a firm of Chartered Certified Accountants. Your specific responsibilities include planning the allocation of professional staff to audit assignments. The following matters have arisen in connection with the audits of three client companies:

(a) The finance director of Almond, a private limited company, has requested that only certain staff are to be included on the audit team to prevent unnecessary disruption to Almond's accounting department during the conduct of the audit. In particular, that Xavier be assigned as accountant in charge (AIC) of the audit and that no new trainees be included in the audit team. Xavier has been the AIC for this client for the last two years.

(5 marks)

(b) Alex was one of the audit trainees assigned to the audit of Phantom, a private limited company, for the year ended 31 March 20X4. Alex resigned from Ebony with effect from 30 November 20X4 to pursue a career in medicine. Kurt, another AIC, has just told you that on the day Alex left he told Kurt that he had ticked schedules of audit work as having been performed when he had not actually carried out the tests.

(5 marks)

(c) During the recent interim audit of Magenta, a private limited company, the AIC, Jamie, has discovered a material error in the prior year financial statements for the year ended 31 December 20X3. These financial statements had disclosed an unquantifiable contingent liability for pending litigation. However, the matter was settled out of court for $4.5 million on 14 March 20X4. The auditor's report on the financial statements for the year ended 31 December 20X3 was signed on 19 March 20X4. Jamie believes that Magenta's management is not aware of the error and has not drawn it to their attention.

(5 marks)

Required:

Comment on the ethical, quality control and other professional issues raised by each of the above matters and their implications, if any, for Ebony's staff planning.

Note: The mark allocation is shown against each of the three issues.

(Total: 15 marks)

Test your understanding 1 – Lambley

The partner in charge of your audit firm has asked your advice on frauds which have been detected in recent audits.

(a) The audited financial statements of Lambley Trading were approved by the shareholders at the AGM on 3 June 20X2. On 7 June 20X2 the managing director of Lambley Trading discovered a petty cash fraud by the cashier. Investigation of this fraud has revealed that it has been carried out over a period of a year. It involved the cashier making out, signing and claiming petty cash expenses which were charged to motor expenses. No receipts were attached to the petty cash vouchers. The managing director signs all cheques for reimbursing the petty cash float. Lambley Trading has sales of $2 million and the profit before tax is $150,000. The cashier has prepared the draft financial statements for audit.

The partner in charge of the audit decided that no audit work should be carried out on petty cash. He considered that petty cash expenditure was small, so the risk of a material error or fraud was small.

Required:

(i) Briefly state the auditor's responsibilities for detecting fraud and error in financial statements.

(ii) Consider whether your firm is negligent if the fraud amounted to $5,000.

(iii) Consider whether your firm is negligent if the fraud amounted to $20,000.

(9 marks)

(b) The audit of directors' remuneration at Colwick Enterprises, a limited company, has confirmed that the managing director's salary is $450,000, and that he is the highest paid director. However, a junior member of the audit team asked you to look at some purchase invoices paid by the company.

Your investigations have revealed that the managing director has had work amounting to $200,000 carried out on his home, which has been paid by Colwick Enterprises. The managing director has authorised payment of these invoices and there is no record of authorisation of this work in the board minutes.

The managing director has refused to include the $200,000 in his remuneration for the year, and to change the financial statements. If you insist on modifying your auditor's report on this matter, the managing director says he will get a new firm to audit the current year's financial statements. The company's profit before tax for the year is $91 million.

Required:

Assuming the managing director owns 60% of the issued shares of Colwick Enterprises and refuses to amend the financial statements:

(i) Consider whether the undisclosed remuneration is a material item in the financial statements.

(ii) Describe the matters you will consider and the action you will take:

- to avoid being replaced as auditor, and
- if you are replaced as auditor.

(iii) Describe the matters you will consider and the action you will take to avoid being replaced as auditor, assuming Colwick Enterprises is a listed company with an audit committee, and the managing director owns less than 1% of the issued shares.

(11 marks)

(Total: 20 marks)

Test your understanding 2

You are the auditor of Promise Co. The Finance Director has asked for a meeting with you. She recently discovered that the purchase ledger manager has diverted company funds into his own bank account. The Finance Director has identified funds of $50,000 to date as being diverted and wants and explanation as to why you did not highlight this issue during the course of your recently completed audit. The profit for the year was $17.5m. Prepare a set of briefing notes to assist you in your meeting with the Finance Director.

Test your understanding 3

You are the auditor of a chain of restaurants. You have noticed a newspaper report that guests at a wedding have fallen ill after eating at one of your client's restaurants.

What impact should this report have on your considerations of compliance with laws and regulations and what audit procedures would you perform?

Test your understanding 4

The directors of Jubilee Co have asked your firm to produce a much more detailed report at the end of the audit than usual, listing all the deficiencies in the internal control system. They are unhappy that during the year discounts had been given to customers who did not qualify for them, as a result of the non-application of an internal control process. They have expressed dissatisfaction with your audit firm as this control deficiency was not reported to them by your firm.

Draft points to include in your reply to Jubilee Co.

Test your understanding 5

A recent industry commentator has written:

"In respect of the many recent corporate collapses, the auditor is often seen as the easy scapegoat. Not least because of their professional indemnity insurance. This damages the reputation of the profession and over time can only lead to reduction in the number and quality of skilled audit practitioners, and a consequential increase in costs to their clients. Legislation has to be changed, in order to protect the auditor and the future of the profession, to allow auditors to agree a contractual cap on their liability for statutory audits."

Required:

Set out the arguments for and against allowing auditors to agree on a contractual cap as described above.

4 Laws and regulations – summary

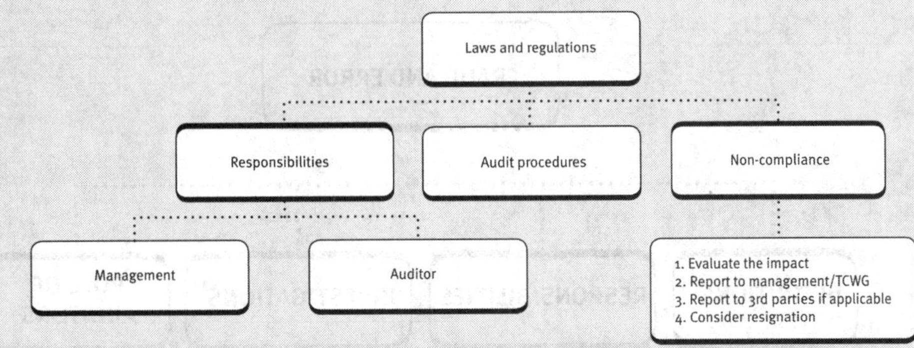

5 Fraud and error – summary

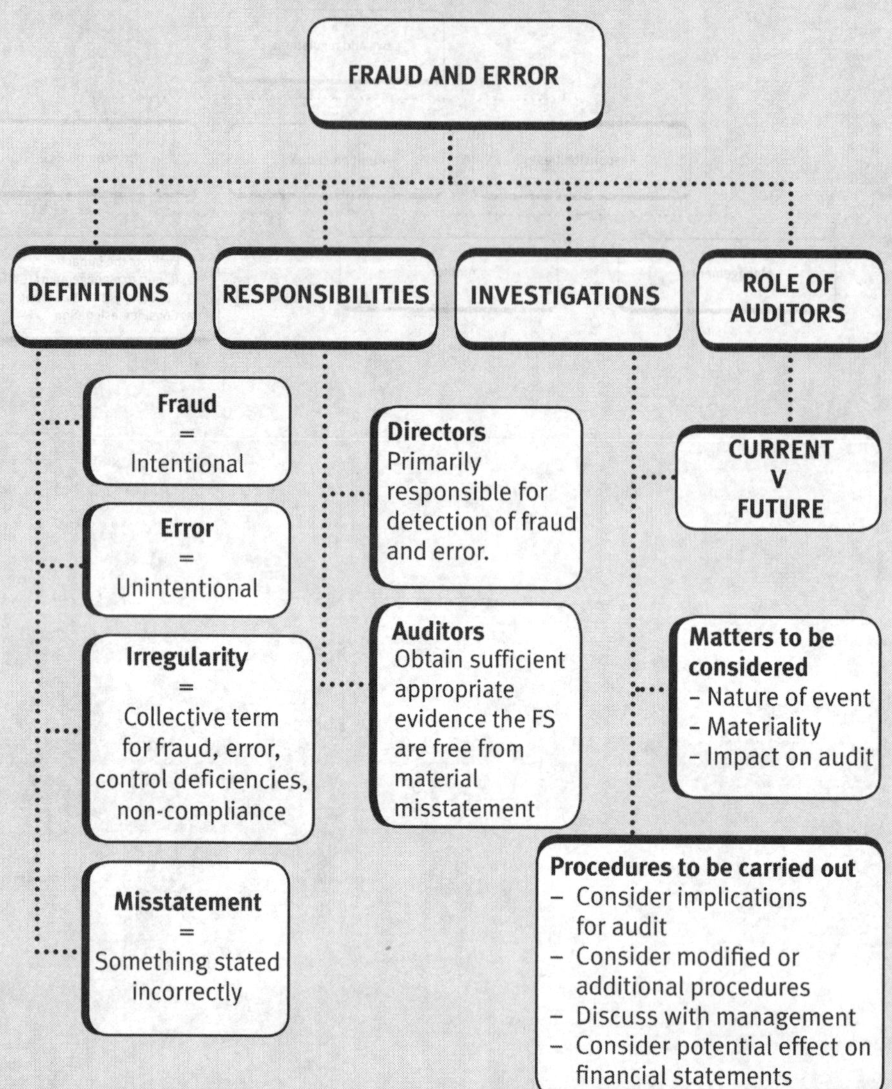

6 Legal liability – summary

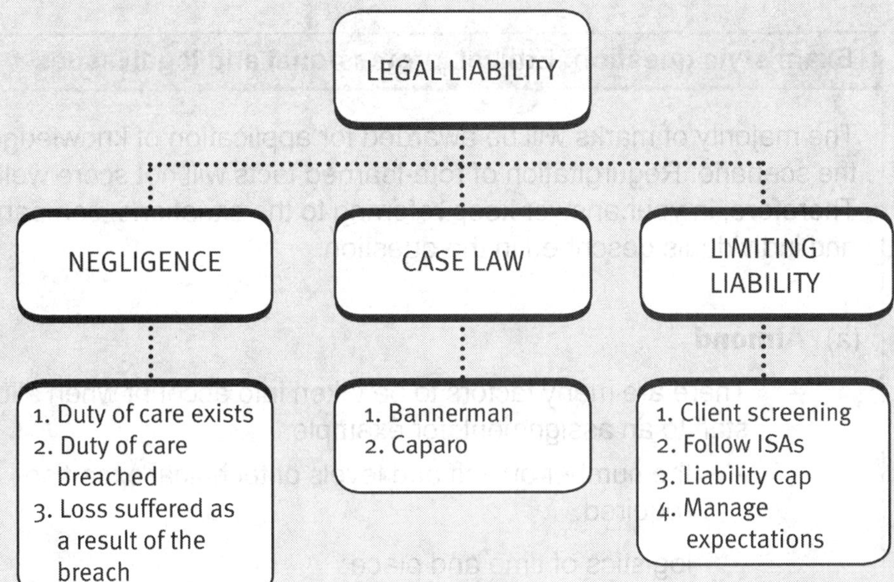

Test your understanding answers

Exam style question: Ethical, professional and legal issues

The majority of marks will be awarded for application of knowledge to the scenario. Regurgitation of rote-learned facts will not score well in P7. Therefore, in your answer keep referring to the situations, companies and individuals described in the question.

(a) **Almond**

- There are many factors to be taken into account when allocating staff to an assignment, for example:
  - the number of staff and levels of technical expertise required.
  - logistics of time and place.
  - the needs of staff (e.g. for study leave).
  - what is in the client's best interest (e.g. an expeditious audit).
- A client should not dictate who staffs their audit. If the finance director's requests are based solely on the premise that to have staff other than as requested would cause disruption then he should be assured that anyone assigned to the audit will be:
  - technically competent to perform the tasks delegated to them.
  - adequately briefed and supervised.
  - mindful of the need not to cause unnecessary disruption.
- Ebony may have other (more complex) assignments on which Xavier (and other staff previously involved in the audit of Almond) could be better utilised.
- To re-assign Xavier to the job may be to deny him other on-the-job training necessary for his personal development. For example, he may be ready to assume a more demanding supervisory role with another client, or he may wish to expand the client base on which he works to obtain a practicing certificate (say).
- To keep Xavier with Almond for a third year may also increase the risk of familiarity with the client's staff. Xavier may be too trusting of the client and lack professional scepticism.

- If it is usual to assign new trainees to Almond then the finance director should be advised that to assign a higher grade of staff is likely to increase the audit fee (as more experienced staff cannot necessarily do the work of more junior staff in any less time).

Conclusion

The finance director's requests should be granted only if:

(1) it is in the interests of Almond's shareholders (primarily).

(2) meets the needs of Ebony's staff.

(3) Almond agrees to the appropriate audit fee.

(b) **Phantom**

- Ebony's quality control procedures should be such that:
  - the work delegated to Alex was within his capability.
  - Alex was supervised in its execution.
  - the work performed by Alex was reviewed by appropriate personnel (i.e. someone of at least equal competence).
- Alex's working papers for the audit of Phantom should be reviewed again to confirm that there is evidence of his work having been properly directed, supervised and reviewed. If there is nothing which appears untoward it should be discussed with Alex's supervisor on the assignment whether Alex's confession to Kurt could have been a joke.
- As Alex has already left not only the firm, but the profession, it may not seem worth the effort taking any disciplinary action against him (e.g. reporting the alleged misconduct to ACCA). However, ACCA's disciplinary committee would investigate such a matter and take appropriate action.
- It is likely that Ebony will have given Alex's new employer a reference. This should be reviewed in the light of any evidence which may cast doubt on Alex's work ethics.
- As there are doubts about the integrity of Alex, his work should now be reviewed again, to determine the risk that the conclusions drawn on his work may be unsubstantiated in terms of the relevance, reliability and sufficiency of audit evidence.
- The review process should have identified the problem. If the reviewer did not detect an evident problem this would indicate the review process was not effective and the reviewer should be (re)trained as necessary.
- The work undertaken by Alex for audit clients other than Phantom should also be subject to scrutiny.

Conclusion

As Kurt is already aware of the potential problem, it may be appropriate that he be assigned as AIC to audits on which Alex undertook audit work, as he will be alert to any ramifications. It is possible that Ebony should not want to make the situation known to its staff generally.

(c) **Magenta**

- It appears that the subsequent events review was inadequate in that the impact of an adjusting event (the out-of-court settlement) was not considered.
- The financial statements for the year ended 31 December 20X3 contained a material error in that they disclosed a contingent liability (of unspecified amount) when a provision should have been made (for a known liability).
- The reasons for the error/oversight should be ascertained. For example:
  - who was responsible for signing off the subsequent events review?
  - when was the review completed?
  - for what reason, if any, was it not extended to the date of signing the auditor's report?
  - on what date was the written representation letter signed?
  - did the written representation letter cover the outcome of pending litigation (for example)?
- The error has implications for the firm's quality control procedures. For example:
  - was the AIC adequately directed and supervised in the completion of the subsequent events review?
  - was the work of the AIC adequately reviewed, to notice (for example) that it was not extended up until the date on which the auditor's report was signed?
- Ebony may need to review and improve on its procedures for the audit of provisions, contingent liabilities and subsequent events.
- If the AIC (or other staff) involved in the prior year audit of Magenta was not as thorough as they should have been, with respect to the subsequent events review, then other audit clients may be similarly affected.
- The auditor has a duty of care to draw the error / oversight to Magenta's attention. This would be an admission of fault for which Ebony should be liable if Magenta decided to take action against the firm.

- If Ebony remains silent and in the hope the error is unnoticed, there is the risk that Magenta will find out anyway.
- As the matter is material, it warrants a prior period adjustment (IAS® 8 *Accounting Policies, Changes in Accounting Estimates and Errors*). If this is not made, the financial statements will be materially misstated with respect to the current year and comparatives because the expense of the out-of-court settlement should be attributed to the prior period and not the current year's profit or loss.
- The most obvious implication for the current year audit of Magenta is that a more thorough subsequent event review will be required than the previous year. This may have a consequent effect on the time/fee/staff budgets of Magenta for the year ended 31 December 20X4.
- As the matter is material, it needs to be brought to the attention of Magenta's management, so that a prior year adjustment is made. In the absence of which a modified opinion (qualified – 'except for') should be required.

Conclusion

The staffing of the final audit of Magenta should be reviewed and perhaps a more experienced person assigned to the subsequent event review than in the prior year. The assignments allocated to the staff responsible for the oversight in Magenta's prior period should be reviewed and their competence / capability re-assessed.

Test your understanding 1 – Lambley

There are three main aspects of auditing examined in this question:

- the role of and potential liability of the auditor in connection with the detection and prevention of fraud
- the concept of materiality
- the position of the auditor when threatened with dismissal and replacement.

Note: Misstatements of > 5% profit before tax and > ½% revenue are considered material.

(a) **Lambley Trading**

(i) Auditors should design their audit procedures to have a reasonable expectation of detecting material fraud and error in the financial statements. An auditor would generally be considered to be at fault if he fails to detect material fraud and error. However, the auditor may not be liable if the fraud is difficult to detect (i.e. the fraud had been concealed and it is unreasonable to expect the auditor to have detected the fraud).

A claim for negligence against the auditor for not detecting immaterial fraud or error would be unsuccessful, except in the circumstances described below.

An auditor may be negligent if he:

– Finds an immaterial fraud while carrying out his normal procedures and does not report it to the company's management. However, he may not be negligent if the evidence to support a suspected fraud is weak.

– Carries out audit procedures on immaterial items, of which the company's management is aware, and these procedures are not carried out satisfactorily, so failing to detect an immaterial fraud. For instance, there may be a teeming and lading fraud, and the auditor may check receipts from sales are correctly recorded in the cash book and sales ledger, but fail to check that the cash from these sales is banked promptly.

– Carries out audit procedures on immaterial items at the specific request of the company's management, and the auditor failed to detect an immaterial fraud due to negligent work. The management would have a good case to claim damages for negligence against the auditor.

(ii) A fraud of $5,000 is 3.3% of the company's profit before tax, so it is immaterial.

As the auditor has carried out no work in this area, and is not responsible for detecting immaterial fraud, it is probable that he is not negligent.

It could be argued that the other audit procedures should have detected an apparent irregularity, such as analytical procedures. This might have indicated an increase in motor expenses compared with the previous year and budget, or the auditor could have looked at petty cash expenditure, which would show an increase compared with the previous year.

It could also be argued that the auditor should have looked at the absolute level of petty cash expenditure in order to decide whether to carry out work on the petty cash system. These arguments against the auditor are relatively weak, and it is unlikely that a claim for negligence would be successful. However, not detecting the fraud is likely to lead to a deterioration of the client's confidence in the auditor.

(iii) A fraud of $20,000 is 13.3% of the company's profit before tax, so it is material. It appears that the auditor may have been negligent in not carrying out any audit work on petty cash.

The auditor should design audit procedures so as to have a reasonable expectation of detecting material fraud or error. As no work was performed on petty cash there is no chance of detecting the fraud.

As a minimum, the auditor should have looked at the level of petty cash expenditure, comparing it with the previous year and the budget. This should have highlighted the increase in expenditure and led to the auditor carrying out further investigations.

As this is a petty cash fraud, it could be difficult to detect, but the cashier writing out and signing the petty cash vouchers, with no receipt attached, should have led the auditor to suspect the fraud.

It could be argued that the company has some responsibility for allowing the fraud to take place, as there was a serious deficiency in the system of internal control (i.e. the cashier recorded and made petty cash payments, and appeared to be able to authorise petty cash vouchers).

A more senior employee (e.g. the managing director) should have checked the cashier's work. Also, the managing director would have signed cheques which reimburse the petty cash, and he should have been aware that these had increased and investigated the reasons for the increase.

(b) **Colwick Enterprises**

(i) In terms of profit before tax, the sum of $200,000 is immaterial. Normally, a material item in terms of profit before tax is a misstatement which exceeds 5% of the profit before tax (i.e. $4.55m), so $200,000 is very small.

However, in terms of the director's remuneration, the $200,000 is 44% of the managing director's annual salary of $450,000.

Directors' remuneration is an important item in financial statements, both as far as legal requirements are concerned, and to the users of the financial statements, therefore is material by nature.

The company is proposing that the financial statements should show only 69% of the managing director's remuneration, so the understatement is material.

(ii) If the managing director refused to change the financial statements, the auditor's opinion should be qualified and the basis for qualified opinion should state his total emoluments are $650,000.

However, it seems probable that he will try to dismiss the audit firm before they issue their auditor's report on the financial statements. In order to change the auditor, he must:

- find another auditor who is prepared to accept appointment as auditor and
- call a general meeting to vote on the change of auditor, and
- notify the shareholders, the new auditor, and the existing auditor.

The auditor has the right to make representations to the shareholders, which can either be sent to the shareholders before the meeting, and/or make the representations at the meeting when the replacement of the auditor is proposed.

Although these representations are likely to have little effect on the change of auditor (as the managing director owns 60% of the shares, and only a majority vote is required to change the auditor), it would alert the other shareholders to the action of the managing director and concealment of information.

As a further point, provided the new auditors are a member of the ACCA or one of the recognised bodies, the ethical rules require the new auditor to contact the outgoing auditor asking if there are any matters to be brought to their attention to enable them to decide whether or not they are prepared to accept the audit appointment. The outgoing auditor should reply to their letter promptly, saying that the managing director has had $200,000 of benefits-in-kind, which he refuses to allow to be disclosed in the financial statements

It has been explained to the managing director that the auditor's opinion will be qualified if these emoluments are not disclosed, and this is the reason why he is proposing replacement of the auditor. If the proposed new auditors have the expected amount of integrity, they should discuss this point with the managing director, and point out that they will have to qualify the opinion if the benefits of $200,000 are not included in his remuneration in the financial statements.

If the new auditors take over the appointment and give an unmodified report, the outgoing auditor should take legal advice. The action taken would include:

- Disclosing information about the director's remuneration to the new auditor's professional body, and the fact that the auditor's report has not been modified.
- Disclosing the benefit to the tax authorities (as it may not have been subject to income tax).

(iii) If the managing director owned less than 1% of the issued shares, the auditor's position would be much stronger than in part (ii) above. If the managing director refuses to increase the remuneration in the draft accounts, the matter should be referred to the audit committee. If he still refuses to change the remuneration, a meeting with the members should be arranged with the chairman of the audit committee. The auditor would explain that the opinion will be qualified unless the remuneration was increased to $650,000. Also, it is likely that either the company or the managing director is committing an offence by not disclosing this benefit to the tax authorities. It seems probable that this meeting will decide to incorporate the benefit in the financial statements.

However if the audit committee believes the financial statements should not be changed, the auditor's report will need to be modified. If, at this stage, the directors decide to replace the audit firm, they will have to call a general meeting for this purpose. Representations should be made in writing to the shareholders, and/or circulated at the general meeting.

As Colwick Enterprises is a listed company, this information is likely to be picked up by the press and financial institutions, and result in adverse publicity for the company. In addition, it will make shareholders suspicious of the honesty of the managing director and the other directors.

Test your understanding 2

Notes for meeting with finance director

- Engagement letter:
  - Refer to any specific points regarding work in this area.
  - Refer to section on auditor's and directors' responsibilities.
  - Client signed the engagement letter agreeing to the terms.
- Responsibility for detection of fraud is primarily the responsibility of management.
- Implementation of an internal control system is the responsibility of management.
- The auditor's role is to obtain *reasonable assurance* that financial statements are free from *material fraud and error*.
- The amounts in question are not material, only 0.3% PBT.
- Ascertain how the FD discovered the fraud.
- Ascertain how the amounts of diverted funds were quantified.
- Discuss whether there might be further unidentified sums.

Test your understanding 3

The auditor should consider whether there has been a breach of laws or regulations (for example laws and regulations over health and safety, food hygiene, product use by dates etc.).

Procedures include:

- Obtain a general understanding of the relevant legal and regulatory framework e.g. by:
  - researching the industry on the internet
  - considering laws and regulations applicable to other clients in the same industry
  - enquiring of management.
- Discuss with the directors and other appropriate management (perhaps at the local level) whether there have been any instances of non-compliance.
- Inspect correspondence with the local authority and hygiene inspectors regarding instances of non-compliance.
- Evaluate the financial impact of the non-compliance, for example, possible penalties, the cost of compensation claims, the cost of remedial action, the impact on the value of the brand name.
- Obtain written representations from management that they have provided the auditor with all information in relation to the non-compliance and its impact.
- Consult experts in the area if considered necessary.

Test your understanding 4

Auditors must determine the most effective approach to each area of the financial statements. This may involve a combination of tests of controls and substantive procedures, or substantive procedures only.

Where the auditors choose to test the internal control systems of the company, they must design their work to have a reasonable expectation of detecting any deficiencies which would be likely to result in a material misstatement in the financial statements.

The area of discounts may have been one which did not involve testing of the internal controls as analytical procedures are likely to be effective.

Even if the controls in this area have been tested, the discounts given to customers may have been recorded accurately in the financial statements. In this case no material misstatement has occurred.

Jubilee must be reminded that the control deficiencies included in the report to management, issued at the conclusion of the audit, is simply a by-product of the audit. It is not intended to be a comprehensive list of all possible deficiencies. Should Jubilee Co require a more comprehensive review, then this could be undertaken as a separate assurance assignment.

Test your understanding 5

For

- Avoid firms exiting from the statutory audit market and thus maintaining choice and competition.
- Management of costs for both audit firms and their clients.
- Clearly quantifies the extent of auditors' liability to the public.
- Reduces the risk of auditors being used as scapegoats.
- Ensures that directors bear their extent of liability.

Against

- Auditors may not feel as accountable or be seen to be as accountable.
- May reduce the perceived value of an audit if risk to auditors is reduced.
- Setting a cap may be a difficult and contentious issue to agree with the client.
- Shareholders, or other parties to whom the auditors owe a duty of care may find themselves inadequately protected.

chapter

9

Planning, materiality and assessing the risk of misstatement

Chapter learning objectives

This chapter covers syllabus areas:

- D1 – Planning, materiality and assessing the risk of misstatement
- G4b – Discuss current developments in business practices, practice management and audit methodology and evaluate the potential impact on the conduct of an audit and audit quality
- G4c – Discuss current developments in emerging technologies, including big data and the use of data analytics and the potential impact on the conduct of an audit and audit quality

Detailed syllabus objectives are provided in the introduction section of the text book.

Exam focus

Risk assessment and planning normally makes up a significant number of marks of the exam. It is also essential for all areas of the exam that you are able to assess the materiality of a matter. Materiality is explained in this chapter.

1 The audit strategy and plan

The auditor should establish an overall strategy for the audit.

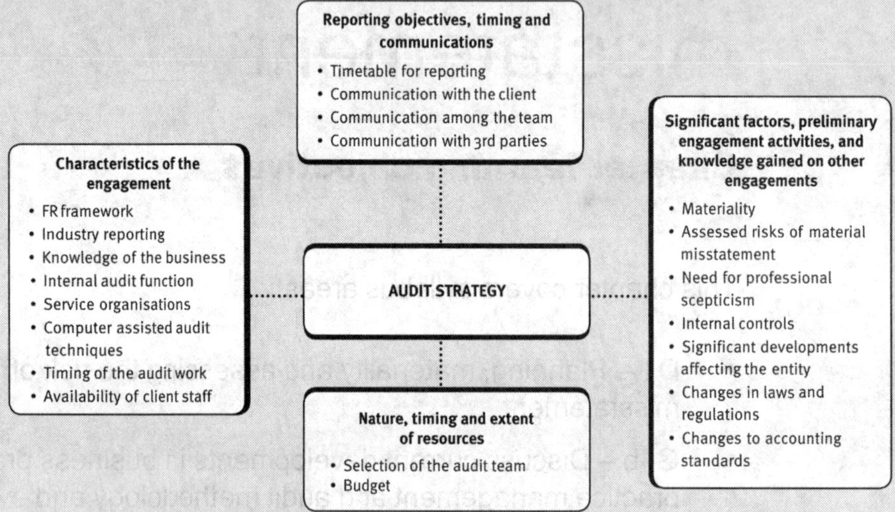

Once the strategy has been established the auditor should develop an audit plan. The audit plan is more detailed than the strategy and should include specific descriptions of:

- the nature, timing and extent of risk assessment procedures.
- the nature, timing and extent of further audit procedures, including:
  - **what** audit procedures are to be carried out
  - **who** should do them
  - **how much** work should be done (sample sizes, etc.)
  - **when** the work should be done (interim vs. final)
- any other procedures necessary to conform to ISAs.

Both the strategy and the plan must be formally documented in the audit working papers.

Planning procedures for initial engagements

In an initial audit engagement there are several factors which should be considered in addition to the planning procedures which are carried out for every audit.

- Arrangements should be made with the predecessor auditor to review their working papers.
- Any matters which were brought to the firm's attention when professional clearance was obtained should be considered for their potential impact on the audit strategy.
- Matters which were discussed with management in connection with the appointment should be considered, for example, discussion of significant accounting policies which may impact on the planned audit strategy.
- Audit procedures necessary to obtain sufficient appropriate audit evidence regarding opening balances, and procedures should be planned in accordance with ISA 510 *Initial Audit Engagements – Opening Balances*.
- Quality control procedures may be increased for initial engagements, for example, the involvement of another partner or senior individual to review the overall audit strategy prior to commencing significant audit procedures. Compliance with any such procedures should be fully documented.
- Additional time and resource may be necessary in the first year of an audit for a new client, in order to obtain the required knowledge of the client, e.g. documenting the internal control systems of the client for the first time, understanding the business including the legal and regulatory framework applicable to the company.
- In addition, it may be difficult to place reliance on analytical procedures as a source of substantive audit evidence as these require knowledge and experience of the client in order to set appropriate expectations, and therefore increased tests of detail may be necessary.
- Given the increased risk associated with initial engagements, consideration should be given to using an experienced audit team in order to reduce detection risk.

The impact of ISAs and IFRS standards

The impact of ISAs

ISA 315 (Revised) *Identifying and Assessing the Risks of Material Misstatement through Understanding the Entity and Its Environment* states that the auditor should adopt a risk based approach to the audit.

"The objective of the auditor is to identify and assess the risks of material misstatement, whether due to fraud or error, at the financial statement and assertion levels, through understanding the entity and its environment, including the entity's internal control, thereby providing a basis for designing and implementing responses to the assessed risks of material misstatement."

ISA 330 *The Auditor's Response to Assessed Risks* further develops the concept by stating that:

"The objective of the auditor is to obtain sufficient appropriate audit evidence regarding the assessed risks of material misstatement, through designing and implementing appropriate responses to those risks."

The importance of financial reporting standards

The audit opinion states whether or not the financial statements have been prepared in accordance with the financial reporting framework.

In order to reach this opinion, the auditor must fully understand the relevant financial reporting standards, and must evaluate whether the financial statements comply with these standards. This knowledge and understanding needs to be applied throughout the audit.

At the planning stage the auditor needs to assess the risk of material misstatement in the financial statements. The auditor must understand the required accounting treatment in order to identify potential omission or incorrect measurement, recognition, presentation or disclosure of an item.

The risk of material misstatement will increase with the complexity of the financial reporting issue, and where the matter requires the use of significant judgment.

F8 recap: Audit risk

Audit risk = Inherent risk × Control risk × Detection risk

Inherent risk is the susceptibility of an assertion about a class of transaction, account balance or disclosure to a misstatement that could be material, before consideration of any related controls.

Control risk is the risk that a misstatement that could occur will not be prevented, or detected and corrected, on a timely basis by the entity's internal control.

Detection risk is the risk that the procedures performed by the auditor to reduce audit risk to an acceptably low level will not detect a misstatement that exists that could be material.

(ISA 200 *Overall Objectives of the Independent Auditor and the Conduct of an Audit in Accordance with International Standards on Auditing*)

2 Risk assessment

ISA 315 (Revised) *Identifying and Assessing the Risks of Material Misstatement through Understanding the Entity and Its Environment* requires auditors to perform the following (minimum) risk assessment procedures:

- **Enquiries** with management, of appropriate individuals within the internal audit function (if there is one), and others with relevant information within the client entity (e.g. about external and internal changes the company has experienced)
- **Analytical procedures** to identify trends/relationships that are inconsistent with other relevant information or the auditor's understanding of the business. The purpose of this is to identify risk areas and guide the design of further audit procedures that are aimed at detecting and quantifying material misstatement.

  The term 'analytical procedure' means the evaluation of financial information through the analysis of plausible relationships among both financial and non-financial data.

- **Observation** (e.g. of control procedures)
- **Inspection** (e.g. of key strategic documents and procedural manuals).

The auditor may also consider how management has responded to the findings and recommendations of the internal audit function regarding identified deficiencies in internal control relevant to the audit, including whether and how such responses have been implemented, and whether they have been subsequently evaluated by the internal audit function.

Example risk assessment procedures

It is impossible to prepare a comprehensive list of risk assessment procedures that need to be carried out. The procedures need to be prepared in light of the unique circumstances of the client. However, examples include:

Enquiries of management:

- Have any share issues occurred during the year?

- Has the company invested in any new capital assets during the year?
- Have any new competitors or products entered the market?
- How does the company manage exposure to exchange rate risk?
- Have there been any changes in senior management during the year?

Analytical procedures:

- Compare actual results to forecast to identify any significant changes to plan.
- Compare the client's performance and position to any available industry data to identify significant variations.
- Compare the client's financial statements in comparison to the prior year to identify any unexpected changes in performance or position.

Observe:

- The application of controls over the counting of inventory during the year.
- The performance of year-end reconciliations (bank, supplier statement) to ensure they are performed regularly.
- Month-end adjustments/reconciliations being performed during an interim visit to ensure controls are applied throughout the year.

Inspect:

- Organisation charts to identify changes in key staff.
- Examples of controls operating throughout the year, e.g. evidence of review of month end reconciliations, evidence of review of aged receivables on a monthly basis.
- HR records/payroll records to identify movements in staff.
- News/media reports to identify any significant issues, such as potential legal action.

The entity and its environment

Auditors should obtain an understanding of:

- Relevant industry, regulatory and other external factors.
- The nature of the entity, including:
  - Its operations
  - Its ownership and governance structures
  - The types of investment the entity makes
  - The way the entity is structured and financed.
- The entity's selection and application of accounting policies.
- The entity's objectives and strategies, and those related business risks that may result in material misstatement.
- The measurement and review of the entity's financial performance.

If the entity has an internal audit function, obtaining an understanding of that function also contributes to the auditor's understanding of the entity and its environment, including internal control, in particular the role that the function plays in the entity's monitoring of internal control over financial reporting.

The entity's internal control

The components of internal control include:

- The control environment.
- The entity's risk assessment process.
- The information system relevant to financial reporting.
- The control activities.
- The monitoring system.

The auditor must evaluate the design of the controls to determine whether they have been implemented during the financial reporting period and whether they are effective at preventing and detecting potentially material fraud and error.

3 Materiality

As stated in ISA 200 *Overall Objectives of the Independent Auditor and the Conduct of an Audit in Accordance with International Standards on Auditing*, the objective of an audit is to express an opinion as to whether the financial statements are prepared, in all **material** respects, in accordance with an applicable financial reporting framework. It is therefore of vital importance for auditors to apply the concept of materiality in the planning and performance of the audit.

"Misstatements, including omissions, are considered to be material if they, individually or in aggregate, could reasonably be expected to influence the economic decisions of users taken on the basis of the financial statements."

Calculation

ISA 320 *Materiality in Planning and Performing an Audit*, recognises, and permits, the use of benchmark calculations of materiality.

A traditional calculation basis is as follows:

	Value	**Comments**
Pre-tax profit	5 – 10%	Users usually interested in profitability of the company.
Revenue	½ – 1%	Materiality relates to the size of the business, which can be measured in terms of revenue
Total assets	1 – 2%	Size can also be measured in terms of the asset base

These benchmarks should be used in the initial assessment of materiality.

The auditor must then use judgment to modify materiality to ensure it is relevant to the unique circumstances of the client.

When deciding on an appropriate benchmark the auditor must consider:

- The elements of the financial statements.
- Whether particular items tend to be the focus of the users.
- The nature of the entity, its life cycle and its environment.
- The ownership and financing structure.
- The relative volatility of the benchmark.

Material by nature

Materiality is not just a purely financial concern. Some items may be material by nature i.e. the impact they have on the financial statements.

Examples of items which are material by nature include:

- Misstatements that affect compliance with regulatory requirements.
- Misstatements that affect compliance with debt covenants.
- Misstatements that, when adjusted, would turn a reported profit into a loss for the year.
- Misstatements that, when adjusted, would turn a reported net-asset position into a net-liability position (or net-current asset to net-current liability).
- Related party transactions including transactions with directors, e.g. salary and benefits, personal use of assets, etc.
- Disclosures in the financial statements relating to possible future legal claims or going concern issues, for example, could influence users' decisions and may be purely narrative. In this case a numerical calculation is not relevant.

Performance materiality

It is unlikely, in practice, that auditors will be able to identify individually material misstatements. It is much more common that misstatements are material in aggregate (i.e. in combination). For this reason auditors must also consider what is known as 'performance materiality.'

This is an amount, established by the auditor, set below the materiality to be used when designing the nature, timing and extent of further procedures. The aim is to reduce the risk that misstatements in aggregate exceed materiality for the financial statements as a whole.

Performance materiality also considers the significance of individual classes of transaction, account balances or disclosures to the users of accounts.

Case Study: Performance materiality

LeJoG Co is a company that organises accommodation, luggage transportation, and support for charitable sporting enthusiasts attempting to travel from one end of the country to the other. All customers pay in full when booking their trip. LeJoG has a complicated cancellation policy, the amount refundable decreases with the length of time before the start of the trip.

The audit engagement team has planned the audit of the financial statements for the year ended 30 June 20X4. The team has determined a materiality level for the financial statements as a whole, of $100,000, which has been calculated using an average of 1% of revenue, 2% total assets and 10% profit before tax. Performance materiality needs to be applied to revenue and the associated liabilities recognised when taking payment from customers in advance, as revenue recognition is an area of audit risk.

Performance materiality could be determined as a percentage of financial statement materiality, say 75%, i.e. a performance materiality of ($100,000 × 75%) $75,000 could be set for the audit of revenue and the associated liabilities. The audit team could use a higher or lower percentage, or use a different calculation, depending on their professional judgment.

The aim of performance materiality is to reduce the risk that misstatements in aggregate exceed materiality for the financial statements as a whole. For example, if a misstatement was identified of, say $80,000, without performance materiality the auditor would conclude that revenue is not materially misstated. However, the audit may not have detected further misstatements which when added to the $80,000 identified would result in a material misstatement. By using performance materiality, the auditor would conclude that a misstatement of $80,000 could be material, thereby prompting them to do additional work. If no additional misstatements are detected, an unmodified opinion may be issued.

Risk and the exam

In the exam it is likely that you will be asked to perform a risk assessment for an audit client. The three types of risk examinable are:

- Risk of material misstatement
- Audit risk
- Business risk

It is vital that you understand the difference between these types of risk to ensure you answer the question appropriately.

4 Risk of material misstatement

Risk of material misstatement is the risk the financial statements are materially misstated (either due to fraud or error), prior to the audit. Risk of material misstatement is comprised of **inherent and control risk**.

The financial statements may be materially misstated for 3 main reasons:

- Numbers are misstated – e.g. overstatement of receivables due to bad debts not being written off.
- Disclosures are missing or inadequate – e.g. going concern disclosures being omitted.
- The basis of preparation is inappropriate – the going concern basis has been used when the break up basis should have been used.

The financial statements will be materially misstated if they are not prepared in accordance with IFRS Standards. In order for the auditor to identify material misstatement they need to know what the appropriate accounting treatment is and whether it has been complied with.

When evaluating the risk of material misstatement it is crucial to discuss the specific impact of the risk on the **financial statements**, i.e.

- the specific account balance, transaction or disclosure affected
- whether the item might be overstated, understated, omitted, inappropriately recognised, etc.

The auditor is also required to determine whether any of the risks are a significant risk. A significant risk is a risk of material misstatement that requires special audit consideration.

The importance of financial reporting standards

In the exam you will have to comment on whether the accounting treatment is appropriate therefore your knowledge from P2 will be required in the P7 exam. The chapter 'Financial reporting revision' summarises the key points from these standards.

You should also read the examiner's article called 'The importance of financial reporting standards to auditors' which is available on the ACCA website in the P7 Technical Articles section.

5 Audit risk

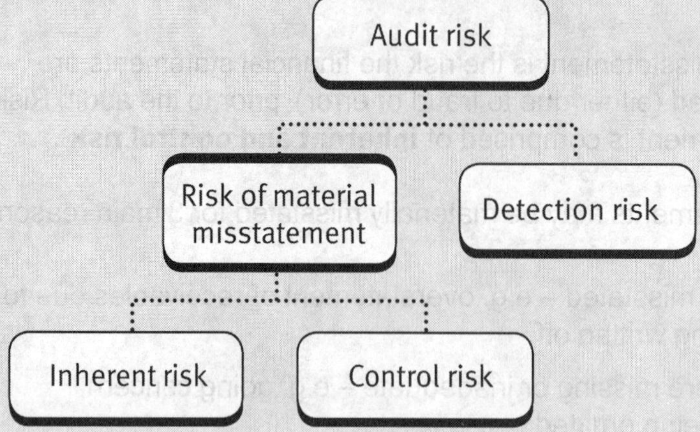

Audit risk is the risk that the auditor expresses an inappropriate opinion.

The auditor will express an inappropriate opinion if the financial statements are materially misstated and they fail to detect that misstatement.

Detection risks include situations such as:

- first year of auditing the client therefore a lack of cumulative knowledge and experience.
- the client is putting the auditor under undue time pressure resulting in the audit being rushed and misstatements possibly going undetected.
- The client operates from multiple sites and the auditor may not be able to visit each site during the audit. This will be an issue, for example, if a material amount of inventory is held at sites not visited by the auditor.

If no detection risks are given in the scenario, an answer to an audit risk question will be identical to an answer to a risk of material misstatement question.

6 Business risk

A business risk is one resulting from "significant events, conditions, circumstances, actions or inactions that could adversely affect an entity's ability to achieve its objectives and execute its strategies".

Auditors must assess business risk in order to:

- develop business understanding
- increase the likelihood of identifying specific risks of material misstatement
- evaluate overall audit risk.

The relationship between business risk and the risk of material misstatement/audit risk

Most business risks will eventually have financial consequences, and therefore an effect on the financial statements. If the client does not account for these issues in the correct manner, the financial statements could be materially misstated.

Business risk v risk of material misstatement

Operating in a technologically fast paced market could lead to a company's products being outdated by superior products. This is a **business risk** because it may stop a company achieving desired profit margins.

The **risk of material misstatement** is that inventory may be overstated in the financial statements: the net realisable value of inventory may have fallen below cost, requiring a write-down of the inventory balance.

Examples of business risks

These risks are often categorised as being 'external' or 'internal' risks.

Typical 'external risks'	Typical 'internal risks'
Changing legislation	Employees
Changing interest rates	Failure to modernise products, processes, labour relations, marketing
Changing exchange rates	Excessive reliance on a dominant CEO
Public opinion, attitudes, fashions	Cash flow difficulties
Price wars initiated by competitors	Rapidly increasing gearing
Untried technologies and ideas, political factors	Overtrading
Natural hazards	Fraud
	Excessive reliance on one or few products, customers, suppliers
	Computer systems failures

7 Assessing whether a risk is significant

As part of the risk assessment process the auditor should consider the significance of the identified risks, including:

- Whether the risk is one of fraud.
- Whether it is related to recent economic, accounting or other developments that require specific attention.
- The complexity of the related transactions.
- Whether it involves related parties.
- The degree of subjectivity involved in measuring financial information.
- Whether it involves transactions outside the normal course of business.

If the auditor determines that a significant risk exists they must then obtain the necessary understanding of how the entity controls that risk. Only then can the auditor determine an appropriate response in terms of further audit procedures.

Additional information to help plan the audit

In the exam you may be asked to suggest additional information to help plan the audit. The scenario will have provided some information on the client, but in order to fully identify the risks, further information will be required.

By obtaining additional information, a greater understanding of the risk areas can be obtained to allow the impact on the financial statements to be considered. This will enable the audit to be planned more effectively.

Additional information

Example 1 – Purchase of shares during the year

The client has purchased 25% of a company's share capital during the year. Additional information would be required to determine the appropriate accounting treatment. It is possible that it is being treated as an associate when in fact no significant influence can be exercised. In this case it should be treated as an investment. Additional information is required regarding voting rights attached to the shares to determine whether significant influence has been acquired.

Example 2 - New loan taken out during the year

The client has taken out a ten year loan during the year. Additional information would be required to determine whether the loan should be split between current and non-current liabilities and whether any disclosure needs to be made of any security for the loan. Whilst it would be expected that the loan should be split between current and non-current liabilities, if there are no payments due for the first twelve months, the loan will be a non-current liability for the first year. In this case the loan agreement would provide the additional information required regarding payment terms and details of whether the loan is secured over the company's assets.

8 Response to risk assessment

The main purpose of performing risk assessment is to guide the auditor in the design and performance of further audit procedures to obtain sufficient appropriate audit evidence. The only way the auditor can reduce audit risk is by manipulating their **detection risk**. They can manipulate detection risk by:

- Allocating complex or risky areas of the engagement to suitably experienced and competent staff, such as the audit of related party transactions and complex inventory calculations.
- Placing more or less reliance on the results of systems and controls testing.
- Performing more or less substantive analytical procedures as opposed to other, more detailed ones.
- Altering the volume of substantive procedures performed after the year-end.
- Altering the volume of balances tested by changing sample sizes.
- Consulting external experts on technically complex or contentious matters.
- Changing the timing and frequency of review procedures, including using additional partners to review work.
- Emphasising the need for professional scepticism.

Current issue: Data analytics and big data

Data analytics and big data

Definitions

Big data refers to data sets that are large or complex.

Big data technology allows the auditor to perform procedures on very large or complete sets of data rather than samples.

Data analytics is the science of examining raw data (big data) with the purpose of drawing conclusions about that information.

Features of data analytics

- Data analytics allows the auditor to manipulate 100% of the data in a population quickly. Results can be visualised graphically which may increase the user-friendliness of the reports.
- Data analytics can be used throughout the audit to help identify risks, test the controls and as part of substantive procedures. The results of data analytics still need to be evaluated using the professional skills and judgment of the auditor in order to analyse the results and draw conclusions.
- As with analytical procedures in general, the quality of data analytics depends on the reliability of the underlying data used.
- Data analytics can incorporate a wider range of data. For example data can be extracted and analysed from social media, public sector data, industry data and economic data.
- Essentially data analytics are a more comprehensive version of computer assisted audit techniques.

Benefits of data analytics

- Audit quality should increase as sampling risk is reduced or even eliminated as complete data sets are subject to audit.
- As audit quality is increased the auditor's liability risk is reduced.
- Audit procedures can be performed more quickly and to a higher standard. This provides more time to analyse and interpret the results rather than gathering the information for analysis.
- Audit procedures can be carried out on a continuous basis rather than being focused at the year-end.
- Reporting to the client and users will be more timely as the work may be completed within weeks rather than months after the year-end.

- May result in more frequent interaction between the auditor and client over the course of the year.

Risks

- Risk of changing the client's data.
- Data retention – auditors must keep documentation to support the audit conclusions in order to comply with ISAs. This causes problems in that large data sets need to be stored which takes up considerable server space. Personal data may also be stored which breaches data protection.
- Ethical issues – clients may want to use the results of the auditors' analytics. Specific results of audit tests are not usually provided to the client.
- Significant cost of investment in hardware, software and training.
- Reduction in billable hours as audit efficiency increases. Whilst this is good news for the client it will mean lower fees for the auditor.

What it means for the profession

- Larger accountancy firms are developing their own data analytic platforms. This requires significant investment in computer hardware and software, training of staff and quality control.
- Small firms are unlikely to have the resources available to develop their own software as the cost is likely to be too prohibitive. However, external computer software companies have developed audit systems that work with popular accounting systems such as Sage, Xero and Intuit which many clients of small accountancy firms may be using.
- Medium sized firms may also find the level of investment too restrictive and may therefore be unable to compete with the larger audit firms for listed company audits. However, these firms may find that listed companies require systems and controls assurance work which their auditors would not be allowed to perform under ethical standards.
- Currently, ISAs are based on the systems based approach to audit, which seeks to obtain audit evidence by placing reliance on internal controls rather than on carrying out extensive substantive testing. The development of data analytics represents a significant progression away from traditional auditing methods. Therefore, as they become more widely used, ISAs will need to be updated to reflect this innovation in auditing techniques.

Example

The auditor uses data analytics to analyse journals posted. The analysis identifies:

- The total number of journals posted
- The number of journals posted manually
- The number of journals posted automatically by the system
- The number of people processing journals
- The time of day the journals are posted

The auditor may conclude there is a higher risk of fraud this year compared with last if:

- The number of manual versus automatic journals increases significantly.
- The number of people processing journals increases.
- Journals are posted outside of normal working hours.

Professional scepticism

Professional scepticism is defined as: 'An attitude that includes a questioning mind, being alert to conditions which may indicate possible misstatement due to error or fraud, and a critical assessment of audit evidence.'

It is both an ethical and a professional issue. Professional scepticism includes maintaining independence of mind.

The auditor must maintain professional scepticism throughout the planning and performance of the audit, recognising that circumstances may exist that cause the financial statements to be materially misstated.

Professional scepticism requires the auditor to be alert to:

- Audit evidence that contradicts other audit evidence.
- Information that brings into question the reliability of documents and responses to enquiries to be used as audit evidence.
- Conditions that may indicate possible fraud.
- Circumstances that suggest the need for audit procedures in addition to those required by ISAs.

For example, the auditor may make an enquiry of management regarding compliance with laws and regulations. Management may inform the auditor that there have been no instances of non-compliance during the year. Application of professional scepticism would require the auditor to seek alternative, corroborative evidence to support management's claim as they may not wish the auditor to know about any breaches. This may involve speaking with the company's compliance department to confirm management's statement as well as reviewing board minutes for any discussions that indicate non-compliance or reviewing invoices from legal advisers which may indicate advice has been obtained regarding non-compliance.

In February 2012, the IAASB released *Questions and Answers: Professional Scepticism in an Audit of Financial Statements*, which provides additional explanations relating to professional scepticism.

Specifically, professional scepticism:

- is fundamentally a mindset that drives auditor behaviour to adopt a questioning approach.
- is inseparably linked to objectivity and auditor independence.
- forms an integral part of the auditor's skill set and is closely interrelated with professional judgment, both of which are key inputs to audit quality.
- enhances the effectiveness of an audit procedure and reduces the risk of giving an inappropriate opinion.

The Q&A reiterates the importance of the components of quality control in enhancing the awareness of the importance and application of professional scepticism.

In addition, the Q&A emphasises that although professional scepticism is not referred to within each ISA, it is relevant and necessary throughout the audit and is particularly important when considering the risks of material misstatement due to fraud and when addressing areas of the audit that are more complex, significant or highly judgmental (e.g. accounting estimates, going concern, related party transactions, non-compliance with laws and regulations).

Audit documentation is critical in evidencing professional scepticism, particularly documentation demonstrating how significant judgments and key audit issues were addressed, which may provide evidence of the auditor's exercise of professional scepticism.

Effective oversight and inspection of audits by regulators and oversight bodies should incorporate challenging, influencing and stimulating auditors to be sceptical and focusing auditors on the importance of professional scepticism and how it can be appropriately applied through constructive dialogue.

UK syllabus: Professional scepticism

In March 2012, the FRC released a Briefing Paper *Professional Scepticism*.

The briefing paper takes a theoretical approach to discussing the importance of professional scepticism in the audit, specifically:

- Exploring:
  - the roots of scepticism and identifying lessons for its role in the conduct of the audit
  - scientific scepticism
  - the origins of modern audit.
- Concluding about professional scepticism and the audit.
- Discussing the conditions necessary for auditors to demonstrate professional scepticism.

The paper highlights the significance of scepticism to the quality of the audit. It defines scepticism as 'examination, inquiry into, hesitation or doubt' specifically, doubt that stimulates challenge and inquiry.

It explains that scientific scepticism is a 'systematic form of continual informed questioning', or critical appraisal, looking for evidence that contradicts management's assertions and suspending judgment about the validity of those assertions. In the context of an audit, this means actively looking for risks of material misstatement.

Assessing whether professional scepticism has been applied

In the exam you may be required to critically evaluate the planning or performance of an audit engagement. This will include assessing whether an engagement has been planned and performed with an attitude of professional scepticism.

Examples of circumstances where professional scepticism has not been applied include:

- Contradictory evidence has not been questioned.
- The reliability of documents and responses to enquiries from the client has not been evaluated.
- The sufficiency and appropriateness of evidence has not been considered.
- The authenticity of a document has not been considered, when there are indications of possible fraud.
- Past experience of the dishonesty or lack of integrity of the client has been disregarded.
- The auditor has accepted less persuasive evidence because of their past experience of the honesty and integrity of the client.

If professional scepticism is not maintained, the auditor may:

- overlook unusual circumstances
- use unsuitable audit procedures
- reach inappropriate conclusions.

Professional scepticism reduces audit risk.

Approach to exam questions

Risk questions in the exam usually contain the largest single allocation of marks, therefore it is important that you can do well on these questions.

Here are some tips to help you score well:

Use analytical procedures to identify and explain the risks of material misstatement/audit risks

When asked to perform analytical procedures, do your calculations first and present them neatly in a table.

Each calculation is usually worth ½ mark. There will usually be 5 or 6 marks available for calculations.

Refer to your calculations as you perform your risk assessment.

Using the information provided / the results of your analytical procedures, evaluate the risks of material misstatement / audit risks

Each risk is usually worth 1½ or 2 marks. To earn the full marks for each risk you need to properly explain the risk. If your answers are too brief or do not demonstrate sufficient understanding you will not score the marks.

To ensure your answer is sufficiently detailed, use the following approach:

- Identify the information from the scenario that creates the potential risk.
- If numbers are provided, calculate whether the balance is material. This helps to assess whether or not the risk is significant.
- State the required accounting treatment.
- State the risk to the financial statements if the required treatment is not followed.

For example:

Receivables

- A major customer is struggling to pay their debt and as a result the receivables balance is significantly higher than last year.
- The balance outstanding represents 5% of total assets therefore is material and a significant risk.
- Receivables should be valued at the fair value of the economic benefit expected to be received in accordance with IFRS 9 *Financial Instruments*. If the debt is not likely to be paid it should be written off or written down.
- There is a risk that receivables and profit are overstated if the debt is not written off or written down.

Foreign currency transactions

- The company purchases all goods from an overseas supplier resulting in foreign currency transactions.
- Foreign currency purchases should be translated using the spot rate or average rate at the date of the transaction. Any payables balance outstanding at the year-end must be revalued using the year-end rate in accordance with IAS 21 *The Effects of Changes in Foreign Exchange Rates*.
- There is a risk that purchases are misstated if the exchange rate used is incorrect or if errors are made when translating the purchase cost. Payables may be misstated if they have not been revalued at the year-end.

Provisions

- The client has this year started offering warranties with products sold but no provision has been recognised for warranty costs.
- A provision is required to be recognised if there is a present obligation as a result of a past event which can be measured reliably and is probable to lead to a transfer of economic benefits in accordance with *IAS 37 Provisions, Contingent Liabilities and Contingent Assets*.
- The sale of goods with a warranty creates an obligation for the company to repair or replace goods returned within the warranty period.
- Provision liabilities and expenses are understated if a provision for warranty costs is not recognised.

Note how the explanation of the risks focuses on how the financial statements may be materially misstated.

Evaluate the business risks facing the client

Make sure you explain business risks as risks the directors of the business will care about. The focus here should be on adverse impact to profit, revenue, or cash flow.

- Identify the information from the scenario creating the risk.
- Explain the impact it will have on the business operations.
- Explain the financial impact.

Major customer

- A major customer is struggling to pay their debt.
- If the customer cannot pay their balance, the company will not receive the cash which will reduce cash inflows.
- The debt will need to be written off which will reduce profit.
- Future revenues will also decrease as the major customer will no longer be trading with the client.

Foreign currency transactions

- The company purchases all goods from an overseas supplier resulting in foreign currency transactions.
- If the company does not use any hedging instruments it will be exposed to exchange rate fluctuations which will affect the price of purchases.
- If exchange rates move in an adverse direction, the cost of purchases will be higher resulting in a reduction in profit.

Relevance of the information provided

The scenario for the risk question will be quite detailed and require you to evaluate it in the context of the audit. Be aware that it may contain some information that will not necessarily be relevant for planning the audit. Some information may be provided to help set the scene of the scenario and to enable you to understand the client and its operations. If you can't see how the information relates specifically to the requirement, don't try and force it into an answer. This will waste valuable time in the exam that could be better used on a different question.

For example, a supplier may have increased prices to the client. This does not create any audit risk as such. If the client continues to process and record purchases in the usual way there is no risk of material misstatement in the financial statements. However, if the question had asked for business risks, this would be a business risk as it impacts the company's profits.

Professional marks

P7 includes four professional marks in one of the Section A questions, for clarity of explanation or evaluation, the use of logical structure and an appropriate format. In the exam, you should prioritise risks identified as this adds to the professionalism of the risk assessment performed.

Applying ISAs proportionately...

Applying ISAs Proportionately with the Size and Complexity of an Entity (IAASB – August 2009)

The IAASB issued a publication to highlight how the design of the ISAs issued by the IAASB under the Clarity Project enables them to be applied in a manner proportionate to the size and complexity of an entity. Specifically, it focuses on matters that are likely to be of particular relevance to the audits of small and medium-sized entities (SME).

The auditor's objectives are the same for audits of entities of different sizes and complexities. This, however, does not mean that every audit will be planned and performed in exactly the same way. In particular ISAs explain that the appropriate audit approach for designing and performing audit procedures depends on the auditor's risk assessment and the exercise of appropriate professional judgment.

Often, SMEs engage in relatively simple business transactions, which means that their audits will generally be relatively straightforward. For example, consider the requirement in ISA 315 for the auditor to obtain an understanding of the entity and its environment. The typically simpler structure and processes in a SME often mean that the auditor may obtain understanding quite readily and document this in a straightforward manner. Similarly, internal control in the context of a SME may be simpler.

Of particular relevance is the fact that the ISAs include useful guidance that assists the auditor in applying specific requirements in the context of a SME audit. Where appropriate, guidance is included in ISAs under the subheading 'Considerations Specific to Smaller Entities'.

For example:

- Standard audit programs drawn up on the assumption of few relevant control activities may be used for the audit of a SME provided that they are tailored to the circumstances of the engagement.
- In the absence of interim or monthly financial information the auditor may need to plan analytical procedures when an early draft of the entity's financial statements becomes available.
- Given the potential lack of documentary evidence concerning control activities, the attitudes, awareness, and actions of management are of particular importance to the auditor's understanding of a SME's control environment.

Other guidance indicates that specific aspects of the audit will vary with the size, complexity, and nature of the entity, for example:

- The nature and extent of the auditor's planning activities.
- The auditor's consideration of fraud risk factors.
- The communication process between the auditor and those charged with governance.
- The level of detail at which to communicate significant deficiencies in internal control.
- The judgment as to whether a control is relevant to the audit.

Not all of the ISAs are necessarily relevant in every audit, that is, the circumstances in which an ISA applies may not exist in the engagement. For example, some of the ISAs that may not be relevant in a SME audit include:

- ISA 402 *Audit Considerations Relating to An Entity Using a Service Organisation*, if the client does not use a service organisation.
- ISA 600 *Special Considerations - Audit of Group Financial Statements (including the work of component auditors),* if it is not a group audit.
- ISA 610 *Using the Work of Internal Auditors*, if there is no internal audit function.

Even if an ISA is relevant, not all of its requirements may be relevant in the particular circumstances of an audit. A few examples include:

- Holding an engagement team meeting if it is only a one person team.
- Performing the specified substantive procedures if the auditor has not identified previously unidentified or undisclosed related parties or related party transactions.
- Obtaining sufficient appropriate audit evidence to determine whether a material uncertainty exists if the auditor has not identified any event or condition that casts doubt on the entity's ability to continue as a going concern.

Finally, to further assist the auditor, the ISAs provide examples of how the documentation in a SME audit can be approached in an efficient and effective manner. For example:

- It may be helpful and efficient to record various aspects of the audit together in a single document, with cross-references to supporting working papers as appropriate.
- The documentation of the understanding of the entity may be incorporated in the auditor's documentation of the overall strategy and audit plan.
- The results of the risk assessment may be documented as part of the auditor's documentation of further procedures.
- It is not necessary to document the entirety of the auditor's understanding of the SME and matters related to it.
- A brief memorandum may serve as the documented audit strategy. At the completion of the audit, a brief memorandum could be developed and then updated to serve as the documented audit strategy for the following year's audit engagement.

Auditing significant, unusual or highly complex transactions

In September 2010, the IAASB issued a Questions & Answers publication, *Auditor considerations regarding significant unusual or highly complex transactions* in response to specific requests for information on how the ISAs deal with this particular topic.

The publication highlights that because of their nature, these transactions may give rise to risks of material misstatement of the financial statements and, accordingly, may merit heightened attention by auditors.

The publication does not provide any additional guidance beyond that which is contained within the ISAs themselves. Instead, it highlights the most salient points from the ISAs for auditors to consider when approaching the audit of significant, unusual or highly complex transactions, and in particular highlights:

- What considerations in the ISAs are relevant when forming an opinion on the financial statements.
- What general considerations in the ISAs are relevant in relation to audit documentation, quality control, and interim reviews of financial statements when dealing with such transactions.
- How the ISAs guide the auditor in the auditor's communication with those charged with governance when dealing with such transactions.

The publication highlights many specific requirements of the ISAs, including:

- The requirement to exercise professional judgment and maintain professional scepticism throughout the planning and performance of an audit.
- The need to identify and assess the risks of material misstatement by performing risk assessment procedures designed to obtain the required understanding of the entity and its environment, including the entity's internal control.
- The requirement to design and implement overall responses to address the assessed risks of material misstatement and to design and perform further audit procedures whose nature, timing, and extent are based on and are responsive to the assessed risks of material misstatement at the assertion level.

When approaching the audit of significant, unusual or highly complex transactions, the auditor should consider the need to obtain more persuasive audit evidence in responding to the assessed risks, as the auditor's assessment of risk is likely to be higher, in particular there is the possibility of increased risk of bias in management's judgments due to the complexity involved therein.

Test your understanding 1 – Yates

Your firm has successfully tendered for the audit of Yates Co, a private national haulage and distribution company with over 2,000 employees. This long-established company provides refrigerated, bulk and heavy haulage transport services to time-sensitive delivery schedules. You have obtained the following financial information from Yates:

Statement of profit and loss	**30 June 20X4 Draft $m**	**30 June 20X3 Actual $m**
Revenue (note 1)	161.5	144.4
Materials expense (note 2)	(88.0)	(74.7)
Staff costs	(40.6)	(35.6)
Depreciation and amortisation	(8.5)	(9.5)
Other expenses	(19.6)	(23.2)
Finance costs	(2.9)	(2.2)
Total expenses	159.6	145.2
Profit/loss before tax	1.9	(0.8)
Statement of financial position	**30 June 20X4**	**30 June 20X3**
	$m	**$m**
Intangible assets (note 3)	7.2	6.2
Tangible assets (note 4)		
– Property and transport equipment	55.1	57.8
– Vehicles	16.4	16.0
– Other equipment	7.4	9.3
Inventories	0.6	0.5
Trade receivables (note 5)	13.7	13.4
Cash and cash equivalents	3.4	2.8
Total assets	**103.8**	**106.0**

Provisions		
– Restructuring (note 6)	9.7	10.8
– Tax provision	3	3.3
Lease liabilities (note 7)	5.4	4.4
Trade payables	13.8	13.1
Other liabilities (note 8)	8.5	7.9
Total liabilities	**40.4**	**39.5**

Note 1: Revenue is net of rebates to major customers that increase with the volume of consignments transported. Rebates are calculated on cumulative sales for the financial year and awarded quarterly in arrears.

Note 2: Materials expense includes fuel, repair materials, transportation and vehicle maintenance costs.

Note 3: Purchased intangible assets, including software and industrial licences, are accounted for using the cost model. Internally generated intangible assets, mainly software developed for customers to generate consignment documents, are initially recognised at cost if the asset recognition criteria are satisfied.

Note 4: Depreciation is charged at the following rates on a straight line basis:

- Property 6 – 60 years
- Vehicles and transport equipment 3 – 8 years
- Other equipment 3 – 15 years

Note 5: Trade receivables are carried at their principal amount, less allowances for impairment.

Note 6: The restructuring provision relates to employee termination and other obligations arising on the closure and relocation of distribution depots in December 20X2.

Note 7: Leases are capitalised at the date of inception of the lease at fair value or the present value of the minimum lease payments, if less.

Note 8: Other liabilities include amounts due to employees for accrued wages and salaries, overtime, sick leave, maternity pay and bonuses.

Required:

(a) Calculate preliminary materiality and justify the suitability of your assessment.

(5 marks)

(b) Prepare briefing notes for the audit partner which identify and explain the risks of material misstatement for the audit of Yates Co for the year ending 30 June 20X4.

(12 marks)

Professional marks for structure, clarity of explanation and logical flow.

(4 marks)

(c) Briefly describe the principal audit work to be performed in respect of the carrying amount of the following items in the statement of financial position:

(i) Trade receivables

(ii) Vehicles

(8 marks)

(d) Explain the extent to which you should plan to place reliance on analytical procedures as audit evidence.

(6 marks)

(Total: 35 marks)

Test your understanding 2 – Ivor

You are the audit senior in a firm of accountants. One of the partners has given you the following financial information for a client, Ivor Co, whose final audit is due to take place in a month's time. The partner has asked you to conduct an analytical review of the management accounts in comparison to the prior year's financial statements.

		31.12.20X3 (Management accounts)		31.12.20X2 (Audited financial statements)
		$000		$000
Statement of profit or loss				
Revenue		13,095		10,160
Sales discounts		(525)		(200)
		12,570		9,960
Cost of sales		(9,556)		(7,603)
Gross profit		3,014		2,357
Distribution costs		(762)		(498)
Admin expenses				
Wages and salaries	1,275		960	
Directors' salaries	125		115	
Rent	35		12	
Profit on disposal	(510)		(75)	
Other expenses	137		153	
		(1,062)		(1,165)
Net profit before tax		1,190		694

Statement of financial position				
Non-current assets				
Tangible assets (note 1)		1,073		2,130
Intangible assets (note 2)		54		75
		1,127		2,205
Current assets				
Inventory	1,640		1,200	
Trade receivables (note 3)	2,204		1,353	
Other receivables	46		42	
Cash	104		–	
		3,994		2,595
		5,121		4,800
Equity and liabilities				
Ordinary share capital		1,700		1,000
Retained earnings		1,894		1,004
		3,594		2,004
Non-current liabilities				
Bank loan		500		1,000
Current liabilities				
Overdrafts	–		129	
Trade payables	703		1,479	
Other payables	32		20	
Tax payable	292		168	
		1,027		1,796
		5,121		4,800

Note 1

	Land & buildings	Plant & machinery	Total
	$000	$000	$000
Cost			
B/fwd at 1 Jan 20X3	2,000	750	2,750
Disposals	(1,100)	–	(1,100)
C/fwd at 31 Dec 20X3	900	750	1,650
Depreciation			
B/fwd at 1 Jan 20X3	200	420	620
Disposals	(110)	–	(110)
Charge	18	49	67
C/fwd at 31 Dec 20X3	108	469	577
Carrying value			
At 31 Dec 20X3	792	281	1,073
At 31 Dec 20X2	1,800	330	2,130

Buildings are depreciated over 50 years on a straight line basis.

Plant and machinery are depreciated at 15% using the reducing balance method.

Note 2 – Development costs

	Total
	$000
B/fwd at 1 Jan 20X3	125
Additions	5
C/fwd at 31 Dec 20X3	130
Amortisation	
B/fwd at 1 Jan 20X3	50
Charge	26
C/fwd at 31 Dec 20X3	76
Carrying value	
At 31 Dec 20X3	54
At 31 Dec 20X2	75

Development costs are being amortised over five years using the straight line method.

Notes:

	31.12.20X3	31.12.20X2
	$000	$000
Trade receivables	2,274	1,423
Allowance for doubtful receivables	(70)	(70)
	2,204	1,353

Required:

Prepare briefing notes for the partner which evaluate the audit risks that should be taken into consideration when planning the final audit of Ivor Co. Four professional marks are available for structure, clarity of explanation and logical flow.

(14 marks)

Test your understanding 3

Engine Co

You are the audit senior in a firm of accountants. You are assisting with the planning for the year-end audit of one of your main clients, Engine Co. The senior manager has asked you to perform an analytical review of the financial statements that she can use to brief the engagement partner of the key audit risks.

	30.06.20X4 (Draft)		30.06.20X3 (Audited)	
	$m	$m	$m	$m
Statement of profit or loss				
Revenue		128		107
Cost of sales				
Opening inventory	9		6	
Purchases	87		74	
Closing inventory	(14)		(9)	
		(82)		71
Gross profit		46		36
Distribution costs		(11)		(9)
Admin expenses (note 1)		(20)		(18)
Profit before tax		15		9

Statement of financial position

Non-current assets				
Tangible assets (note 2)		77		67
Intangible assets (note 3)		17		13
		94		80
Current assets				
Inventory (note 4)	14		9	
Trade receivables	17		13	
Cash	3		3	
		34		25
Total assets		128		105
Equity and liabilities				
Ordinary share capital		20		20
Revaluation reserve		38		30
Retained earnings		30		25
		88		75
Non-current liabilities				
Bank loan		13		11
Current liabilities				
Trade payables	17		13	
Other payables	5		3	
Tax payable	5		3	
		27		19
		128		105

Note 1

Included within operating profits are the following items:

	30.06.20X4	30.06.20X3
	$m	$m
Wages and salaries	7	7
Directors' salaries	2	2
Depreciation	3	3
Amortisation	4	3

Note 2

	Land & buildings	Plant & machinery	Total
	$m	$m	$m
Cost			
B/fwd at 1 July 20X3	70	30	100
Additions	–	5	5
Revaluations	8	–	8
C/fwd at 30 June 20X4	78	35	113
Depn			
B/fwd at 1 July 20X3	10	23	33
Charge	1	2	3
C/fwd at 30 June 20X4	11	25	36
Carrying value			
At 30 June 20X4	67	10	77
At 30 June 20X3	60	7	67

The revaluation relates to a piece of land.

Plant and machinery are depreciated at 25% using the reducing balance method.

Note 3

Development costs	**Total**
	$
Cost	
B/fwd at 1 July 20X3	16
Additions	8
C/fwd at 30 June 20X4	24
Amortisation	
B/fwd at 1 July 20X3	3
Charge	4
C/fwd at 30 June 20X4	7
Carrying value	
At 30 June 20X4	17
At 30 June 20X3	13

During the year significant research and development has taken place with regard to a new product, for which commercial production has now commenced.

Note 4

	30.06.20X4	**30.06.20X3**
	$m	$m
Inventory	3	2
Raw materials	1	1
WIP	11	7
Finished goods	(1)	(1)
Allowance for slow-moving inventory	14	9

Required:

Prepare a memo for your manager that identifies and explains the key audit risks discovered during your analytical review of the financial statements. Your review should conclude by briefly discussing the possible implications for the final audit.

Four professional marks are available for structure, clarity of explanation and logical flow.

(16 marks)

Test your understanding 4

(1) Kingston Co operates in the computer games industry, developing new games for sale in retail stores.

(2) Portmore Co is currently waiting for confirmation from their bank that their overdraft facility will be extended. The bank have requested a copy of the audited financial statements as soon as they are available.

(3) Montego Co has recently started selling their products overseas.

(4) Lucea Co, a manufacturer, has negotiated a contract with a new supplier for all its raw materials.

Required:

For each of the scenarios below identify the business risks and state what, if any, impact this might have on your assessment of the risk of material misstatement for the planning of the audit.

Test your understanding 5

Your firm has recently been appointed as the auditor of Holifex Co. The company provides and erects scaffolding on building sites and other industrial locations.

Your client, Stoke Co, has recently expanded its operations overseas. This is Stoke's first venture outside of its home country, where it has operated as a single entity. The venture has been set up by acquiring an entity overseas which is run and operated by its own, recently appointed, management team.

Chantry Co has been your client for many years. In recent years it has experienced rapid growth. In order to cope with this level of growth, Chantry has introduced a new accounting system and transferred the data from their current software.

Westbourne Co is a major building and construction company focusing mostly on large projects such as the construction of major sporting and entertainment venues. Contracts are usually won through a tender process with construction work on successful tenders taking many years. During the year Westbourne has found itself in dispute with one of its major customers who claim that the concert venue Westbourne has constructed does not meet the specifications per the original contract. As a result the customer is withholding the final completion payment representing 30% of the contract value.

Required:

Identify and explain the risks of material misstatement to assist with the planning for each of the engagements above.

9 Chapter summary

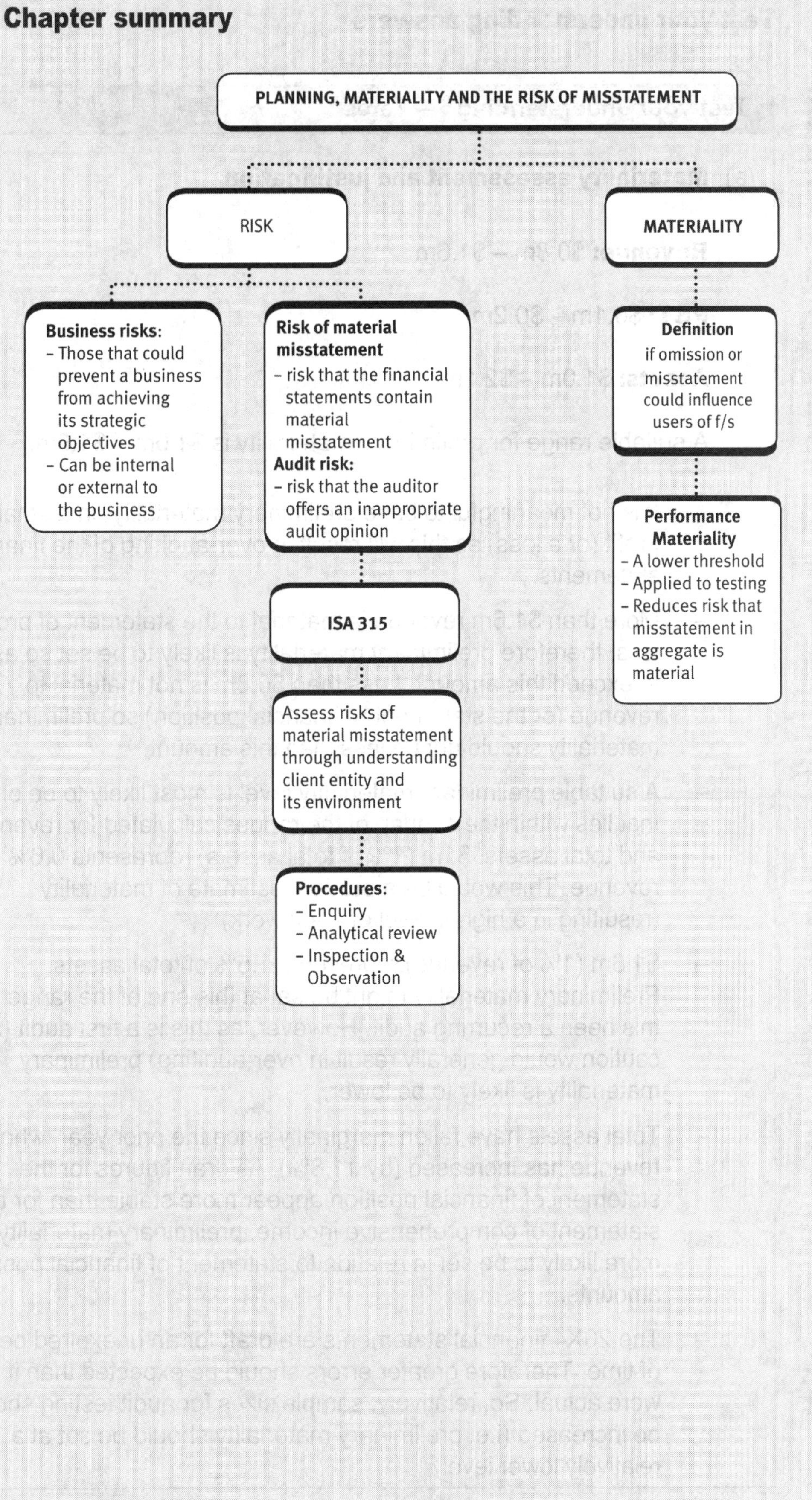

Test your understanding answers

Test your understanding 1 – Yates

(a) **Materiality assessment and justification**

Revenue: $0.8m – $1.6m

PBT: $0.1m – $0.2m

Assets: $1.0m – $2.1m

A suitable range for preliminary materiality is $1.0m – $1.6m.

- It is not meaningful to base preliminary materiality on a small profit (or a loss) as this will result in over-auditing of the financial statements.
- More than $1.6m revenue is material to the statement of profit or loss, therefore preliminary materiality is likely to be set so as not to exceed this amount. Less than $0.8m is not material to revenue (or the statement of financial position) so preliminary materiality should not be less than this amount.
- A suitable preliminary materiality level is most likely to be one that lies within the overlap of the ranges calculated for revenue and total assets. $1m (1% of total assets) represents 0.6% revenue. This would be a prudent estimate of materiality (resulting in a higher level of audit work).
- $1.6m (1% of revenue) represents 1.5% of total assets. Preliminary materiality might be set at this end of the range had this been a recurring audit. However, as this is a first audit (and caution would generally result in over-auditing) preliminary materiality is likely to be lower.
- Total assets have fallen marginally since the prior year, whereas revenue has increased (by 11.8%). As draft figures for the statement of financial position appear more stable than for the statement of comprehensive income, preliminary materiality is more likely to be set in relation to statement of financial position amounts.
- The 20X4 financial statements are draft for an unexpired period of time. Therefore greater errors should be expected than if they were actual. So, relatively, sample sizes for audit testing should be increased (i.e. preliminary materiality should be set at a relatively lower level).

(b) **Briefing Notes**

To: Audit partner

From: Audit manager

Date: 01 June 20X4

Subject: Planning of the audit of Yates for the year ended 30 June 20X4

Introduction

These briefing notes assess materiality for the audit, identify and explain the risks of material misstatement and suggest audit procedures to be included in the audit plan. The notes will also discuss the extent to which analytical procedures can be relied on as a source of audit evidence.

Risks of material misstatement

Revenue

Revenue is recorded net of rebates which are calculated quarterly in arrears. Revenue has increased by 11.8%.

There is a risk of overstatement of revenue if rebates for the last quarter have not been accrued at the year-end.

Intangibles

Intangible assets have increased by $1m and represent 6.9% of total assets therefore are material and an area of significant risk.

IAS 38 *Intangible Assets* states that internally-generated intangibles should not be recognised as they cannot be reliably measured.

Intangible assets may be overstated if the balance includes intangibles which do not meet the criteria of IAS 38.

Restructuring provision

The restructuring provision that was made last year represents 9.3% of total assets therefore are material and an area of significant risk.

IAS 37 *Provisions, Contingent Liabilities and Contingent Assets* requires a provision to be recognised only if there is a present obligation that is probable to result in an outflow of benefits and can be measured reliably.

There is a risk that provisions are overstated as the restructuring occurred 18 months ago and there may no longer be any obligations for the company to fulfil.

Lease liabilities

Lease liabilities represent 5.2% of total assets and are therefore material and an area of significant risk.

Leases of twelve months or longer should be recognised as assets and a corresponding liability recognised for the lease payments, unless the underlying asset has a low value. Leases of less than twelve months should be expensed.

There is a risk of under or overstatement of assets and lease liabilities if leased assets are treated incorrectly.

There is also a risk of inadequate disclosure if the disclosure requirements of IFRS 16 *Leases* are not met.

Opening balances

Yates is a new audit client which means the opening balances were not audited by our firm last year.

There is a risk of misstatement of opening balances if the auditors last year failed to detect any material misstatements.

The predecessor auditor should be contacted and their working papers reviewed as part of our firm's testing on opening balances this year.

Tangible assets

The carrying value of property has fallen by 5%, vehicles increased by 2.5% and other equipment has fallen by 20.4%.

Vehicles and equipment may be overstated if:

- disposals have not been recorded
- depreciation has been undercharged (e.g. not for a whole year)
- impairments have not yet been accounted for.

Depreciation and amortisation

Depreciation and amortisation expense has fallen by 10.5%. This could be valid if Yates has significant assets already fully depreciated or the asset base is lower since last year's restructuring.

However, there is a risk of understatement of depreciation and therefore overstatement of assets, if, for example:

- Not all assets have been depreciated (or depreciated at the wrong rates, or only for 11 months of the year).
- Impairment losses have not been recognised (as compared with the prior year).

Materials expense

Materials expense has increased by 17.8% which is more than the increase in revenue.

This could be legitimate for example if fuel costs have increased significantly. However, the increase could indicate misstatement in relation to capital expenditure treated as revenue (e.g. on overhauls or major refurbishment) or misclassification of expenses.

There is a risk of overstatement of materials expense.

Other expenses

Other expenses have fallen by 15.5% which is unusual given the increase in the level of business.

Expenses may be understated due to:

- expenses being misclassified as materials expense.
- underestimation of accrued expenses (especially as the financial reporting period has not yet expired).

Trade payables

These have increased by only 5.3% compared with the 17.8% increase in materials expense.

There is a risk of understatement of liabilities if supplier invoices are still to be received in respect of goods delivered before the year-end (the month of June being an unexpired period).

Receivables

Trade receivables have increased by just 2.2% although revenue has increased by 11.8%. Receivables days have reduced from 34 days to 31 days.

This seems unusual and may indicate understatement of the receivables balance due to a lack of completeness.

Other liabilities

These may be understated as they have increased by only 7.6% although staff costs have increased by 14%.

For example, balances owing in respect of outstanding holiday entitlements at the year-end may not yet be accurately estimated, or employment taxes may not have been accrued on bonuses.

Conclusion

The above audit risks demonstrate that the audit of Yates Co is a high risk engagement. These risks must be addressed by designing appropriate audit procedures to be included in the audit plan. Appropriately experienced staff must be assigned to the audit team to ensure any material misstatements are detected.

(c) **Audit procedures**

(i) Trade receivables

- Review agreements to determine the volume rebates terms. For example:
  - the % discounts
  - the volumes to which they apply
  - the period over which they accumulate
  - settlement method (e.g. by credit note or other off-set or repayment).
- Perform a direct positive confirmation of a sample of balances (i.e. larger amounts) to identify potential overstatement (e.g. due to discounts earned not being awarded).
- Inspect after-date cash receipts and match against amounts due as shortfalls may indicate disputed amounts.
- Review after-date credit notes to ensure adequate allowance (accrual) is made for discounts earned in the year.
- Enquire with management to identify if prompt payment discounts have been offered and level of take up.

(ii) Vehicles

- Physically inspect a sample of vehicles selected from the asset register to confirm existence and condition (for evidence of impairment). If analytical procedures use management information on mileage records this should be checked (e.g. against millimetres) at the same time.
- Inspect purchase invoices for additions to confirm the cost has been recorded accurately in the asset register.

- Review the terms of all lease contracts entered into during the year to ensure that leases have been capitalised appropriately.
- Recalculate the depreciation charge for a sample of vehicles to ensure arithmetical accuracy.
- Review repairs and maintenance accounts (included in materials expense) to ensure that there are no material items of capital nature that have been expensed (completeness).

(d) **Extent of reliance on analytical procedures as audit evidence**

- Although there is likely to be less reliance on analytical procedures than if this had been an existing audit client, the fact that this is a new assignment does not preclude placing some reliance on such procedures.
- Analytical procedures will not be relied on in respect of material items that require 100% testing. For example, additions to property is likely to represent a very small number of transactions.
- Analytical procedures alone may provide sufficient audit evidence on line items that are not individually material. For example, inventory (less than ½% revenue and less than 1% total assets) may be shown to be materially correctly stated through analytical procedures on consumable stores (i.e. fuel, lubricants, materials for servicing vehicles etc).
- Substantive analytical procedures are best suited to large volume transactions (e.g. revenue, materials expense, staff costs). If controls over the completeness, accuracy and validity of recording transactions in these areas are effective than substantive analytical procedures showing that there are no unexpected fluctuations should reduce the need for substantive detailed tests.
- The extent of planned use will be dependent on the relationships expected between variables. (e.g. between items of financial information and between items of financial and non-financial information). For example, if material costs rise due to an increase in the level of business then a commensurate increase in revenue and staff costs might be expected also.
- A proof in total (reasonableness test) provides substantive evidence that statement of profit and loss items are not materially misstated. In the case of Yates this could be applied to staff costs (number of employees in each category × wage/salary rates, grossed up for social security, etc) and finance expense (interest rate × average monthly overdraft balance).

- However, such tests may have limited application, if any, if the population is not homogenous and cannot be subdivided. For example, all the categories of non-current asset have a wide range of useful life. Therefore it would be difficult/meaningless to apply an 'average' depreciation rate to all assets in the class to substantiate the total depreciation expense for the year.
- Substantive analytical procedures are more likely to be used if there is relevant information available that is being used by Yates. For example, as fuel costs will be significant, Yates may monitor consumption (e.g. miles per gallon).
- Analytical procedures may supplement alternative procedures that provide evidence regarding the same assertion. For example, the review of after-date payments to confirm the completeness of trade payables may be supplemented by calculations of average payment period on a monthly basis.

Test your understanding 2 – Ivor

Briefing Notes

To: Audit partner
From: Audit senior
Date: 24 March 20X4
Subject: Audit risks of Ivor Co to assist the planning of the year-end audit.

Introduction

These briefing notes evaluate the audit risks that should be considered when planning the audit of Ivor Co.

Revenue

Revenue has increased by 29% during the year. This significant increase suggests a risk that revenue could be overstated.

The increase in revenue has been partly fuelled by offering greater discounts, totalling 4% of revenue as compared with 2% in the prior year. It is possible that extended credit terms have been offered due to the lengthening of the receivables collection period from an average 49 days last year to an average of 61 days this year.

The significant increase may indicate inappropriate cut-off or revenue recognition procedures which are not in accordance with IFRS 15 *Revenue from contracts with customers*.

Sale of buildings

During the year buildings with a carrying value of $990,000 have been sold for $1,500,000. At the same time the company's rental expenses have increased by 190%. It appears the company has entered into a sale and leaseback arrangement as it is unlikely that the company would be able to increase production so much having sold half of their buildings.

There is a risk that this has not been accounted for in accordance with IFRS 16 *Leases*. If the sale is not a genuine sale the asset building should continue to be recognised by Ivor and a financial liability recognised equal to the proceeds received.

As there is no financial liability included in the statement of financial position, this would indicate that Ivor has treated the sale and leaseback as a sale.

There is a risk of understatement of tangible assets and financial liabilities. In addition, the relevant disclosures for the transaction may not be made adequately.

Development costs

Development costs of $54k represent 1% of total assets and are material.

The costs may not be accounted for in accordance with IAS 38 *Intangible Assets*. The amortisation policy is 5 years. This may not be the expected life of the product and therefore may be inappropriate.

There is a risk of overstatement of development costs if the amortisation charge is not appropriate.

Inventory

Inventory represents 32% of total assets therefore is material and an area of significant risk.

Inventory should be valued at the lower of cost and net realisable value in accordance with IAS 2 *Inventories*. The discounts offered must be taken into account when determining the net realisable value. Some products may be used as loss leaders in a drive to tempt new customers.

As inventory days have increased from 58 days to 63 days, this could indicate an increased risk of overvaluation of inventory.

Receivables

The overall increase in credit sales, coupled with the greater credit period increases the risk of irrecoverable receivables. However, the allowance for receivables has not been adjusted from the previous balance of $70,000, which represented 5% of total receivables last year but only 3% of receivables this year. Receivable days have increased from 49 days to 61 days.

There is a risk of overstatement of trade receivables and understatement of the allowance for receivables.

Going concern

During the year there appears to have been an improvement in the liquidity of the company, with the current and quick ratios improving from 1.4 and 0.8 last year to 3.9 and 2.3 this year, respectively.

Ivor has raised a significant amount of cash from the disposal of buildings and the issuing of new shares during the year. In total $2.2m has been raised ($1.5m disposal + $700k share issue) and it appears as though this has been used to pay off significant external debts, most notably the bank loan and trade payables. The result is a healthier statement of financial position.

However, there is very little residual cash left over and the company appears to be having difficulty generating trading cash balances. Inventory days and receivables days have both increased and this increase in the operating cycle could be caused by offering extended credit in an attempt to win new customers.

The inability to generate cash balances could indicate the company is unable to meet loan or lease repayments. A failure to pay trade payables could lead to a loss of supplier goodwill and have implications for future trade relationships.

If the business is no longer a going concern then the break up basis should be used. There is a risk the financial statements are prepared on an inappropriate basis.

If the basis of preparation is deemed appropriate, there is a risk of inadequate disclosure of going concern issues.

Cost of sales

Cost of sales has increased by 25.7% when revenue has increased by 28.9%. Cost of sales may be understated or revenue overstated as it would be expected that these balances would increase by the same proportion.

Purchases including accruals may not be completely recorded or closing inventory may be overstated (see below).

Distribution costs

These have increased by over 53% during the financial year which is much higher than the increase in revenue. This could be due to greater geographical dispersement of customers, rising fuel costs or misallocation of expenses.

Conclusion

The above evaluation demonstrates that the audit of Ivor Co is a high risk engagement. The audit plan will need to include audit procedures to address these risks. The audit team selected will need to have the relevant skills to address the risks.

Appendix: Analytical procedures

Annual movements

Revenue (gross)	2,935/10,160 × 100	28.9%
Cost of sales	1,953/7,603 × 100	25.7%
Distribution Costs	264/498 × 100	53%
Wages/salaries	315/960 × 100	32.8%
Directors' Salaries	10/115 × 100	8.7%
Rent	23/12 × 100	191.7%
Other	16/153 × 100	(10.5%)

Ratio analysis

	20X3		20X2	
Gross margin	3,014/13,095 × 100	23%	2,357/10,160 × 100	23.2%
Operating margin	1,190/13,095 × 100	9.1%	694/10,160 × 100	6.8%
ROCE	1,190/4,094 × 100	29.1%	694/3,004 × 100	23.1%
Asset turnover	13,095/4,094	3.2	10,160/3,004	3.4
Current ratio	3,994/1,027	3.9:1	2,595/1,796	1.4:1
Quick ratio	2,354/1,027	2.3:1	1,395/1,796	0.8:1
Inventory days	1,640/9,556 × 365	62.6	1,200/7,603 × 365	57.6
Receivable days	2,204/13,095 × 365	61.4	1,353/10,160 × 365	48.6
Payable days	703/10,150 × 365	25.3	1,479/7,830 × 365	68.9

Test your understanding 3

Memorandum

To: Audit Manager

From: Audit senior

Date: 27 September 20X4

Subject: Engine Co - audit risk assessment

Introduction

As requested, please find a summary of the key audit risks identified during the analytical review of the financial statements of Engine Co and the possible implications for the year-end audit.

Profitability

Gross margins have increased during the year from 34% to 36%. Operating margins, however, have increased significantly from 8% to 12%.

The change in gross margin appears to have been achieved through economies in purchasing, which could be due to bulk purchasing consistent with the increase in revenue.

If this is not the case, there is a risk that cost of sales are understated possibly by overvaluation of closing inventory or incomplete recording of purchases.

The gains made due to savings at the operational level appear to be driven through administrative efficiencies. These costs have increased by 11% in the year in comparison to an overall 20% increase in revenue. A review of operating costs suggests that this has been achieved through labour efficiencies, given the stable salary costs.

There is a risk that expenses have not been completely recorded and attention should be paid to cut-off at the year-end.

Salary costs

There is a risk that salary costs are understated and at the same time intangible development costs are overstated.

During the year Engine Co capitalised $8m of development costs relating to a project which has now begun commercial production. These costs should have been capitalised in line with IAS 38 *Intangible Assets* meaning only those development costs meeting all the capitalisation criteria may be taken to the statement of financial position. Research costs must be expensed.

It is unclear from the financial statements whether any salary costs relating to research have been included in the statement of profit and loss. However, given the fall in salary as a percentage of revenue it is possible that these costs have been capitalised incorrectly.

Inventory

Closing inventory levels have increased by over 50% since 20X3, possibly due to increased demand. This has led to an increase in inventory days (from 46 to 62).

Whilst the inventory balance has increased by 50% in the year the allowance has remained static. Increases in inventory could indicate damage or obsolescence which could reduce the NRV to below cost.

There is a risk that the slow-moving inventory allowance is understated and, therefore, inventory is overstated.

Non-current assets

Land has been revalued by $8m. Care should be taken at the final audit to assess the appropriateness of the revaluation and ensure that all appropriate disclosures have been made in the notes to the financial statements.

The credentials of the valuer should be assessed (competence and independence) to ensure their valuation is reliable.

During the year $5m of plant and machinery assets were acquired. However it appears as though these items have not been depreciated during the year. Using a rough method of calculation (closing carrying value x 25%) the depreciation charge for plant and machinery should be $3m, not the $2m presented in the accounts. It therefore appears as though depreciation has not been accounted for as per IAS 16 *Property, Plant and Equipment*.

There is a risk that the depreciation charge is understated and profit and non-current assets are overstated.

Loan

During the year the company has taken out a loan of $2m , presumably to help finance the purchases of new plant and machinery. This has had a minimal effect on gearing, which has risen from 12.8% in 20X3 to 12.9% in the current year. However, if the effect of the revaluation is removed from equity this would mean gearing is actually 14%.

Whilst this is not a significant amount it will be important to assess the terms of the new loan in case there are any covenants in place. Given the possibility that the directors are excluding salaries, depreciation and inventory allowances from profits, there could be a significant adjustment required to the reported profit, which would adversely affect profitability ratios.

The financial statement figures may be being manipulated in order to meet the terms of the covenants. If so, going concern issues may result which would require disclosure in the notes. There is a risk this disclosure is not made.

Conclusion

The above audit risks demonstrate that the audit of Engine Co is a high risk engagement. These risks must be addressed by designing appropriate audit procedures to be included in the audit plan. Appropriately experienced staff must be assigned to the audit team to ensure any material misstatements are detected.

Appendix: Ratio analysis

	20X4		20X3	
Gross margin	46/128 × 100	35.9%	35/107 × 100	33.6%
Operating margin	15/128 × 100	11.7%	9/107 × 100	8.4%
ROCE	15/101 × 100	14.8%	9/86 × 100	10.5%
Asset turnover	128/101	1.27	107/86	1.24
Current ratio	34/27	1.3:1	25/19	1.3:1
Quick ratio	20/27	0.7:1	16/19	0.8:1
Inventory days	14/82 × 365	62	9/71 × 365	46
Receivables days	17/128 × 365	48	13/107 × 365	44
Payables days	17/87 × 365	71	13/74 × 365	64
Gearing	13/101 × 100	12.9%	11/86 ×100	12.8%

Test your understanding 4

	Business risk	**Audit risk**
Kingston Co	Rapidly changing industry with constant product developments. They may not have the resources or expertise to keep up with the pace of change.	Risk of overstatement of inventory (and WIP) where products become obsolete. In the extreme could lead to going concern issues which would require disclosure in the notes to the financial statements.
Portmore Co	Failure of the bank to renew overdraft facility may increase the risk of insufficient financing or more costly financing.	Directors of Portmore will be under pressure to present the financial statements in the best light possible leading to possible manipulation of the financial statements. Lack of confirmation from the bank represents a fundamental uncertainty surrounding going concern which would require disclosure in the notes to the financial statements.

Montego Co	• The new venture overseas may not be successful. • The market may have been overestimated. • Foreign currency fluctuations may affect profits.	Translation errors may occur. Revaluation of foreign currency balances at year-end may not be performed.
Lucea Co	Disruption to the manufacturing process if the new supplier does not deliver the right quality of products or at the right time, leading to delays in supplying customers.	Increased risk that inventory is overstated due to poor quality items leading to reduced selling prices resulting in NRV being lower than cost.

Test your understanding 5

Holifex Co

Holifex operates in an industry where health and safety is paramount. Any breaches in regulations may lead to fines. There is a risk that provisions are understated or that contingent liabilities are not disclosed.

There is a further risk of understatement of provisions because Holifex could be exposed to potential claims by injured parties if they have been negligent in erecting scaffolding.

If the claims are significant, this could threaten the going concern status which might not be adequately disclosed in the notes to the financial statements.

There is a possible overstatement of non-current assets. These are dispersed across many different locations. Controls over the storage and valuation of the assets might not be effective.

Use of scaffolding by customers is likely to span the year-end in some instances. There is also a risk that revenue is overstated due to cut-off errors.

Stoke Co

Lack of experience of recording this type of acquisition increases the risk of misstatement both in recording and measuring transactions.

The new entity will require consolidation into the group accounts. There is a risk that this has not been performed correctly. The overseas operation will require translation prior to consolidation.

There is a risk that incorrect rates have been used to translate the statement of financial position and statement of profit or loss.

The overseas entity is operated by its own management team. This increases control risk, as these may not be in line with group controls.

Chantry Co

The period of rapid growth could indicate the possibility of increased control risk due to systems and procedures not being able to cope with the expansion before the new system was introduced.

Staff may not be familiar/adequately trained to use new accounting system, which increases the risk of human error.

Data has been transferred from the old accounting system. There is a risk that the transfer was not performed accurately or completely.

Each of these issues increases the risk of errors in the financial records and therefore the financial statements.

Westbourne Co

Long term contracts in building and construction could present the risk that revenue is overstated and that related balances (WIP, receivables, payables) are also misstated.

The disputed receivable increases the risk that receivables are overstated and allowance for doubtful receivables is understated.

There are several going concern issues affecting Westbourne with the risk that these are not adequately disclosed in the notes.

- Over reliance on a few customers with no guarantee that contracts will be renewed.
- The dispute with one of its customers may lead to negative PR consequences.
- 30% of the contract value is being withheld and impacts cash flow.
- The shortfall in cash could lead to problems meeting debt requirements, particularly as liquidity is also an issue.

chapter

10

Group and transnational audits

Chapter learning objectives

This chapter covers syllabus areas:

- D4 – Group audits
- G2 – Transnational audits

Detailed syllabus objectives are provided in the introduction section of the text book.

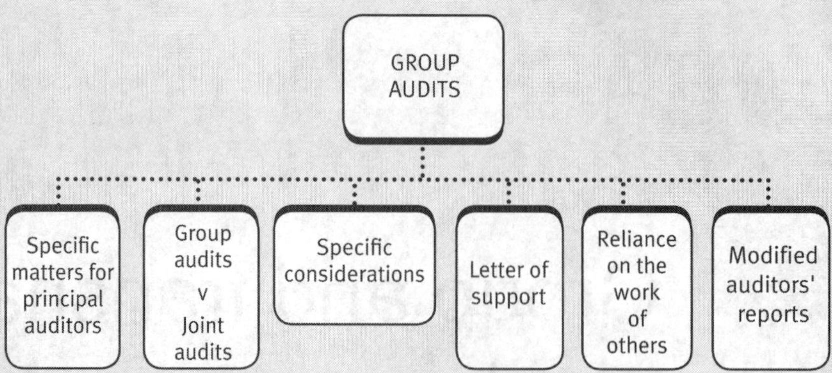

Exam focus

- A group could appear in any question in the exam, and is relevant to all stages of an engagement.
- You should identify early in the exam whether the scenario is for a single entity or a group.
- Also take care to identify whether you are the auditor for the entire group (including subsidiaries) or just the parent company as reliance on the work of other auditors will only be relevant if you are not responsible for the audit of the subsidiaries.

Revision of consolidation

Consolidation involves taking a number of sets of individual company financial statements and adding them all together to form one combined set. Due to various complications, such as companies using different currencies and intergroup trading, a number of adjustments have to be made before the consolidated financial statements can be finalised.

Before the group financial statements can be audited, the individual company's financial statements have to be prepared and audited. In the diagram below this includes Parent Co, Subsidiary Co 1 and Subsidiary Co 2. It is the responsibility of individual company directors/management to prepare their financial statements. These may be audited by the group auditor or another firm of auditors.

Once this process is complete the financial statements are combined to create a single set of consolidated financial statements. This process is the responsibility of the group's directors.

Once the consolidated financial statements have been prepared the group auditor performs an audit of the consolidated financial statements.

As the group is a summary of the trading results and positions of the various components of the group (and is itself not a trading entity) the group auditor does not need to audit the group financial statements in the same way. They rely on the audited figures of the individual financial statements to confirm the majority of balances and then audit the consolidation process and adjustments.

Consolidation adjustments do not pass through the usual transaction processing systems and may not be subject to the same internal controls as other transactions. Therefore the group auditor needs to:

- Evaluate whether the adjustments appropriately reflect the events and transactions underlying them.
- Determine whether adjustments have been correctly calculated, processed and authorised.
- Determine whether adjustments are supported by sufficient appropriate documentation.
- Ensure intra-group balances and transactions reconcile and have been eliminated.

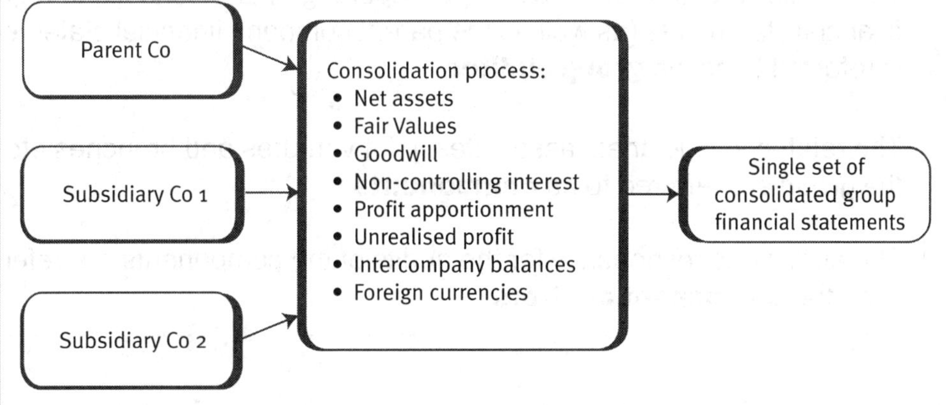

1 Group audits – specific considerations

The principles of auditing a group are the same as the audit of a single company and all of the ISAs are still relevant to a group audit. There are, however, some specific considerations relevant to the audit of a group:

- Group financial statements require numerous and potentially complicated consolidation adjustments.
- Specific accounting standards relating to group financial statements must be complied with.
- The components of the group (i.e. the subsidiaries) **may** be audited by firms other than the group auditor.
- The organisation and planning of a group audit may be significantly more complex than for a single company.

The objectives of an auditor with regard to these matters are identified in ISA 600 *Special Considerations – Audits of Group Financial Statements (Including the Work of Component Auditors)* as follows:

- To determine whether it is appropriate to act as the auditor of the group financial statements, and
- If acting as the auditor of the group financial statements:
  - To communicate clearly with the component auditors about the scope and timing of their work on financial information related to components and their findings.
  - To obtain sufficient appropriate evidence regarding the financial information of the components and the consolidation process to express an opinion on whether the group financial statements are prepared, in all material respects, in accordance with the applicable financial reporting framework.

Key terms

The auditor with the responsibility for reporting on the consolidated group financial statements (as well as the parent company financial statements) is referred to as the **group auditor**.

The related subsidiaries, associates, joint ventures and branches etc of the group are referred to as **components**.

The audit firms responsible for the audits of the components are referred to as the **component auditors**.

2 Acceptance

Acceptance as group auditor

In addition to the normal acceptance considerations discussed in the chapter 'Professional appointments', firms should consider whether to accept the role of group auditor. To assist the decision they must consider:

- Whether sufficient appropriate audit evidence can reasonably be expected to be obtained in relation to the consolidation process and the financial information of the components of the group.
- Where component auditors are involved, the engagement partner shall evaluate whether the group engagement team will be able to be involved in the work of the component auditors.
- Whether reliance can be placed on the component auditor's work.
- The materiality of the portion of the group not audited by them.
- Understanding of the group, the components and their environments:

- Group structure (changes to group structure due to acquisitions, disposals or changes in the level of investment)
- Business activities
- Use of service organisations
- Group-wide controls
- Complexity of the consolidation process and risk of material misstatement
- Whether auditors from a different firm will be used
- Whether there will be unrestricted access to those charged with governance, management and information of the group

- Any other risks identified which affect the group and its financial statements.

This understanding can be obtained from information provided by and discussions with group management, component auditors and previous auditors.

If the engagement partner concludes that it will not be possible to obtain sufficient appropriate evidence due to restrictions imposed by group management and that the possible effect of this will result in a disclaimer of opinion then they must not accept the engagement. If it is a continuing engagement, the auditor should withdraw from the engagement, where possible under applicable laws and regulations.

Acceptance as component auditor

The component auditor will consider the following before accepting appointment:

- Whether they are independent of the parent and component companies and can comply with ethical requirements applying to the group audit.
- Whether they possess any special skills necessary to perform the audit of the component and are competent to perform the work.
- Whether they have an understanding of the auditing standards relevant to group audits and can comply with them.
- Whether they have an understanding of the relevant financial reporting framework applicable to the group.
- Whether they can comply with the group audit team instructions including the deadlines.
- Whether they are willing to have the group auditor involved in their work and evaluate it before relying on it for group audit purposes.

3 Planning the group audit

Overall audit strategy and plan

The group auditor is responsible for establishing an overall group audit strategy and plan (in accordance with ISA 300 *Planning an Audit of Financial Statements*). The group engagement partner is ultimately responsible for reviewing and approving this.

The planning stage for a group audit incorporates the usual planning activities such as:

- Understanding the client
- Materiality
- Communication
- Risk assessment

Understanding the client

During the planning stage the group auditor must:

- Enhance its understanding of the group, its components and their environments including group-wide controls, obtained during the acceptance/continuance stage.
- Obtain an understanding of the consolidation process, including instructions issued by group management to components.
- Confirm or revise its initial identification of components that are likely to be significant.
- Assess the risks of material misstatement.

Significant components

ISA 600 requires the auditor to perform a full audit of components which are classed as significant components. A significant component is identified by using an appropriate benchmark (such as assets, liabilities, cash flows, profit, revenue). The benchmark is a matter of auditor judgment. Some auditors may consider a component to be significant if it exceeds normal materiality thresholds.

Analytical procedures (rather than a full audit) may be performed on components which are not significant.

Understanding the component auditor

Group auditors cannot simply rely on the work of other auditors, they must always evaluate the work of others before relying on it. Therefore the group auditor should obtain an understanding of:

- Whether the component auditor understands and will comply with the code of ethics.
- The professional competence of the component auditor.
- Whether the group auditor will be able to be involved in the work of the component auditor.
- Whether the component auditor operates in a regulatory environment that actively oversees auditors.

If the group auditor has serious concerns about any of the above issues then they shall obtain sufficient appropriate evidence relating to the financial information of the component, without requesting that the component auditor performs any work.

Materiality

The group auditor is responsible for establishing:

- Materiality and performance materiality for the group financial statements as a whole.
- Materiality for components where they are to be audited by other auditors.

Items that are material in individual financial statements may not be material in the consolidated financial statements. This will affect the amount of evidence that needs to be obtained to support the group audit opinion.

In order to reduce the risk of material misstatement in the group financial statements, materiality for the components should be set at an amount below materiality for the group as a whole.

Examples of matters to be understood

In order to perform their risk assessment thoroughly, the group auditor must obtain a wide ranging understanding of matters relevant to the unique circumstances of the group and its components. Whilst the list below is not exhaustive, it provides a range of common examples to be considered specific to the circumstances of a group:

- Group-wide controls:
  - Regularity of meetings between group and component management.
  - Monitoring process of component's operations and financial results.
  - Group management's risk assessment process.
  - Monitoring, controlling, reconciling and elimination of intra-group transactions.
  - Centralisation of IT systems.
  - Activities of internal audit.
  - Consistency of policies across the group.
  - Group wide codes of conduct and fraud prevention.
- Consolidation process:
  - The extent to which component management understand the consolidation process.
  - The process for identifying and accounting for components.
  - The process for identifying reportable segments.
  - The process for identifying related party transactions.
  - How changes to accounting policies are managed.
  - The procedures for dealing with differing year-ends.
  - The procedures for dealing with differing accounting policies.
  - Group's process for ensuring complete, accurate and timely financial reporting.
  - The process for translating foreign components.
  - How IT is used in the consolidation.
  - Procedures for reporting subsequent events.
  - The preparation and authorisation of consolidation adjustments.
  - Frequency, nature and size of transactions between components.
  - Steps taken to arrive at fair values.

Communication with component auditors

The group auditor is responsible for communicating with the auditors of the components on a timely basis. Communication shall include:

- The work to be performed by the component and the use made of this.
- The form and content of the communications made by the component auditor to the group auditor.
- A request that the component auditor cooperates with the group team.
- The ethical requirements relevant to the group audit.
- Component materiality and the threshold for triviality.
- Identified significant risks of material misstatement of the group financial statements.
- A list of identified related parties.

As part of the communication process the group auditor should also request that the component auditor communicates matters that are relevant to the group audit on a timely basis. Such matters include:

- Compliance with ethical standards.
- Compliance with audit instructions.
- Identification of financial information upon which the component auditor is reporting.
- Instances of non-compliance with laws and regulations.
- Uncorrected misstatements.
- Indications of management bias.
- Significant deficiencies in internal control.
- Other significant matters to be communicated to those charged with governance.
- Any other matters relevant to the group audit.
- The component auditor's overall conclusion.

Further communications

As well as the matters identified above, the group auditor should also communicate further matters in a letter of instruction. This is likely to include:

- Matters relevant to the planning of the component audit:
  - The timetable for completion.
  - Dates of planned visits by the group auditor.
  - A list of key contacts.
  - Work to be performed on intra-group balances.
  - Guidance on other statutory reporting responsibilities.
  - Instructions for subsequent events review.
- Matters relevant to the conduct of component auditor work:
  - The findings of the group auditor's tests of controls on common systems.
  - The findings of internal audit relevant to the component.
  - A request for timely communication of evidence that contradicts evidence used in the group risk assessment.
  - A request for written representations on component management's compliance with the applicable financial reporting framework.
  - Matters to be documented by the component auditor.
- Other information:
  - A request that the following be reported in a timely fashion:
  - Significant accounting, financial reporting and auditing matters, including accounting estimates and related judgments.
  - Matters relating to the going concern status of the component.
  - Matters relating to litigation and claims.
  - Significant deficiencies in internal control and information that indicates the existence of fraud.
  - A request that the group auditor be notified of any unusual events as early as possible.

4 Audit risks specific to a group audit

Risk assessment

The group audit team has to determine the type of work to be performed on the financial information of the components, whether performed by the group team or another auditor.

If, however, the audit of a significant component is to be performed by another auditor then the group auditor shall be involved in the component's risk assessment. This includes:

- Discussing with the component auditor the susceptibility of the component to material misstatement.
- Reviewing the component auditor's documentation of identified risks of material misstatement.
- Performing risk assessment procedures themselves.

If significant risks of material misstatement are identified in a component that is audited by another auditor then the group auditor shall evaluate the appropriateness of the further audit procedures performed.

Audit risks

In addition to the risks covered in chapter 9 which could affecting any audit, specific risks affect group audits. There are specific accounting standards which relate to groups such as:

- IFRS 3 *Business Combinations*
- IFRS 10 *Consolidated Financial Statements*
- IFRS 11 *Joint Arrangements*
- IAS 27 *Separate Financial Statements*
- IAS 28 *Investments in Associates and Joint Ventures*

As always, there is a risk that the client does not comply with the relevant accounting treatment which would mean the financial statements are materially misstated. Some examples include:

- Valuation of goodwill
- Translation of foreign subsidiaries in the consolidation process
- Non-coterminous year-ends
- Inconsistent accounting policies used across the group
- Fair value adjustments
- Calculation of non-controlling interests
- Elimination of inter-company balances and trading
- Profit apportionment where there has been an acquisition or disposal
- Simple transposition or arithmetical errors in the consolidation process

The auditor must ensure that audit procedures are designed and performed to address these specific risks.

Dealing with non-coterminous year-ends

IFRS 10 *Consolidated Financial Statements*, requires the parent and subsidiaries to have the same year-end or to consolidate based on additional financial information prepared by the subsidiary (or if impracticable, the most recent financial statements adjusted for significant transactions or events). The difference between the parent and subsidiary's year-end must be no more than three months.

This increases audit risk as there may be transactions and adjustments in the consolidated financial statements that have not been audited.

The group auditor must plan to obtain sufficient appropriate evidence about transactions or events that have not been subject to audit.

Risk indicators

The following examples, whilst not exhaustive, cover a wide range of conditions or events that could indicate an increased risk of material misstatement of the group financial statements:

- A complex group structure.
- Frequent acquisitions, disposals and/or reorganisations.
- Poor corporate governance systems.
- Non-existent or ineffective group-wide controls.
- Components operating under foreign jurisdictions that may be subject to unusual government intervention.

- High risk business activities of components.
- Unusual related party transactions.
- Prior occurrences of intra-group balances that did not reconcile.
- The existence of complex transactions that are accounted for in more than one component.
- Differing application of accounting policies.
- Differing financial year-ends.
- Prior occurrences of unauthorised or incomplete consolidation adjustments.
- Aggressive tax planning.
- Frequent changes of auditor.

5 Auditing the consolidated financial statements

Procedures over the consolidation schedule

- Agree the figures from the component financial statements into the consolidation schedule to ensure accuracy.
- Recalculate the consolidation schedule to ensure arithmetical accuracy.
- Recalculate the translation of any foreign components to ensure accuracy.
- Recalculate any non-controlling interest balances to verify accuracy.
- Agree the date of any acquisitions or disposals and recalculate the time apportionment of the results for these components included in the consolidation.
- Evaluate the classification of the component (i.e. subsidiary, associate, joint venture etc) to ensure this is still appropriate.
- For investments in associates ensure that these are accounted for using the equity method of accounting and not consolidated.
- Review the financial statement disclosures for related party transactions.
- Review the policies and year-ends applied by the components to ensure they are consistent across the group.
- Reconcile inter-company balances and ensure they cancel out in the group financial statements.
- Assess the reasonableness of the client's goodwill impairment review to ensure goodwill is not overstated.

- Calculate any goodwill on acquisition arising in the year paying special attention to:
  - Consideration paid – agree to bank statements.
  - Acquisition related costs – ensure they have been expensed and not capitalised.
  - Contingent consideration – whether this has been valued at fair value taking into account the probability and timing of payment.
  - Deferred consideration – should be discounted to present value.

6 Completion and review

Review of the work of the component auditor

The group auditor must review the work of the component auditor to ensure it is sufficient and appropriate to rely on for the purpose of the group auditor's report.

This may be achieved by the component auditor sending the group auditor a questionnaire or checklist which identifies the key aspects of the audit.

The group auditor can then make an assessment as to whether any further work is needed.

- If any significant matters have arisen they should discuss with the component auditor or group management, as appropriate.
- If necessary the group auditor should then also review other relevant parts of the component auditor's working papers.
- If the group auditor is not satisfied with the component auditor's work they should determine what additional procedures are required.
- If it is not feasible for the component auditor to perform this then the group auditor must perform the procedures.
- When all procedures on the components have been completed, the group engagement partner must consider whether the aggregate effect of any uncorrected misstatements will have a material impact on the group financial statements.

Other completion activities

Subsequent events, going concern and final analytical procedures will need to be considered for the group in the same way as they are considered for single entity audits.

Letters of support

A situation may arise where a subsidiary may have going concern issues. The parent company may offer support to the subsidiary to enable it to continue trading in the foreseeable future. If this is the case the directors must give the group auditor formal documentation, usually called a 'comfort' or 'support' letter which confirms their intention to support the subsidiary.

The group auditor should not take this at face value. They should consider the position of the group to help identify whether it has the resources to fulfil its promise of support before accepting the letter as sufficient appropriate evidence of the going concern basis for the subsidiary.

7 Reporting

Modified auditors' reports

Where one or more of the subsidiaries has a modified auditor's report (regardless of who audited the subsidiary) the group auditor must consider the impact of the issue on the group financial statements, according to group materiality levels.

- If the matter is not material in a group context, an unmodified report will be issued.
- If the matter is material to both the component and the group the auditor should consider whether the issue causing the modification can be resolved as a consolidation adjustment and aim to resolve the matter with the client. If so, an unmodified report can be issued.
- If the matter cannot be resolved through the consolidation process, the modification should be carried through to the group auditor's report, (e.g. if the evidence is not available to support the balance).
- Note that a matter which is pervasive to the component may be material but not pervasive to the group. In which case, a disclaimer of opinion or adverse opinion in a subsidiary will be altered to a qualified opinion in the group auditor's report.

Reporting to those charged with governance

The following matters should be reported to those charged with governance of the group:

- Overview of the work performed and involvement in the component auditor's work.
- Areas of concern over the quality of the component auditor's work.
- Difficulties obtaining sufficient appropriate evidence.
- Fraud identified or suspected.

Any frauds or deficiencies in the group-wide controls identified by either the group auditor or the component auditor should be reported to management of the group.

8 Joint audit

What is a joint audit?

This is when two audit firms are appointed to provide an opinion on a set of financial statements. They will work together planning the audit, gathering evidence, reviewing the work and providing the opinion.

Benefits

- Retention of subsidiary auditor (and therefore their cumulative audit knowledge and experience) following acquisition.
- Availability of a wider range of resources (particularly important across national boundaries).
- Possible efficiency improvements.

Disadvantages

- Cultural clashes.
- Difficulty setting a joint approach.
- Both firms will need to be paid a fee.

Before accepting a joint audit, the firm must consider the level of risk associated with issuing a report alongside the other firm. The auditor's report will be signed by both firms and they will be jointly responsible if the report is wrong.

The firm should consider the experience and quality of the other firm to ensure they are competent.

If accepted, an engagement letter should be signed and the planning can commence which will involve agreeing an acceptable and fair division of the workload.

Joint audit – recent trends

Joint auditing allows small and medium sized entities to continue to be involved in an audit once their client has been acquired or merged with another organisation. Given recent trends in globalisation the alternative would likely be the replacement of the existing auditor with a larger firm.

Given the nature of the current economy and the level of acquisition activity, this could significantly reduce the pool of business for small and medium sized accountancy practices. Joint audit is therefore considered to be an important tool in combating the increased power of the 'Big 4' and the more significant medium tier firms.

9 Transnational audits

Transnational audit means an audit of financial statements which may be relied upon outside the audited entity's home jurisdiction.

Reliance on these audits might be for purposes of significant lending, investment or regulatory decisions.

The differences between a 'normal' audit, conducted within the boundaries of one set of legal and regulatory requirements, and a transnational audit are largely due to variations in:

- Auditing standards
- Regulation and oversight of auditors
- Financial reporting standards
- Corporate governance requirements.

Auditors must be aware of the different regimes that apply to the audit of a transnational entity because they will be bound by the varying laws and regulations. Given the globalisation of businesses and stock markets this is an increasingly significant concern for many firms of auditors.

Specific differences with transnational audit

Auditing standards

Despite the prevalence of International Standards on Auditing, many countries use modified versions and many continue to use local standards. As a result, in a group audit with components from a wide range of geographical backgrounds, it is possible that the audits of the components will be performed according to different standards. This could lead to inconsistency and poor quality for the group audit as a whole.

Regulation and oversight of auditors

As well as differing audit standards there are many different ways that the auditing profession is regulated. This can also affect the quality of the audit of components from different regimes, which will also lead to inconsistency in the quality of a group audit.

Financial reporting standards

Within a multinational group it is likely that adjustments will be required due to the application of differing financial reporting standards. These standards will be reflected in the component financial statements but, upon consolidation, must be adjusted to reflect the parent's accounting policies. These can lead to some very technically complex consolidation adjustments, which will increase the risk of material misstatement.

Corporate governance requirements

In some countries there are very strict corporate governance requirements that not only affect the directors of the company but their auditor. Often the auditor is required to perform, and report on, compliance with corporate governance requirements. In other countries the corporate governance requirements, particularly with regard to internal controls, are much more relaxed. However, this also affects the audit because this could indicate that internal controls may be less effective than those of a component that operates in a highly regulated environment.

The Transnational Audit Committee

The International Federation of Accountants (IFAC) has a committee with specific responsibilities for transnational audits: the Transnational Audit Committee (TAC).

Globalisation

Advantages	Disadvantages
• Wide ranging expertise • Global facilities • Can invest in expensive systems and necessary IT to meet needs of international clients	• Lack of competition and choice, particularly for large companies.

The concentration of the audit market into a few very large firms has come about because of globalisation. The larger firms found that amalgamations amongst the audit firms were the way forward leading to a more concentrated audit market:

- **Affiliation** is used by the larger accounting firms to develop an internationally recognised brand name.
- **Co-operation** is used by the mid-tier firms who join international co-operatives of firms who send each other business, but retain their own trading name in their home countries.

Current trends

Current trends still lean towards mergers:

- of firms in the countries where the profession is more highly developed, for example USA and many European countries, and
- between firms in the more developed arenas with practices in less developed locations.

In the mid-tier sector, the fastest way for firms to grow and achieve dominance in the sector is to merge with other similar sized companies. Recent mergers and acquisitions of firms include:

- BDO and PKF, now BDO
- Baker Tilly and RSM Tenon, now Baker Tilly.

Test your understanding 1

You are an audit manager in Ross & Co, a firm of Certified Public Accountants. The principal activity of one of your audit clients, Murray Co, is the manufacture and retail sale of women's fashions and menswear throughout the capital cities of Western Europe.

The following financial information has been extracted from Murray's most recent consolidated financial statements:

	20X4 $000	20X3 $000
Revenue	36,367	27,141
Gross profit	22,368	16,624
Profit before tax	5,307	4,405
Intangible assets:		
– Goodwill	85	85
– Trademarks	52	37
Property, plant and equipment	7,577	4,898
Current assets	13,803	9,737
Total assets	21,517	14,757

Equity	13,226	10,285
Non-current liabilities:		
Provisions	201	87
Current liabilities:		
Trade and other payables	8,090	4,385
Total equity and liabilities	21,517	14,757

In May 20X3 Murray purchased 100% of the shareholding of Di Rollo Co. Di Rollo manufactures fashion accessories (for example, jewellery, scarves and bags) in South America that are sold throughout the world by mail order. Murray's management is now planning that clothes manufacture will expand into South America and sold into Di Rollo's mail order market. Additionally, Di Rollo's accessories will be added to the retail stores' product range.

Murray is a member of an ethical trade initiative that aims to improve the employment conditions of all workers involved in the manufacture of its products. Last week Di Rollo's chief executive was dismissed following allegations that he contravened Di Rollo's policy relating to the environmentally-friendly disposal of waste products. The former chief executive is now suing Di Rollo for six months' salary in lieu of notice and a currently undisclosed sum for damages.

Ross & Co has recently been invited to accept nomination as auditor to Di Rollo. Murray's management has indicated that the audit fee for the enlarged Murray group should not exceed 120% of the fee for the year ended 31 March 20X3.

You have been provided with the following information relating to the acquisition of Di Rollo:

	Carrying amount	**Fair value adjustment**	**Fair value to the group**
	$000	$000	$000
Di Rollo brand name	–	–	600
Plant and equipment	95	419	514
Current assets	400	–	400
Current liabilities	(648)	–	(648)
Net assets at date of acquisition	(153)	419	866
Goodwill arising on acquisition			859
Cash consideration			1,725

Required:

(a) Using the information provided, explain the matters that should be considered before accepting the engagement to audit the financial statements of Di Rollo Co for the year ending 31 March 20X4.

(b) Explain what effect the acquisition of Di Rollo Co will have on the planning of your audit of the consolidated financial statements of Murray Co for the year ending 31 March 20X4.

Test your understanding 2

You are the manager responsible for the audit of the Nassau Group, which comprises a parent company and six subsidiaries. The audit of all individual companies' financial statements is almost complete, and you are currently carrying out the audit of the consolidated financial statements. One of the subsidiaries, Exuma Co, is audited by another firm, Jalousie & Co. Your firm is satisfied as to the competence and independence of Jalousie & Co.

You have received from Jalousie & Co the draft auditor's report on Exuma Co's financial statements, an extract from which is shown below:

Qualified Opinion (extract)

In our opinion, except for effects of the matter described in the Basis for Qualified Opinion paragraph, the financial statements give a true and fair view of the financial position of Exuma Co as at 31 March 20X1...'

Basis for Qualified Opinion (extract)

The company is facing financial damages of $2 million in respect of an ongoing court case, more fully explained in note 12 to the financial statements. Management has not recognised a provision but has disclosed the situation as a contingent liability. Under International Financial Reporting Standards, a provision should be made if there is an obligation as a result of a past event, a probable outflow of economic benefit, and a reliable estimate can be made. Audit evidence concludes that these criteria have been met, and it is our opinion that a provision of $2 million should be recognised. Accordingly, net profit and shareholders' equity would have been reduced by $2 million if the provision had been recognised.

An extract of Note 12 to Exuma Co's financial statements is shown below:

Note 12 (extract)

The company is the subject of a court case concerning an alleged breach of planning regulations. The plaintiff is claiming compensation of $2 million. The management of Exuma Co, after seeking legal advice, believe that there is only a 20% chance of a successful claim being made against the company.

Figures extracted from the draft financial statements for the year ending 31 March 20X1 are as follows:

	Nassau Group $ million	Exuma $ million
Profit before tax	20	4
Total assets	85	20

Required:

(a) **Identify and explain the matters that should be considered, and actions that should be taken by the group audit engagement team, in forming an opinion on the consolidated financial statements of the Nassau Group.**

A trainee accountant, Jo Castries, is assigned to your audit team. This is the first group audit that Jo has worked on. Jo made the following comment regarding the group audit:

'I understand that in a group audit engagement, one of the requirements is to design and perform audit procedures on the consolidation process. Please explain to me the principal audit procedures that are performed on the consolidation process.'

(b) **Required:**

Respond to the trainee accountant's question.

10 Chapter summary

GROUP AUDITS

Specific matters for principal auditors

- complex FS adjustments
- group accounting standards
- involvement of component auditors
- complexity organising a group audit

Specific considerations

- correct classification of investments
- differing accounting policies and frameworks
- fair values on acquisition
- intangibles
- taxation
- goodwill on consolidation
- intra-group balances, transactions and profits
- related parties
- share options
- subsequent events

Reliance on the component auditors

- compliance with the code of ethics
- competence of component auditors
- involvement of group auditor in audit of component
- regulatory environment of component auditor
- assess materiality and risk at group and component level
- communications with the component auditors

Test your understanding answers

Test your understanding 1

(a) Matters to consider

Ross & Co should be sufficiently competent and experienced to undertake the audit of Di Rollo as it has similar competence and experience in auditing the larger Murray Co. However, Ross needs knowledge of conducting businesses in South America including legal and tax regulations.

Factors that might impair Ross's objectivity in forming an opinion on the financial statements of Di Rollo (and the consolidated financial statements of Murray). For example, if Ross was involved in any due diligence review of Di Rollo, the same senior staff should not be assigned to the audit.

Adequacy of resources in South America (e.g. in representative/associated offices). Ross must have sufficient time to report on Di Rollo within the timeframe for reporting on the consolidated financial statements of Murray.

Ross should not accept the nomination if any limitation imposed by management would be likely to result in the need to issue a disclaimer of opinion on Di Rollo's financial statements.

The proposed restriction in audit fee may compromise the quality of the audit of Di Rollo and/or the Murray group. The 20% increase needs to be sufficient to cover the cost of the audit of Di Rollo and the incremental costs associated with auditing Murray's consolidated financial statements (as well as any general annual price increase that might be applied to audit fees).

Di Rollo is material to the Murray group. At acquisition the fair values of Di Rollo's tangible non-current assets, current assets and current liabilities represent 6.8%, 2.9% and 8%, respectively, of those in Murray's consolidated financial statements at 31 March 20X3.

It is usual that a parent company should want its auditors to audit its subsidiaries. If Ross declined the nomination, Murray's management may seek an alternative auditor for the group.

Murray should give Ross written permission to communicate with Di Rollo's current auditor to enquire if there is any professional reason why they should not accept this assignment.

Murray may provide Ross with additional fee-earning opportunities (e.g. due diligence reviews, tax consultancy, etc) if it continues to expand in future.

(b) Effect of acquisition on planning the audit of Murray's consolidated financial statements for the year ending 31 March 20X4.

Group structure

The new group structure must be ascertained to identify all entities that should be consolidated into the Murray group's financial statements for the year ending 31 March 20X4.

Materiality assessment

Preliminary materiality for the group will be much higher, in monetary terms, than in the prior year. For example, if a % of total assets is a determinant of the preliminary materiality, it may be increased by 10% (as the fair value of assets acquired, including goodwill, is $2,373,000 compared with $21.5m in Murray's consolidated financial statements for the year ended 31 March 20X3).

The materiality of each subsidiary should be reassessed, in terms of the enlarged group as at the planning stage. For example, any subsidiary that was just material for the year ended 31 March 20X3 may no longer be material to the group.

This assessment will identify, for example:

– significant components requiring a full audit, and
– components for which analytical procedures will suffice.

As Di Rollo's assets are material to the group, Ross should plan to inspect the South American operations. The visit may include meeting with Di Rollo's previous auditors to discuss any problems that might affect the balances at acquisition and a review of the prior year audit working papers, with their permission.

Di Rollo was acquired two months into the financial year therefore its post-acquisition results should be expected to be material to the consolidated statement of profit and loss.

Goodwill acquired

The assets and liabilities of Di Rollo at 31 March 20X4 will be combined on a line-by-line basis into the consolidated financial statements of Murray and goodwill arising on acquisition recognised.

Audit work on the fair value of the Di Rollo brand name at acquisition, $600,000, may include a review of a brand valuation specialist's working papers and an assessment of the reasonableness of assumptions made.

Significant items of plant are likely to have been independently valued prior to the acquisition. It may be appropriate to plan to place reliance on the work of expert valuers. The fair value adjustment on plant and equipment is very high (441% of carrying amount at the date of acquisition). This may suggest that Di Rollo's depreciation policies are over-prudent (e.g. if accelerated depreciation allowed for tax purposes is accounted for under local GAAP).

As the amount of goodwill is material (approximately 50% of the cash consideration) it may be overstated if Murray has failed to recognise any assets acquired in the purchase of Di Rollo. For example, Murray may have acquired intangible assets such as customer lists or franchises that should be recognised separately from goodwill and amortised (rather than tested for impairment).

Subsequent impairment

The audit plan should draw attention to the need to consider whether the Di Rollo brand name and goodwill arising have suffered impairment as a result of the allegations against Di Rollo's former chief executive.

Liabilities

Proceedings in the legal claim made by Di Rollo's former chief executive will need to be reviewed. If the case is not resolved at 31 March 20X4, a contingent liability may require disclosure in the consolidated financial statements, depending on the materiality of amounts involved. Legal opinion on the likelihood of Di Rollo successfully defending the claim may be sought. Provision should be made for any actual liabilities, such as legal fees.

Group (related party) transactions and balances

A list of all companies in the group (including any associates) should be included in group audit instructions to ensure that intra-group transactions and balances (and any unrealised profits and losses on transactions with associates) are identified for elimination on consolidation. Any transfer pricing policies (e.g. for clothes manufactured by Di Rollo for Murray and sales of Di Rollo's accessories to Murray's retail stores) must be ascertained and any provisions for unrealised profit eliminated on consolidation.

It should be confirmed at the planning stage that inter-company transactions are identified as such in the accounting systems of all companies and that inter-company balances are regularly reconciled.

Other auditors

If Ross plans to use the work of other auditors in South America (rather than send its own staff to undertake the audit of Di Rollo), group instructions will need to be sent containing:

- a request for confirmation of independence
- proforma statements
- a list of group and associated companies
- a list of related parties
- a statement of group accounting policies (see below)
- the timetable for the preparation of the group financial statements (see below)
- a request for copies of written representations from management
- an audit work summary questionnaire or checklist
- contact details (of senior members of Ross's audit team).

Accounting policies

Di Rollo may have material accounting policies which do not comply with the rest of the Murray group. As auditor to Di Rollo, Ross will recalculate the effect of any non-compliance with a group accounting policy that Murray's management would be requested to adjust on consolidation.

Timetable

The timetable for the preparation of Murray's consolidated financial statements should be agreed with management as soon as possible. Key dates should be planned for:

- agreement of inter-company balances and transactions
- submission of proforma statements
- completion of the consolidation package
- tax review of group financial statements
- completion of audit fieldwork by other auditors
- subsequent events review
- final clearance on the financial statements of subsidiaries
- Ross's final clearance of consolidated financial statements.

Test your understanding 2

(a) **Matters that should be considered when forming an opinion on the group financial statements**

Significant component

A significant component is a component identified by the group audit engagement team that is of individual significance to the group. Exuma Co meets the definition of a significant component because it contributes 20% of group profit before tax, and 23.5% of group total assets. Exuma Co is therefore material to the group financial statements.

Materiality of accounting issue

The legal case against Exuma Co involves a claim against the company of $2 million. This is material to the individual financial statements of Exuma Co as it represents 50% of profit before tax, and 10% of total assets. The matter is also material to the group financial statements, representing 10% of group profit before tax, and 2.4% of group total assets.

Qualified Opinion – Exuma Co financial statements

Jalousie & Co has expressed a modified opinion due to a material misstatement regarding the accounting treatment of the court case. Management has treated the matter as a contingent liability, as they believe that it is possible, but not probable, that the court case will go against the company, but the auditors believe that it should have been recognised as a provision according to IAS 37 *Provisions, Contingent Liabilities and Contingent Assets*. Given the materiality of the matter to the individual financial statements, this opinion seems appropriate (rather than an adverse opinion), as long as the audit evidence concludes that a provision is necessary.

Review and discussion of audit work relating to the court case

Due to the significance of this matter, the audit work performed by Jalousie & Co should be subject to review by the group audit engagement team. Specifically, the evidence leading to the conclusion that a probable outflow of cash will occur should be reviewed, and the matter should be discussed with the audit partner responsible for the opinion on Exuma Co's financial statements.

Evidence should include copies of legal correspondence, a copy of the actual claim showing the $2 million claimed against the company, and a written representation from management detailing management's reason for believing that there is no probable cash outflow.

Further audit procedures

Given the subjective nature of this matter, the group engagement partner may consider engaging an external expert to provide an opinion as to the probability of the court case going against Exuma Co.

Discussion with Nassau Group management

The matter should be discussed with the Group management team as to whether a provision is necessary. Their views should be documented in a written representation. There should also be discussion with management, and communication with those charged with governance regarding the potential impact of the matter on the group audit opinion. The impact depends on whether an adjustment is made in the individual accounts of Exuma Co, on consolidation, or not made at all, as explained below.

Adjustment to Exuma Co financial statements

Exuma Co is a subsidiary of Nassau, and by definition is under the control of the parent company. Therefore, management of Exuma Co can be asked to adjust the financial statements to recognise a provision. If this happens, Jalousie & Co's auditor's report can be redrafted as unmodified, and the group audit opinion will also be unmodified.

Adjustment on consolidation

Even if Exuma Co's financial statements are not amended, an adjustment could be made on consolidation of the group financial statements to include the provision. In this case, the opinion on Exuma Co's financial statements would remain qualified, but the group audit opinion would not be qualified as the matter causing the material misstatement has been rectified.

No adjustment made

If no adjustment is made, either to Exuma Co's individual financial statements, or as a consolidation adjustment in the group financial statements, and if the group engagement partner disagrees with this accounting treatment, then the group audit opinion should be qualified due to a material misstatement. In this case, a paragraph entitled Basis for Qualified Opinion should explain the reason for the qualification, i.e. non-compliance with IAS 37, and should also quantify the financial effect on the consolidated financial statements. Reference to the work performed by a component auditor should not be made.

(b) **Procedures**

- Agree the figures from the component financial statements into the consolidation schedule to ensure accuracy.
- Recalculate the consolidation schedule to ensure arithmetical accuracy.
- Recalculate the translation of any foreign components to ensure accuracy.
- Recalculate any non-controlling interest balances to verify accuracy.
- Agree the date of any acquisitions or disposals and recalculate the time apportionment of the results for these components included in the consolidation.
- Evaluate the classification of the component (i.e. subsidiary, associate, joint venture etc) to ensure this is still appropriate.
- Review the financial statement disclosures for related party transactions.
- Review the policies and year-ends applied by the components to ensure they are consistent with the group.
- Reconcile inter-company balances and ensure they cancel out in the group financial statements.
- Assess the reasonableness of the client's goodwill impairment review to ensure goodwill is not overstated.
- Review and recalculate the deferred tax consequences of any fair value adjustments.

chapter

11

Evidence

Chapter learning objectives

This chapter covers syllabus areas:

- D2 – Evidence
- E5c – Recognise and evaluate the impact of outsourced functions on the conduct of an audit

Detailed syllabus objectives are provided in the introduction section of the text book.

Exam focus

More than one question in the exam is likely to feature a requirement to design relevant audit or assurance procedures. It is essential that you understand the principles of audit evidence and can apply this knowledge to the scenario and design procedures relevant to the area of the subject matter being tested or the risk to be addressed.

1 The principles of evidence

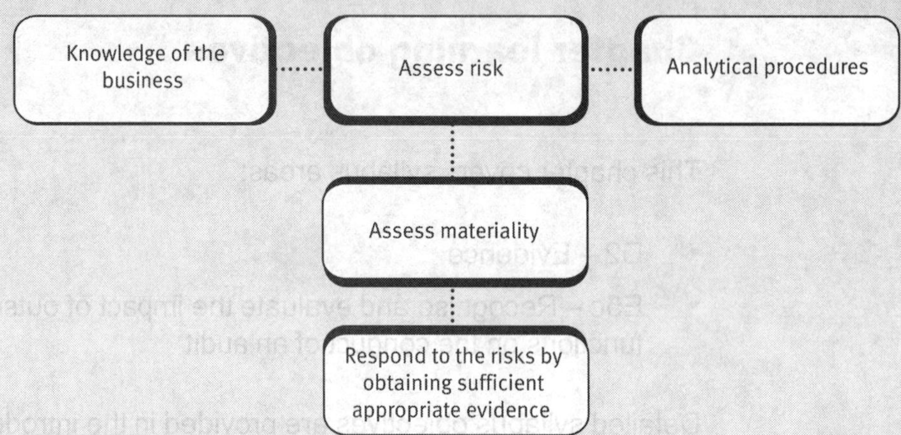

- Audit procedures are designed to obtain evidence in response to the assessment of risk at the planning stage.
- Evidence gathered must be sufficient and appropriate to reduce assessed risk to an acceptable level.
- If, at the review stage, the senior audit staff deem that the risk of misstatement has not been reduced to an acceptable level, more evidence will be required.

2 Obtaining audit evidence

ISA 500 *Audit Evidence*, requires the auditor to obtain sufficient appropriate evidence to be able to draw reasonable conclusions.

Sufficient evidence

- A measure of quantity, i.e. does the auditor have enough evidence to draw a conclusion.
- Affected by risk and materiality of the balances.

Appropriate evidence

- Measures quality of evidence – **relevance** and **reliability**.
- Reliability of evidence depends on several factors:
  - Independent, externally generated evidence is better than evidence generated internally by the client.
  - Effective controls imposed by the entity, generally improve the reliability of evidence.
  - Evidence obtained directly by the auditor is more reliable than evidence obtained indirectly or by inference.
  - It is better to get written, documentary evidence rather than verbal confirmations.
  - Original documents provide more reliable evidence than photocopies or facsimiles.
- Relevance means the evidence relates to the financial statement assertions being tested.

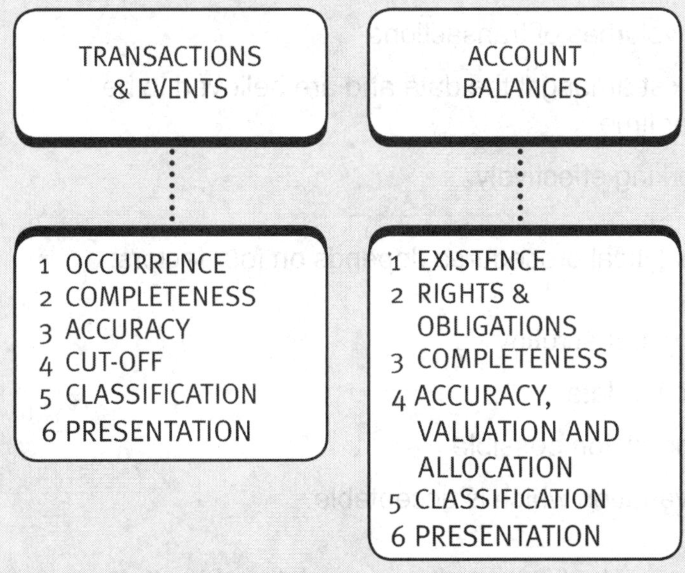

Audit procedures for obtaining evidence

The methods of obtaining evidence are:

- Inspection of records, documents or physical assets.
- Observation of processes and procedures, e.g. inventory counts.
- External confirmation obtained in the form of a direct written response to the auditor from a third party.
- Recalculation to confirm the numerical accuracy of documents or records.

- Re-performance by the auditor of procedures or controls.
- Analytical procedures.
- Enquiry of knowledgeable parties.

The auditor obtains evidence to draw conclusions on which to base the audit opinion. This is achieved by performing procedures to:

- Obtain an understanding of the entity and its environment, including internal control, to assess the risks of material misstatement.
- Test the operating effectiveness of controls in preventing, detecting and correcting material misstatements.
- Detect material misstatements.

3 Substantive analytical procedures

The use of analytical procedures as substantive evidence is generally more applicable where:

- there are large volumes of transactions
- relationships exist amongst the data and are believed to be predictable over time
- controls are working effectively.

The suitability of analytical procedures depends on four factors:

- the assertion/s under scrutiny
- the reliability of the data
- the degree of precision possible
- the amount of variation which is acceptable.

If analytical procedures identify fluctuations or relationships that are inconsistent with the auditor's knowledge of the business then the auditor should investigate those peculiarities through:

- Enquiry of management.
- Other procedures, as deemed necessary, for example, when management's response is considered inadequate.

Substantive procedures vs tests of control

Tests of controls are designed to check that the audit client's internal control systems operate effectively.

Examples of tests of controls:

- Inspect purchase invoices for evidence of authorisation by a manager before payment is made.
- Observe the process for despatch of goods to ensure the warehouse staff check the goods to the order before despatch.
- Using test data, enter a dummy order over a customer's credit limit to verify that the system won't allow the order to be accepted.

Substantive procedures are designed to detect material misstatement at the assertion level in the financial statements (i.e. designed to detect errors and, possibly, fraud).

Substantive procedures can be tests of detail or analytical procedures.

Substantive tests of detail looks at the supporting evidence for individual transactions and traces them through to the financial statements to ensure they are dealt with appropriately.

Examples of tests of detail:

- Inspect a purchase invoice for the amount and trace it into the purchase listing to ensure it has been recorded accurately.
- Inspect a title deed for the name of the client to verify rights and obligations.
- Recalculate an allowance for doubtful receivables using the client's formula to verify arithmetical accuracy.

Substantive analytical procedures test the balances as a whole to identify any unusual relationships e.g. comparison of a gross profit margin year on year might highlight that revenue is overstated if there is no known reason for the GPM to increase. An analytical procedure tests the 'reasonableness' of a balance.

Examples of analytical procedures:

- Calculate receivables days ratio and compare with credit terms offered to customers to identify any possible overstatement. If receivables days appears too high, discuss with management the need for an increase in the allowance for doubtful receivables.
- Obtain a breakdown of sales by month and analyse the seasonal trend to ensure it is consistent with the auditor's knowledge of the business. Discuss any unusual fluctuations with management.
- Calculate the expected interest charge for a loan by multiplying the outstanding loan amount with the interest rate and compare with the client's figure. Discuss any significant difference with management.

ISA 505 External confirmations

External confirmations are written responses received from third parties directly by the auditor to help them obtain sufficient appropriate evidence. Examples include: receivables circularisations and bank letters.

As these form external, written evidence, they are considered to be reliable sources of evidence. In order to ensure that the evidence sought remains reliable auditors should maintain control over this process.

To do this they should:

- Determine the information to be confirmed.
- Select the appropriate third party.
- Design the confirmation requests and instructions to return directly to the auditor.
- Send the requests, including a follow up when no response is received.

If management refuses to allow the auditor to send such requests the auditor should consider whether this is reasonable or not in the circumstances. This may affect the auditor's fraud risk assessment and reliance upon written representations from management.

If the auditor concludes that management's request is unreasonable and they cannot obtain sufficient appropriate evidence by any other means, the matter should be communicated to those charged with governance.

The auditor must be alert to the risk of interception, alteration or fraud and maintain appropriate professional scepticism when considering the reliability of responses which may have been received indirectly or appear not to come from the intended party.

Sampling

Auditors rarely test every transaction, balance and disclosure relevant to a set of financial statements. ISA 530 *Audit Sampling* states that auditors should select appropriate samples for testing that provide a reasonable basis to draw conclusions about the population from which the sample is selected.

When selecting samples auditors should consider the following concepts:

- Materiality and performance materiality.
- Sampling risk: the risk that the conclusions reached based on the sample would be different than the conclusions reached applying the same procedures to the whole population.
- The nature (and risk) of the population being tested, including the number of items within the population, their size relative to the total of the population and the coverage required to reduce audit risk to an acceptable level.
- The need to project, or extrapolate, the results of misstatements identified in the sample to the whole population.

When choosing a sampling method there are two broad approaches:

- Statistical sampling, where items in the population are selected randomly so that probability theory may be used to evaluate the results (through extrapolation to the whole population).
- Non-statistical, which is a method that does not meet the characteristics of statistical. This is usually employed when the auditor uses judgment to select sample items (e.g. focusing on high value, or known high risk items). Extrapolation cannot be used when bias has been introduced into the sample because the sample is no longer representative of the whole population.

Specific sampling methods include:

- Random: through use of random selectors/number tables.
- Systematic: number of items divided by a specific testing interval (e.g. every 50th balance to be tested). The starting point should be determined haphazardly/randomly.
- Monetary unit: value weighted selection so that conclusions are permitted in monetary amounts.
- Haphazard: no structured technique but avoids bias.
- Block: selection of contiguous items (i.e. sequential and rarely appropriate for statistical analysis).

4 Written representations

The value of written representations from management

ISA 580 *Written Representations* requires the auditor to obtain written representations from management:

- That they have fulfilled their responsibilities for the preparation of the financial statements.
- That they have provided the auditor with all relevant information.
- That all transactions have been recorded and reflected in the financial statements.
- To support other audit evidence relevant to the financial statements or specific assertions if deemed necessary by the auditor.
- As required by specific ISAs.

However, as a form of evidence, representations are low down in the order of reliability because they are internally produced.

On their own, written representations **do not provide sufficient appropriate evidence** about any of the matters with which they deal.

If, having received the representations considered necessary to gather sufficient appropriate evidence, the auditor concludes that there is sufficient doubt about the integrity of management to the extent that the representations are unreliable, then the auditor shall disclaim an opinion in accordance with ISA 705 *Modifications to the Opinion in the Independent Auditor's Report*.

The limitations of written representations

When asked for procedures or evidence in the exam, students should be careful not to suggest written representations for all areas of testing. The examiner has stated this is a common concern with weaker students who do not appreciate the nature of 'appropriate' evidence and that it detracts from the quality of an answer. Written representations are only appropriate for matters where better evidence is not available. This is generally areas requiring judgment of management.

Other written representations

The typical subjects of other representations include:

- Whether the selection and application of accounting policies are appropriate.
- Whether the following matters have been measured, presented and disclosed in accordance with the relevant financial reporting framework:
  - Plans or intentions that may affect the carrying value or classification of assets and liabilities.
  - Liabilities, both contingent and actual.
  - Title to, or control over, assets.
  - Aspects of laws, regulations and contractual agreements that may affect the financial statements, including non-compliance.
- That the directors have communicated all deficiencies in internal control to the auditor.
- Specific assertions about classes of transactions, accounts balances and disclosures requiring management judgment.

Written representations required by specific ISAs

Management must confirm they have informed the auditor of:

- all known and suspected frauds (ISA 240 *The Auditor's Responsibilities Relating to Fraud in an Audit of Financial Statements*)
- all instances of non-compliance with laws and regulations (ISA 250 *Consideration of Laws and Regulations in an Audit of Financial Statements*)
- all related parties and related party transactions (ISA 550 *Related Parties*)
- all subsequent events (ISA 560 *Subsequent Events*)
- all going concern issues (ISA 570 *Going Concern*)

Management must also confirm that they consider the effect of uncorrected misstatements to be immaterial (ISA 450 *Evaluation of Misstatements Identified During the Audit*).

5 Relying on the work of others

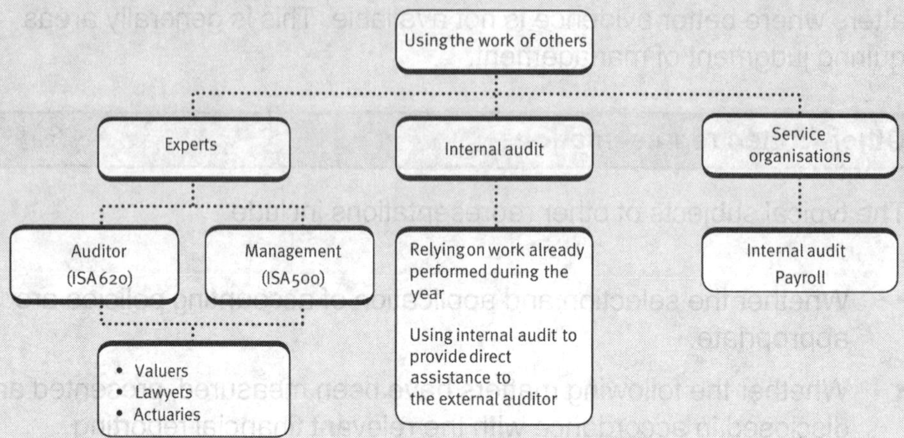

Relying on the work of an auditor's expert

Occasionally, when the auditor lacks the required technical knowledge to gather sufficient appropriate evidence to form an opinion, they may have to rely on the work of an expert. Examples of such circumstances include:

- The valuation of complex financial instruments, land and buildings, works of art, jewellery and intangible assets.
- Actuarial calculations associated with insurance contracts or employee benefit plans.
- The estimation of oil and gas reserves.
- The interpretation of contracts, laws and regulations.
- The analysis of complex or unusual tax compliance issues.

ISA 620 *Using the Work of an Auditor's Expert* suggests that, whilst this is acceptable, the auditor still needs to obtain sufficient appropriate evidence that such work is adequate for the purposes of the audit.

To fulfil this responsibility the auditor must **evaluate whether the expert has the necessary competence, capability and objectivity for the purpose of the audit**. The auditor also needs to obtain an understanding of the field of expertise of the expert to:

- Determine the nature, scope and objectives of the expert's work for audit purposes.
- Evaluate the adequacy of that work for audit purposes.

Once the auditor has considered the above issues they must then agree the following matters in writing with the expert:

- The nature, scope and objectives of the expert's work.
- The roles and responsibilities of the auditor and the expert.
- The nature, timing and extent of communication between the two parties.
- The need for the expert to observe confidentiality.

Once the expert's work is complete the auditor must scrutinise it and evaluate whether it is appropriate for audit purposes. In particular, the auditor should consider:

- The reasonableness of the findings and their consistency with other evidence.
- The significant assumptions made.
- The use and accuracy of source data.

Reference to the work of an expert

Auditors cannot devolve responsibility for forming an audit opinion, or for reaching conclusions with regard to specific assertions, onto an expert. The auditor has to use their professional judgment whether the evidence produced by the expert is sufficient and appropriate to support the audit opinion.

Finally, the auditor **should not make reference to the use of an expert in their auditor's report** unless it is required to aid the understanding of a modification to the audit opinion. In such circumstances the auditor shall indicate that the reference to the expert does not diminish the auditor's responsibility for the opinion.

The competence, capability and objectivity of the expert

Information regarding the competence, capability and objectivity on an expert may come from a variety of sources, including:

- Personal experience of working with the expert.
- Discussions with the expert.
- Discussions with other auditors.
- Knowledge of the expert's qualifications, memberships of professional bodies and licences.
- Published papers or books written by the expert.
- The audit firm's quality control procedures.

Assessing the objectivity of the expert is particularly difficult, as they may not be bound by a similar code of ethics as the auditor and, as such, may be unaware of the ethical requirements and threats with which auditors are familiar. It may therefore be relevant to:

- Make enquiries of the client about known interests or relationships with the chosen expert.
- Discuss applicable safeguards with the expert.
- Discuss financial, business and personal interests in the client with the expert.
- Obtain written representation from the expert.

Relying on internal audit

An internal audit department forms part of the client's system of internal control. If this is an effective element of the control system it may reduce control risk, and therefore reduce the need for the auditor to perform detailed substantive testing.

Additionally, auditors may be able to co-operate with a client's internal audit department and place reliance on their procedures in place of performing their own.

ISA 610 (Revised) *Using the Work of Internal Auditors* states that before relying on the work of internal audit, the external auditor must assess the effectiveness of the internal audit function and assess whether the work produced by the internal auditor is adequate for the purpose of the audit.

Evaluating the internal audit function

- The extent to which the internal audit function's **organisational status** and relevant policies and procedures support the **objectivity** of the internal auditors).
- The **competence** of the internal audit function.
- Whether the internal audit function applies a systematic and disciplined **approach**, including quality control.

If the auditor considers it appropriate to use the work of the internal auditors they then have to determine the areas and extent to which the work of the internal audit function can be used (by considering the nature and scope of work) and incorporate this into their planning to assess the impact on the nature, timing and extent of further audit procedures.

Evaluating the internal audit work

- The work was properly planned, performed, supervised, reviewed and documented.
- Sufficient appropriate evidence has been obtained.
- The conclusions reached are appropriate in the circumstances.
- The reports prepared are consistent with the work performed.

To evaluate the work adequately, the external auditor may re-perform some of the procedures that the internal auditor has performed to ensure they reach the same conclusion.

The extent of the work to be performed on the internal auditor's work will depend on the amount of judgment involved and the risk of material misstatement in that area.

When reviewing and re-performing some of the work of the internal auditor, the external auditor must consider whether their initial expectation of using the work of the internal auditor is still valid.

Note that the auditor is not required to rely on the work of internal audit. In some jurisdictions, the external auditor may be prohibited or restricted from using the work of the internal auditor by law.

Responsibility for the auditor's opinion cannot be devolved and no reference should be made in the auditor's report regarding the use of others during the audit.

The objectivity and competence of internal audit

When evaluating the competence of the internal audit function, the external auditor will consider:

- Whether the resources of the internal audit function are appropriate and adequate for the size of the organisation and nature of its operations.
- Whether there are established policies for hiring, training and assigning internal auditors to internal audit engagements.
- Whether internal auditors have adequate technical training and proficiency, including relevant professional qualifications and experience.
- Whether the internal auditors have the required knowledge of the entity's financial reporting and the applicable financial reporting framework.

- Whether the internal audit function possesses the necessary skills (e.g. industry-specific knowledge) to perform work related to the entity's financial statements.
- Whether the internal auditors are members of relevant professional bodies that oblige them to comply with the relevant professional standards including continuing professional development.

When evaluating whether the internal audit function applies a systematic and disciplined approach, the external auditor will consider:

- Whether there are adequate documented internal audit procedures or guidance.
- Whether the internal audit function has appropriate quality control procedures.

(ISA 610 *Using the Work of Internal Auditors*)

Using the internal audit to provide direct assistance

External auditors can consider whether the internal auditor can provide direct assistance with gathering audit evidence under the supervision and review of the external auditor. ISA 610 provides guidance to aim to reduce the risk that the external auditor over uses the internal auditor.

The following considerations will be made:

- Direct assistance cannot be provided where laws and regulations prohibit such assistance, e.g. in the UK.
- The competence and objectivity of the internal auditor. Where threats to objectivity are present, the significance of them and whether they can be managed to an acceptable level must be considered.
- The external auditor must not assign work to the internal auditor which involves significant judgment, a high risk of material misstatement or with which the internal auditor has been involved.
- The planned work must be communicated with those charged with governance so agreement can be made that the use of the internal auditor is not excessive.

Where it is agreed that the internal auditor can provide direct assistance:

- Management must agree in writing that the internal auditor can provide such assistance and that they will not intervene in that work.
- The internal auditors must provide written confirmation that they will keep the external auditors information confidential.
- The external auditor will provide direction, supervision and review of the internal auditor's work.
- During the direction, supervision and review of the work, the external auditor should remain alert to the risk that the internal auditor is not objective or competent.

Documentation

The auditor should document:

- The evaluation of the internal auditor's objectivity and competence.
- The basis for the decision regarding the nature and extent of the work performed by the internal auditor.
- The name of the reviewer and the extent of the review of the internal auditor's work.
- The written agreement of management mentioned above.
- The working papers produced by the internal auditor.

Note that for **UK syllabus**, direct assistance by the internal auditor is not allowed.

Use of service organisations

Many companies use service organisations to perform business functions such as:

- Payroll processing
- Receivables collection
- Pension management.

If a company uses a service organisation this will impact the audit as audit evidence will need to be obtained from the service organisation instead of, or in addition to, the client. This needs to be taken into consideration when planning the audit.

Planning the audit

The service organisation is an additional element to be taken into account when planning the audit and greater consideration needs to be made regarding obtaining sufficient appropriate evidence.

Risk assessment

The auditor should determine the effect on their assessment of risk. The following issues should be considered:

- the reputation of the service organisation
- the existence of external supervision
- the extent of controls operated by service provider.
- the experience of errors and omissions.
- the degree of monitoring by the user.

Factors the auditor should consider during the audit

The auditor should:

- Gain an understanding of the services being provided.
- Assess the design and implementation of the internal controls of the service provider.
- Visit the service provider to perform tests of controls.
- Contact the service provider's auditors to request a type 1 or type 2 report:

  A Type 1 report provides a description of the design of the controls at the service organisation prepared by the management of the service organisation. It includes a report by the service auditor providing an opinion on the description of the system and the suitability of the controls.

  A Type 2 report is a report on the description, design and operating effectiveness of controls at the service organisation. It contains a report prepared by management of the service organisation. It includes a report by the service auditor providing an opinion on the description of the system, the suitability of the controls, the effectiveness of the controls and a description of the tests of controls performed by the auditor.

If the auditor intends to use a report from a service auditor they should consider:

- the competence and independence of the service organisation auditor.
- the standards under which the report was issued.

- Consider whether sufficient appropriate evidence has been obtained and the implications for the auditor's report.

ISA 402 Use of a Service Organisation

ISA 402 *Audit Considerations Relating to an Entity Using a Service Organisation* provides guidance to auditors on the audit impact of outsourcing.

Objectives of the auditor in relation to the use of a service organisation

- Obtain an understanding of the service organisation sufficient to identify and assess the risks of material misstatement.
- Design and perform audit procedures responsive to those risks.

Obtaining an understanding of the service provided

- Nature of the services and their effect on internal controls.
- Nature and materiality of the transactions to the entity.
- Level of interaction between the activities of the service organisation and the entity.
- Nature of the relationship between the service organisation and the entity including contractual terms.

Sources of information for obtaining an understanding

- From the client entity.
- Obtaining a type 1 or type 2 report from the service organisation's auditor.
- Contacting the service organisation through the client.
- Visiting the service organisation.
- Using another auditor to perform tests of controls.

Responding to assessed risks

If controls are expected to operate effectively:

- Obtain a type 2 report if available
- Perform tests of controls at the service organisation
- Use another auditor to perform tests of controls.

When using a type 2 report, the auditor should consider

- whether the date covered by the report is appropriate for the audit
- whether the client has any complementary controls in place
- the time lapsed since the tests of controls were performed
- whether the tests of controls performed by the auditor are relevant to the financial statement assertions.

The auditor should enquire of the client whether the service organisation has reported any frauds to them or whether they are aware of any frauds.

Impact on the auditor's report

If sufficient appropriate evidence has not been obtained, a qualified or disclaimer of opinion will be issued.

The use of a service organisation auditor is not mentioned in the auditor's report as the auditor is fully responsible for their opinion.

Benefits to the audit

- **Independence:** because the service organisation is external to the client, the audit evidence derived from it is regarded as being more reliable than evidence generated internally by the client.
- **Competence:** because the service organisation is a specialist, it may be more competent in executing its role than the client's internal department resulting in fewer errors.
- **Possible reliance on the service organisation's auditors:** it may be possible for the client's auditors to confirm information directly with the service organisation's auditors.

Drawbacks

- The main disadvantage of outsourced services from the auditor's point of view concerns access to records and information.
- Auditors generally have statutory rights of access to the client's records and to receive answers and explanations that they consider necessary to enable them to form their opinion.
- They do not have such rights over records and information held by a third party such as a service organisation.
- If access to records and other information is denied by the service organisation, this may impose a limitation on the scope of the auditor's work. If sufficient appropriate evidence is not obtained this will result in a modified auditor's report.

ISAE 3402: Reporting on Controls at a Service Organisation

ISAE 3402 *Assurance Reports on Controls at a Service Organisation* deals with assurance engagements undertaken to provide a report for use by entities engaging the services of another organisation and the user entities' auditors.

It provides guidance to the assurance provider to ensure that where the service is relevant to the user entity's internal controls relating to financial reporting, the reports prepared provide sufficient appropriate audit evidence, as required by ISA 402.

In order to provide sufficient appropriate evidence, these assurance engagements are required to provide **reasonable assurance**. The engagements are performed as attestation engagements.

The objective of the engagement is to obtain reasonable assurance that:

- the service organisation's description of its system fairly presents the system as designed and implemented
- the controls were suitably designed
- the controls operated effectively throughout the specified period, and
- to report on the above matters.

The evaluation of the suitability of the design and operating effectiveness of the controls would need to be performed to the same standard as an evaluation performed by the external auditor.

The assurance provider can rely on the service entity's internal audit function, in the same way that the external auditor would, where the work of the internal audit function is relevant to the engagement and the work is adequate for the purposes of the engagement – the assessment of the internal audit function required is the same as that required by ISA 610.

6 Related parties

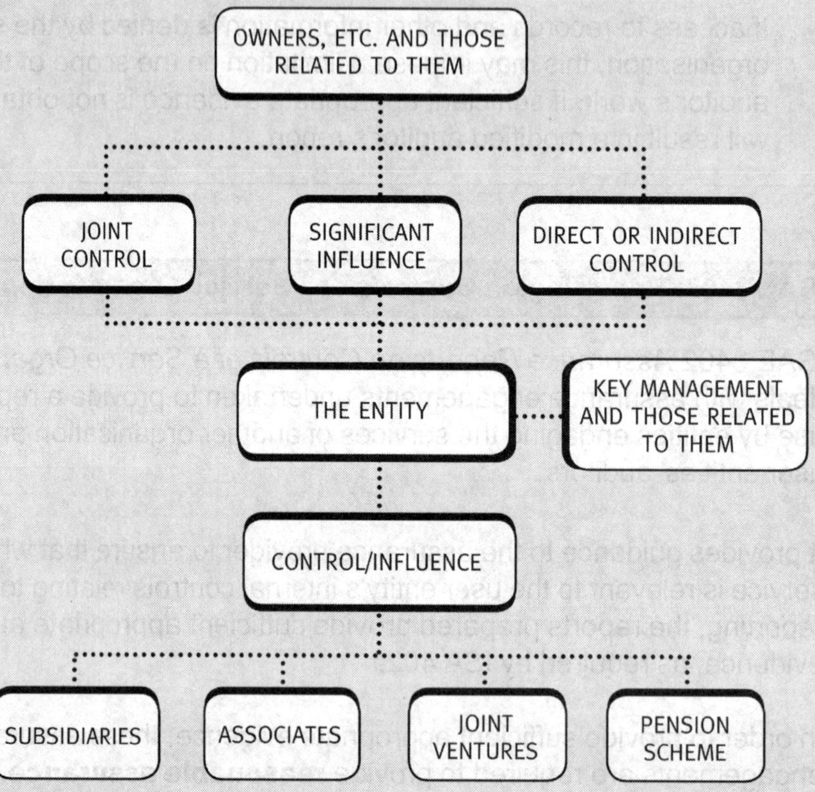

Related parties to a business

- Those who control, directly or indirectly, the entity.
- Those related to those who control the entity.
  - Family
  - Entities under their control (including group entities)
  - Parent company management.
- Those who manage the entity.
- Those related to those who manage the entity.

- Those under the control or influence of the entity.
  - Subsidiaries
  - Associates
  - Joint ventures
  - Pension schemes.

Risks with related party transactions

There is nothing wrong with an entity dealing with a related party.

Related party transactions may increase the potential for the financial results to be manipulated as transactions may be carried out on a basis other than 'arms length'. In these circumstances it is appropriate for such transactions to be brought to the attention of shareholders (IAS 24 *Related Party Disclosures*).

The auditor should obtain sufficient appropriate evidence that transactions have been identified and disclosed in accordance with IAS 24.

Disclosure should be made of the following:

- the nature of the related party relationship.
- information about the transactions including the amount and any balances outstanding at the year-end.
- any allowance for doubtful receivable or expense recognised in respect of irrecoverable debts.

If transactions have not been disclosed in accordance with those requirements, the potentially significant deficiency in the internal control system should be reported to those charged with governance.

Even once related parties have been identified it can be difficult to spot associated transactions with them:

- Directors may be reluctant to disclose transactions, particularly in the case of family members.
- Transactions may not be easy to identify from the accounting systems because they are not separately identified from 'normal' transactions.
- Transactions may be concealed in whole, or in part, from auditors for fraudulent purposes.

As a result of the risks above, related party transactions are generally deemed material by nature.

Audit procedures

Typical procedures to identify related party transactions include:

- Inspecting prior year working papers.
- Assessing the entity's procedures for identifying, authorising and recording related party transactions.
- Enquiring about relationships between those charged with governance and management and other entities.
- Inspecting shareholder records for details of principal shareholders.
- Inspecting minutes of shareholders' meetings and other relevant minutes and records.
- Enquiring of other auditors involved with the audit.
- Inspecting the entity's income tax returns and other information supplied to the regulatory authorities.
- Reviewing transactions with abnormal terms of trade or appear not to have a logical business reason.

ISA 550 Related Parties

Indicators of related party transactions

Related parties are often difficult to identify in practice. It can be hard to establish exactly who, or what, are the related parties of an entity. Indicators of related party transactions include:

- Transactions with abnormal terms of trade.
- Transactions that appear not to have a logical business reason.
- Transactions where substance and form differ.
- Transactions that are not processed in the usual or routine way.
- High volumes of transactions, or high value or otherwise significant transactions with individual customers or suppliers.
- Unrecorded transactions such as rent free accommodation, or services provided at no cost.

Members of the audit team need to be aware that they should consider the possibility of undisclosed related party transactions when they carry out audit procedures such as examining documents, inspecting minutes of meetings, etc. If the auditor identifies related parties that were not previously identified or disclosed they should:

- Communicate that information to the rest of the engagement team.
- Request that management identifies all transactions with the related party and enquire why they failed to identify them.

- Perform appropriate substantive procedures relating to transactions with these entities.
- Reconsider the risk that other, unidentified, related parties may exist.
- Evaluate the implications if the non-disclosure by management appears intentional.

If the auditor identifies related party transactions outside the entity's normal course of business they should also:

- Inspect the underlying contracts or agreements to establish:
  - the business rationale
  - the terms of the transaction
  - whether appropriate disclosures have been made.
- Obtain evidence that the transactions were appropriately authorised.

7 Estimates and fair values

ISA 540 *Auditing Accounting Estimates, Including Fair Value Accounting Estimates and Related Disclosures* requires auditors to obtain sufficient appropriate evidence about whether estimates (including fair values) are reasonable and adequately disclosed in the financial statements.

Examples of balances where fair values are relevant include:

- Defined benefit pension schemes
- Share based payment schemes
- Investments in shares
- Investment property
- Property within PPE if the revaluation model is used
- Net assets of a subsidiary at the acquisition date

Risk assessment

The auditor should consider:

- How management identifies transactions and balances requiring estimation such as fair values and financial instruments.

- How management makes the estimates including:
  - models used
  - relevant controls (control environment, risk management processes, information systems, documented system of internal control, appropriate accounting policies)
  - use of an expert
  - assumptions underlying the estimates
  - changes since the prior period
  - how management assesses the effect of uncertainty.
- Whether the valuation techniques are commonly used by other market participants.
- The competence and objectivity of those responsible for the valuations.

To assist with this process the auditor should consider the outcome of estimates made in the prior period.

Professional scepticism is required for the auditor to be alert to possible management bias.

Audit procedures

- Determining whether events up to the date of the auditor's report provide additional evidence with regard to the appropriateness of estimates.
- Testing how management made their estimates and evaluating whether the method is appropriate.
- Testing the effectiveness of controls over estimations.
- Developing a point estimate to use in comparison to managements'.
- If there are significant risks associated with estimates the auditor should also enquire whether management considered any alternative assumptions and why they rejected them and whether the assumptions used are reasonable in the circumstances.
- Obtain written representations from management confirming that they believe the assumptions used in making estimates are reasonable.
- Verify the external prices used to value financial instruments.

Challenges in Auditing Fair Value Accounting Estimates

IAASB Practice Alert (IAASB – October 2008): Challenges in Auditing Fair Value Accounting Estimates in the Current Market Environment

The practice alert has been prepared in light of difficulties in the credit markets and therefore has a focus on financial instruments. Recent market experience has highlighted the difficulties that arise in valuing financial instruments when market information is either not available or sufficient information is difficult to obtain.

In the current environment obtaining reliable information relevant to fair values has been one of the greatest challenges faced by preparers, and consequently by auditors. The nature and reliability of information available to management to support the making of a fair value accounting estimate vary widely, and thereby affect the degree of estimation uncertainty associated with that fair value.

The alert is a comprehensive and lengthy document. A summary of some of the key points is included below:

- Due to the complex nature of certain financial instruments, it is vital that both the entity and the auditor understand the instruments in which the entity has invested or to which it is exposed, and the related risks.
- The auditor's understanding of the instruments may be developed by understanding the entity's processes for investing in particular instruments.
- Factors that may influence the auditor's risk assessment with regard to financial instruments include:
  - Whether the entity has control procedures in place for making investment decisions
  - The level of due diligence associated with particular investments
  - The expertise of those responsible for making investment decisions
  - Whether the entity has the ability to subsequently value the instruments
  - Management's track record for assessing the risks of particular instruments.

- In the case of fair value accounting estimates, it is necessary that the audit engagement team include one or more members sufficiently skilled and knowledgeable about fair value accounting in order to comply with the required quality control procedures.
- Depending on the nature, materiality and complexity of fair values, management representations about fair value measurements and disclosures contained in the financial statements may also include representations about the following:
  - The appropriateness of the measurement methods and the consistency in application of the methods.
  - The completeness and appropriateness of disclosures related to fair values.
  - Whether subsequent events require adjustment to the fair value measurements.

ISA 501 Specific Considerations

In accordance with ISA 501 auditors are required to obtain sufficient appropriate evidence with regard to three specific matters, as follows:

(1) The existence and condition of inventory
- Attendance at the inventory count
  - evaluate management's instructions
  - observe the count procedures
  - inspect the inventory
  - perform test counts
- Perform procedures with regard to final inventory records to ensure they reflect actual inventory count results.

(2) The completeness of litigation and claims involving the entity
- Enquiry of management and in-house legal counsel.
- Inspecting minutes of board meetings and meetings with legal counsel.
- Inspecting legal expense accounts.
- If there is a significant risk of material misstatement due to unidentified litigation or claims the audit should seek direct communication with the entity's external legal counsel.

(3) The presentation and disclosure of segmental information

- Understand, evaluate and test methods used by management to determine segmental information.
- Perform analytical procedures.

Addressing disclosures

Addressing disclosures in the audit of financial statements

Disclosures are an important part of the financial statements and seen as a way for communicating further information to users. Poor quality disclosures may obscure understanding of important matters.

Concerns have been raised about whether auditors are giving sufficient attention to disclosures during the audit. The IAASB believes that where the term financial statements is used in the ISAs it should be clarified that this is intended to include all disclosures subject to audit.

Recent changes to ISAs include:

- Emphasis on the importance of giving appropriate attention to addressing disclosures.
- Focus on matters relating to disclosures to be discussed with those charged with governance, particularly at the planning stage.
- Emphasis on the need to agree with management their responsibility to make available the information relevant to disclosures, early in the audit process.

ISAs affected by these changes are:

- ISA 200 *Overall Objectives of the Independent Auditor and the Conduct of an Audit in Accordance with International Standards on Auditing.*
- ISA 210 *Agreeing the Terms of Audit Engagements.*
- ISA 240 *The Auditor's Responsibilities Relating to Fraud in an Audit of Financial Statements*
- ISA 260 (Revised) *Communication with Those Charged With Governance.*
- ISA 300 *Planning an Audit of Financial Statements.*
- ISA 315 (Revised) *Identifying and Assessing the Risks of Material Misstatement through Understanding the Entity and Its Environment.*
- ISA 320 *Materiality in Planning and Performing an Audit.*

- ISA 330 *The Auditor's Responses to Assessed Risks.*
- ISA 450 *Evaluation of Misstatements Identified during the Audit.*
- ISA 700 (Revised) *Forming an Opinion and Reporting on Financial Statements.*

Audit documentation

The need for documentation

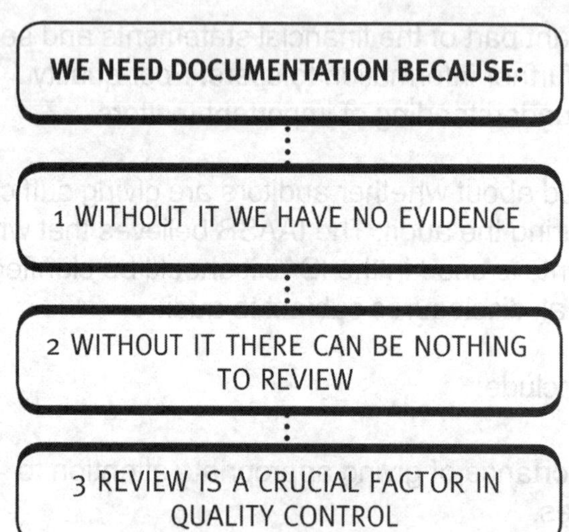

ISA 230 *Audit Documentation* deals specifically with audit documentation and requires:

- timely preparation of audit documentation necessary to provide a sufficient and appropriate record of the basis for the auditor's report, and evidence that the audit was carried out in accordance with ISAs and applicable legal and regulatory requirements.
- audit documentation sufficient to enable an experienced auditor, having no previous connection with the audit, to understand the audit work performed, the results and audit evidence obtained, and the significant matters identified and conclusions reached thereon.

Recap: Example audit procedures

Non-current assets

- Select a sample of assets from the asset register and physically inspect them to verify existence.
- Select a sample of assets visible at the client premises and inspect the asset register to ensure they are included to verify completeness.
- Recalculate the depreciation charge to verify arithmetical accuracy.
- Inspect the physical condition of assets to assess valuation.
- Review any valuers' reports to confirm valuation.
- Inspect title deeds or registration documents for the client's name to verify rights and obligations.

Inventory

- Inspect the inventory listing to ensure damaged/obsolete items have been written down to NRV.
- Inspect the inventory listing for the items on the last GRNs and GDNs obtained to ensure cut-off is correctly applied.
- Trace items on the count sheets obtained during the count into the inventory listing to ensure the quantities have not been changed.
- Calculate inventory days ratio and compare with prior year to identify any slow-moving items requiring write down.
- Inspect the aged inventory listing for old items and discuss the need for write down with management.
- Inspect purchase invoice to verify cost.
- Inspect post year-end sales invoices to verify NRV.
- Review calculations of overheads included in WIP and ensure only production related overheads are included.

Receivables

- Request direct confirmation from customers to confirm existence and rights.
- Inspect GDNs and invoices included in the listing to confirm accuracy of the amount recorded.
- Inspect cash received post year-end to confirm valuation.
- Calculate receivables days and compare with credit terms to assess the recoverability of the debts.
- Enquire with management about any long overdue debts and discuss the need for write down with management.
- Inspect correspondence with customers for evidence of disputes which may indicate overvaluation.

Bank

- Obtain a bank confirmation letter for all bank accounts held to verify rights and existence.
- Obtain bank reconciliations for all bank accounts and cast to confirm accuracy.
- Agree the balance per the cash book to the ledger.
- Agree the balance per the bank statement to the bank letter.
- Agree unpresented cheques to the post year-end bank statements to confirm they have cleared in a reasonable time.
- Agree outstanding lodgements to the paying in book and post year-end bank statements.

Payables

- Inspect purchase invoices and GRNs included on the listing to confirm accuracy of recording.
- Obtain/perform supplier statement reconciliations to identify discrepancies which could impact completeness, existence or valuation.
- Obtain direct confirmation of balances from suppliers where supplier statements are not available.
- Inspect post year-end bank statements for payments made which may indicate unrecorded liabilities.
- Calculate payables days ratio and compare with credit terms given to identify unusual differences and discuss with management.
- Inspect GRNs for before the year-end to ensure completeness.

Provisions

- Enquire with management the basis of the provision to assess reasonableness.
- Recalculate the provision to confirm arithmetical accuracy.
- Obtain written representation from management as to the adequacy and completeness of the provision.
- For a legal provision obtain confirmation from lawyers regarding the amount and probability.
- Inspect board minutes to confirm an obligation exists at year-end.
- Review subsequent events for further evidence.

Use of IT in auditing

Computer assisted audit techniques (CAATs) are the means by which the auditor uses IT to carry out audit procedures in place of manual ones. CAATs include test data and audit software.

Test data is used to test the programmed controls within a computer system allowing the auditor to test aspects that would otherwise not be capable of testing manually.

Audit software is used to:

- Calculate ratios for use in analytical procedures.
- Identify exceptional transactions, i.e. those unusual transactions that exceed predefined limits, i.e. a member of management being paid in excess of $20,000 in any one month. This helps identify balances that require further audit testing.
- Extract samples in a non-biased manner.
- Check the calculations in client prepared reports.
- Prepare lead schedules for the auditor to use in working papers.

CAATs have obvious benefits:

- Allowing continual auditing of processes and delivery of more frequent reports.
- Processing large volumes of data and performing large volumes of calculations, many more than could reasonably be performed manually.
- Test data tests the underlying system data, rather than copies and printouts.

- Once software has been written for a client it can then be applied to their system with few further costs.
- Reduced need for audit staff to perform procedures, hence further cost savings for clients.
- Reduced need for paper audit trails (hence reduced environmental impact of the audit process).

However, there are many concerns that need to be addressed before an audit firm actually implements computer based auditing techniques:

- There is an initial high cost of designing the software package, although this cost can be recouped over a number of years of use.
- Software may interfere with the client's system and could potentially increase the risk of viruses and data corruption.
- Clients may be concerned for the security of their data.
- They are only usually cost effective if the client's accounting systems are integrated, otherwise auditors would need different software programmes for different systems.
- Lead times tend to be long and the planning has to be carried out well in advance – not just three or four weeks before the start of fieldwork, but perhaps a whole year in advance.
- Audit firms will need to recruit increasingly from an IT, rather than an accounting, background.
- Software has to be tested on a 'live' system before the auditor knows whether it will work or not (i.e. high risk of corrupting that system).
- If the client wishes to change their system the auditor has to incur further costs changing their audit software.

UK syllabus: PN 16

Bank reports

In February 2011, the FRC issued a revised Practice Note (16) *Bank Reports for Audit Purposes in the United Kingdom*.

ISA 330 *The Auditor's Responses to Assessed Risks* requires the auditor to consider whether external confirmation procedures are to be performed as substantive procedures in order to perform the audit in an effective manner.

Practice Note 16 summarises the process agreed between the UK auditing profession and the British Bankers Association (BBA) regarding the procedures auditors use when requesting confirmation of balances, transactions or arrangements from the bankers of an entity being audited, using bank reports (bank confirmations).

The Practice Note includes templates for the different types of bank reports available and the circumstances in which they should be used:

- **Standard:** in most circumstances, when the auditor is not able to supply sufficient references to identify the bank accounts for which information is required.
- **Fast Track:** in exceptional circumstances, e.g. to meet a reporting deadline within a month or less of the accounting year-end.
- **Incomplete Information:** when the auditor is unable to provide the main account sort code and number for all the entities in a group.

UK syllabus: PN 23

Special considerations in auditing financial instruments

Financial instruments are susceptible to estimation uncertainty which is the susceptibility of an accounting estimate and related disclosures to an inherent lack of precision in its measurement.

Detection risks when auditing financial instruments

- The auditor may not understand the financial instruments.
- Evidence may be difficult to obtain.
- Undue reliance may be placed on certain individuals who exert significant influence on the financial instrument transactions.
- Transactions may not be significant in value but the risks and exposures associated with them may be significant.

Risk of material misstatement

The risk of material misstatement increases when those responsible for the fair values and estimates:

- Do not fully understand the risks and have insufficient experience to manage those risks.
- Do not have the expertise to value them appropriately in accordance with the financial reporting framework.
- Do not have sufficient controls in place over the financial instruments.
- Inappropriately hedge risks.

Significant transactions may increase the risk of misappropriation of assets.

The risk of fraud may be higher if the employees responsible for accounting for financial instruments are more knowledgeable than management and those charged with governance.

Audit planning considerations

- Understanding the accounting and disclosure requirements.
- Understanding the purpose and risks of the financial instruments.
- Determining whether specialised skills and knowledge are needed in the audit.
- Understanding and evaluating the system of internal control.
- Understanding the internal audit function.
- Understanding management's process for valuing financial instruments.
- Assessing and responding to the risks of material misstatement.

Assessing and responding to the risks of material misstatement

- Testing the controls will be effective in an organisation with well established controls and systems and where there are significant volumes of transactions which would mean substantive procedures alone would not suffice.
- Organisations with few financial instrument transactions are less likely to have effective controls in place and management may only have a limited understanding which would lead to a substantive approach being taken.
- Substantive analytical procedures may not be effective as complex interplay of the drivers of the valuation may mask unusual trends.
- For non-routine transactions, a substantive approach will be the most effective means of obtaining audit evidence.
- As valuations can change significantly in a short period of time, these will need to be tested at the year-end rather than during the interim audit.

UK syllabus: PN 25

Attendance at Stocktaking

In February 2011, the FRC issued a revised Practice Note (25) *Attendance at Stocktaking*.

ISA 501 *Audit Evidence – Specific Considerations for Selected items* includes requirements and application material relating to inventory (stock) and in particular, obtaining audit evidence by attendance at physical inventory counts (stock takes).

The Practice Note contains further guidance including how the requirements of other ISAs may be applied in relation to attendance at stocktaking, in particular in relation to obtaining evidence relating to the existence assertion.

The Practice Note covers:

- Assessment of risks and internal controls including factors relating to risk of material misstatement in the context of the existence of stocks (e.g. timing of stocktakes relative to the year-end date).
- Audit evidence obtained from attendance at stocktaking, in particular the principal sources of evidence relating to the existence of stocks (e.g. substantive evidence from physical inspection of stock).

- The principal procedures that should be performed when attending a stocktake, including:
  - the need for procedures to be performed by audit staff who are familiar with the entity's business.
  - the need for advance planning.
  - procedures before, during and after the stocktake.
  - inspection of work-in-progress.
  - the use of expert valuers and stocktakers.
  - the need to obtain sufficient appropriate evidence over stock held by third parties or in public warehouses.

UK syllabus: PN 26

Smaller Entities

In December 2009, the FRC issued a revised Practice Note (26) *Guidance on Smaller Entity Audit Documentation*. The Practice Note provides guidance on the application of documentation requirements contained within ISAs to the audit of financial statements of smaller entities in an efficient manner.

The guidance is aimed at auditors of smaller, simpler entities, including entities which are exempt from audit but which choose to have a voluntary audit such as small subsidiary companies, small charities, and simple larger entities. It excludes smaller entities with complex operations or the audit of complex and subjective matters.

The Practice Note highlights that it is neither practicable nor necessary to document every matter considered, or professional judgment made, in an audit. It encourages:

- the use of structured forms (instead of narrative notes) to document understanding of the entity.
- focusing on how the main transaction cycles operate at highlighting the risks of material misstatement when documenting smaller entities' accounting systems.
- not documenting matters that would normally have been documented solely to inform or instruct members of the audit team, when the engagement partner is performing the work themselves (as smaller audit teams are common in audits of smaller entities).

Exam style question – Queens Cars

Study Note: this is an example of a typical section A case study style question. The examiner has indicated that risk assessment and audit procedures are core areas and will be examined in every sitting. The format below represents how these topics have been examined so far.

Your firm has recently been appointed as auditor of Queens Cars Co, a new and second hand motor vehicle dealer with six sites. You are currently planning the audit for the year ended 29 February 20X4. The draft financial statements show revenue of $23.3m (20X3: $18.1m), profit before tax of $2.6m (20X3: $1.4m) and total assets of $15.8m (20X3: $12.6m).

New cars are purchased on a consignment basis from a single supplier. Queens Cars pays the invoice price (plus a 2% display fee) six months after delivery, or on sale of the vehicle if sooner. Currently Queens Cars records the purchase of the vehicles when the invoice is paid because their supplier legally owns the vehicles and may demand their return at any point prior to settlement. Although, the FD has told you that this has yet to happen.

The value of all new cars held across the various sites at the year-end, according to management records, was $2.4m (20X3: $1.9m). The value of used cars held at the year-end, according to inventory records, was $0.6m (20X3: $0.6m).

Whilst less popular with new cars, many customers like to pay cash, using this as leverage to barter for a cash discount. In addition, Queens Cars also accept cars in part exchange. One of their current promotions is that they will accept any vehicle for a minimum of $500 trade in value.

The MD of Queens Cars has informed you that he has employed his nephew, a trainee accountant, to manage and record the spare parts inventory across all branches. It was his responsibility to conduct the year-end count. However, you have been told that the year-end fell during the nephew's reading week and he was on holiday at the time. Therefore he conducted the count the week before the year-end and then reconciled the movements on his return. The year-end valuation of spare parts inventory was $0.2m (20X3: $0.15m).

During the year Queens Cars purchased a brand of simple fitting replacement parts that it will now supply on all servicing and repair jobs. As part of this purchase $0.7m was paid for the brand name "Quick Fit." This has been capitalised as an intangible asset. However, Queens Cars are not amortising the brand following the advice of the MD's nephew, who argued that the brand was so strong that its useful life was indefinite.

All new cars come with a warranty of three years or 30,000 miles, whichever is sooner. Second hand cars are offered with a six month guarantee. At the end of the year the warranty provision was \$0.8m (20X3: \$0.7m). The FD believes that despite the increase in the number of cars sold there is no need to increase the warranty provision because the company has focused more heavily on new car sales this year, which, according to him, require less after sales repairs than used cars.

Required:

Prepare briefing notes for the engagement partner that:

(a) Identifies and explains the principal audit risks that need to be considered when planning the final audit of Queens Cars for the year ended 29 February 20X4.

(9 marks)

(b) Describes the principal audit procedures that would be carried out in respect of the amortisation of the Quick Fit brand.

(5 marks)

Professional marks will be awarded in part (a) for the format of the answer and for the clarity of assessment provided.

(4 marks)

Test your understanding 1 – Financial instruments

You are planning the audit of Gig Co for the year ended 31 December 20X1. During the period, Gig Co entered into the following transactions:

On 1 April 20X1 Gig Co purchased 1 million shares in Concert Co for $5 per share. This amounts to a 6% holding of Concert Co's issued share capital, and is not sufficient to give significant influence or control. The shares of Concert Co are not listed.

Gig Co required additional finance and on 1 January 20X1, it issued 1 million $10 bonds at par. Interest is payable at a rate of 5% of the par value annually in arrears. The bonds will be redeemed at a premium on 31 December 20X3. The bonds are held in the financial statements at $10 million and the interest paid during the period has been charged to profit or loss.

Required:

Explain the principal audit procedures to be performed in respect of:

(a) **The investment in the shares of Concert Co.**

(b) **The bonds.**

8 Chapter summary

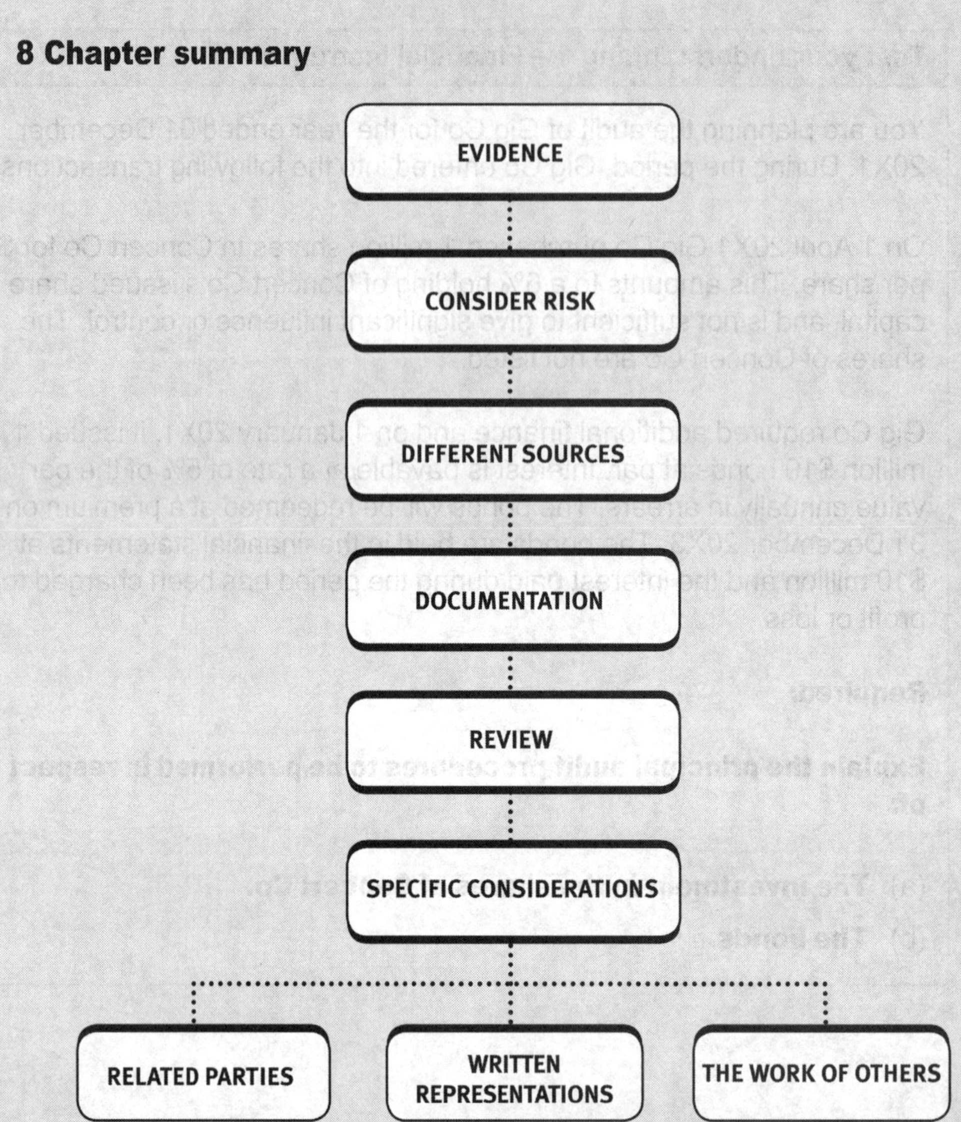

Test your understanding answers

Exam style question – Queens Cars

Study Note: Throughout your answer you must remain specific to the scenario presented in the question. The majority of the marks are for **application** of knowledge. Simply restating the information from the scenario will not score enough for a pass.

Note the use of structure (short paragraphs, headings, briefing note format). This generally leads to more succinct answers, which are easier to mark. There are also professional marks available for use of appropriate format, introduction, conclusion and the quality of the presentation/flow.

(a) **Briefing notes**

To: A. Partner

From: A.N. Accountant

Date: 8 April 20X4

Subject: Planning of the year-end audit of Queens Cars Co

Introduction

These briefing notes identify and explain the audit risks to be considered when planning the audit of Queens Cars Co. Procedures to be performed in respect of the useful life of the brand name are also included.

New car inventories

In legal terms Queens Cars do not own the consignment inventory held on site at the year-end. However, Queens have never returned a vehicle and in substance they should record the purchase of inventory in their accounting records at the point of delivery. There is therefore a risk that new car inventories, and the consequent liabilities, are understated.

Finance costs

There is also an associated risk that finance costs are understated in the statement of profit or loss. The 2% display fee should be treated as a finance cost in the statement of profit or loss.

Second hand inventories

There is a risk that second hand inventories are overstated. At $0.6m these are material to total assets. The case suggests that it is common for customers to barter for discounts, which could lead to vehicles being sold for less than cost.

Queens also offer a fixed part exchange value for any vehicle and it is therefore likely that they may receive vehicles in part exchange that do not have a resale value of $500 or more. It will be necessary to establish whether such vehicles have a resale value above their part exchange value.

Spare parts inventories

Spare parts inventory total $0.2m and are therefore material to total assets. There is a risk that these have been incorrectly valued at the year-end due to the fact that the year-end count was performed before the year-end. This increases the risk that inventory balances are overstated.

Brand

There is also a risk that the acquired brand, 'Quick Fit' is overstated at the year-end. The balance of $0.7m is material to total assets. According to IAS 38 *Intangible Assets* 'indefinite' does not mean "infinite." Indefinite suggests the company has sufficient resources to maintain the brand strength. However other factors, such as competition, new technology and substitutes, suggest that this could be difficult to maintain in the long term.

Regardless, according to IAS 38 if Queens Cars rebuts the presumption that the useful life is less than 20 years they must still perform an annual impairment review. Therefore there is further risk that the asset is overstated and impairment charges are understated.

Revenue

There is a risk that revenue is misstated due to discounts for cash sales. There is a risk that the sale may be recorded at the original amount, rather than the renegotiated value. There is also an increased risk of theft by sales persons, who could record a higher cash discount in the accounts and keep some of the cash for themselves.

Warranty provision

There is a risk that the warranty provision is understated on the statement of financial position. $0.8m is material to total assets. Whereas revenue has increased by 29% the provision has only increased by 14%, which suggests that the provision does not reflect the increased activity of the business. IAS 37 *Provisions, Contingent Liabilities and Contingent Assets* suggests that a provision should be recorded for all probable liabilities and given that all cars are sold with a warranty there is a suggestion that the provision should be increased accordingly.

New audit client

This is our first year of audit. Given our lack of cumulative audit knowledge and experience there is a greater exposure to audit risk. In response it may be prudent to perform increased substantive procedures this year.

Given the multiple sites it will be necessary to visit at least a sample to assess the accounting/control environment. This could increase the time taken to perform the audit and will have consequences for the budget.

(b) **Audit work on useful life**

- Review the history of the Quick Fit brand. Most importantly assess how long the brand has been trading under that name.
- Inspect advertising invoices to confirm the amount spent on marketing the Quick Fit brand during the accounting year which may extend the life of the brand.
- Compare the amortisation policies of known competitor brands within the same industry. The accounts should be publicly available and an accounting policy note should be included for amortisation of intangibles.
- Inspect any forecasts/budgets available to assess the level of marketing considered necessary to maintain the brand name.
- Compare the performance of the brand on a month by month basis since acquisition to the present day to identify if performance continues to improve, or at least remain healthy to confirm management's assumption of brand strength.
- Inspect a breakdown of the repairs and maintenance account after the year-end to identify any possible concerns over the quality of the replacement parts which would indicate possible impairment of the brand.
- Review industry journals to identify the risk of new entrants or substitute products to the spare parts industry which may indicate impairment of the brand.
- Inspect any impairment tests carried out by management, or make enquiries of management to the same effect.
- Make enquiries of management about the basis of their assumptions with regard to the strength of the brand and their strategy for maintaining its market position.
- Obtain written representations from management to corroborate the results of enquiries with management with regard to areas of judgment and estimation.

Conclusion

The audit risks explained above indicate that the audit of Queens Cars is a relatively high risk engagement. Appropriate audit responses will need to be designed to address these risks and ensure that audit risk is reduced to an acceptable level.

Test your understanding 1 – Financial instruments

(a) **Shares**

- Agree the cash paid of $5 million on the purchase of the shares to bank statements and the cash book.
- Inspect the board minutes of Gig Co, or other internal documents, for evidence that the investment has been classified to be measured at fair value through other comprehensive income (FVOCI).
- If classified to be measured at fair value through other comprehensive income, enquire of management to confirm that they do not intend to trade the shares in the short-term.
- Inspect profit and cash flow forecasts to verify that the shares are not expected to be sold within the next year.
- Review past share sales and assess if Gig Co has a history of trading shares in the short-term.
- Enquire of management if legal or broker fees were incurred on the share issue. If so, agree to invoices and ensure that the treatment is appropriate (they should be expensed if the investment is measured at fair value through profit or loss (FVPL), but added onto the carrying amount if measured at FVOCI).
- Enquire of management as to how the fair value of non-listed shares has been determined.
- Review the fair value calculation for accuracy and assess the reasonableness of the assumptions used. Assess the level of input used as per IFRS 13 *Fair Value Measurement.*
- Inspect the financial statements to see where the revaluation loss has been recorded and assess if this is consistent with the classification of the financial asset (FVPL or FVOCI).
- Inspect the financial statement disclosures, particularly around the level of input used to measure the fair value of the shares.

(b) **Bonds**

- Agree the cash receipt of $10 million to the bank statements and cash book.
- Agree the interest payment to the bank statement and cash book.
- Obtain documentation relating to the bond issue to verify the interest rate and the redemption premium.
- Enquire of management if legal or broker fees were incurred on the bond issue. If so, agree to invoices. An audit adjustment would need to be proposed to deduct these from the initial carrying amount of the liability.
- Recalculate the effective rate of interest on the bonds to confirm arithmetical accuracy.
- Calculate the audit adjustment required so that the finance cost in profit or loss is based on the effective rate of interest.
- Inspect the financial statements to ensure that the liability in respect of the bonds is correctly classified as non-current.

chapter

12

Completion

Chapter learning objectives

This chapter covers syllabus areas:

- D3 – Evaluation and review

Detailed syllabus objectives are provided in the introduction section of the text book.

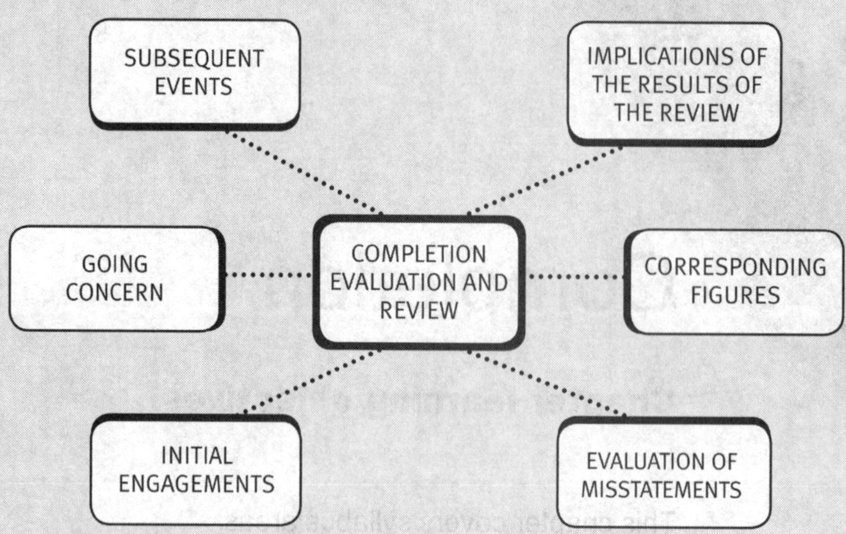

Exam focus

Often a question asks for the 'matters to consider' and 'evidence you would expect to find' in your review of the engagement files. Matters to consider include materiality, accounting treatment required and whether the client is complying with the relevant accounting standard and the risk of material misstatement. However, a requirement could also test a specific area of the completion stage in more detail such as going concern or subsequent events.

1 Subsequent events

ISA 560 *Subsequent Events*, requires the auditor to gather sufficient appropriate evidence that events occurring between the period end and the date of the auditor's report, and facts discovered after the date of the auditor's report have been accounted for in accordance with IAS 10 *Events After the Reporting Period*.

IAS 10 identifies two types of event after the reporting period:

- adjusting
- non-adjusting.

Illustration 1 – Adjusting and non-adjusting events

Adjusting events

These are events that provide additional evidence relating to conditions existing at the reporting date. Such events provide new information about the items included in the financial statements and hence the financial statements should be adjusted to reflect the new information.

Examples of **adjusting** events include:

- Allowances for damaged inventory and doubtful receivables.
- Amounts received or receivable in respect of insurance claims which were being negotiated at the reporting date.
- The determination of the purchase or sale price of non-current assets purchased or sold before the year-end.
- Agreement of a tax liability.
- Discovery of errors/fraud revealing that the financial statements are incorrect.

Non-adjusting events

These are events concerning conditions which arose after the reporting date. In order to prevent the financial statements from presenting a misleading position, disclosure is required in the notes to the financial statements indicating what effect the events may have. Such events, therefore, will not have any effect on items in the statements of financial position or statement of profit or loss for the period.

Examples of **non-adjusting** events include:

- Issue of new share or loan capital.
- Major changes in the composition of the group (for example, mergers, acquisitions or reconstructions).
- Losses of non-current assets or inventory as a result of fires or floods.
- Strikes, government action such as nationalisation.
- Purchases/sales of significant non-current assets.

(IAS 10 *Events After the Reporting Period*)

Auditor responsibilities

Subsequent events

Definition: Subsequent events are events occurring between the date of the financial statements and the date of the auditor's report, and facts that become known to the auditor after the date of the auditor's report

Auditors responsibility

ACTIVE DUTY	PASSIVE DUTY	PASSIVE DUTY
Must obtain sufficient appropriate evidence that all subsequent events that require adjustment or disclosure have been identified.	No requirement to perform audit procedures. If fact becomes known, must take the necessary action.	No requirement to perform audit procedures. If fact becomes known, must take the necessary action.

Between the date of the financial statements and the date of the auditor's report

- The auditor should perform procedures to identify events that might require adjustment or disclosure in the financial statements.
- If material adjusting events are not adjusted for, or material non-adjusting events are not disclosed, the auditor will ask management to make the necessary amendments to the financial statements.
- If the identified adjustments or disclosures necessary are not made then the auditor should consider the impact on the auditor's report and whether a modification is necessary.

Between the date of the auditor's report and the date the financial statements are issued

- The auditor is under no obligation to perform audit procedures after the auditor's report has been issued, however, if they become aware of a fact which would cause them to issue a modified report, they must take action.
- This will normally be in the form of asking the client to amend the financial statements, auditing the amendments and reissuing the auditor's report.
- If management do not amend the financial statements and the auditor's report has not yet been issued to the client, the auditor can still modify the opinion.
- If the auditor's report has been provided to the client, the auditor shall notify management and those charged with governance not to issue the financial statements before the amendments are made.

If the client issues the financial statements despite being requested not to by the auditor, the auditor shall take action to prevent reliance on the auditor's report.

After the financial statements are issued

- The auditor is under no obligation to perform audit procedures after the financial statements have been issued, however, if they become aware of a fact which would have caused them to modify their report, they must take action.
- The auditor should discuss the matter with management and consider if the financial statements require amendment.
- Request management to make the necessary amendments. Management must also take the necessary actions to ensure anyone who is in receipt of the previously issued financial statements is informed.
- The auditor should perform audit procedures on the amendments to ensure they have been put through correctly.
- Issue a new auditor's report including an emphasis of matter paragraph to draw attention to the fact that the financial statements and auditor's report have been reissued.
- If management refuses to recall and amend the financial statements, the auditor shall take action to prevent reliance on the auditor's report.

Subsequent events procedures

- Enquiring into management procedures/systems for the identification of events after the reporting period.
- Reading minutes of members' and directors' meetings.
- Reviewing accounting records including budgets, forecasts, cash flows, management accounts and interim information.
- Reviewing the progress of known risk areas and contingencies.
- Enquiring of the directors if they are aware of any events, adjusting or non-adjusting, that have not yet been included or disclosed in the financial statements.
- Considering relevant information which has come to the auditor's attention, from sources outside the entity, including public knowledge, competitors, suppliers and customers.
- Obtaining a written representation from management confirming that they have informed the auditor of all subsequent events and accounted for them appropriately in the financial statements.

2 Going concern

Going concern is the assumption that the entity will continue in business for the foreseeable future.

Responsibilities

Management

Going concern is a fundamental principle in the preparation of financial statements.

Management are responsible for preparing the financial statements and must make a specific assessment of the entity's ability to continue as a going concern. This requires making judgments about the future outcome of events or conditions which are inherently uncertain.

Management must prepare the financial statements on the most appropriate basis – going concern or break-up basis.

The **'break up' basis** requires that all assets and liabilities are reclassified as 'current' and revalued at net realisable value. Further provisions for liquidation, such as redundancy and legal costs, may also be required.

If management are aware of any material uncertainties which may affect this assessment, IAS 1 *Presentation of Financial Statements* requires them to disclose such uncertainties in the financial statements.

Auditor

ISA 570 (Revised) *Going Concern* states that the auditor shall:

- obtain sufficient appropriate evidence regarding the appropriateness of management's use of the going concern basis of accounting in the preparation of the financial statements.
- conclude on whether a material uncertainty exists about the entity's ability to continue as a going concern.
- report in accordance with ISA 570.

Going concern procedures

Audit procedures to assess management's evaluation of going concern

- Evaluate management's assessment of going concern.
- Assess the same period that management have used in their assessment and if this is less than 12 months, ask management to extend their assessment.

- Consider whether management's assessment includes all relevant information.

Audit procedures to perform where there is doubt over going concern

- Analyse and discuss cash flow, profit and other relevant forecasts with management.
- Analyse and discuss the entity's latest available interim financial statements.
- Review the terms of debentures and loan agreements and determining whether any have been breached.
- Read minutes of the meetings of shareholders, the board of directors and important committees for reference to financing difficulties.
- Enquire of the entity's lawyer regarding the existence of litigation and claims and the reasonableness of management's assessments of their outcome and the estimate of their financial implications.
- Confirm the existence, legality and enforceability of arrangements to provide or maintain financial support with related and third parties and assessing the financial ability of such parties to provide additional funds.
- Review subsequent events to identify those that either mitigate or otherwise affect the entity's ability to continue as a going concern.
- Review correspondence with customers for evidence of any disputes that might impact recoverability of debts and affect future sales.
- Review correspondence with suppliers for evidence of issues regarding payments that might impact the company's ability to obtain supplies or credit.
- Review correspondence with the bank for indication that a bank loan or overdraft may be recalled.
- Obtain written representations from management regarding its plans for the future and how it plans to address the going concern issues.

Exam tip

Audit procedures should focus on cash flows rather than profits. A company can continue to trade as long as it can pay its debts when they fall due. Therefore identify procedures to obtain evidence about the amount of cash that is likely to be received and the amount of cash that it likely to be paid out and consider whether there is any indication of cash flow difficulties.

Disclosures

Disclosures relating to going concern are required to be made by the directors in the following circumstances:

(1) Where there is any **material uncertainty over the future of a company**, the directors should include disclosure in the financial statements. A material uncertainty exists when the magnitude of its potential impact and likelihood of occurrence is such that disclosure of the nature and implications of the uncertainty is necessary for the fair presentation of the financial statements and for the financial statements not to be misleading. The disclosure should explain:

- the principal events or conditions that cast significant doubt on the entity's ability to continue as a going concern and management's plans to deal with them.
- the company may be unable to realise its assets and discharge its liabilities in the normal course of business.

(2) Where the directors have been **unable to assess going concern in the usual way** (e.g. for less than one year beyond the date on which they sign the financial statements), this fact should be disclosed.

(3) Where the **financial statements are prepared on a basis other than the going concern basis**, the basis used should be disclosed.

Audit conclusions and reporting

Based on the audit evidence obtained, the auditor should determine if, in their judgment:

(a) a material uncertainty exists that may cast significant doubt on the entity's ability to continue as a going concern.

(b) the basis of preparing the financial statements is or is not appropriate in the circumstances.

Situation	Impact on audit opinion	Impact on auditor's report
No material uncertainty exists regarding going concern	Unmodified – Financial statements give a true and fair view	INT syllabus: Unmodified UK syllabus: The auditor will report by exception in a section headed 'Conclusions Relating to Going Concern' whether they have anything to add or draw attention to in relation to the directors' statement about the appropriateness of the use of the going concern basis.
Material uncertainty exists and is adequately disclosed by management	Unmodified – Financial statements give a true and fair view	Modified with a section headed: 'Material Uncertainty Related to Going Concern'.
Material uncertainty exists which is not adequately disclosed or is omitted altogether	Modified – qualified or adverse	Modified. Basis for qualified/adverse opinion explaining the going concern issues management have failed to disclose adequately
Company is not a going concern and has prepared the financial statements on the break up basis appropriately and made adequate disclosure of this fact	Unmodified – Financial statements give a true and fair view	Modified with Emphasis of Matter paragraph
Company is not a going concern and has prepared the FS on the going concern basis	Modified – adverse opinion	Modified. Basis for adverse opinion explaining the going concern issues management have failed to account for appropriately
The period assessed by management is less than twelve months from the statement of financial position date and management is unwilling to extend the assessment	Modified – qualified or disclaimer due to an inability to obtain sufficient appropriate audit evidence regarding the use of the going concern assumption	Modified. Basis for qualified/disclaimer opinion explaining that sufficient appropriate evidence was not obtained to form a conclusion on the going concern assumption

Indicators of going concern risk

Auditors should consider the following indicators as possible reasons for doubt over the going concern assumption:

- rapidly increasing costs
- shortages of supplies
- adverse movements in exchange rates
- business failures amongst customers or suppliers
- loan repayments falling due in the near future
- high gearing
- nearness to present borrowing limits
- loss of key staff
- loss of key suppliers/customers
- technical obsolescence of product range
- impact of major litigation
- other fundamental uncertainties

The foreseeable future

The auditor should remain alert to the possibility of events or conditions that will occur beyond management's period of assessment that may bring into question the appropriateness of the going concern assumption. However, due to the uncertainty surrounding such distant events, the indicator needs to be significant to prompt the auditor into further action. If such an event is identified the auditor should request that management consider the significance of the event of condition.

Other than enquiry, the auditor has no other responsibility to perform any other procedures to identify events or conditions beyond the period assessed by management (i.e. at least 12 months from the financial statements date).

UK syllabus: FRC Bulletin 2008/01

During times of economic hardship, particularly during recession, there is always an increase in the number of failed businesses. This does not just include small businesses, even significant institutions fail, for example Lehman Brothers, a large Wall Street investment bank, filed for Chapter 11 bankruptcy protection in September 2008.

During such times auditors must be aware that there is a heightened risk that companies may not be a going concern and that the basis of preparing the financial statements and the nature of disclosures relating to uncertainty must be closely scrutinised.

In response to the economic crisis, several bulletins have been issued to provide guidance to auditors.

FRC Bulletin 2008/01 – Audit issues when financial market conditions are difficult and credit facilities may be restricted (January 2008)

The bulletin focuses on the risks and uncertainties relating to companies that may not be a going concern due to difficulties obtaining finance as a result of the credit crunch and the risk associated with the valuation of investments where the company invested in may have significantly curtailed its operations or may have ceased trading.

Difficulties obtaining credit

Whilst the credit crunch mostly affects financial institutions, risks of material misstatement are also higher in other types of company as credit facilities are significantly more difficult to obtain which may cast significant doubt over the going concern assumption.

The audit partner must have particular regard to:

- his own involvement in the direction, supervision and performance of the audit.
- the capabilities and competence of the audit team.
- consultation with other professionals on difficult and contentious matters.
- the nature and timing of communications with those charged with governance.

Where there is an inability to obtain confirmation of borrowing facilities, this must be disclosed in the financial statements in order to give a true and fair view. The auditor's report may also need to be modified due to insufficient appropriate evidence.

Valuation of investments

Auditors should evaluate whether the significant assumptions used by management are a reasonable basis for the fair value measurements and disclosures, including whether the assumptions reflect current market conditions and information.

Disclosure requirements include:

- Management judgments in the application of accounting policies.
- Information about key assumptions concerning the future.
- As required by IFRS 7 *Financial Instruments: Disclosures*.

UK syllabus: FRC Bulletin 2008/10

FRC Bulletin 2008/10 – Going Concern Issues During the Current Economic Conditions (December 2008)

This bulletin, along with IAASB practice alert Audit Considerations in Respect of Going Concern in the Current Economic Environment (January 2009), explains the particular challenges the current economic conditions create including the need for increased disclosure about going concern and liquidity risk. It aims to raise auditors' awareness about matters relevant to the consideration of the use of the going concern assumption.

UK syllabus: Going concern and liquidity risk

FRC Going Concern and Liquidity Risk: Guidance for Directors of UK Companies 2009

Requires directors to:

- Make a rigorous assessment of whether the company is a going concern by preparing budgets and forecasts and ensure they have adequate borrowing facilities in place.
- Consider all available information for a period of at least 12 months from the date of approval of the financial statements.
- Make balanced proportionate and clear disclosures about going concern.

UK syllabus: ISA (UK) 570 (Revised) Going Concern

ISA (UK) 570 (Revised June 2016) *Going Concern* requires management to assess going concern for a period of at least one year from the (expected) date of approval of the financial statements (rather than 12 months from the reporting date).

The Companies Act 2006 requires company directors to include a business review which describe the principal risks and uncertainties the company faces in the directors' report. The review should be balanced and comprehensive analysis of the development and performance of the business and the position of the company at the year-end. This review will include risks and uncertainties surrounding the going concern status of the company.

For companies that report on compliance with the UK Corporate Governance Code, the auditor shall determine whether they have anything material to add or to draw attention to in the auditor's report on the financial statements in relation to the directors' disclosures on:

- the assessment of the principal risks facing the entity including those that would threaten its business model, future performance, solvency or liquidity
- how the risks are mitigated
- the assessment of the going concern basis and identification of material uncertainties related to going concern
- how they have assessed the prospects of the entity, over what period they have done so and why they consider that period to be appropriate.

The auditor should auditor consider whether they are aware of information that would indicate that the annual report and accounts taken as a whole are not fair, balanced and understandable.

3 Final analytical procedures and review

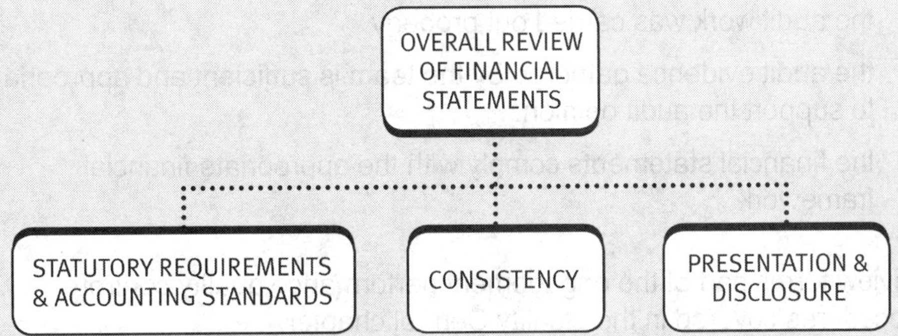

Before forming an opinion on the financial statements and deciding on the wording of the auditor's report, the auditor should conduct **an overall review**.

The auditor should perform the following procedures:

(1) Review the financial statements to ensure:

- compliance with accounting standards and local legislation disclosure requirements. This is sometimes performed using a disclosure checklist.
- accounting policies are sufficiently disclosed and to ensure that they are in accordance with the accounting treatment adopted in the financial statements.
- they adequately reflect the information and explanations previously obtained and conclusions reached during the course of the audit.

(2) Perform analytical procedures to corroborate conclusions formed during the audit and assist when forming an overall conclusion as to whether the financial statements are consistent with the auditor's understanding of the entity.

(3) Review the aggregate of the uncorrected misstatements to assess whether a material misstatement arises. If so, discuss the potential adjustment with management. See below.

The purpose of review procedures

As part of the overall review, the auditor should assess whether:

- initial assessments made at the start of the audit are still valid in light of the information gathered during the audit.
- the audit plan was properly flexed to meet any new circumstances.
- there is a need to revise the nature, timing and extent of the work performed
- the audit work was carried out properly.
- the audit evidence gathered by the team is sufficient and appropriate to support the audit opinion.
- the financial statements comply with the appropriate financial framework.

Review forms part of the engagement performance quality control procedures covered in the Quality Control chapter.

Final analytical procedures

Final analytical procedures involve similar procedures to analytical procedures performed at the planning stage. Differences to note between the two stages:

- At the completion stage the financial statements are almost finalised and therefore there should be no further changes to the figures. At the planning stage the figures were draft and still subject to change.
- The audit work is almost complete and therefore the auditor should have a full understanding of the client's performance during the year. When analysing the figures, the reasons for the movements should be documented on the audit file and as a result this analysis should be confirming what the auditor already knows.

If something new is identified, or if a relationship between balances is not understood, it will highlight that further work is necessary and the auditor does not yet have sufficient appropriate evidence for the opinion.

The auditor will calculate the movements from year to year and will check that the justifications for any unusual fluctuations are on file.

Key ratios such as GPM, receivables days, payables days, inventory days will be calculated and reasons for movements tied through to the audit file to ensure the outcome is consistent with what is recorded on file.

A review of the financial statements as a whole will be performed to ensure the presentation complies with the applicable financial reporting framework.

4 Evaluation of misstatements

The auditor must consider the effect of misstatements on both the audit procedures performed and ultimately, if uncorrected, on the financial statements as a whole. Guidance on how this is performed is given in ISA 450 *Evaluation of Misstatements Identified During the Audit.*

In order to achieve this the auditor must:

- Accumulate a record of all identified misstatements, unless they are clearly trivial.
- Consider if the existence of such misstatements indicates that others may exist, which, when aggregated with other misstatements, could be considered material.
- If so, consider if the audit plan and strategy need to be revised.

- Assess the materiality of the matter (both quantitative and qualitative).
- Report all misstatements identified during the course of the audit to an appropriate level of **management** on a timely basis.
- Request that **all** misstatements are corrected.
- If management refuses to correct some or all of the misstatements the auditor should consider their reasons for refusal and take these into account when considering if the financial statements are free from material misstatement.

Evaluation of uncorrected misstatements

If management have failed to correct all of the misstatements reported to them, the auditor should:

- Revisit their assessment of materiality to determine whether it is still appropriate in the circumstances.
- Determine whether the uncorrected misstatements, either individually or in aggregate, are material to the financial statements as a whole. In so doing the auditor must consider both the size and nature of the misstatements and the effect of misstatements related to prior periods (e.g. on corresponding figures, comparatives and opening balances). If an individual misstatement is considered material it cannot be offset by other misstatements.
- Report the uncorrected misstatements to **those charged with governance** and explain the effect this will have on the audit opinion.
- Request a written representation from those charged with governance that they believe the effects of uncorrected misstatements are immaterial.

Evaluating misstatements - example

You are at the completion stage of the audit of a client. The PBT for the year is $8m and total assets are $35m. The following matters have not been corrected by management and have been left for your attention:

(1) A major customer has gone into liquidation owing an amount of $200,000 which has not been written off.

(2) A provision of $300,000 has not been recognised.

The irrecoverable debt of $200,000 represents 2.5% of PBT and 0.57% of total assets therefore is not material.

The provision of $300,000 represents 3.75% of PBT and 0.86% of total assets therefore is not material.

Cumulatively they have a bigger effect on the financial statements:

$500,000 represents 6.25% of PBT and 1.4% of total assets which is material. The two amounts will need to be adjusted to avoid a modified opinion.

The auditor should ask for both issues to be corrected in accordance with ISA 450.

5 Initial engagements – audit considerations

ISA 510 *Initial Engagements – Opening Balances* requires that when auditors take on a new client, they must ensure that:

- opening balances do not contain material misstatements.
- prior period closing balances have been correctly brought forward or, where appropriate, restated.
- appropriate accounting policies have been consistently applied, or changes adequately disclosed.

Audit procedures

Where the prior period was audited by another auditor or unaudited, the auditors will need to perform additional work in order to satisfy themselves regarding the opening position. Such work would include:

- Consulting the client's management.
- Reviewing records and accounting and control procedures in the preceding period.
- Consulting with the previous auditor and reviewing (with their permission) their working papers and relevant management letters.
- Substantive testing of any opening balances where the above procedures are unsatisfactory.

Some evidence of the opening position will also usually be gained from the audit work performed in the current period.

[UK syllabus: The predecessor auditor is required to provide access to all relevant information concerning the entity including information concerning the most recent audit in accordance with ISQC 1 (UK).]

Opening balances – implications for the auditor's report

If there is an inability to obtain sufficient appropriate evidence over the opening balances, a qualified or disclaimer of opinion will be issued.

If the opening balances are materially misstated or the accounting policies have not been consistently applied, a qualified or adverse opinion will be issued.

If a prior year adjustment has been put through to correct material misstatements arising in the prior year, an unmodified opinion can be issued. An emphasis of matter paragraph will be needed to draw attention to the disclosure note explaining the reason for the restatement of the opening balances.

Initial engagements

Considerations:

- Were the previous financial statements audited?
- If the previous financial statements were audited, was the opinion modified?
- If the previous opinion was modified, has the matter been resolved since then?
- Were any adjustments made as a result of the audit? If so, has the client adjusted their accounting ledgers as well as the financial statements?

Difficulties may arise where the prior period auditor's report was modified and the matter remains unresolved. If the matter is material to the current period's financial statements then the current auditor's report will also need to be modified.

For example, if there was a modification on the grounds of a material misstatement of closing inventory in the prior period, this will affect the current period's statement of profit or loss. This is because last year's closing inventory is this year's opening inventory and the auditor may need to modify this year's auditor's report on that basis.

6 Corresponding figures and comparative financial statements

ISA 710 *Comparative Information – Corresponding Figures and Comparative Financial Statements* requires that comparative figures comply with the identified financial reporting framework and that they are free from material misstatement.

Two categories of comparatives exist:

- *Corresponding figures* where preceding period figures are included as an integral part of the current period financial statements (i.e. figures shown to the right of the current year figures).

- *Comparative financial statements* where preceding period amounts are included for comparison with the current period (i.e. the prior year's full financial statements are included within the current year annual report).

Corresponding figures

Audit procedures in respect of corresponding figures should be significantly less than for the current period and are limited to ensuring that:

- Corresponding figures have been correctly reported and appropriately classified.
- Accounting policies are consistently applied.
- Corresponding figures agree to the prior period financial statements.

Comparative financial statements

Sufficient appropriate evidence should be gathered to ensure that:

- Comparative financial statements meet the requirements of an applicable financial reporting framework.
- Accounting policies are consistently applied.
- Comparative figures agree to the prior period financial statements.

Comparative information and the auditor's report

Corresponding figures and the auditor's report

The auditor's report only refers to the financial statements of the current period which encompasses the prior period figures. If a matter in respect of which the prior period auditor's report was modified is unresolved, the current auditor's report may also have to be modified in respect of corresponding figures.

Comparative financial statements and the auditor's report

Where figures are presented as comparative financial statements the auditor should issue a report in which the comparatives are specifically identified because the auditor's opinion is expressed individually on the financial statements of each period presented.

It is therefore possible for the auditor to express a modified opinion with respect to one year of financial statements while issuing a different report on the other financial statements.

Approach to completion questions in the exam

Completion questions usually ask for **matters to consider and evidence you would expect to find during your review of the audit file**.

The approach the examiner expects you to take when dealing with matters is:

- **M**ateriality assessment – calculate whether the issue is material.
- **A**ccounting treatment – state what the relevant accounting standard requires and whether the client is complying with that treatment. If they are not compliant, state what they are doing wrong.
- **R**isk of material misstatement – state which balances or disclosures in the financial statements will be materially misstated as a result.

Evidence refers to the audit evidence that should have been obtained and put on file by the auditor performing the work. Evidence is essentially the audit procedure but without the action e.g.

- Copies of board minutes to identify management discussions about the legal provision.
- Copies of bank statements to verify the payment was made by the client during the year.
- Notes of discussions with management regarding their approach for determining the estimate.

Note how the examples above still make reference to the reason for obtaining the documentation. Sometimes you may be asked for procedures instead of evidence.

Procedures should be an action, applied to a source, to achieve an objective e.g.

- Review board minutes to identify management discussions about the legal provision.
- Inspect bank statements to verify the payment was made by the client during the year.
- Discuss with management their approach for determining the estimate.

Test your understanding 1

You are the manager responsible for the audit of Phoenix, a private limited liability company, which manufactures super alloys from imported zinc and aluminium. The company operates three similar foundries at different sites under the direction of Troy Pitz, the chief executive. The draft accounts for the year ended 31 March 20X4 show profit before taxation of $1.7m (20X3 – $1.5m). The audit senior has produced a schedule of 'Points for the Attention of the Audit Manager' as follows:

(a) A trade investment in 60,000 $1 ordinary shares of Pegasus, one of the company's major shipping contractors, is included in the statement of financial position at cost of $80,000. In May 20X4, the published financial statements of Pegasus as at 30 September 20X3 show only a small surplus of net assets. A recent press report now suggests that Pegasus is insolvent and has ceased to trade. Although dividends declared by Pegasus in respect of earlier years have not yet been paid, Phoenix has included $15,000 of dividends receivable in its draft accounts as at 31 March 20X4.

(6 marks)

(b) Current liabilities include a $500,000 provision for future maintenance. This represents the estimated cost of overhauling the blast furnaces and other foundry equipment. The overhaul is planned for August 20X4 when all foundry workers take two weeks annual leave.

(7 marks)

(c) All industrial waste from the furnaces ('clinker') is purchased by Cleanaway, a government-approved disposal company, under a five-year contract that is due for renewal later this year. A recent newspaper article states that 'substantial fines have been levied on Cleanaway for illegal dumping'. Troy Pitz is the majority shareholder of Cleanaway.

(7 marks)

Required:

For each of the above points:

(i) comment on the matters that you would consider; and

(ii) state the audit evidence that you would expect to find, in undertaking your review of the audit working papers and financial statements of Phoenix.

(Total: 20 marks)

Test your understanding 2

You are the manager responsible for the audit of Aspersion, a limited liability company, which mainly provides national cargo services with a small fleet of aircraft. The draft accounts for the year ended 30 September 20X3 show profit before taxation of $2.7m (20X2: $2.2m) and total assets of $10.4m (20X2: $9.8m).

The following issues are outstanding and have been left for your attention:

(a) The sale of a cargo carrier to Abra, a private limited company, during the year resulted in a loss on disposal of $400,000. The aircraft cost $1.2 million when it was purchased nine years ago and was being depreciated on a straight-line basis over 20 years. The minutes of the board meeting at which the sale was approved record that Aspersion's finance director, Iain Joiteon, has a 30% equity interest in Abra.

(7 marks)

(b) As well as cargo carriers, Aspersion owns two light aircraft which were purchased at the end of 20X0 to provide business passenger flights to a small island under a three year service contract. It is now known that the contract will not be renewed when it expires at the end of March 20X4. The aircraft, which cost $450,000 each, are being depreciated over 15 years.

(7 marks)

(c) Deferred tax amounting to $570,000 as at 30 September 20X3 has been calculated relating to tangible non-current assets at a tax rate of 30% using the full provision method (IAS 12 *Income Taxes*). On 1 December 20X3, the government announced an increase in the corporate income tax rate to 34%. The directors are proposing to adjust the draft accounts for the further liability arising.

(6 marks)

Required:

For each of the above points:

(i) comment on the matters that you should consider; and

(ii) state the audit evidence that you should expect to find, in undertaking your review of the audit working papers and financial statements of Aspersion.

(Total: 20 marks)

7 Chapter summary

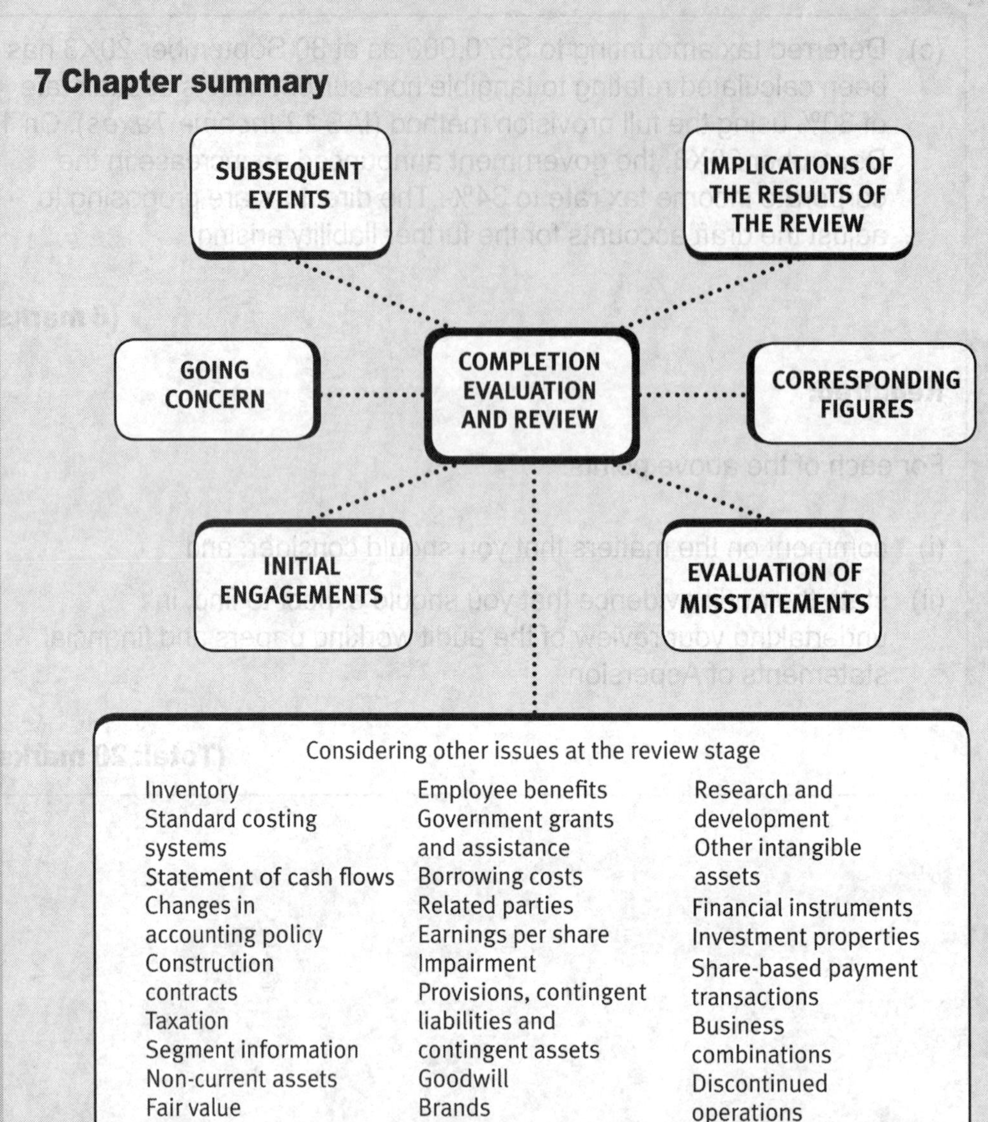

Test your understanding answers

Test your understanding 1

(a) **Trade investment**

(i) **Matters**

Assuming that Pegasus is insolvent (e.g. a receiver or liquidator has been appointed) this is an adjusting event (IAS 10 *Events After the Reporting Period*).

As the recoverable amounts of the investment and dividends receivable are likely to be nil, they should be written off.

The total expense of $95,000 represents 5.6% of draft profit before tax and is therefore material. As is it not expected to recur, separate disclosure (IAS 1 *Presentation of Financial Statements*) may be appropriate to explaining Phoenix's performance for the year.

There is a risk that investments and receivables are overstated if these amounts are not written off.

As the adjustments are material, a qualified opinion would need to be issued with the 'except for' wording.

(ii) **Audit evidence**

- A copy of the press report confirming the liquidation of Pegasus.
- The audited accounts of Pegasus for the year ended 30 September 20X3 showing whether there are assets with market values in excess of book values.
- The receiver's (or liquidator's) statement of affairs indicating whether any distribution is possible.
- If a meeting of the shareholders of Pegasus has been held to consider the company's state of affairs, a copy of the minutes (may be obtained by Phoenix).
- Notes of discussions with the client as to who, if anyone, has replaced Pegasus as one of their major shipping contractors. Also, whether any consignments have been held up while negotiating for an alternative shipping contractor.

(b) **Future maintenance**

(i) **Matters**

The provision represents 29% of draft profit before tax and is therefore material.

This provision does not appear to meet the definition of IAS 37 *Provisions, Contingent Liabilities and Contingent Assets* which requires there to be an obligation at the year-end to make payment which is probable and can be measured reliably.

Overhaul expenditure to restore or maintain the future economic benefits expected from the plant and equipment should normally be recognised as an expense when it is incurred.

The components (blast furnace interiors) which require replacement are separate assets that should be depreciated over the replacement cycle. To the extent that the $500k includes the cost of replacing separate assets, it represents future capital cost.

It is not clear whether an obligation exists at the year-end, for example if there was industry legislation requiring the overhaul to take place within a certain timescale.

If the provision is not allowable under IAS 37 and is not released, provisions will be overstated and profits will be understated.

Draft profit before tax ($1.7m) shows a 13% increase on the previous year. If adjustments are made for points (1) and (2), profit will be increased by at least $400,000 (i.e. (1) $95k decrease plus (2) $500k increase). Profit before tax of $2.1m would be a 40% increase on the prior year.

The management of Phoenix may have decided that $1.7m is what is to be reported. Management may have made the future maintenance provision as a way of 'setting aside' a reserve. For example, in anticipation of increased costs expected to arise in respect of waste disposal in (3).

Tutorial note: It is a 'higher skill' to be able to demonstrate an ability to stand back from the individual items and take an overall view in this part of the question, considering the overall impact on the draft PBT.

(ii) **Audit evidence**

- Client's schedule showing the make-up of provision.
- Notes of discussions with senior management about their reasons for having made the provision and whether any costs have been contracted for.
- External tenders or quotes for subcontracted work (and/or internal costings) to verify the amount.
- Prior year working papers (and/or the permanent audit file) showing the cost and frequency of overhauls in previous periods (whether all sites done at once or on a cyclical basis).

(c) **Cleanaway**

(i) **Matters**

The matter is likely to be material as all Phoenix's industrial waste is disposed of by Cleanaway. The issue is material by nature as Cleanaway is a related party through Troy Pitz. Troy Pitz has authority and responsibility for Phoenix's operational activities (as chief executive) and a controlling interest in Cleanaway.

IAS 24 *Related Party Disclosures* requires the following to be disclosed in the notes to the financial statements:

- the nature of the related party relationship
- the amount of the transactions entered into
- any balances outstanding at the year-end.

Whether Phoenix has been implicated in Cleanaway's illegal dumping (e.g. by Phoenix's clinker having been dumped, or by Troy Pitz's relationship with the two companies).

Whether the integrity of Troy Pitz has been questioned (either by the media or other key personnel in Phoenix) and, if so, its impact on the audit. For example, any assessment of control risk as less than high should be reassessed in the light of his role in the control environment.

If the contract is not renewed a legal alternative will need to be found for disposal of clinker, for example, another approved provider of waste disposal services or a suitable landfill site (taxes may be substantial), otherwise there may be doubts about going concern.

Possible consequences for Phoenix of the contract being renewed:

- A substantial increase in costs of disposal, e.g. because terms were last agreed five years ago.
- Loss of customer goodwill through associations with Cleanaway.
- Risk of investigation by a government agency into the company's environmental practices.

(ii) **Audit evidence**

- A copy of the contract, in particular whether:
  - early termination could be an option for Phoenix (in the light of Cleanaway's illegal activities).
  - any clauses are relevant to its renewal (e.g. restricting price increases).
- Newspaper articles including any editorial comment or letters from Cleanaway or Troy Pitz regarding the issue.
- Notes of discussions with senior management (Troy Pitz and others) whether a suitable alternative service provider exists.
- Prior year working papers and financial statements to identify the disclosure made last year.
- Copies of board minutes to indicate what action, if any, management propose to take to mitigate the adverse publicity surrounding Cleanaway.

Test your understanding 2

(a) **Related party transaction – sale of cargo carrier**

Matters

The $400,000 loss represents 15% of profit before tax and is therefore material. Disclosure as a separate line item may therefore be appropriate.

The cargo carrier was in use for 9 years and would have had a carrying value of $720,000 at 30 September 20X2.

Abra appears to be a related party as lain:

- is one of the key management personnel of Aspersion (being the finance director), and
- has an equity interest in Abra which is presumed to constitute significant influence (being greater than 20%).

The related party relationship and the sale of the cargo carrier to Abra should be disclosed in a note to the financial statements for the year to 30 September 20X3. The elements of such a material transaction which are likely to be necessary (for an understanding of the financial statements) are:

- the amount(s) involved (i.e. sale proceeds and loss).
- any outstanding balance of amounts due from Abra.
- the nature of the relationship.

If suitable disclosure is not made, there will be a material misstatement with regard to non-compliance with IAS 24 *Related Party Disclosures*.

The reason for the loss on sale should also be considered e.g. whether the:

- sale was below market value (if the sale to the related party was not at arm's length)
- aircraft had a bad maintenance history (or was otherwise impaired)
- useful life of a cargo carrier is less than 20 years.

If the latter, it is likely that non-current assets are materially overstated in respect of cargo carriers still in use. This would lead to a risk of overstatement of non current assets and profits as the depreciation policies may not be appropriate and compliant with IAS 16 *Property plant and equipment*.

(ii) **Audit evidence**

- Copy of bank statements confirming the sales proceeds.
- Copy of sales invoice confirming the party it was sold to and the amount.
- Copy of board minutes authorising the disposal at the low value.
- Notes of discussions with management regarding the appropriateness of depreciation policies for other assets.
- Documentation of analysis of profits/losses on disposal in previous years to obtain further evidence that depreciation policies are not appropriate.
- Documentation noting whether the related party transaction has been disclosed in the financial statements.

(b) **Impairment – light aircraft**

(i) **Matters**

The annual depreciation charge for each of these two aircraft is \$30,000 (1/15 × 450,000). The aircraft have been depreciated for only 2½ years to 30 September 20X3 (assuming time apportionment in 20X1 when the aircraft were brought into use) and have a total carrying amount of \$750,000 (2 × [450,000 – (2½ × 30,000)]). This represents 7.2% of total assets and is therefore material.

Tutorial note: Alternatively it could be assumed that a full year's depreciation was charged in the year to 30.9.X1 (i.e. three years' accumulated depreciation to 30.9.X3).

The aircraft were purchased for a specific use which will cease six months after the reporting date. The value of the aircraft may be impaired and Aspersion should have made a formal estimate of their recoverable amount (IAS 36 *Impairment of Assets*).

The auditor should consider management's intentions, for example:

- to sell the aircraft
- to find an alternative use for the aircraft (e.g. providing other business or pleasure flights).

If the client can sell the aircraft for more than the current carrying value or if the aircraft can be used in another part of the business, the assets may not be impaired.

There is a risk that non-current assets and profits are overstated if an impairment charge is necessary but hasn't been made.

Additional point: If the passenger business constitutes a business segment, cessation of the contract may result in a discontinued operation (IFRS 5 *Non-current Assets Held for Sale and Discontinued Operations*).

(ii) **Audit evidence**

- A copy of the service contract confirming expiry in March 20X4.
- Physical inspection of aircraft (evidence of existence and condition at 30 September 20X3).
- Notes of discussions with Aspersion's management concerning negotiations for:
  - the sale of the aircraft, or
  - obtaining new service contracts.
- Extracts from any correspondence regarding any new contract or sale.
- A copy of any (draft) agreement for:
  - the sale of the aircraft after the contract expires
  - new business or pleasure contracts.
- Discounted cash flow projections for any proposed new venture/contracts (i.e. value in use).
- Comparison of projected cash flows with budgets and assumptions (e.g. aircraft days available and average daily utilisation per aircraft).

(c) **Deferred tax – change in tax rate**

(i) **Matters**

The total provision amounts to 21% of PBT and is therefore material. (However the deferred tax expense/income for the year may not have been material.)

The increase in liability if calculated at 34% ($570,000 (34/30 – 1) = $76,000) represents 2.8% of PBT. Considered in isolation, this amount is not material.

Under IAS 12 *Income Taxes* the tax rate in force at the reporting date should be used for the calculation. The increase in tax rate announced on 1 December is a non-adjusting event (IAS 10 *Events After the Reporting Period*).

If the directors adjust the draft accounts there will be non-compliance with IAS 10 and IAS 12. The tax expense and associated liability will be misstated as a result.

(ii) **Audit evidence**

- A copy of the computations of:
  - deferred tax liability (SFP)
  - current tax expense (SPL)
  - deferred tax expense/income.
- Agreement of tax rate(s) to tax legislation.
- Reconciliation between tax expense and accounting profit multiplied by the applicable tax rate.
- Schedules of carrying amount (i.e. cost of revalued amounts net of accumulated depreciation) of non-current assets agreed to:
  - the asset register (individual assets and in total)
  - general ledger account balances (totals).
- Completed audit program for non-current assets (e.g. inspecting invoices for additions, agreeing depreciation rates to prior year accounting policies, etc).
- Client's schedules of tax base agreed to:
  - the asset register (for completeness)
  - prior year working papers (completeness and accuracy of brought forward balances).

chapter

13

Auditors' reports

Chapter learning objectives

This chapter covers syllabus areas:

- F1 – Auditor's reports

Detailed syllabus objectives are provided in the introduction section of the text book.

Exam focus

Reporting could appear in any question in the exam, and could appear as a requirement within more than one question. Therefore it is important you are comfortable with this syllabus area. Common requirements in the past have asked for a critical evaluation of draft extracts of the auditor's report or for the reporting implications of issues which remain unresolved.

1 The objectives of the auditor

According to ISA 700 (Revised) *Forming an Opinion and Reporting on Financial Statements,* the auditor's objectives are:

- To form an opinion on the financial statements based on an evaluation of the conclusions drawn from the audit evidence obtained, and
- To express clearly that opinion through a written report that also describes the basis for that opinion.

When the auditor concludes that the financial statements are prepared, in all material respects, in accordance with the applicable financial reporting framework they issue an **unmodified opinion** in the auditor's report.

If there are no other matters which the auditor wishes to draw to the attention of the users, they will issue an **unmodified report**.

2 The independent auditor's report

ISA 700 (Revised) and ISA (UK) 700 prescribe the following structures for the auditor's report:

INT syllabus **ISA 700 (Revised)**	**UK syllabus** **ISA (UK) 700**
1. Title	1. Title
2. Addressee	2. Addressee
3. Auditor's opinion	3. Auditor's opinion
4. Basis for opinion	4. Basis for opinion
5. [Material uncertainty related to going concern] (if applicable)	5. Conclusions relating to going concern/[Material uncertainty related to going concern]

6. [Emphasis of matter] (if applicable)	6. [Emphasis of matter] (if applicable)
7. Listed entities: Key audit matters	7. Listed entities: Key audit matters Our application of materiality An overview of the scope of our audit
8. Other information	8. Other information
9. Responsibilities of management	9. Opinions on other matters prescribed by the Companies Act 2006
10. Auditor's responsibilities	10. Matters on which we are required to report by exception
11. Report on other legal and regulatory requirements	11. Responsibilities of directors
12. [Other matter] (if applicable in accordance with ISA 706)	12. Auditor's responsibilities
13. Name of the engagement partner Signature	13. [Other matter] (if applicable in accordance with ISA (UK) 706)
14. Auditor's address	14. Signature
15. Date	15. Auditor's address
	16. Date

INT syllabus: Illustrative auditor's report

INDEPENDENT AUDITOR'S REPORT

To the Shareholders of XYZ Company

Report on the Audit of the Financial Statements [sub-title is not included if there is no separate Report on Other Legal and Regulatory Requirements]

Opinion

We have audited the financial statements of the XYZ Company (the Company), which comprise the statement of financial position as at 31 December, 20X4, and the statement of comprehensive income, statement of changes in equity and statement of cash flows for the year then ended, and notes to the financial statements, including a summary of significant accounting policies.

In our opinion, the accompanying financial statements present fairly, in all material respects, (or give a true and fair view of) the financial position of the Company as at December 31, 20X4, and its performance and its cash flows for the year then ended in accordance with International Financial Reporting Standards.

Basis for Opinion

We conducted our audit in accordance with International Standards on Auditing (ISAs). Our responsibilities under those standards are further described in the Auditor's Responsibilities for the Audit of the Financial Statements section of our report. We are independent of the Company in accordance with the ethical requirements that are relevant to our audit of the financial statements in [jurisdiction], and we have fulfilled our other ethical responsibilities in accordance with these requirements. We believe that the audit evidence we have obtained is sufficient and appropriate to provide a basis for our opinion.

Key Audit Matters

Key audit matters are those matters that, in our professional judgment, were of most significance in our audit of the financial statements of the current period. These matters were addressed in the context of our audit of the financial statements as a whole, and in forming our opinion thereon, and we do not provide a separate opinion on these matters.

[Description of each key audit matter in accordance with ISA 701]

Other information

Management is responsible for the other information. The other information comprises the [description of other information, for example] Chairman's statement, but does not include the financial statements and the auditor's report thereon.

Our opinion on the financial statements does not cover the other information and we do not express any form of assurance conclusion thereon.

In connection with our audit of the financial statements, our responsibility is to read the other information and, in doing so, consider whether the other information is materially inconsistent with the financial statements or our knowledge obtained in the audit or otherwise appears to be materially misstated. If based on the work we have performed, we conclude that there is a material misstatement of this information, we are required to report that fact. We have nothing to report in this regard.

Responsibilities of Management and Those Charged With Governance for the Financial Statements

Management is responsible for the preparation and fair presentation of these financial statements in accordance with International Financial Reporting Standards, and for such internal control as management determines is necessary to enable the preparation of financial statements that are free from material misstatement, whether due to fraud or error.

In preparing the financial statements, management is responsible for assessing the Company's ability to continue as a going concern, disclosing as applicable, matters related to going concern and using the going concern basis of accounting unless management either intends to liquidate the Company or to cease operations, or has no realistic alternative but to do so.

Those charged with governance are responsible for overseeing the Company's financial reporting process.

Auditor's Responsibilities for the Audit of the Financial Statements

Our objectives are to obtain reasonable assurance about whether the financial statements as a whole are free from material misstatement, whether due to fraud or error, and to issue an auditor's report that includes our opinion. Reasonable assurance is a high level of assurance, but is not a guarantee that an audit conducted in accordance with ISAs will always detect a material misstatement when it exists. Misstatements can arise from fraud or error and are considered material if, individually or in the aggregate, they could reasonably be expected to influence the economic decisions of users taken on the basis of these financial statements.

As part of an audit in accordance with ISAs, we exercise professional judgment and maintain professional scepticism throughout the audit. We also:

- Identify and assess the risks of material misstatement of the financial statements, whether due to fraud or error, design and perform audit procedures responsive to those risks, and obtain audit evidence that is sufficient and appropriate to provide a basis for our opinion. The risk of not detecting a material misstatement resulting from fraud is higher than for one resulting from error, as fraud may involve collusion, forgery, intentional omissions, misrepresentations, or the override of internal control.
- Obtain an understanding of internal control relevant to the audit in order to design audit procedures that are appropriate in the circumstances, but not for the purpose of expressing an opinion on the effectiveness of the Company's internal control.
- Evaluate the appropriateness of accounting policies used and the reasonableness of accounting estimates and related disclosures made by management.
- Conclude on the appropriateness of management's use of the going concern basis of accounting and, based on the audit evidence obtained, whether a material uncertainty exists related to events or conditions that may cast significant doubt on the Company's ability to continue as a going concern. If we conclude that a material uncertainty exists, we are required to draw attention in our auditor's report to the related disclosures in the financial statements or, if such disclosures are inadequate, to modify our opinion. Our conclusions are based on the audit evidence obtained up to the date of our auditor's report. However, future events or conditions may cause the Company to cease trading as a going concern.
- Evaluate the overall presentation, structure and content of the financial statements, including the disclosures, and whether the financial statements represent the underlying transactions and events in a manner that achieves fair presentation.

We communicate with those charged with governance regarding, among other matters, the planned scope and timing of the audit and significant findings, including any significant deficiencies in internal control that we identify during our audit.

We also provide those charged with governance with a statement that we have complied with relevant ethical requirements regarding independence, and to communicate with them all relationships and other matters that may reasonably be thought to bear on our independence, and where applicable, related safeguards.

From the matters communicated with those charged with governance, we determine those matters that were of most significance in the audit of the financial statements of the current period and are therefore the key audit matters. We describe these matters in our auditor's report unless law or regulation precludes public disclosure about the matter or when, in extremely rare circumstances, we determine that a matter should not be communicated in our report because the adverse consequences of doing so would reasonably be expected to outweigh the public interest benefits of such communication.

Report on Other Legal and Regulatory Requirements

[*As required by local law, regulation or national auditing standards*]

The engagement partner on the audit resulting in this independent auditor's report is [name].

Signature (the name of audit firm, the name of the auditor, or both)

Auditor address

Date

UK syllabus: Illustrative auditors' report

INDEPENDENT AUDITOR'S REPORT TO THE MEMBERS OF XYZ PLC

Opinion

We have audited the financial statements of (name of company) for the year ended ... which comprise [specify the titles of the primary statements such as the Statement of Financial Position, the Statement of Comprehensive Income, the Statement of Cash Flows, the Statement of Changes in Equity] and notes to the financial statements, including a summary of significant accounting policies. The financial reporting framework that has been applied in their preparation is applicable law and International Financial Reporting Standards as adopted by the European Union.

In our opinion the financial statements:

- give a true and fair view of the state of the company's affairs as at [date] and of its [profit/loss] for the year then ended;
- have been properly prepared in accordance with IFRS Standards as adopted by the European Union; and
- have been prepared in accordance with the requirements of the Companies Act 2006.

Basis for opinion

We conducted our audit in accordance with International Standards on Auditing (UK) (ISAs (UK)) and applicable law. Our responsibilities under those standards are further described in the Auditor's responsibilities for the audit of the financial statements section of our report. We are independent of the company in accordance with the ethical requirements that are relevant to our audit of the financial statements in the UK, including the FRC's Ethical Standard as applied to listed entities, and we have fulfilled our other ethical responsibilities in accordance with these requirements. We believe that the audit evidence we have obtained is sufficient and appropriate to provide a basis for our opinion.

Conclusions relating to going concern

We have nothing to report in respect of the following matters in relation to which the ISAs (UK) require us to report to you where:

- the directors' use of the going concern basis of accounting in the preparation of the financial statements is not appropriate; or
- the directors have not disclosed in the financial statements any identified material uncertainties that may cast significant doubt about the company's ability to continue to adopt the going concern basis of accounting for a period of at least twelve months from the date when the financial statements are authorised for issue.

Key audit matters

Key audit matters are those matters that, in our professional judgment, were of most significance in our audit of the financial statements of the current period and include the most significant assessed risks of material misstatement (whether or not due to fraud) we identified, including those which had the greatest effect on: the overall audit strategy, the allocation of resources in the audit; and directing the efforts of the engagement team. These matters were addressed in the context of our audit of the financial statements as a whole, and in forming our opinion thereon, and we do not provide a separate opinion on these matters.

[Description of each key audit matter in accordance with ISA (UK) 701.]

Our application of materiality

[Explanation of how the auditor applied the concept of materiality in planning and performing the audit. This is required to include the threshold used by the auditor as being materiality for the financial statements as a whole but may include other relevant disclosures.]

An overview of the scope of our audit

[Overview of the scope of the audit, including an explanation of how the scope addressed each key audit matter and was influenced by the auditor's application of materiality.]

Other information

The directors are responsible for the other information. The other information comprises the information included in the annual report, other than the financial statements and our auditor's report thereon. Our opinion on the financial statements does not cover the other information and, except to the extent otherwise explicitly stated in our report, we do not express any form of assurance conclusion thereon.

In connection with our audit of the financial statements, our responsibility is to read the other information and, in doing so, consider whether the other information is materially inconsistent with the financial statements or our knowledge obtained in the audit or otherwise appears to be materially misstated. If we identify such material inconsistencies or apparent material misstatements, we are required to determine whether there is a material misstatement in the financial statements or a material misstatement of the other information. If, based on the work we have performed, we conclude that there is a material misstatement of this other information, we are required to report that fact. We have nothing to report in this regard.

Opinions on other matters prescribed by the Companies Act 2006

In our opinion, based on the work undertaken in the course of the audit:

- the information given in the strategic report and directors' report for the financial year for which the financial statements are prepared is consistent with the financial statements; and
- the strategic report and director's report have been prepared in accordance with applicable legal requirements.

Matters on which we are required to report by exception

In the light of the knowledge and understanding of the company and its environment obtained in the course of the audit, we have not identified material misstatements in the strategic report or the directors' report.

We have nothing to report in respect of the following matters in relation to which the Companies Act 2006 requires us to report to you if, in our opinion:

- adequate accounting records have not been kept, or returns adequate for our audit have not been received from branches not visited by us; or
- the financial statements are not in agreement with accounting records and returns: or

- certain disclosures of directors' remuneration specified by law are not made; or
- we have not received all the information and explanations we require for our audit.

Responsibilities of directors

As explained more fully in the directors' responsibilities statement [set out on page …], the directors are responsible for the preparation of the financial statements and for being satisfied that they give a true and fair view, and for such internal control as the directors determine is necessary to enable the preparation of financial statements that are free from material misstatement, whether due to fraud or error.

In preparing the financial statements, the directors are responsible for assessing the company's ability to continue as a going concern, disclosing, as applicable, matters related to going concern and using the going concern basis of accounting unless the directors either intend to liquidate the company or to cease operations, or have no realistic alternative but to do so.

Auditor's responsibilities for the audit of the financial statements

Our objectives are to obtain reasonable assurance about whether the financial statements as a whole are free from material misstatement, whether due to fraud or error, and to issue an auditor's report that includes our opinion. Reasonable assurance is a high level of assurance, but is not a guarantee that an audit conducted in accordance with ISAs (UK) will always detect a material misstatement when it exists. Misstatements can arise from fraud or error and are considered material if, individually or in the aggregate, they could reasonably be expected to influence the economic decisions of users taken on the basis of these financial statements.

A further description of our responsibilities for the audit of the financial statements is located on the Financial Reporting Council's website at: [website link]. This description forms part of our auditor's report.

[Signature]
John Smith (Senior statutory auditor)
For and on behalf of ABC LLP, Statutory Auditor
Address
Date

Explanation of the sections

Section	Purpose
1. Title	To clearly identify the report as an Independent Auditor's Report.
2. Addressee	To identify the intended user of the report.
3. Auditor's opinion	Provides the auditor's conclusion as to whether or not the financial statements give a true and fair view.
4. Basis for opinion	Provides a description of the professional standards applied during the audit to provide confidence to users that the report can be relied upon.
5. Key audit matters	To draw attention to any other significant matters of which the users should be aware to aid their understanding of the entity. (**Note:** This section is only compulsory for listed entities)
6. Other information	To clarify that management are responsible for the other information. The auditor's opinion does not cover the other information and the auditor's responsibility is only to read the other information and report in accordance with ISA 720.
7. Responsibilities of management	To clarify that management are responsible for preparing the financial statements and for the internal controls. Included to help minimise the expectations gap.

8. Auditor responsibilities	To clarify that the auditor is responsible for expressing reasonable assurance as to whether the financial statements give a true and fair view and express that opinion in the auditor's report. The section also describes the auditor's responsibilities in respect of risk assessment, internal controls, going concern and accounting policies. Included to help minimise the expectations gap.
9. Other reporting responsibilities	To highlight any additional reporting responsibilities, if applicable. This may include responsibilities in some jurisdictions to report on the adequacy of accounting records, internal controls over financial reporting, or other information published with the financial statements.
10. Name of the engagement partner	To identify the person responsible for the audit report in case of any queries.
11. Signature	Shows the engagement partner or firm accountable for the opinion.
12. Auditor's address	To identify the specific office of the engagement partner in case of any queries.
13. Date	To identify the date up to which the audit work has been performed. Any information that comes to light after this date will not have been considered by the auditor when forming their opinion. The report must be signed and dated after the directors have approved the financial statements. Often the financial statements and the auditor's report are signed on the same day.

UK specific sections

Conclusions relating to going concern

The auditor must state within the auditor's report whether there are any matters to report in relation to the basis of preparation or disclosures of going concern. If there are no matters to report i.e. the auditor is satisfied with the basis of preparation and disclosures relating to going concern, the auditor must make a statement to this effect.

Opinions on other matters prescribed by the Companies Act 2006

In the UK there is a requirement for auditor's to report on whether the strategic report and directors' report are consistent with the financial statements and prepared in accordance with the applicable legal requirements i.e. Companies Act 2006.

All companies must prepare a strategic report unless they are entitled to the small companies exemption.

The purpose of the strategic report is to inform members and help them assess how the directors have performed in their duty to promote the success of the company.

The strategic report must contain:

- A fair review of the company's business including a detailed analysis of the performance of the company and the position of the company at the year-end.
- A description of the principal risks and uncertainties facing the company.

The strategic report must be approved by the board of directors and signed on behalf of the board by a director or secretary.

Matters on which we are required to report by exception

Under the Companies Act 2006, the auditor is required to report by exception on certain matters such as whether they have received all information and explanations for their audit and whether the directors' remuneration has been disclosed as required. In the past these matters were only mentioned in the auditor's report if problems were encountered but are now included in the UK auditor's report specifically and will state whether or not there is anything to report.

The expectation gap

The sections of the auditor's report are set out in **ISA 700 (Revised)**.

Over time the wording of the auditor's report has grown longer in an attempt to counteract what has become known as the **expectation gap**, i.e. the difference between what an auditor's responsibility actually is and what the public perceives the auditor's responsibility to be.

The auditor's report is not:

- a certificate of the accuracy of the contents of financial statements
- a guarantee against fraud
- confirmation that an entity is being run in accordance with the principles of good corporate governance.

The wording is intended to ensure that users of the financial statements understand what level of assurance they are being given and how much reliance they may place on a set of audited financial statements.

3 Forming an opinion

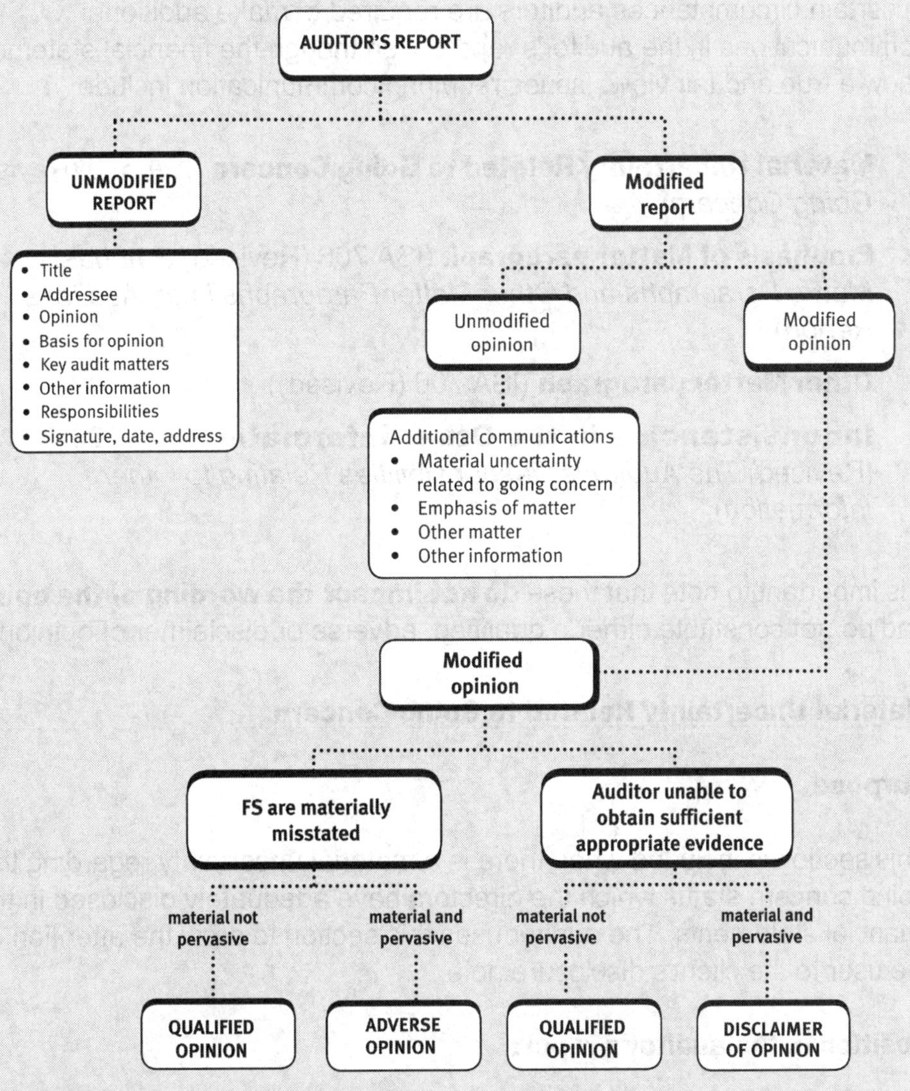

As can be seen from the diagram above, the report can be:

- Unmodified – the financial statements show a true and fair view (ISA 700 Revised).
- Modified without modifying the opinion – the financial statements show a true and fair view but there is additional communication required to bring something to the attention of the user.
- Modified with a modified opinion – the financial statements don't fully show a true and fair view or the auditor has not obtained sufficient appropriate evidence to make that conclusion (ISA 705 (Revised) *Modifications to the Opinion in the Independent Auditor's Report*).

4 Modified report with unmodified opinion

In certain circumstances auditors are required to make additional communications in the auditor's report even though the financial statements show a true and fair view. Issues requiring communication include:

- **Material Uncertainty Related to Going Concern** (ISA 570 (Revised) *Going Concern*)
- **Emphasis of Matter paragraph** (ISA 706 (Revised) *Emphasis of Matter Paragraphs and Other Matter Paragraphs in an Auditor's Report*)
- **Other Matter paragraph** (ISA 706 (Revised))
- **Inconsistencies in the Other Information** (ISA 720 (Revised) *The Auditor's Responsibilities Relating to Other Information*)

It is important to note that these **do not impact the wording of the opinion** and do not constitute either a qualified, adverse or disclaimer of opinion.

Material Uncertainty Related to Going Concern

Purpose

This section is included when there is a material uncertainty regarding the going concern status which the directors have adequately disclosed in the financial statements. The auditor uses this section to draw the attention of the user to the client's disclosure note.

Position in the auditor's report

Below the Basis for Opinion section.

Emphasis of Matter paragraph

Purpose

An Emphasis of Matter paragraph is used to refer to **a matter that has been adequately presented or disclosed in the financial statements** by the directors. The auditor's judgment is that these matters are **of such fundamental importance to the users' understanding** of the financial statements that the auditor should emphasise the disclosure.

Examples of such fundamental matters include:

- Where the financial statements have been prepared on a basis other than the going concern basis.
- An uncertainty relating to the future outcome of exceptional litigation or regulatory action.
- A significant subsequent event occurs between the date of the financial statements and the date of the auditor's report.
- Early application of a new accounting standard.
- Major catastrophes that have had a significant effect on the entity's financial position.
- Where the corresponding figures have been restated.
- Where the financial statements have been recalled and reissued or when the auditor provides an amended auditor's report.

Position in the auditor's report

Below the Basis for Opinion section.

When a Key Audit Matters section is presented in the auditor's report, an Emphasis of Matter paragraph may be presented either directly before or after the Key Audit Matters section, based on the auditor's judgment as to the relative significance of the information included in the Emphasis of Matter paragraph.

Tutorial notes

An Emphasis of Matter paragraph is not used to draw attention to immaterial misstatements. The fact that they are immaterial means they do not warrant the attention of the shareholders.

An Emphasis of Matter paragraph can only be used when adequate disclosure has been made of the matters mentioned above. The auditor can only emphasise something that is already included.

Where adequate disclosure has not been made the opinion will need to be modified and an Emphasis of Matter paragraph **should NOT be used**.

The heading of the paragraph can be amended to provide further context, for example, Emphasis of Matter – Subsequent event.

INT syllabus: An Emphasis of Matter should not be used to highlight an issue already included in the Key Audit Matters section. The auditor must use judgment to determine which section they consider is the most appropriate to highlight the issue.

UK syllabus: Law or regulation may require a matter to be emphasised in the auditor's report in addition to communicating such a matter as a key audit matter in accordance with ISA (UK) 701.

Example wording of an 'Emphasis of Matter' paragraph

Emphasis of Matter

We draw attention to Note 12 of the financial statements, which describes the effects of a fire at the premises of a third party warehouse provider. Our opinion is not modified in respect of this matter.

BP plc

The auditors of BP plc, Ernst & Young LLP, have issued a modified auditor's report on the financial statements since 2010 in relation to the Gulf of Mexico oil spill. A fund of $20bn was established to settle claims made against the company as a result of the Deepwater Horizon accident and oil spill, however, the full cost still isn't known. BP plc have included several disclosures in the notes to the financial statements relating to the uncertainty over the provisions and contingencies. An **Emphasis of Matter** paragraph has been included in the auditor's report referring to these disclosure notes.

Other Matter Paragraphs

Purpose

An Other Matter paragraph is included in the auditor's report if the auditor considers it necessary to communicate to the users regarding **matters that are not presented or disclosed in the financial statements** that, in the auditor's judgment, are **relevant to understanding the audit, the auditor's responsibilities, or the auditor's report**.

Examples of its use include:

- To communicate that the auditor's report is intended solely for the intended users, and should not be distributed to or used by other parties.
- When law, regulation or generally accepted practice requires or permits the auditor to provide further explanation of their responsibilities.
- To explain why the auditor has not resigned, when a pervasive inability to obtain sufficient appropriate evidence is imposed by management (e.g. denying the auditor access to books and records) but the auditor is unable to withdraw from the engagement due to legal restrictions.
- To communicate audit planning and scoping matters where laws or regulations require.
- Where an entity prepares one set of accounts in accordance with a general purpose framework and another set in accordance with a different one (e.g. one according to UK and one according to International standards) and engages the auditor to report on both sets.

Position in the auditor's report

When an Other Matter paragraph is included to draw the users' attention to a matter relating to other reporting responsibilities addressed in the auditor's report, the paragraph may be included in the Report on Other Legal and Regulatory Requirements section.

When relevant to all auditor's responsibilities or users' understanding of the auditor's report, the Other Matter paragraph may be included as a separate section following the Report on the Other Legal and Regulatory Requirements.

Tutorial notes

An Other Matter paragraph does not include confidential information or information required to be provided by management.

The heading may be amended to provide further context, for example, Other Matter – Scope of the audit.

Example wording of 'Other Matter' paragraph

Other Matter

The financial statements of ABC Company for the year ended December 31, 20X0, were audited by another auditor who expressed an unmodified opinion on those statements on March 31, 20X1.

Other Information

Other information refers to financial or non-financial information, other than the financial statements and auditor's report thereon, included in the entity's annual report, that is not necessarily subject to audit.

Examples of other information include:

- Chairman's report
- Operating and financial review
- Social and environmental reports
- Corporate governance statements

Purpose

If the auditor obtains the final version of the other information before the date of the auditor's report, they must read it to identify any material inconsistencies with the financial statements or the auditor's knowledge obtained during the audit.

If the auditor identifies a material inconsistency they should:

- Perform limited procedures to evaluate the inconsistency. The auditor should consider whether it is the financial statements or the other information that requires amendment.
- Discuss the matter with management and ask them to make the correction.
- If management refuse to make the correction, communicate the matter to those charged with governance.
- If the matter remains uncorrected the auditor should withdraw from the engagement if possible under applicable law or regulation as the issue casts doubt over management integrity.
- If withdrawal is not possible, the auditor must describe the material misstatement in the auditor's report.

A separate section is included in the auditor's report under the heading 'Other Information' which:

- Identifies the other information obtained by the auditor prior to the date of the auditor's report.
- States that the auditor has not audited the other information and accordingly does not express an opinion or conclusion on that information.
- Includes a description of the auditor's responsibilities with respect to the other information.

- States either that the auditor has nothing to report or provides a description of the material misstatement if applicable.

Position in the auditor's report

The Other Information section is included in the auditor's report below the Basis for Opinion and Key Audit Matters section (if applicable) and above the Responsibilities of Management.

Tutorial notes

Misstatement of other information exists when the other information is incorrectly stated or otherwise misleading (including because it omits or obscures information necessary for a proper understanding of a matter).

Material misstatements or inconsistencies in the other information may undermine the credibility of the financial statements and the auditor's report.

The auditor must not be knowingly associated with information which is misleading.

The auditor must retain a copy of the final version of the other information on the audit file.

UK syllabus: ISA (UK) 720

ISA (UK) 720 The Auditor's Responsibilities Relating to Other Information (Revised June 2016)

In addition to the requirements of ISA 720, ISA 720 (UK) (Revised) contains additional requirements for UK auditors.

In the UK, an annual report includes at least:

- The statutory other information
- Any other documents that are incorporated by cross-reference in, or distributed to shareholders with, statutory other information either voluntarily or pursuant to law or regulation or the requirements of a stock exchange listing.

A misstatement of the other information exists when the statutory other information has not been prepared in accordance with the legal and regulatory requirements applicable to the statutory other information.

In the UK, the statutory other information includes, where required to be prepared:

- The directors' report
- The strategic report
- The separate corporate governance statement.

For entities that are required to prepare statutory other information, as part of obtaining an understanding of the entity and its environment, the auditor shall obtain an understanding of:

- The legal and regulatory requirements applicable to the statutory other information
- How the entity is complying with those legal and regulatory requirements.

The auditor shall perform such procedures as are necessary to identify whether the statutory other information appears to be materially misstated in the context of the auditor's understanding of the legal and regulatory requirements applicable to the statutory other information.

5 Key Audit Matters – Listed companies only

ISA 701 *Communicating Key Audit Matters in the Independent Auditor's Report* requires auditors of **listed companies** to determine key audit matters and to communicate those matters in the auditor's report.

Auditors of non-listed entities may voluntarily, or at the request of management or those charged with governance, include key audit matters in the auditor's report.

Key audit matters are those that in the auditor's professional judgment were of most significance in the audit and are selected from matters communicated to those charged with governance.

The purpose of including these matters is to assist users in understanding the entity, and to provide a basis for the users to engage with management and those charged with governance about matters relating to the entity and the financial statements.

Each key audit matter should describe why the matter was considered to be significant and how it was addressed in the audit.

Key audit matters include:

- Areas of higher assessed risk of material misstatement, or significant risks identified in accordance with ISA 315 (Revised) *Identifying and Assessing the Risks of Material Misstatement through Understanding the Entity and Its Environment*.
- Significant auditor judgments relating to areas in the financial statements that involved significant management judgment, including accounting estimates that have been identified as having high estimation uncertainty.
- The effect on the audit of significant events or transactions that occurred during the period.

Specific examples include:

- Significant fraud risk
- Goodwill
- Valuation of financial instruments
- Fair values
- Effects of new accounting standards
- Revenue recognition
- Material provisions such as a restructuring provision
- Implementation of a new IT system, or significant changes to an existing system

Note that a matter giving rise to a qualified or adverse opinion, or a material uncertainty related to going concern are by their nature key audit matters. However, they would not be described in this section of the report. Instead, a reference to the Basis for qualified or adverse opinion or the going concern section would be included.

If there are no key audit matters to communicate, the auditor shall:

- Discuss this with the engagement quality control reviewer, if one has been appointed.
- Communicate this conclusion to those charged with governance.
- Explain in the key audit matters section of the auditor's report that there are no matters to report.

Illustration of Key Audit Matters

Goodwill

Under IFRS Standards, the Group is required to annually test the amount of goodwill for impairment. This annual impairment test was significant to our audit because the balance of XX as of December 31, 20X1 is material to the financial statements. In addition, management's assessment process is complex and highly judgmental and is based on assumptions, specifically [describe certain assumptions], which are affected by expected future market or economic conditions, particularly those in [name of country or geographic area].

Effects of New Accounting Standards

As of January 1, 2013, IFRS 10 (Consolidated Financial Statements), 11 (Joint Arrangements) and 12 (Disclosure of Interests in Other Entities) became effective. IFRS 10 requires the Group to assess for all entities whether it has: power over the investee; exposure, or rights, to variable returns from its involvement with the investee; and the ability to use its power over the investee to affect the amount of the investor's returns. The complex structure, servicing and ownership of each vessel, requires the Group to assess and interpret the substance of a significant number of contractual agreements.

6 Modified report with modified opinion

Actions when the opinion is to be modified

Modification of the audit opinion is always the final course of action. As the directors have a legal responsibility to prepare the financial statements to show a true and fair view, the number of modified opinions in real life is very low.

If the auditor is expecting to modify the opinion the following actions will be taken:

(1) Discuss the matter with those charged with governance

This may lead to the matter being resolved as the client may decide to amend the financial statements or the auditor may be provided with further evidence to conclude that a modification is not necessary.

(2) Consider management integrity

It is generally expected that the client would want to avoid a modified opinion, therefore if the issue cannot be resolved satisfactorily it casts doubt over management integrity. This will mean that any representations from management may not be reliable. If representations cannot be relied on, this would lead to a disclaimer of opinion in accordance with ISA 580 *Written Representations*.

(3) Seek external advice

Before resigning, the auditor may decide to seek legal advice or consult with the ACCA about the issues.

(4) Resign

Where the auditor has reason to doubt management integrity or where the auditor expects in future that there will be a need to issue a disclaimer, resignation must be considered. These are both matters that would have been considered at the acceptance stage and they must be reconsidered at the end of the audit to decide whether to continue with the engagement.

Modifications to the audit opinion

The auditor may decide they need to modify the opinion when they conclude that:

- Based upon the evidence obtained **the financial statements** as a whole **are not free from material misstatement**. This is where the client has not complied with the applicable financial reporting framework.
- They have been **unable to gather sufficient appropriate evidence** to be able to conclude that the financial statements as a whole are free from material misstatement. This is evidence the auditor would expect to exist to support the figures in the financial statements.

The nature of the modification depends upon whether the auditor considers the matter to be material but not pervasive, or material and pervasive, to the financial statements.

Material but not pervasive – Qualified opinion

- If the misstatement or lack of sufficient appropriate evidence is **material but not pervasive**, a **qualified opinion** will be issued.
- This means the matter is material to the area of the financial statements affected but does not affect the remainder of the financial statements.
- **'Except for'** this matter, the financial statements give a true and fair view.
- Whilst significant to users' decision making, a material matter can be isolated whilst the remainder of the financial statements may be relied upon.

Material and pervasive

A matter is considered '**pervasive**' if, in the auditor's judgment:

- The effects are not confined to specific elements, accounts or items of the financial statements
- If so confined, represent or could represent a substantial proportion of the financial statements, or
- In relation to disclosures, are fundamental to users' understanding of the financial statements.

In brief, a pervasive matter must be fundamental to the financial statements, therefore rendering them unreliable as a whole.

Adverse opinion

An **adverse opinion** is issued when a misstatement is considered material and pervasive. This will mean the financial statements **do not give a true and fair view**. Examples include:

- Preparation of the financial statements on the wrong basis.
- Non-consolidation of a subsidiary.
- Material misstatement of a balance which represents a substantial proportion of the assets or profits e.g. would change a profit to a loss.

Disclaimer of opinion

A **disclaimer of opinion** is issued when the auditor has not obtained sufficient appropriate evidence and the effects of any possible misstatements could be pervasive. The auditor **does not express an opinion** on the financial statements in this situation.

Examples include:

- Failure by the client to keep adequate accounting records.
- Refusal by the directors to provide written representation.
- Failure by the client to provide evidence over a single balance which represents a substantial proportion of the assets or profits or over multiple balances in the financial statements.

Impact of a disclaimer of opinion

Where a disclaimer of opinion is being issued:

- the statement that sufficient appropriate evidence to provide a basis for the auditor's opinion has been obtained is not included.
- the statement that the financial statements have been audited is changed to 'we were engaged to audit the financial statements'.
- the statements regarding the audit being conducted in accordance with ISAs, and independence and other ethical responsibilities, are positioned within the Auditor Responsibilities section rather than the Basis for Disclaimer of Opinion section.
- the Key Audit Matters section is not included in the report as to do so would suggest the financial statements are more credible in relation to those matters which would be inconsistent with the disclaimer of opinion on the financial statements as a whole.

Basis for modified opinion

When the auditor decides to modify the opinion, they must amend the heading 'Basis for Opinion' to 'Basis for Qualified Opinion', 'Basis for Adverse Opinion' or 'Basis for Disclaimer of Opinion', as appropriate.

- The section will explain the reason why the opinion is modified e.g. which balances are misstated, which disclosures are missing or inadequate, which balances the auditor was unable to obtain sufficient appropriate evidence over and why.
- If possible, a quantification of the financial effect of the modification will be included.
- If the material misstatement relates to narrative disclosures, an explanation of how the disclosures are misstated should be included, or in the case of omitted disclosures, the disclosure should be included if the information is readily available.
- Where a qualified or adverse opinion is being issued, the auditor must amend the statement '...the audit evidence is sufficient and appropriate to provide a basis for the auditor's qualified/adverse opinion.'

The following table illustrates the impact on the audit opinion and auditor's report:

	Material but Not Pervasive	**Material & Pervasive**
Financial statements are materially misstated	Qualified Opinion Except for ... Basis for qualified opinion	Adverse Opinion FS do not give a true and fair view Basis for adverse opinion
Inability to obtain sufficient appropriate audit evidence	Qualified Opinion Except for ... Basis for qualified opinion	Disclaimer of Opinion Do not express an opinion Basis for disclaimer of opinion

Management imposed limitation of scope

- If after accepting the engagement management impose a limitation of scope that will result in a modified opinion, the auditor will request management remove the limitation.
- If management refuse, the matter must be discussed with those charged with governance.
- The auditor should perform alternative audit procedures to obtain sufficient appropriate evidence, if possible.
- If the auditor is unable to obtain sufficient appropriate evidence and the matter is material but not pervasive, the auditor must issue a qualified audit opinion.
- If the matter is considered pervasive, the auditor must withdraw from the audit.
- If withdrawal is not possible before issuing the auditor's report, a disclaimer of opinion should be issued.
- If the auditor decides to withdraw from the audit, the auditor must communicate any material misstatements identified during the audit to those charged with governance before withdrawing.

University of Oxford

The auditors of the University of Oxford, Deloitte, have issued a **Qualified Opinion** due to material misstatement for a number of years. The results of Oxford University Press (OUP), a department of the University, are not consolidated in the financial statements of the University because the financial regulations of the Council of the University do not apply to OUP. The financial statements do not comply with UK GAAP in this respect, and are therefore materially misstated.

Example wording of a Qualified Opinion (a)

Example where the auditor concludes that the financial statements are materially (but not pervasively) misstated:

Qualified Opinion

We have audited the financial statements of ABC Company (the Company), which comprise the statement of financial position as at December 31, 20X1, and the statement of comprehensive income, statement of changes in equity and statement of cash flows for the year then ended, and notes to the financial statements, including a summary of significant accounting policies.

In our opinion, except for the effects of the matter described in the Basis for Qualified Opinion section of our report, the accompanying financial statements give a true and fair view.................. (remainder of wording as per an unmodified report).

Basis for Qualified Opinion

The Company's inventories are carried in the statement of financial position at xxx. Management has not stated the inventories at the lower of cost and net realisable value but has stated them solely at cost, which constitutes a departure from IFRS Standards. The Company's records indicate that, had management stated the inventories at the lower of cost and net realisable value, an amount of xxx would have been required to write the inventories down to their net realisable value. Accordingly, cost of sales would have been increased by xxx, and income tax, net income and shareholders' equity would have been reduced by xxx, xxx and xxx, respectively.

We conducted our audit in accordance with International Standards on Auditing (ISAs). Our responsibilities under those standards are further described in the Auditor's Responsibilities for the Audit of the Financial Statements section of our report. We are independent of the Company in accordance with the ethical requirements that are relevant to our audit of the financial statements in [jurisdiction], and we have fulfilled our other ethical responsibilities in accordance with these requirements. We believe that the audit evidence we have obtained is sufficient and appropriate to provide a basis for our qualified opinion.

Example wording of a Qualified Opinion (b)

Example where the auditor concludes that they have been unable to gather sufficient appropriate evidence and the possible effects are deemed to be material but not pervasive:

Qualified Opinion

We have audited the financial statements of the ABC Company (the Company), which comprise the statement of financial position as at 31 December, 20X1, and the statement of comprehensive income, statement of changes in equity and statement of cash flows for the year then ended, and notes to the financial statements, including a summary of significant accounting policies.

In our opinion, except for the possible effects of the matter described in the Basis for Qualified Opinion section of our report, the accompanying financial statements give a true and fair view.................. (remainder of wording as per an unmodified report).

Basis for Qualified Opinion

The Group's investment in XYZ Company, a foreign associate acquired during the year and accounted for by the equity method, is carried at xxx on the consolidated statement of financial position as at December 31, 20X1, and ABC's share of XYZ's net income of xxx is included in ABC's income for the year then ended. We were unable to obtain sufficient appropriate audit evidence about the carrying amount of ABC's investment in XYZ as at December 31, 20X1 and ABC's share of XYZ's net income for the year because we were denied access to the financial information, management, and the auditors of XYZ. Consequently, we were unable to determine whether any adjustments to these amounts were necessary.

We conducted our audit in accordance with International Standards on Auditing (ISAs). Our responsibilities under those standards are further described in the Auditor's Responsibilities for the Audit of the Consolidated Financial Statements section of our report. We are independent of the Group in accordance with the ethical requirements that are relevant to our audit of the consolidated financial statements in [jurisdiction], and we have fulfilled our other ethical responsibilities in accordance with these requirements. We believe that the audit evidence we have obtained is sufficient and appropriate to provide a basis for our qualified opinion.

Example wording of an Adverse Opinion

Example where the auditor has concluded that the financial statements are misstated and deemed pervasive to the financial statements:

Adverse Opinion

In our opinion, because of the significance of the matter discussed in the Basis for Adverse Opinion paragraph, the consolidated financial statements do not give a true and fair view .... (remainder of wording as per an unmodified report).

Basis for Adverse Opinion

As explained in Note X, the Group has not consolidated subsidiary XYZ Company that the Group acquired during 20X1 because it has not yet been able to determine the fair values of certain of the subsidiary's material assets and liabilities at the acquisition date. This investment is therefore accounted for on a cost basis. Under IFRS Standards, the Company should have consolidated this subsidiary and accounted for the acquisition based on provisional amounts. Had XYZ Company been consolidated, many elements in the accompanying consolidated financial statements would have been materially affected. The effects on the consolidated financial statements of the failure to consolidate have not been determined.

We conducted our audit in accordance with International Standards on Auditing (ISAs). Our responsibilities under those standards are further described in the Auditor's Responsibilities for the Audit of the Consolidated Financial Statements section of our report. We are independent of the Group in accordance with the ethical requirements that are relevant to our audit of the consolidated financial statements in [jurisdiction], and we have fulfilled our other ethical responsibilities in accordance with these requirements. We believe that the audit evidence we have obtained is sufficient and appropriate to provide a basis for our adverse opinion.

Example wording of a Disclaimer of Opinion

Example where the auditor was unable to obtain sufficient appropriate evidence and has concluded that the possible effects of this matter are both material and pervasive to the financial statements:

Disclaimer of Opinion

We were engaged to audit the consolidated financial statements of ABC Company and its subsidiaries (the Group), which comprise the consolidated statement of financial position as at December 31, 20X1, and the consolidated statement of comprehensive income, consolidated statement of changes in equity and consolidated statement of cash flows for the year then ended, and notes to the consolidated financial statements, including a summary of significant accounting policies.

We do not express an opinion on the accompanying consolidated financial statements of the Group. Because of the significance of the matter described in the Basis for Disclaimer of Opinion section of our report, we have not been able to obtain sufficient appropriate audit evidence to provide a basis for an audit opinion on these consolidated financial statements.

Basis for Disclaimer of Opinion

The Group's investment in its joint venture XYZ Company is carried at xxx on the Group's consolidated statement of financial position, which represents over 90% of the Group's net assets as at December 31, 20X1. We were not allowed access to the management and the auditors of XYZ Company, including XYZ Company's auditors' audit documentation. As a result, we were unable to determine whether any adjustments were necessary in respect of the Group's proportional share of XYZ Company's assets that it controls jointly, its proportional share of XYZ Company's liabilities for which it is jointly responsible, its proportional share of XYZ's income and expenses for the year, and the elements making up the consolidated statement of changes in equity and the consolidated cash flow statement.

Responsibilities of Management and Those Charged with Governance for the Consolidated Financial Statements

[Wording as per ISA 700]

Auditor's Responsibilities for the Audit of the Consolidated Financial Statements

Our responsibility is to conduct an audit of the Group's consolidated financial statements in accordance with International Standards on Auditing and to issue an auditor's report. However, because of the matter described in the Basis for Disclaimer of Opinion section of our report, we were not able to obtain sufficient appropriate audit evidence to provide a basis for an audit opinion on these consolidated financial statements.

We are independent of the Group in accordance with the ethical requirements that are relevant to our audit of the financial statements in [jurisdiction], and we have fulfilled our other ethical responsibilities in accordance with these requirements.

UK syllabus: Recent developments affecting UK Auditor's reports

ISA 700 (UK) (Revised June 2016)

For audits of financial statements of public interest entities, the auditor's report shall:

- State by whom or which body the auditor(s) was appointed.
- Indicate the date of the appointment and the period of total uninterrupted engagement including previous renewals and reappointments of the firm.
- Explain to what extent the audit was considered capable of detecting irregularities, including fraud.
- Confirm that the audit opinion is consistent with the additional report to the audit committee. The auditor's report shall not contain any cross-references to the additional report to the audit committee unless specifically required.
- Declare that the non-audit services prohibited by the FRC's Ethical Standard were not provided and that the firm remained independent of the entity in conducting the audit.
- Indicate any services, in addition to the audit, which were provided by the firm to the entity and its controlled undertaking(s), and which have not been disclosed in the annual report or financial statements.

ISA 701 (UK) Communicating Key Audit Matters in the Independent Auditor's Report

ISA 701 (UK) requires the auditor to communicate other audit planning and scoping matters in the auditor's report.

KAM include the most significant assessed risks of material misstatement (whether or not due to fraud) identified by the auditor, including those which had the greatest effect on the overall audit strategy, the allocation of resources in the audit, and directing the efforts of the engagement team.

In describing each of the key audit matters, the auditor's report shall provide:

- A description of the most significant assessed risks of material misstatement, (whether or not due to fraud)
- A summary of the auditor's response to those risks
- Where relevant, key observations arising with respect to those risks.

Where relevant to the above information provided in the auditor's report concerning each of the most significant assessed risks of material misstatement (whether or not due to fraud), the auditor's report shall include a clear reference to the relevant disclosures in the financial statements.

In describing why the matter was determined to be a key audit matter, the description shall indicate that the matter was one of the most significant assessed risks of material misstatement (whether or not due to fraud) identified by the auditor.

Communicating Other Audit Planning and Scoping Matters

The auditor's report shall provide:

- An explanation of how the auditor applied the concept of materiality in planning and performing the audit, specifying the threshold used by the auditor as being materiality for the financial statements as a whole.
- An overview of the scope of the audit, including an explanation of how such scope:
  - Addressed each KAM relating to one of the most significant risks of material misstatement disclosed.
  - Was influenced by the auditor's application of materiality disclosed.

Auditing the Directors' Remuneration Report

The Companies Act 2006 requires the directors to prepare a directors' remuneration report. Some of this information is required to be audited. The auditor's report must therefore describe accurately which sections of the remuneration report have been audited. The auditor will ask the directors to make the disclosure of the audited information clearly distinguishable from that which is not audited.

The auditor must form an opinion as to whether the auditable part of the company's directors' remuneration report:

- has been properly prepared in accordance with the Companies Act 2006
- is in agreement with the accounting records and returns.

If this is not the case, the auditor should include in their report the required information.

Companies disclosing compliance with the UK Corporate Governance Code

ISA (UK) 700 requires the auditor to report by exception on the following matters in the auditors' reports of companies disclosing compliance with the UK Corporate Governance Code where the annual report includes:

- A statement given by the directors that they consider the annual report and accounts taken as a whole is fair, balanced and understandable and provides the information necessary for shareholders to assess the entity's performance, business model and strategy, that is inconsistent with the knowledge acquired by the auditor in the course of performing the audit.
- A section describing the work of the audit committee that does not appropriately address matters communicated by the auditor to the audit committee.
- An explanation, as to why the annual report does not include such a statement or section, that is materially inconsistent with the knowledge acquired by the auditor in the course of performing the audit.
- Other information that, in the auditor's judgment, contains a material inconsistency or a material misstatement of fact.

The auditor shall include a suitable conclusion on these matters in the auditor's report.

Bulletin 2009/4 *Developments in corporate governance affecting responsibilities of auditors of UK companies* provides guidance for auditors and require the auditors to review:

- the statement of directors responsibilities in relation to going concern.

- the part of the corporate governance statement relating to compliance with the nine provisions of the UK Corporate Governance Code. The corporate governance statement may be included within the directors' report or may be a separate statement within the annual report or cross referenced to the company's website.

FRC Extended auditor's reports – A review of experience in the first year

A review of experience in the first year found that investors:

- Would like to see more information about why the level of materiality was chosen.
- Liked discussion of what the auditor found, whether the company's approach was satisfactory or whether the auditor questioned management's judgment.
- Liked reports that had an engaging layout, particularly through use of tables and charts.

UK syllabus: Senior statutory auditor

Senior statutory auditor under the Companies Act 2006

Senior statutory auditor (SSA) has the same meaning as engagement partner when the audit is conducted in accordance with ISAs and is the person responsible for signing the auditor's report.

The SSA signs the auditor's report in his own name on the original report but is not required to physically sign the copies of reports which are sent to the Registrar. Copies of reports just need to state the name of the SSA.

If there is a change to the SSA during the engagement, the new SSA must review the work performed to date to ensure it has been properly planned and performed in accordance with regulations.

If the SSA is absent for any reason at the time the report needs to be signed, the SSA may sign the report electronically by email or fax.

If the auditor's report needs to be signed by a certain date, a contingency plan should be put in place in case the SSA is unable to sign the report. If another partner is actively involved in the audit, the contingency plan should be for the other partner to work in parallel with the SSA and can therefore take over as SSA if the need arises.

A SSA cannot be appointed a quality control review partner for a client as objectivity will be affected by having been the SSA.

UK syllabus: Bulletin 2010/1 XBRL tagging of information

In February 2010, the IAASB issued Bulletin 2010/1 XBRL: Tagging of information in audited financial statements – guidance for auditors.

XBRL (eXtensible Business Reporting Language), is a language for the electronic communication of business and financial data. XBRL assigns all individual disclosure items within business reports a unique, electronically readable tags (like a barcode). HMRC requires companies to file their tax returns online using XBRL for returns submitted after 31 March 2011.

As we have seen, ISA 720 sets out the auditor's responsibilities relating to other information in documents containing audited financial statements. XBRL – tagged data does not represent "other information" as referred to in ISA 720.

Auditors are not required to provide assurance on XBRL data in the context of an audit of financial statements.

However, auditors may be able to provide other services in relation to XBRL data, including:

- Performing the tagging exercise.
- Agreed-upon procedures engagements such as the accuracy of the tagging by management.
- Providing advice on the selection of tags.
- Supplying accounts preparation software which automates the tagging process.
- Training management in XBRL tagging.

As a result of these other services, self-review and management threats may arise which would need to be assessed and safeguarded as discussed in the ethics section.

Exam question approach

There are two common styles of exam question for P7

(1) Explain the implications for the auditor's report

(2) Critically appraise the suggested auditor's report

Below are suggested approaches/considerations you can make when answering these questions.

Explain the implications for the auditor's report

(1) Materiality assessment – if the issue is not material it won't affect the auditor's report. Calculate the percentage of assets and profit the issue represents and state whether this is material or not material.

(2) Identify the type of issue

- material misstatement – non compliance with an accounting standard
- inability to obtain sufficient appropriate evidence – evidence the auditor would expect to obtain hasn't been obtained
- material uncertainty – significant events where the outcome will only be known in the future
- inconsistency with the other published information – contradiction between the financial statements and the other information which is not subject to audit e.g. directors report, chairman's statement, CSR report, etc.
- a matter that is of importance to the scope of the audit, the auditor's assessment of materiality, assessment of risk of material misstatement or other key audit matter that the auditor should specifically refer to in their report.

(3) Comment on the issue

- which accounting standard has not been complied with and why.
- which piece of evidence has not been obtained and why.
- what event/outcome is uncertain
- what is the contradiction in the unaudited information
- explain why the auditor focused specifically on the key audit matters described in greater detail in the auditor's report e.g. involved a high degree of management judgment, required complex accounting treatment creating significant risk of material misstatement.

(4) State whether the issue is material or material and pervasive – is it isolated or relatively small in impact or does it make the financial statements as a whole unreliable.

(5) Conclude on the opinion

- unmodified – if no material misstatements or lack of evidence
- qualified – if there is a material (but not pervasive) misstatement or a lack of evidence over a material balance.
- adverse – if there is a pervasive misstatement
- disclaimer – if there is a lack of evidence which is considered pervasive

(6) State any other reporting implications

- Basis for modified opinion if the opinion is modified
- Going concern section
- Emphasis of matter paragraph
- Other matter paragraph
- Requires inclusion in the Key Audit Matters section for a listed entity
- UK syllabus: Requires reporting by exception under ISAs or Companies Act.

Critically appraise the suggested auditor's report

In order to say what is wrong with the suggested report you must understand the following:

- The main elements of an auditor's report.
- The order of the paragraphs within the report.
- Appropriate titles for the opinion and basis for opinion paragraphs.
- Professional and appropriate wording and content.
- Which opinion is the appropriate opinion to use in the circumstances.
- When it is appropriate to use emphasis of matter and other matter paragraphs.

Look out for:

- Paragraphs being included in the wrong order.
- Titles of paragraphs using the wrong wording.
- Incorrect use of EOM and OM paragraphs.
- Inappropriate opinion being suggested for the issue.
- Inconsistent opinion wording with the name of the opinion e.g. adverse opinion being suggested but the wording within the opinion. using 'except for' which is the wording for a qualified opinion..
- Unprofessional wording of the report in general.
- Insufficient explanation of the reason for the modification.

Exam style question: Reporting

This question is typical of the style and wording of a reporting question. In order to ensure a good mark you must discuss relevant accounting guidance, why there appears to be a departure from that guidance, whether you are able to gather sufficient appropriate evidence to support an opinion and how these issues affect your opinion.

Ultimately you will have to suggest an opinion. You must reach a specific conclusion (i.e. the wording of your report) based upon your discussion. Do not offer a range of possible solutions as there is very rarely a range of possible opinions to these questions. The examiner has indicated that she would like to see students be able to draw conclusions from their work.

You are a partner of Finbar & Sons, a firm of accountants. You are conducting a review of the draft financial statements of a major client, Holly & Ivy Co, for the year ended 30 April 20X4. According to the draft accounts revenue for the year was $125m, profit before tax was $9m and total assets were $100m. You also identify the following issues:

(1) The accounting policies note state that all development costs are expensed as incurred. The audit work performed shows that these costs totalled $6m during the year and that of these $1.3m should have been capitalised as development assets in accordance with relevant financial reporting standards.

The audit senior has suggested a qualified audit opinion with a disclaimer paragraph, given the highly material nature of the matter above in comparison to profit before tax. She has also included an emphasis of matter paragraph, due to the perceived significance of the issue.

(2) The directors of Holly & Ivy have, for the first time, stated their intention to publish the annual report on the company's website.

Required:

Identify and comment upon the implications of the above matters and the impact they will have on the final auditor's report for the year ended 30 April 20X4.

(10 marks)

Test your understanding 1

(a) Explain the responsibility of the auditor in respect of corresponding figures and comparatives.

(5 marks)

(b) Libra & Leo, a small firm of chartered certified accountants, has provided audit services to Delphinus Co for many years. The company, which makes hand-crafted beds, is undergoing expansion and has recently relocated its operations. Having completed the audit of the financial statements for the year ended 31 December 20X3 and issued an unmodified opinion thereon, Libra & Leo have now indicated that they do not propose to offer themselves for re-election.

The chief executive of Delphinus, Mr Pleiades, has now approached your firm to audit the financial statements for the year to 31 December 20X4. However, before inviting you to accept the nomination he has asked for your views on the following extracts from an auditors' report:

'However, the evidence available to us was limited because we were not appointed auditors of the company until (date 20X4) and in consequence we were not able to attend the inventory count at 31 December 20X3. There were no satisfactory alternative means that we could adopt to confirm the amount of inventory and work- in-progress included in the preceding period's financial statements at $ ....

'In our opinion, except for any adjustments that might have been found to be necessary had we been able to obtain sufficient evidence concerning inventory and work-in-progress as at 1 January 20X4, the financial statements give a true and fair view of the state of the company's affairs as at 31 December 20X4 and of its profit [loss] for the year then ended.

Mr Pleiades has been led to understand that such a modified opinion must be given on the financial statements of Delphinus for the year ended 31 December 20X4, as a necessary consequence of the change in audit appointment. He is anxious to establish whether you would issue anything other than a modified opinion.

Required:

Comment on the proposed auditors' report. Your answer should consider whether and how the chief executive's concerns can be overcome.

(10 marks)

(Total: 15 marks)

Test your understanding 2

(a) The purpose of ISA 250 *Consideration of Laws and Regulations in an Audit of Financial Statements* is to establish standards and provide guidance on the auditor's responsibility to consider laws and regulations in an audit of financial statements.

Required:

Explain the auditor's responsibilities for reporting non-compliance that comes to the auditor's attention during the conduct of an audit.

(5 marks)

(b) You are an audit manager in a firm of Chartered Certified Accountants currently assigned to the audit of Cleeves Co for the year ended 30 September 20X6. During the year Cleeves acquired a 100% interest in Howard Co. Howard is material to Cleeves and audited by another firm, Parr & Co. You have just received Parr's draft auditor's report for the year ended 30 September 20X6. The wording is that of an unmodified report except for the opinion paragraph which is as follows:

Audit opinion

As more fully explained in notes 11 and 15 impairment losses on non-current assets have not been recognised in profit or loss as the directors are unable to quantify the amounts.

In our opinion, provision should be made for these as required by International Accounting Standard 36 (*Impairment*). If the provision had been so recognised the effect would have been to increase the loss before and after tax for the year and to reduce the value of tangible and intangible non-current assets. However, as the directors are unable to quantify the amounts we are unable to indicate the financial effect of such omissions.

In view of the failure to provide for the impairments referred to above, in our opinion the financial statements do not present fairly in all material respects the financial position of Howard Co as of 30 September 20X6 and of its loss and its cash flows for the year then ended in accordance with International Financial Reporting Standards.

Your review of the prior year auditor's report shows that the 20X5 audit opinion was worded identically.

Required:

(i) Critically appraise the appropriateness of the report extracts given by Parr & Co on the financial statements of Howard Co, for the years ended 30 September 20X6 and 20X5.

(7 marks)

(ii) Briefly explain the implications of Parr & Co's audit opinion for your audit opinion on the consolidated financial statements of Cleeves Co for the year ended 30 September 20X6.

(3 marks)

(Total: 15 marks)

7 Chapter summary

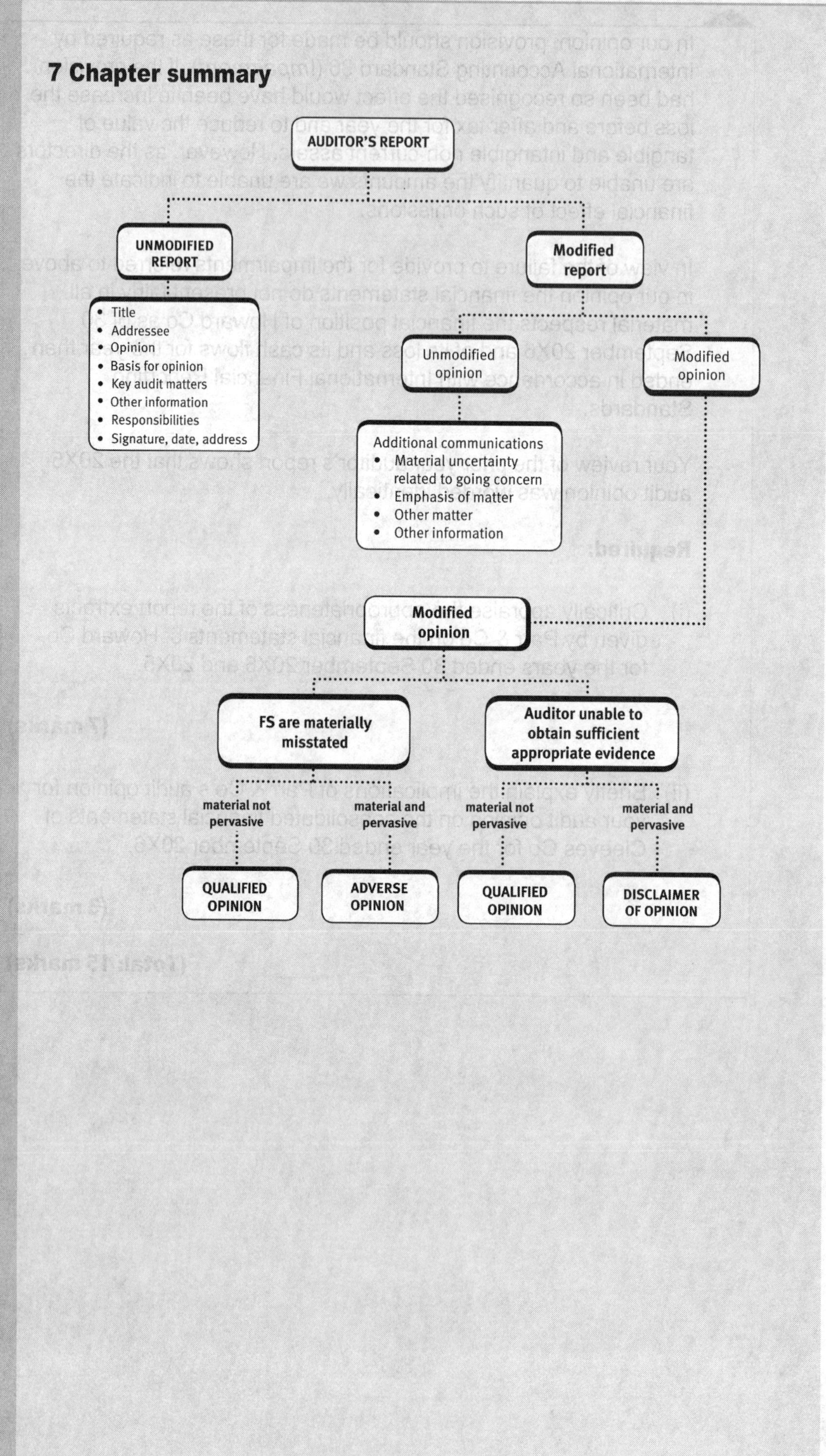

Test your understanding answers

Exam style question: Reporting

Development costs

The misstatement of $1.3m represents 1.3% of assets and 14.4% of profit before tax and is material to the financial statements.

According to IAS 38 *Intangible Assets*, if the costs of a project can be measured separately and reliably, if the project is commercially viable and technically feasible and if an overall profit is expected then the development costs MUST be capitalised.

The expensing of development costs does not comply with IAS 38.

In addition the directors will be required to update the accounting policy notes. If this policy were adopted in the prior year, and development costs expensed again, then a restatement of opening reserves may be required. This would require an explanatory note in the accounts discussing the nature of the prior year adjustment.

Therefore an adjustment should be proposed and the directors of Holly & Ivy should be requested to amend the financial statements. To achieve this the directors must restate the accounts, removing the $1.3m from the statement of profit or loss and capitalising them as intangible development costs on the statement of financial position, as per IAS 38.

Failure to make the required adjustments would mean intangible assets and profits are materially overstated requiring a modified opinion.

The audit opinion should be qualified 'except for' as a result of the material misstatement.

The issue is material but not pervasive as the matter is isolated to this one area of the financial statements and does not mean the financial statements as a whole are unreliable.

The 'basis for opinion' section will be amended to a 'basis for qualified opinion' and will explain the reason for the qualified opinion and quantify the extent of the misstatement.

With regard to the suggested audit opinion, a disclaimer of opinion is being suggested which is not appropriate. A disclaimer of opinion is given when the auditor is unable to gather sufficient appropriate audit evidence, which is not the case here. In this instance the auditor has identified a material misstatement in the financial statements.

The use of a disclaimer suggests that the matter is being treated as a pervasive issue. This means that the misstatement is so significant to the users' understanding of the financial statements that it renders them unreliable on the whole. If this was the case then an adverse opinion would be given.

However, whilst the error represents 14% of profit before tax and 1.3% of total assets and is material, it is unlikely to be pervasive. With full knowledge of the error the users should still be able to rely on the other information contained in the financial statements as there is no indication of further misstatement.

In this instance, a qualified 'except for' opinion would be given on the basis of a failure to comply with relevant financial reporting guidelines for capitalising development costs.

The emphasis of matter paragraph is not required in this circumstance. Emphasis of matter paragraphs should not be used to refer to the nature of a modification to the audit opinion. That information is contained in the 'Basis for Qualified Opinion' paragraph.

Internet report

There is no extension to the auditor's duty of care simply because the report is being published electronically as well as in hard copy. All financial statements are publicly available. The main concern is the extent to which audited information is published on the web. The directors may choose to exclude some parts of the financial statements. The information will need to be uploaded to the internet and information may be corrupted during this process.

The auditor must check the following:

(a) that the information uploaded is derived from the information contained in the manually signed financial statements (e.g. conversion to PDF or HTML).

(b) that the electronic copy agrees to the hard copy, by proof reading.

(c) that the auditor's signature copied onto the electronic document is protected from modification.

(d) that the conversion has not distorted the information in any way.

Most importantly, the auditor needs to make it clear in the audit opinion which information has and has not been audited (e.g. by use of page numbers).

A point should be included in the written representation that the directors acknowledge their responsibility for implementing a security system that prevents the deliberate corruption or manipulation of the electronic financial statements.

Test your understanding 1

It is important that you should not make issues out of information given in a question which is not relevant to answering the question set. For example, this question refers to a predecessor auditor.

Addressing or speculating upon the reasons for the change will not earn marks because (i) it is not relevant; (ii) the tone of the introductory paragraph ('expansion', 'relocation', 'unmodified opinion') does not suggest anything untoward about the change.

(a) **Corresponding figures**

Amounts and disclosures derived from preceding financial statements are included with, and are intended to be read in relation to, the current period figures. When comparatives are presented as corresponding figures they are not specifically identified in an auditor's report because the auditor's opinion is on the current period financial statements as a whole, including the corresponding figures.

For initial engagements, the auditor seeks to obtain sufficient, appropriate audit evidence to confirm that:

- opening balances do not contain misstatements that materially affect the current period's financial statements.
- the prior period closing balances have been properly brought forward as the current period's opening balances.
- accounting policies have been consistently applied.

The auditor must be satisfied with the opening position. A new auditor, however, has not previously obtained audit evidence to support transactions and accounting policies of the prior period.

To obtain the necessary assurance on the opening position, additional procedures can be performed, for example:

- a review of working papers and accounting records for the previous year-end kept by the client's management or obtained from the previous auditor.
- audit work on the current year's transactions and balances will also provide some evidence to support the completeness, valuation, existence and rights or obligations of the opening balances.

In rare circumstances, if these procedures are unsatisfactory, some of the opening balances may need to be substantively tested in order to form an opinion on them.

If the scope of a new auditor's work with respect to the opening position is effectively limited, the lack of audit evidence may result in a modification.

(b) **Proposed auditors' report**

If it is not possible to form an opinion on a material matter, due to lack of evidence, a modified opinion ('except for' qualification or disclaimer) will be required.

The fact that an auditor was not previously appointed to perform procedures on the prior period closing balances is not grounds for modification. For example, a new auditor does not obtain direct confirmations in respect of prior period trade receivable balances, but that does not mean that he cannot form an opinion about the opening trade receivables balance.

Inventory is likely to be a very significant balance in a manufacturing business such as Delphinus. It will be more difficult to form an opinion on the opening balance if:

- inventory is not accounted for in the double-entry bookkeeping system
- inventory records are not maintained
- quantities are ascertained by a year-end physical count
- values of work-in-progress, slow-moving and damaged items are a matter of judgment.

Where a modification is warranted (e.g. because sufficient evidence regarding opening inventory quantities cannot be ascertained by alternative means) the 'except for' opinion is a modification of the opinion on the current period's result (i.e. profit or loss) only and not its financial position.

For Delphinus, it is likely that sufficient evidence will be available to a new auditor in respect of inventory. In particular:

- inventory quantities as at 31 December 20X3 and the valuation thereof should be available from Delphinus (if Delphinus does not have this, Mr Pleaides would be able to request a copy from Libra and Leo).
- hand-crafted beds are not small or inexpensive items, therefore the auditor will be able to compare quantities as at 31 December 20X4 with those of the prior year.
- gross profit margins might be expected to be relatively stable, so if opening inventory was materially overstated the current year margin would be deflated and the prior year inflated.

How to overcome chief executive's concerns

Audit procedures such as those outlined above should be undertaken to confirm the opening position. In particular:

- reviewing prior year-end inventory sheets and comparing quantities of raw materials, WIP and finished beds.
- comparison of key ratios (e.g. gross profit percentages and inventory turnover) and the relative proportions of raw materials, WIP and finished beds.

Such analytical procedures would take into account known fluctuations which, in the case of Delphinus, would arise through recent acquisitions.

To assist the audit, Mr Pleaides should ensure that the following information is readily available:

- records of physical inventory taking at 31 December 20X3.
- full details of write-downs and allowances for slow-moving inventory.
- adjustments, if any, requested to be made by Libra & Leo.
- an analysis of revenue by business segment.

Libra & Leo should make their working papers available to their successor as a matter of professional courtesy.

Whether the chief executive's concerns can be overcome

The change in audit appointment does not necessitate a modified auditor's report. For a company such as Delphinus, minimal additional procedures should provide sufficient appropriate evidence over the opening position including that of inventory.

However, it is not possible to state, unequivocally, that an unmodified opinion will be issued (since the audit has yet to be performed). If, for example, a material misstatement was to arise in respect of the current year, the auditor would need to report this to the members.

Tutorial note: To agree that the proposed modification is unavoidable or, at the other extreme, promising an unmodified opinion without any reservation would not be a professional stance.

Test your understanding 2

(a) **Reporting non-compliance**

Non-compliance refers to acts of omission or commission by the entity being audited, either intentional or unintentional, that are contrary to the prevailing laws or regulations.

To management

Non-compliance that comes to the auditor's attention should be communicated to management.

If the auditor suspects that members of senior management are involved in non-compliance, the auditor should report the matter to the next higher level of authority at the entity, if it exists (e.g. an audit committee or a supervisory board).

Where no higher authority exists, or if the auditor believes that the report may not be acted upon, or is unsure as to the person to whom to report, the auditor would consider seeking legal advice.

To the users of the auditor's report on the financial statements

If the auditor concludes that the non-compliance has a material effect on the financial statements, and has not been properly reflected in the financial statements, the auditor should express a qualified ('except for') or an adverse opinion.

If the auditor is precluded by the entity from obtaining sufficient appropriate audit evidence to evaluate whether or not non-compliance that may be material to the financial statements has (or is likely to have) occurred, the auditor should express an 'except for' qualified opinion or a disclaimer of opinion on the financial statements due to being unable to obtain sufficient appropriate evidence.

If the auditor is unable to determine whether non-compliance has occurred because of limitations imposed by circumstances rather than by the entity, the auditor should consider the effect on the auditor's report.

To regulatory and enforcement authorities

The auditor's duty of confidentiality ordinarily precludes reporting non-compliance to a third party. However, in certain circumstances, that duty of confidentiality is overridden by statute, law or by a court of law (e.g. in some countries the auditor is required to report non-compliance by financial institutions to the regulatory authority). The auditor may need to seek legal advice in such circumstances, giving due consideration to the auditor's responsibility to the public interest.

(i) **Appropriateness of audit opinion**

Heading

The opinion paragraph is not properly headed. It does not state the form of the opinion that has been given nor the grounds for modification.

The opinion 'the financial statements do not give a true and fair view' is an 'adverse' opinion.

The opinion paragraph should be headed 'Adverse Opinion'.

Content

It is not appropriate that the opinion paragraph should refer to the note(s) in the financial statements where the matter giving rise to the modification is more fully explained. This should be included in the 'Basis for...' paragraph.

The 'Basis for...' paragraph should include:

- The reason for impairment.
- Quantification of the effect. The maximum possible loss would be the carrying amount of the non-current assets identified as impaired.

It is not clear why the directors have been 'unable to quantify the amounts'. Since impairments should be quantifiable, any inability suggests an inability to gather sufficient appropriate evidence, in which case a qualified or disclaimer of opinion should be issued on grounds of lack of evidence rather than material misstatement.

That 'provision should be made', but has not, should be clearly stated as non-compliance with IAS 36. The title of IAS 36 *Impairment of Assets* should be given in full.

The wording is confusing. There must be sufficient evidence to support a claim of material misstatement. Although the directors cannot quantify the amounts it seems the auditors must have been able to (estimate at least) in order to form an opinion that the amounts involved are sufficiently material to warrant a modification.

The first paragraph refers to non-current assets. The second paragraph specifies tangible and intangible assets. There is no explanation why or how both tangible and intangible assets are impaired.

The first paragraph refers to profit or loss and the second and third paragraphs to loss. It may be clearer if the first paragraph referred to recognition in the statement of profit or loss.

It is not clear why the failure to recognise impairment warrants an adverse opinion rather than 'except for'. The effects of non-compliance with IAS 36 are to overstate the carrying amount(s) of non-current assets (that can be specified) and to understate the loss. The matter does not appear to be pervasive and so an adverse opinion looks unsuitable as the financial statements as a whole are not incomplete or misleading. A loss is already being reported so it is not that a reported profit would be turned into a loss which is sometimes judged to be pervasive.

Prior year

As the 20X5 auditor's report included an adverse opinion, and the matter that gave rise to the modification is unresolved, the 20X6 report should also be modified regarding the corresponding figures (ISA 710 *Comparative Information – Corresponding Figures and Comparative Financial Statements*).

The 20X6 auditor's report does not refer to the prior period modification nor highlight that the matter resulting in the current period modification is not new. For example, the report could say 'As previously reported and as more fully explained in notes ….' and state 'increase the loss by $x (20X5 – $y)'.

(ii) **Implications for audit opinion on consolidated financial statements of Cleeves**

If the potential adjustments to non-current asset carrying amounts and loss are not material to the consolidated financial statements there will be no implication for the audit opinion. However, as Howard is material to Cleeves and the modification appears to be pervasive, giving rise to adverse opinion, this seems unlikely.

As Howard is wholly-owned, the management of Cleeves must be able to request that Howard's financial statements are adjusted to reflect the impairment of the assets.

The auditor's report on Cleeves will then be unmodified (assuming that any impairment of the investment in Howard is properly accounted for in the consolidated financial statements of Cleeves).

If the impairment losses are not recognised in Howard's financial statements they can nevertheless be adjusted on consolidation (by writing down assets to recoverable amounts). The audit opinion on Cleeves should then be unmodified in this respect.

If there is no adjustment of Howard's asset values (either in Howard's financial statements or on consolidation) it is most likely that the audit opinion on Cleeves' consolidated financial statements would be modified (qualified 'except for').

It is unlikely to require an adverse opinion as it is doubtful whether the opinion on Howard's financial statements should be adverse.

chapter

14

Reports to those charged with governance

Chapter learning objectives

This chapter covers syllabus areas:

- F2 – Reports to those charged with governance and management

Detailed syllabus objectives are provided in the introduction section of the text book.

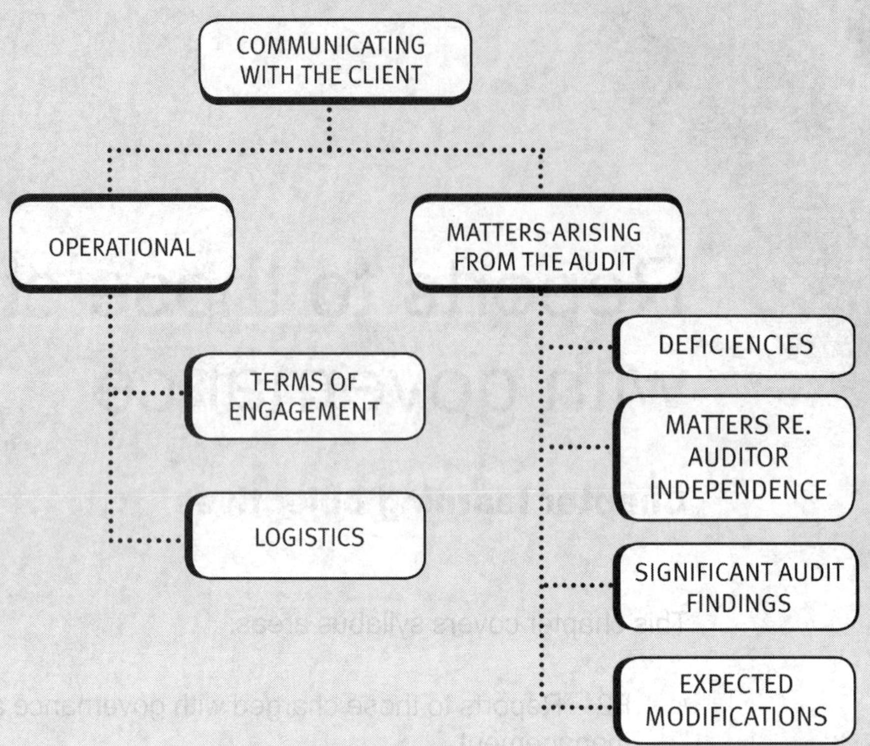

Exam focus

Reporting to management and those charged with governance does not appear in every exam. A typical requirement might incorporate identification of the matters to be reported from a scenario.

To clarify the examination perspective on such audit outputs, the examiner published an article entitled 'Auditor's Reports to Those Charged with Governance' (April 2008). This can be found on the P7 section of the ACCA website.

1 Management and those charged with governance

Those charged with governance are defined in ISA 260 *Communication with Those Charged With Governance* as:

"The persons with responsibility for overseeing the strategic direction of the entity and obligations related to the accountability of the entity." This includes the directors (executive and non-executive) and the audit committee.

In contrast, management are defined as:

"The persons with executive responsibility for the conduct of the entity's operations."

Problems with these definitions

One of the areas of difficulty is that there is assumed to be a distinction between management and those charged with governance. For small and medium-sized entities and particularly for owner-managed businesses, this is often not the case.

There is a possibility, therefore, that the auditor could find themselves reporting to the owners of the business, matters already discussed with them in their capacity as management.

2 Communicating with those charged with governance

Reasons for communicating to those charged with governance

- To communicate responsibilities of the auditor and an overview of the scope and timing of the audit.
- To obtain information relevant to the audit.
- To report matters from the audit on a timely basis.
- To promote effective two-way communication.

Matters that should be reported to those charged with governance

- The auditor's responsibilities in relation to the financial statements audit.
- The planned scope and timing of the audit including, for example:
  - the auditor's approach to internal control relevant to the audit.
  - the extent to which the auditor is planning to use the work of internal audit and the arrangements for so doing.
  - business risks that may result in material misstatements.
  - communications with regulators.

- Significant findings from the audit, such as:
  - the auditor's views about qualitative aspects of the entity's accounting practices/policies.
  - significant difficulties encountered during the audit.
  - significant matters arising during the audit that were discussed with management.
  - written representations the auditor is requesting.
  - circumstances that affect the form and content of the auditor's report, if any. This includes any expected modifications to the report and key audit matters to be communicated in accordance with ISA 701 *Communicating Key Audit Matters in the Independent Auditor's Report*.
  - other matters that, in the auditor's opinion, are significant to the oversight of the reporting process.
- Matters of auditor independence.

Ultimately what constitutes a matter requiring the attention of those charged with governance is a matter of professional judgment. Typical examples include:

- Expected limitations on the audit, either imposed by management or other circumstances.
- The selection of, or changes in, significant accounting policies and practices that have, or could have, a material effect on the entity's financial statements.
- The potential effect on the financial statements of any material risks and exposures, such as pending litigation, that are required to be disclosed in the financial statements.
- A summary of identified misstatements, whether corrected or not by the entity and a request that they are adjusted.
- Material uncertainties related to events and conditions that may cast significant doubt on the entity's ability to continue as a going concern.
- The nature and wording of expected modifications to the auditor's report.
- Any other matters agreed upon in the terms of the audit engagement.
- Delays in obtaining information for the audit.
- An unreasonably brief time within which to complete the audit.

3 Communicating deficiencies in internal control

ISA 265 *Communicating Deficiencies in Internal Control to Those Charged with Governance and Management* requires the auditor to communicate identified deficiencies in internal control that, in the auditor's judgment, are of sufficient importance to merit attention by the entity.

The first task of the auditor, therefore, is to distinguish between simple deficiencies, which do not require communication, and significant ones that do. Deficiencies have been defined as occurring when:

- A control is designed, implemented or operated in such a way that it is unable to prevent, or detect and correct misstatements in the financial statements on a timely basis, or
- A control necessary to prevent, or detect and correct, misstatements in the financial statements on a timely basis is missing.

Significant deficiencies are those which could have a material effect on the financial statements or affect multiple balances.

In their communication the auditor includes:

- A description of the deficiencies and their potential effects.
- An explanation of the purpose of the auditor (i.e. to express an opinion on the financial statements, not to help redesign internal systems).
- An explanation of why consideration of internal control is relevant to the audit.
- An explanation that the matters being reported are only those identified during the audit and considered to be significant enough to report.

As well as reporting to those charged with governance, the auditor should communicate deficiencies to management on a timely basis (including those significant ones reported to those charged with governance and other, less significant ones, meriting the attention of management).

UK syllabus

ISA (UK) 260 *Communication with those charged with governance (Revised)*:

- Clarifies that those charged with governance are both executive and non-executive directors (or equivalent), including members of the audit committee, whereas management would not normally include non-executive directors.
- Sets out additional information that the auditors are required to report to those charged with governance:
  - information relevant to compliance with the UK Corporate Governance Code for relevant entities
  - business risks relevant to financial reporting
  - significant accounting policies
  - management's valuation of material assets and liabilities and related disclosures
  - effectiveness of internal controls relevant to financial reporting
  - other business risks and effectiveness of other internal controls where the auditor has obtained an understanding of these matters.
- In respect of public interest entities, the following must be communicated:
  - Declaration of independence
  - The quantitative level of materiality applied to perform the audit
  - Events or conditions identified during the audit that may cast doubt over the entities ability to continue as a going concern.
  - Significant deficiencies in the internal financial control systems and whether the deficiency has been resolved by management
  - Significant matters involving actual or suspected non-compliance with laws and regulations
  - Any work performed by other auditors that are not part of the same network as the audit firm.

Test your understanding 1

Mandolin Co is an unlisted medium-sized company. It has eight directors including two non-executives. The directors together own 60% of Mandolin's share capital. The following issues have been highlighted by the audit team during the audit:

(1) The passwords to access the accounting system are written on a sticky label on the inside of the top right-hand drawer of the finance director's desk. The finance director's office is usually locked and access is usually observable by the two personal assistants who assist the directors.

(2) The payroll clerk has access to all aspects of the payroll system and is responsible for processing changes to salary rates, tax deduction codes, and all other payroll items. No one reviews the payroll in detail, although the directors do review the management accounts that are produced promptly each month. The finance director is an experienced, qualified accountant and the CEO and one of the non-executive directors also have financial expertise.

(3) The company has used the same freight company for despatching its goods to customers for many years. The audit team has noticed that freight costs have increased considerably as a proportion of sales revenue over the past two years.

(4) The company's inventory includes a material amount of spares inventory against which allowances are made based on a formula calculated on the basis of the period since the last inventory movement. Broadly, the longer the period since the last movement, the higher the allowance. It has emerged that any adjustments to the inventory files, whether or not they represent valid sales, are interpreted by the system as if the inventory is active and therefore current. Such adjustments might include changes of location, the scrapping of small amounts of damaged inventory, or the correction of errors.

(5) The client's system for segregating expenditure on non-current assets from repairs is haphazard. The client's staff are happy to correct mistakes uncovered by the audit team, but seem unconcerned by the distinction between capital and revenue expenditure.

Required:

For each issue, draft a suitable paragraph for inclusion in the management letter or, if appropriate, explain what other action, if any, you would take.

4 Chapter summary

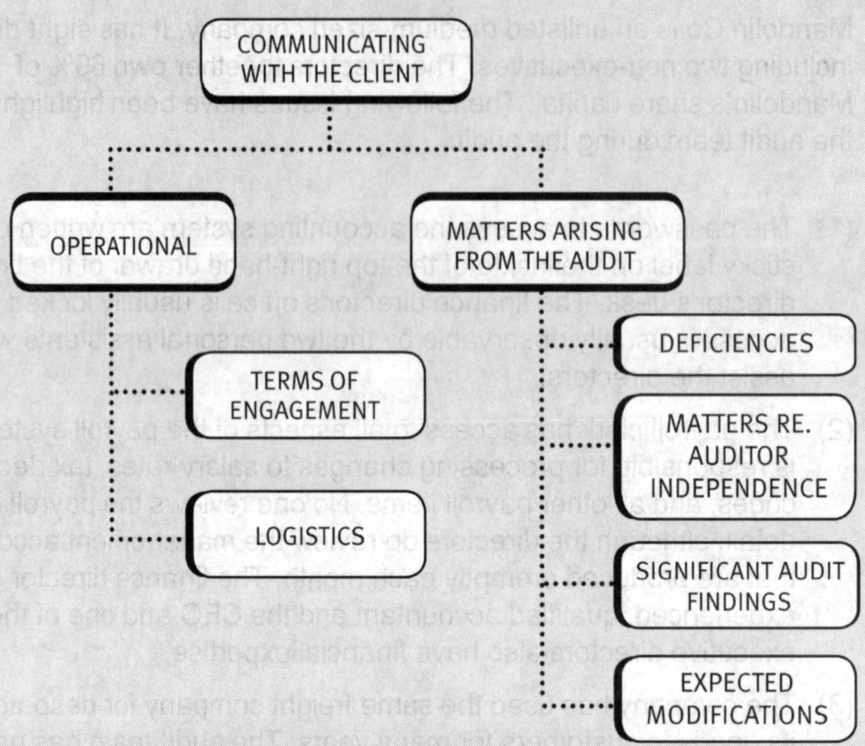

Test your understanding answers

Test your understanding 1

(1) This issue should initially be addressed by discussion with the finance director.

If there is a real risk of abuse, this may indicate a lack of controls throughout the company, which should be brought to the attention of the non-executive directors.

A possible paragraph for the management letter might be:

'We found a number of instances where the passwords giving access to the company's accounting systems were written down and kept in accessible locations.

We recommend that passwords should always be kept confidential to the intended user. Ideally passwords should be memorised. If this is not feasible, a password management system should be used.'

(2) It is possible that the budgetary controls operated by the board in reviewing the management accounts are sufficient for the detection of possible abuse of the payroll system. If not, the following might be appropriate.

'The payroll clerk has sole control of the payroll system and puts all changes into effect. This provides opportunity to create fictitious employees in the payroll system and commit fraud causing loss to the company.

In our view, the monthly review of the management accounts conducted by the board is insufficiently detailed to detect modest abuses of the system, which, although unlikely to be material on an individual basis, could amount to substantial sums over time.

We recommend that before the instruction to make the monthly transfers is given to the bank, the payroll should be reviewed in detail by either the finance director or the CEO.'

(3) 'We draw your attention to the fact that ABC Co has been the sole contractor for the company's outward freight business for a number of years.

We have noted that freight charges as a proportion of sales revenue have increased at the rate of x% per annum on average over the past five years and may not be giving best value for money.

We recommend that you consider asking ABC Co to review their charges, or invite tenders for the business from other companies.'

(4) We have identified a flaw in the operation of the spares inventory system, which has led to an overstatement of spares inventory that we estimate to be \$x at the year-end (PY \$x). The impact on operating profit for the current year was \$x (PY \$x).

The errors have arisen because the system recognises any adjustment to spares inventory as a movement on inventory and therefore treats the relevant inventory lines as being current, even though the movements may be minor technical adjustments or, even, write-downs.

Although the impact on profit is not material year on year, it is possible that the cumulative overstatement of spares inventory values is material.

We recommend that the company should investigate further the actual level of the overstatement of spares inventory, and should take immediate steps to ensure that only valid sales of inventory are recognised as movements for the purpose of deciding whether or not a particular line of inventory is current.

(5) Misallocations between capital and revenue expenditure tend to have tax implications, so the concept of audit materiality may not be relevant.

Possible wording might be:

'We have identified \$x of capital expenditure which has been incorrectly treated as repairs. Such errors have an equal impact on the company's profit for the year, which in turn affects its tax liability.

We recommend that your accounts staff should receive training about the impact of tax sensitive expenditure so that such misallocations do not occur in the future.'

chapter

15

Other assignments

Chapter learning objectives

This chapter covers syllabus areas:

- E1 – Audit-related and assurance services
- F3a – Analyse the form and content of the professional accountant's report for an assurance engagement as compared with an auditor's report
- F3c – Discuss the effectiveness of the 'negative assurance' form of reporting and evaluate situations in which it may be appropriate to modify a conclusion

Detailed syllabus objectives are provided in the introduction section of the text book.

Exam focus

There will usually be one question in the exam that will test your ability to apply your knowledge to a non-audit engagement. The question could cover any area of the engagement process - acceptance, planning, procedures or reporting.

Non-audit engagements include:

Assurance engagements

- Review of financial statements
- Review of interim financial statements
- Due diligence review
- Examination of prospective financial information
- Social and environmental information review

Agreed upon procedures

- Fraud investigation
- Verifying an insurance claim
- Due diligence

The first three of these are covered in this chapter. The remainder are covered in subsequent chapters.

1 Audit related services

Audit-related services are those services that professional accountants offer which are not statutory audits, although they are conceptually related and use similar skills.

An **assurance engagement** is an engagement in which a practitioner expresses a conclusion designed to enhance the degree of confidence of the intended users other than the responsible party about the outcome of the evaluation or measurement of a subject matter against criteria.

Agreed upon procedures require the accountant to report on factual findings and hence no assurance (conclusion) is expressed.

The elements of an assurance engagement

The five elements of an assurance engagement are:

- A 'tripartite' relationship between the practitioner (i.e. accountant), the responsible party (usually directors) and the users of the report.
- A subject matter (the items about which assurance is being sought, e.g. compliance with environmental requirements).
- Suitable criteria (the benchmarks against which the subject matter is being evaluated, e.g. compliance with International Financial Reporting Standards).
- Sufficient appropriate evidence.
- A written assurance report.

The engagement process usually involves:

- Agreeing the terms of the engagement in an engagement letter.
- Deciding on a methodology for evidence gathering to support a conclusion.
- Agreeing on the type of report to be produced at the end of the engagement and expressing the opinion in the written report.

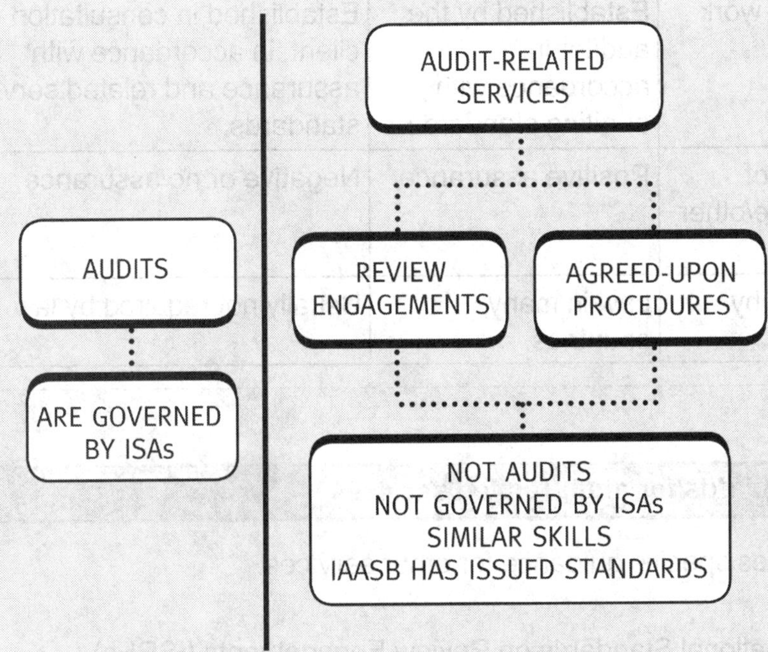

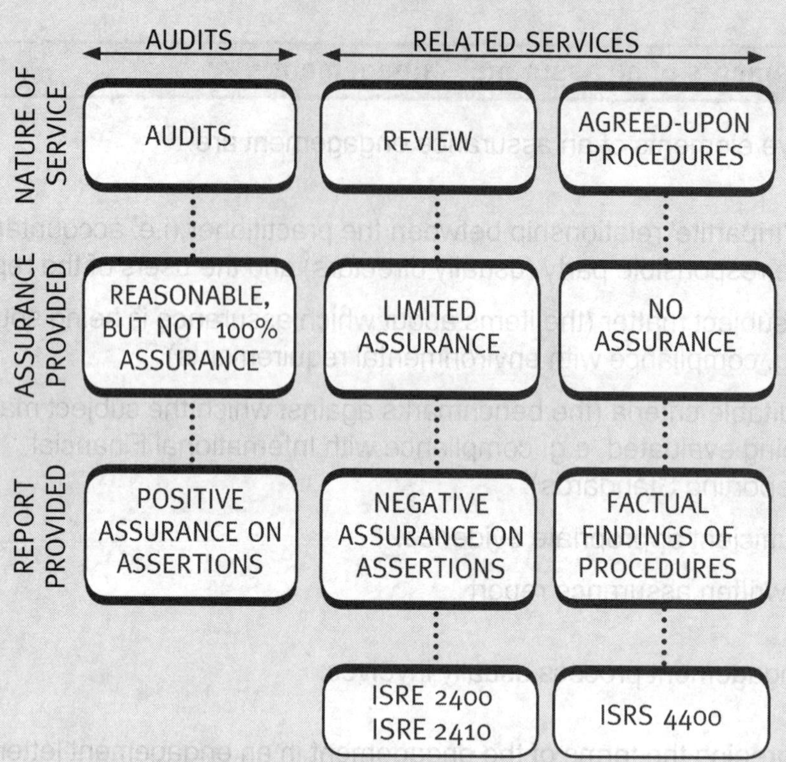

Differences between an audit and audit-related services

	Audit	**Audit-related Services**
Level of assurance	Reasonable assurance	Either limited or no assurance
Scope of work	Established by the auditor in accordance with auditing standards.	Established in consultation with client, in accordance with assurance and related services standards.
Wording of assurance/other reports	Positive assurance	Negative or no assurance
Required by	Law in many countries	Usually not required by law

IFAC standards for audit-related services

IFAC issues specific guidance for other services:

- International Standards on Review Engagements (ISREs)
- International Standards on Related Services (ISRSs)
- International Standards on Assurance Engagements (ISAEs)

Specific examples include:

- ISRE 2400 *Engagements to Review Historical Financial Statements.*
- ISRE 2410 *Review of Interim Financial Information Performed by the Independent Auditor of the Entity.*
- ISAE 3000 *Assurance Engagements other than Audits or Reviews of Historical Financial Statements.*
- ISAE 3420 *Assurance Engagements to Report on the Compilation of Pro Forma Financial Information Included in a Prospectus.*
- ISRS 4400 *Engagements to Perform Agreed-upon Procedures Regarding Financial Information.*
- ISRS 4410 *Engagements to Compile Financial Information.*

Provision of other assurance services

Businesses need to know if their systems are reliable and their business procedures are sound. They may need to demonstrate this to third parties, e.g. a company may wish to persuade influential shareholders that their business plans are sensible and are supported by sound infrastructures. It would be desirable if a third party with the necessary skills and reputation reassured the shareholders.

The auditor is in a strong position to carry out these additional assurance services for their clients. They are professionally trained and already familiar with the business systems in operation at the company. Although this does raise a number of questions regarding the objectivity of the reporting accountant.

In practice, the skills required to offer a comprehensive range of assurance services mean that it is only the largest firms that can offer a complete range of services to clients. Other firms still offer these services and many specialise in certain areas.

The implications of assurance services being provided by auditors are wide-ranging.

- There will be further pressures on the audit firm to maintain its independence as the proportion of fees earned from non-audit work continues to grow and the self-review threat increases.
- Practitioners specialising in a range of disciplines (e.g. IT systems, public sector specialists, etc.) will be needed in the firm as well as traditional financial auditors.

- Many assurance services involve reporting on risk (operational, financial, environmental, etc.). Reporting on such matters will increase the auditor's exposure to professional liability claims.
- The pressures on traditional audit fees will continue to drive them down, since clients will be willing to pay for value-adding assurance services but correspondingly less willing to pay for the statutory audit where they perceive less value for their money.

Levels of assurance provided

The Framework provides the overall guidance for carrying out assurance engagements such as audits and reviews. It permits only two types of assurance engagement to be performed: either a 'reasonable assurance' or a 'limited assurance' engagement.

- The objective of a '**reasonable assurance engagement**' is to obtain sufficient appropriate evidence to conclude that the subject matter conforms in all material respects with identified suitable criteria. The accountant expresses their conclusion in a positive form, giving an opinion on whether the subject matter is free from material misstatement, e.g. statutory audit.
- The objective of a '**limited assurance engagement**' is to obtain sufficient appropriate evidence to be satisfied that the subject matter 'appears plausible' in the circumstances. The accountant expresses their conclusion in a negative form, stating that their procedures have not identified any material misstatement of the subject matter, e.g. a review engagement.

The procedures for a limited assurance engagement are therefore less comprehensive than for a reasonable assurance engagement.

Attestation and Direct Engagements

The framework also permits assurance engagements to be performed as either an **attestation** (or **assertion based**) engagement or a **direct** engagement.

In an **attestation engagement**, the accountant's conclusion relates to an assertion made by the party who is responsible for the subject matter. The accountant can either express a conclusion about this assertion, or can provide a conclusion about the subject matter.

In a **direct engagement**, the accountant expresses a conclusion on the subject matter based on identified criteria, regardless of whether the responsible party has made a written assertion on the subject matter.

For example: a professional accountant may be engaged to report on a company's internal financial controls.

Structured as an attestation engagement:

- management would first make a written assertion about the effectiveness of the company's control structure, and
- the accountant would then give an opinion on management's assertion.

Care must be taken to ensure that management's assertion is clearly understandable and is not subjective. For example, an assertion that the control structure is 'very effective' would be unacceptable since this is a subjective opinion.

Alternatively the engagement could be structured as a direct engagement and the accountant would simply report directly on the effectiveness of the control structure in accordance with predetermined performance criteria.

2 Review engagements

Review of financial statements

- A company which does not require a statutory audit may decide to have a review of its financial statements in order to provide some assurance over, and improve the credibility of, those financial statements.
- **ISRE 2400** ***Engagements to Review Historical Financial Statements*** states that:

  'The objective of a review of financial statements is to enable an auditor to state whether, **on the basis of procedures that do not provide all the evidence that would be required in an audit**, anything has come to the auditor's attention that causes the auditor to believe that the financial statements are not prepared, in all material respects, in accordance with an identified financial reporting framework.'

Review of interim financial statements

- In many countries, listed companies are required to publish a half-yearly interim report containing a summarised statement of profit or loss for the first six months of the financial year as well as certain statement of financial position information and notes.
- Companies may choose to, or be required to, have this report reviewed by the company's auditors.
- **ISRE 2410 *Review of Interim Financial Information Performed by the Independent Auditor of the Entity*** states that:

'The objective of an engagement to review interim financial information is to enable the auditor to express a conclusion whether, on the basis of the review, anything has come to the auditor's attention that causes the auditor to believe that the interim financial information is not prepared, in all material respects, in accordance with an applicable financial reporting framework.'

Main principles of review engagements

To ensure an appropriate standard of work is performed for any type of assurance engagement, practitioners should:

- Comply with the ethical requirements of ACCA's code of conduct.
- Implement appropriate quality control procedures.
- Consider whether the engagement should be accepted such as whether the practitioner has the necessary competence and available resources.
- Agree the terms of engagement in an engagement letter.
- Plan the engagement so that it will be performed effectively including:
  - Applying professional scepticism.
  - Obtaining an understanding of the subject matter and other engagement circumstances to identify and assess the risks of material misstatement.
  - Assessing the suitability of the criteria to evaluate the subject matter.
  - Consideration of materiality and engagement risk.
- Obtain sufficient appropriate evidence on which to base the conclusion.
- Consider subsequent events.
- Document matters significant in providing evidence that supports the engagement report.
- Provide a clear written expression of their conclusion about the subject matter information.

As such, the approach and work may be similar to an audit.

Procedures in review engagements

The accountant must carry out sufficient work to enable them to express limited assurance on the financial statements.

In deciding on the scope of the review (i.e. the procedures deemed necessary in the circumstances), the accountant will consider:

- any knowledge acquired previously about the client.
- the nature of the accounting systems.
- types of material misstatement and the likelihood of occurrence.
- the extent to which items are affected by management judgment.
- the materiality of transactions and balances.

Procedures concentrate primarily on:

- enquiries of relevant parties (usually management).
- analytical procedures.

Analytical procedures should be designed to identify relationships and individual items that appear unusual. Such procedures might include:

- Comparison of the current financial statements vs. prior periods.
- Comparison of the current financial statements vs. forecasts or budgets.
- Review for any relationships within the financial statements that would be expected to conform to a predictable pattern based on previous patterns for the entity or industry norms:
  - Gross profit margin
  - Net profit margin
  - Interest cover
  - Receivables days
  - Payables days
  - Inventory days.

Reporting

The assurance report should include the following elements:

- Title – clearly indicating the report is an independent assurance report.
- Addressee – identifies the intended user.

- Identification and description of the subject matter including period of the information, name of the entity to which the subject matter relates.
- Identification of the criteria.
- Description of any significant, inherent limitations.
- Restriction on the use of the report to specific users.
- Statement of responsibilities of the responsible party and practitioner.
- Statement that the engagement was performed in accordance with professional standards.
- Summary of the work performed.
- Practitioner's conclusion.
- Date.
- Name of the firm or practitioner and location.

Conclusion

The conclusion of an assurance report may be:

- Unmodified
- Qualified
- Adverse
- Disclaimer

If the conclusion is modified, a basis for qualified/adverse/disclaimer of conclusion will be included to explain the circumstances causing the modification.

ISRE 2410 Detailed procedures

ISRE 2410 procedures:

- Reading prior year files relating to the audit and interim financial statement review to enable the auditor to identify matters that may affect the current period interim financial information.
- Considering any significant risks, including the risk of management override of controls, that were identified in the audit of the prior year's financial statements.
- Reading the most recent annual and comparable prior period interim financial information.
- Considering materiality with reference to the applicable financial reporting framework as it relates to interim financial information to assist in determining the nature and extent of the procedures to be performed and evaluating the effect of misstatements.

- Considering the nature of any corrected material misstatements and any identified uncorrected immaterial misstatements in the prior year's financial statements.
- Considering significant financial accounting and reporting matters that may be of continuing significance such as significant deficiencies in internal control.
- Considering the results of any audit procedures performed with respect to the current year's financial statements.
- Considering the results of any internal audit performed and the subsequent actions taken by management.
- Enquiring of management about the results of management's assessment of the risk that the interim financial information may be materially misstated as a result of fraud.
- Enquiring of management about the effect of changes in the entity's business activities.
- Enquiring of management about any significant changes in internal control and the potential effect of any such changes on the preparation of interim financial information.
- Enquiring of management of the process by which the interim financial information has been prepared and the reliability of the underlying accounting records to which the interim financial information is agreed or reconciled.

The review report on a set of financial statements

Illustration 1 Example of an unmodified review report

INDEPENDENT PRACTITIONER'S REVIEW REPORT TO ... ...

Report on the Financial Statements

We have reviewed the accompanying financial statements of ABC Company, which comprise the statement of financial position as at 31 December 20X1, and the statement of profit or loss, statement of changes in equity and statement of cash flows for the year then ended, and a summary of significant accounting policies and other explanatory information.

Management's Responsibility for the Financial Statements

Management is responsible for the preparation of these financial statements in accordance with International Financial Reporting Standards, and for such internal controls as management determines necessary to enable the preparation of financial statements that are free from material misstatement, whether due to fraud or error.

Practitioner's Responsibility

Our responsibility is to express a conclusion on the accompanying financial statements. We conducted our review in accordance with the International Standard on Review Engagements 2400 *Engagements to Review Historical Financial Statements* (or refer to relevant national standards or practices applicable to assurance engagements). ISRE 2400 requires us to conclude whether anything has come to our attention that causes us to believe that the financial statements, taken as a whole, are not prepared in all material respects in accordance with the applicable financial reporting framework. This standard also requires us to comply with relevant ethical requirements.

A review of financial statements in accordance with ISRE 2400 is a limited assurance engagement. The practitioner performs procedures primarily consisting of making inquiries of management and others within the entity, as appropriate, and applying analytical procedures, and evaluates the evidence obtained.

The procedures performed in a review are substantially less than those performed in an audit conducted in accordance with International Standards on Auditing. Accordingly, we do not express an audit opinion on these financial statements.

Conclusion

Based on our review, nothing has come to our attention that causes us to believe that these financial statements do not present fairly, in all material respects, (or 'do not give a true and fair view') the financial position of ABC Company as at December 31 20X1 and of its financial performance and cash flows for the year then ended, in accordance with International Financial Reporting Standards.

Signature

Date

Address

3 Due diligence

Due diligence is a fact finding exercise and is usually conducted to reduce the risk of poor investment decisions.

Purpose and benefits of due diligence

In the context of the P7 exam due diligence is conducted in relation to potential company mergers and acquisitions. An advisor is engaged by the potential acquirer of a company to undertake a comprehensive survey of the target company.

The main purpose of due diligence is **information gathering**: gathering of financial, operational, commercial and market information to ensure the acquirer has full knowledge of the financial performance and position, operations, commercial and market position of the target company. The aim is to reveal any potential problems before a decision regarding the acquisition is made and enables the potential acquirer to enter into the transaction with open eyes.

Due diligence provides the directors of an acquiring company with the information they need to decide whether or not to go ahead with an acquisition; when to go ahead with the acquisition; and how much should be paid for the target company.

Due diligence can increase stakeholder confidence in the acquisition decision, for example, if the acquisition is to be financed by a bank loan, the bank has confidence that the investment is sound and the loan is more likely to be repaid.

Depending upon the client's requirements, a professional conclusion may be expressed. Alternatively, the investigations may result in the presentation of factual findings. Therefore it may **either be conducted as an assurance assignment or an agreed upon procedures assignment**.

Reasons for engaging an advisor to carry out a due diligence review are:

- **Decrease management time spent assessing the acquisition decision**

  Due diligence reviews can be performed internally, by the management of an acquiring company. However, this can be time consuming and the directors may lack the knowledge and experience necessary to perform the review adequately. Engaging an external advisor to carry out the review allows management to focus on strategic matters and running the existing group as well as ensuring an impartial review.

- **Identification of operational issues and risk assessment of the target company**

  For example:

  – possible contractual disputes following a takeover
  – potential breaches of covenants attached to any finance
  – the adequacy of the skills and experience of key management within the target company
  – operational issues such as high staff turnover; issues with supplies/suppliers, quality issues with products or the retention of key customers.

- **Liabilities evaluated and identified**

  It is particularly important that the potential acquirer identifies contingent liabilities that may crystallise in the future, and considers the likelihood of them crystallising and the potential financial consequences. These will affect the price the acquirer wishes to pay for the target.

- **Identify assets not capitalised**

  Internally generated intangibles, such as internal brands, will not be included on the statement of financial position but are vital to purchasing decisions as they increase the value of the business.

- **Gathering information**

  The external advisor will gather any other relevant information that could influence the decision of the client.

- **Enhance the credibility of the investment decision**

  Engaging an external advisor to carry out the due diligence will ensure an independent, objective view is obtained on the investment decision, including the price to be paid.

- **Planning the acquisition**

  The due diligence provider can advise on change management following the acquisition, including integrating the new company into the group, which key staff to retain, help with any restructuring as well as the more immediate issues of determining an appropriate price and reviewing the terms of the sale and purchase agreement.

- **Claims made by the vendor can be substantiated**

  For example, future order levels and current finance agreements.

- **Evaluation of possible post-acquisition synergies and economies of scale and potential further costs**

  The combined entity may be able to utilise distributions systems, non-current assets and management, allowing for surplus assets to be sold and duplicate roles to be made redundant.

The acquiring company may decide the issues and risks identified are so significant they do not want to go ahead with the acquisition. They may use the issues to negotiate a reduced price, or require the vendor to resolve the issues before the acquisition completes.

Procedures

Due diligence procedures will involve:

- enquiries of relevant parties
- analytical procedures
- inspection of documents and records.

Example of a due diligence assignment

Due diligence prior to a flotation

Company A has decided to float part of its share capital on the stock market, so it engages its auditor to conduct a due diligence review. The practitioner will investigate:

- the structure of the business – how it is currently owned and constituted.
- the financial health of the business – looking at past financial statements.
- the credibility of the senior management of the business – looking at the career histories of the directors and ensuring that a balance of skills is available.
- the future potential of the business – planned products and likely future earnings.
- the risk involved in the business.
- the business plan – whether it is realistic.

Types of due diligence

This type of due diligence can be categorised into three areas:

(1) **Financial due diligence:** analysing and validating the target's revenue; maintainable earnings; future cash flows; and financial position including identification and valuation of contingent liabilities and key assets.

(2) **Operational due diligence:** investigation of the operational risks; cost base; asset base; capex requirements; quality of IT and other systems; key customers and suppliers; and performance gaps of the target company.

(3) **Commercial and market due diligence:** a comprehensive review of the target's business plan in the context of the industry and market conditions; including compliance with relevant legal, taxation, and regulatory frameworks.

The advisor will investigate and advise on post-acquisition issues such as consideration of staffing requirements, including the roles of management and key personnel to identify who will need to be retained post-acquisition as well as redundancy, training and other restructuring costs; and identification of potential synergies. The advisor may also provide practical recommendations regarding the acquisition process.

Comparison to external audit

The objective of an audit is to form an opinion regarding whether the financial statements are free from material misstatement.

The aim of due diligence is not to form an opinion on the financial statements, but instead to provide the acquirer with sufficient information to make an informed decision about the acquisition.

Due diligence tends to draw upon wider information resources that include:

- historical financial statements
- management accounts
- business plans, profit and cash flow forecasts
- correspondence with tax authorities and legal advisors
- results of enquiries with management, employees and third parties.

Unless there are specific issues that cause concern, or specific tests have been requested by the client, no detailed audit procedures will be performed on a due diligence investigation. It will also focus more heavily on forecasts and projections, rather than just historical data in order to assess the future prospects of the company and to help decide whether it is a worthwhile investment.

An audit will primarily examine forecasts in order to form an opinion on whether the going concern basis is appropriate, but they are not the focus of an audit.

Finally, it is unlikely that any internal control assessment/testing will be performed on a due diligence exercise unless specifically requested by the client.

Approach to due diligence exam questions

Exam questions will often ask for procedures to be performed for a due diligence engagement. These procedures need to identify the information relevant to the client's investment decision. Based on this information, the client will decide whether to go ahead with the acquisition or it will help them decide what price they are willing to pay.

One way to approach the question is to put yourself in the position of the client.

- What would affect your decision?
- What would make you want to go ahead with the acquisition?
- What would make you think it's not such a good investment?

Examples include:

- Pending legal actions
- Outstanding tax investigations
- Declining market
- Increasing competition
- Damage to reputation
- Old assets in need of replacing
- Declining financial performance
- Quality issues
- Reliability of asset valuations
- Completeness of liabilities

- Human resource issues – e.g. strike action, poor productivity, low morale.

Current issue: Emerging forms of external reporting

Discussion paper: Supporting Credibility and Trust in Emerging Forms of External Reporting: Ten Key Challenges

Emerging External Reports (EER) background

External reporting by companies is increasingly providing non-financial information to meet the needs of stakeholders. This includes environmental, social and governance matters.

Many types of professional services can be performed in relation to this information, including advisory services, agreed-upon procedures, compilation engagements, assurance engagements and internal reporting to management on the entity's reporting processes and controls.

Whilst some countries have developed their own reporting standards on these matters, there is a need for global guidance to provide consistency and quality around the world.

The auditor will read the additional information in the annual report to identify any inconsistencies between the information and the financial statements and their knowledge obtained during the audit. However, they do not express a conclusion about this this information. A separate assurance engagement covering this information may add credibility to the EER report.

Reason for the discussion paper

The IAASB is looking into whether a specific standard should be developed to address a more specific type of engagement. This will keep international standards fit for purpose, support practitioners and support the quality of assurance engagements.

At present there is a lack of guidance for practitioners performing these assurance engagements. The main form of guidance comes from ISAE 3000 which is a framework neutral standard intended to be applied to a wide range of assurance engagements.

Credibility and trust in relation to EER reports

Credibility and trust are enhanced if there are 4 key factors:

(i) Sound reporting framework – the framework should address the reporting objectives and qualitative characteristics of the information.

(ii) Strong governance – the company should have a strong internal control system to ensure the information in the EER is reliable and available on a timely basis.

(iii) Consistent wider information – the information in the EER report should be consistent with other sources of information likely to be available to users of the report.

(iv) External professional service reports e.g. assurance reports – an accompanying report prepared by an external practitioner can add credibility due to their competence, objectivity, professional scepticism and judgment, and quality control procedures.

Ten key challenges

The IAASB has identified ten key challenges which are barriers to more widespread use of assurance reports in relation to Emerging External Reports (EER):

(1) Determining the scope of the assurance engagement – the scope may be broader and more diverse. It may be difficult to provide a full scope engagement as the costs may outweigh the benefits.

(2) Evaluating the suitability of criteria – EER frameworks are less prescriptive and more ambiguous providing opportunity for management bias.

(3) Addressing materiality – EER has no common unit of measurement making materiality judgments difficult to benchmark. Due to the diversity of users, establishing materiality that applies to all will be difficult.

(4) Establishing appropriate assertions – the diverse nature of EER subject matter makes it more difficult to develop appropriate assertions.

(5) Maturity of governance and internal control processes – entities may not have sufficiently robust EER reporting systems and controls in place. As a result the EER report may not be capable of being assured.

(6) Obtaining assurance over narrative information – narrative information may include management judgments and be more susceptible to management bias.

(7) Obtaining assurance over future-oriented information – future-oriented information is more common in EER reports. There is greater uncertainty over this information. Therefore the assurance may have to be limited to obtaining evidence about the process used in arriving at the future-oriented information.

(8) Professional scepticism and judgment – EER reports are likely to contain information that is more susceptible to management bias resulting in a greater need to apply professional scepticism and judgment.

(9) Competence of practitioners – this type of engagement may call for broad specialised subject matter competence, greater need for experts and the use of multi-disciplinary teams.

(10) Form of the assurance report – to effectively communicate the conclusions to users, the report may need to include the following to ensure they are of use and not seen as ambiguous or difficult to interpret:

- a summary of the work performed which provides the basis for the conclusion,
- additional information such as the terms of engagement, criteria, findings, competencies of the individuals involved, materiality levels and recommendations.
- separate conclusions on one or more aspects of the subject matter

Exam style question: Due Diligence

Plaza, a limited liability company, is a major food retailer with a chain of national supermarkets. It has extended its operations throughout Europe and most recently to Asia, where it is expanding rapidly.

You are a manager in Andando, a firm of Chartered Certified Accountants. You have been approached by Duncan Seymour, the chief finance officer of Plaza, to advise on a bid that Plaza is proposing to make for the purchase of MCM. You have ascertained the following from a briefing note received from Duncan. MCM provides training in management, communications and marketing to a wide range of corporate clients, including multi-nationals. The 'MCM' name is well regarded in its areas of expertise. MCM is currently wholly-owned by Frontiers, an international publisher of textbooks, whose shares are quoted on a recognised stock exchange. MCM has a National and an International business.

The National business comprises 11 training centres. The audited financial statements show revenue of $12.5 million and profit before taxation of $1.3 million for this geographic segment for the year to 31 December 20X3. Most of the National business's premises are owned or held on long leases. Trainers in the National business are mainly full-time employees.

The International business has five training centres in Europe and Asia. For these segments, revenue amounted to $6.3 million and profit before tax $2.4 million for the year to 31 December 20X3. Most of the International business premises are leased. International trade receivables at 31 December 20X3 amounted to $3.7 million. Although the International centres employ some full-time trainers, the majority of trainers provide their services as freelance consultants.

Required:

(a) Define 'due diligence' and describe the nature and purpose of a due diligence review.

(4 marks)

(b) Explain the matters you should consider before accepting an engagement to conduct a due diligence review of MCM.

(10 marks)

(c) Illustrate how:

(i) enquiry **(5 marks)**

(ii) analytical procedures **(6 marks)**

might appropriately be used in the due diligence review of MCM.

(Total: 25 marks)

Test your understanding 1

Describe FOUR procedures that can be performed when reviewing interim financial statements.

(4 marks)

Risk assessment

Risk assessment engagements

Corporate governance best practice requires that boards of directors conduct, at least annually, a review of the effectiveness of the group's system of internal controls.

The entity's risk assessment process is an essential component of an effective internal control system.

Management must therefore have a process for identifying, assessing and responding to business risks.

Identifying the risks considers all aspects of the business and what might go wrong. A risk register can then be created.

Assessing the risks involves estimating the possible impact to the organisation if the risk occurs and the probability of the risk occurring.

Possible responses are:

- **Transfer** the risk to someone else, e.g. by insurance or by outsourcing the risky activity or by requiring third parties to sign indemnities.
- **Avoid** the risk, e.g. terminate the risky operation and move the resources to a less risky activity.
- **Reduce** the risk by establishing controls.
- **Accept** the risk, particularly if it is of low impact and/or low likelihood.

The auditor may be engaged to report on the effectiveness of the company's internal controls, especially where evident criteria exist such as the company applying a specific control framework.

Risk audit is also an integral element of P1 *The Professional Accountant*. The P1 examiner published an article entitled "Risk and Environmental Auditing" that may also be of use to candidates studying P7.

ISAE 3420

ISAE 3420 Assurance Engagements to Report on the Compilation of Pro Forma Financial Information Included in a Prospectus

The standard deals with reasonable assurance engagements to report on the compilation of pro forma financial information included in a prospectus where it is required by relevant law or regulation (note, it does not cover situations where a practitioner is engaged to compile the information).

- A **prospectus** is a document that provides details of an entity's securities (debt or equity) offered for sale to the public, containing the information that potential investors need to make an informed investment decision.
- **Pro forma financial information** models the impact of a significant event or transaction, as though the event had occurred or the transaction had been undertaken at an earlier date (selected for the purpose of the illustration) for example:
  - to illustrate the impact of a recent acquisition on the financial position of the entity.
  - to illustrate what the results of the entity might have been if the acquisition was made earlier.
- Pro forma financial information is normally presented alongside the unadjusted financial information, with the adjustments made in arriving at the pro forma financial information also shown separately.
- Pro forma financial information does not represent the entity's actual financial position, financial performance, or cash flows.
- Pro forma financial information is necessary because the most recent financial statements would not show the impact of the event or transaction, and the prospective investors would not be able to make an informed investment decision without this information.

The objectives of the engagement are:

- to obtain reasonable assurance about whether the pro forma financial information has been compiled, in all material respects, by the responsible party on the basis of the applicable criteria, and
- to report on the above.

In performing the engagement, the practitioner must determine that:

- the unadjusted financial information has been obtained from and agrees to an appropriate source (e.g. the audited financial statements)
- the pro forma adjustments are:
  - directly attributable to the event or transaction
  - factually supportable, and
  - consistent with the entity's applicable financial reporting framework and accounting policies.
- the information is presented appropriately, and appropriate disclosures are made to enable the intended users to understand the information conveyed.
- all necessary pro forma adjustments have been included.
- the calculations within the pro forma financial information are arithmetically accurate.

The other information within the prospectus should be read to identify any inconsistencies with the pro forma information.

4 Chapter summary

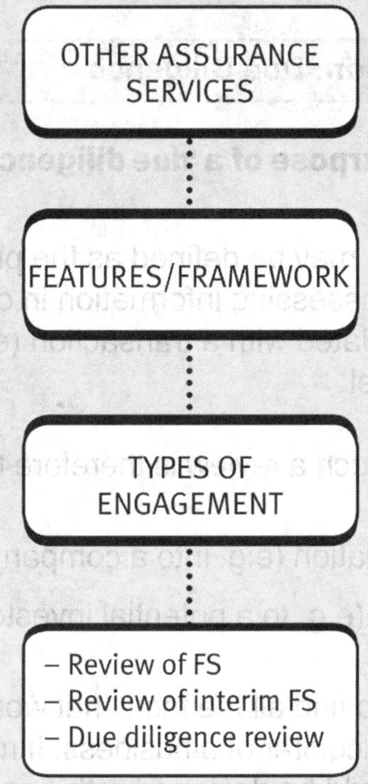

	Audits	**Reviews**	**Agreed-upon procedures**
Assurance provided	Reasonable but not absolute assurance	Limited assurance	No assurance
Guidance given in ...	ISAs	ISRE 2400 ISRE 2410	ISRS 4400
Scope of work decided by ...	Auditor, as much as he deems necessary to give positive opinion	Reviewer, as much as he deems necessary to give negative opinion	The party engaging the accountant's services (to carry out the procedures)
Type of report provided	Positive assurance	Negative assurance	Factual findings of the procedures carried out

Test your understanding answers

Exam style question: Due Diligence

(a) **Nature and purpose of a 'due diligence' review**

'Due diligence' may be defined as the process of systematically obtaining and assessing information in order to identify and contain the risks associated with a transaction (e.g. buying a business) to an acceptable level.

The nature of such a review is therefore that it involves:

– an investigation (e.g. into a company whose equity may be sold)

– disclosure (e.g. to a potential investor) of findings.

Its purpose is to find all the facts that would be of material interest to an investor or acquirer of a business. It may not uncover all such factors but should be designed with a reasonable expectation of so doing.

Professional accountants will not be held liable for non-disclosure of information that failed to be uncovered if their review was conducted with 'due diligence'.

(b) **Matters to be considered (before accepting the engagement)**

Tutorial note: Although candidates may approach this part from a rote-learned list of 'matters to consider' it is important that answer points be tailored, in so far as the information given in the scenario permits, to the specifics of Plaza and MCM. It is critical that answer points should not contradict the scenario (e.g. assuming that it is Plaza's auditor who has been asked to undertake the assignment).

Information about Duncan Seymour

What is the relationship of the chief finance officer to Plaza (e.g. is he on the management board)? By what authority is he approaching Andando to undertake this assignment?

Purpose of the assignment

The purpose must be clarified. Duncan's approach to Andando is 'to advise on a bid'. However, Andando cannot make executive decisions for a client but only provide the facts of material interest. Plaza's management must decide whether or not to bid and, if so, how much to bid.

Scope of the due diligence review

It seems likely that Plaza will be interested in acquiring all of MCM's business as its areas of operation coincide with Plaza's. However it must be confirmed that Plaza is not merely interested in acquiring only the National or International business of MCM.

Andando's competence and experience

Andando should not accept the engagement unless the firm has experience in undertaking due diligence assignments. Even then, the firm must have sufficient knowledge of the territories in which the businesses operate to evaluate whether all facts of material interest to Plaza have been identified.

Resources available

Whether the firm has sufficient resources available (e.g. representative/associated offices) in Europe and Asia to investigate MCM's International business.

Threats to objectivity and independence

For example, if Duncan is closely connected with a partner in Andando or if Andando is the auditor of Frontiers.

Tutorial note: Candidates will not be awarded marks for going into 'autopilot' on independence issues. For example, this is a one-off assignment so size of fee is not relevant. Andando holding shares in MCM is not possible (since wholly owned).

Rationale for the acquisition

Presumably it is significant that MCM operates in the same territories as Plaza. Plaza may be wanting to provide extensive training programs in management, communications and marketing to its workforce.

Relationship between Plaza and MCM

Plaza may be a major client of MCM. That is, Plaza is currently outsourcing training to MCM. Acquiring MCM would bring training in-house.

Tutorial note: Ascertaining what a purchaser hopes to gain from an acquisition before the assignment is accepted as important. The facts to be uncovered for a merger from which synergy is expected will be different from those relevant to acquiring an investment opportunity.

Time available

Andando must have sufficient time to find all facts that would be of material interest to Plaza before disclosing their findings.

Access to information

Whether there will be restrictions on Andando's access to information held by MCM (e.g. if there will not be access to board minutes) and personnel.

Degree of secrecy required

This may go beyond the normal duties of confidentiality not to disclose information to outsiders (e.g. if unannounced staff redundancies could arise).

Plaza's current auditors

Why have they not been asked to conduct the due diligence review, especially as they are responsible for (and therefore capable of undertaking) the group audit covering the relevant countries.

Communication with the current auditor

Andando should be allowed to communicate with Plaza's current auditor:

- to inform them of the nature of the work they have been asked to undertake, and
- to enquire if there is any reason why they should not accept this assignment.

Other services that can be offered

In taking on Plaza as a new client Andando may have a later opportunity to offer external audit and other services to Plaza (e.g. internal audit).

C **Due diligence review**

(i) **Enquiries**

Tutorial note: These should be focused on uncovering facts that may not be revealed by the audited financial statements (e.g. contingencies, commitments and contracts) especially where knowledge may be confined to management.

- Do any members of MCM's senior/executive management have contractual terms that will result in significant payouts to them (e.g. on change of ownership of the company or their being made redundant)?
- What contracts with clients, if any, will lapse or be made void in the event that MCM is purchased from Frontiers?
- Are there any major clients who are likely to be lost if MCM is purchased by Plaza (e.g. any competitor food retailers)?
- What are the principal terms of the leases relating to the International business's premises?
- What penalties should be expected to be incurred if leases and/or contracts with training consultants are terminated?
- Has MCM entered into any purchase commitments since the last audited financial statements (e.g. to buy or lease further premises)?
- Who are the best trainers that Plaza should seek to retain after the purchase of MCM?
- What events since the last audited financial statements were published that have made a significant impact on MCM's assets, liabilities, operating capability and/or cash flows? (For example, storm damage to premises, major clients defaulting on payments, significant interest/foreign-exchange rate fluctuations, etc.)
- Are there any unresolved tax issues which have not been provided for in full?
- What effect will the purchase have on loan covenants? For example, term loans may be rendered repayable on a change of ownership.

(ii) **Analytical procedures**

Tutorial note: The range of valid answer points is very broad for this part.

- Review the trend of MCM's profit (gross and net) for the last five years (say). Similarly earnings per share and gearing.
- For both the National and International businesses compare:
  - gross profit, net profit, and return on assets for the last five years
  - actual monthly revenue against budget for the last 2 years
  - actual monthly salary costs against budget for the last 2 years
  - actual monthly freelance consultancy fees against budget for the last 2 years
  - actual monthly premises costs (e.g. depreciation, lease rentals, maintenance, etc) against budget for the last 2 years.
- Review projections of future profitability of MCM against net profit percentage for:
  - the National business (10.4%)
  - the International business (38.1%)
  - overall (19.9%).
- Review of disposal value of owned premises against carrying values.
- Compare actual cash balances with budget on a monthly basis and compare borrowings against loan and overdraft facilities.
- Compare the average collection period for International trade receivables month on month since 31 December (when it was nearly seven months, i.e. \$3.7/\$6.3 × 365 days) and compare with the National business.

- Compare financial ratios for each of the national centres against the National business overall (and similarly for the International Business), for example:
  - gross and net profit margins
  - return on centre assets
  - average collection period
  - average payment period
  - liquidity ratio.
- Compare key performance indicators across the centres for the last two year's, for example:
  - number of corporate clients
  - number of delegates
  - number of training days
  - average revenue per delegate per day
  - average cost per consultancy day.

Test your understanding 1

- Compare the interim financial information to the prior year interim financial information.
- Calculate key ratios such as receivables days, payables days, inventory days, etc and compare with the ratios calculated from the last audited financial statements.
- Compare the accounting policies used in the interim information with the accounting policies used in the audited financial statements to ensure they are consistent.
- Enquire of management if there have been any significant control deficiencies during the period which could affect the reliability of the figures.
- Review the audit file from the year-end audit to identify issues arising in the subsequent events review which could impact the figures.
- Enquire of management of any significant changes that have happened to update understanding of the entity.

chapter

16

Prospective financial information

Chapter learning objectives

This chapter covers syllabus areas:

- E2 – Prospective financial information
- F3b – Discuss the content of a report for an examination of prospective financial information

Detailed syllabus objectives are provided in the introduction section of the text book.

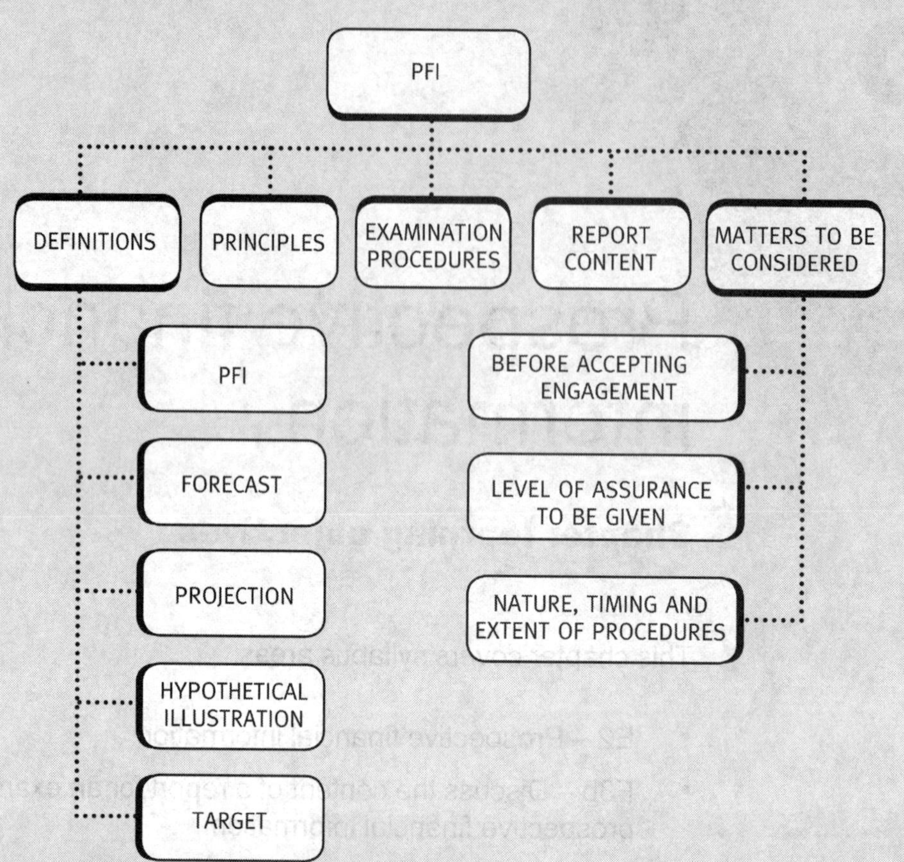

Exam focus

Assurance engagements to examine projections and forecasts, often to support an application for a loan, are very common in real life and feature regularly in the exam. As the transactions haven't happened yet, procedures will focus on testing the reasonableness of the assumptions management have used when preparing the forecast.

1 What is 'prospective financial information'?

A reporting accountant may be asked to give an assurance opinion on prospective (i.e. future) financial information. Guidance on examining PFI is given in **ISAE 3400** *The Examination of Prospective Financial Information*.

Definitions

Prospective financial information (PFI) means financial information based on assumptions about events that may occur in the future and possible actions by an entity. It may be in the form of a forecast or a projection, or a combination of both.

A forecast is:

- PFI prepared on the basis of assumptions as to future events that management expects to take place and the actions management expects to take (best-estimate assumptions).

A projection is:

- PFI prepared on the basis of hypothetical assumptions about future events and management actions that are not necessarily expected to take place, or a mixture of best estimate and hypothetical assumptions.

A hypothetical illustration is a depiction of anticipated outcomes based on uncertain future events and actions.

A target is a desired future outcome aimed for by an organisation.

Principles of useful PFI

PFI can be issued:

- as an internal management tool, e.g. to support a possible capital investment, or
- for distribution to third parties, for example:
  - in a prospectus
  - in an annual report
  - to inform lenders or to support an application for finance.

Ultimately the usefulness of PFI depends on the requirements of the end user. Consider, for example, the different decisions and information needs of a prospective lender and shareholder. The unifying qualities of good PFI are that reports must:

- address the specific needs of the user
- be prepared on a timely basis to enable decisions to be taken.

2 Acceptance of PFI engagements – matters to consider

In general, like an audit engagement, the reporting accountant must consider the risk of involvement with the PFI. The greater the risk of giving an inappropriate report, the greater the risk of legal claims and loss of reputation. Ultimately, if the risk is too high the engagement should be politely declined.

ISAE 3400 requires the reporting accountant to consider the following:

Matter under consideration	Reason
The intended use of the information, such as internal management or external users.	Information for external use will be relied upon by third parties, potentially for making investment decisions. This makes it riskier for the accountant because the consequences of inappropriate reports will be more severe.
Whether the information will be for general or limited distribution.	Information for general distribution will result in the assignment being potentially more risky as a larger audience will be relying on it.
The nature of the assumptions (e.g. best-estimate or hypothetical).	Forecasts and projections cannot be verified with any certainty because the outcome is unknown, however: • If information is best-estimate, it should be a reasonable approximation as to what might actually happen. • Where the assumptions are hypothetical, they will be much more difficult to validate as there is likely to be little to support them and therefore the assignment holds higher risk. The engagement should not be accepted if the assumptions are clearly unrealistic or if it is expected that the PFI will be inappropriate for its intended use.
The elements to be included in the information.	The engagement will be higher risk if the PFI includes elements of which the accountant has little knowledge or that are extremely complex or highly subjective.
The period covered by the information.	Short-term forecasts are likely to be more easily verified than projections looking out over a longer period.

3 Level of assurance

Due to the uncertainty surrounding forecasts and projections, and due to the limited nature of the procedures performed during the accountant's review, only **limited assurance** can be offered for PFI engagements.

The conclusion will be expressed negatively, i.e. 'Nothing has come to our attention to suggest the assumptions used in the forecast don't provide a reasonable basis for the forecast'.

The terms of engagement

An engagement to report on PFI does not constitute an audit. However, the prospective client may not appreciate this fact. Agreeing the terms of engagement is therefore critical in the avoidance of conflict with the client.

Typically the engagement letter should specify the following terms:

- The nature of procedures performed.
- The type of assurance offered, i.e. limited.
- The form of conclusion given, i.e. negative.
- Management's responsibilities, which are to prepare the PFI and to establish appropriate assumptions.
- Restrictions on the use and distribution of the assurance report.
- The basis of setting the fees.

4 Procedures

The practitioner should obtain a sufficient level of knowledge of the business to be able to evaluate whether all significant assumptions required for the preparation of the PFI have been identified.

This requires knowledge of the processes used to prepare the PFI including:

- Internal controls over the system used to prepare the PFI.
- Nature of documentation to support management's assumptions.
- The extent to which statistical, mathematical and computer assisted techniques are used.
- Methods used to develop and apply assumptions.
- Accuracy of PFI prepared in prior periods and reasons for significant variances.

Analytical procedures can be used to identify any unusual fluctuations between the forecast and past performance of the company or industry expectations for the forecast period.

Enquiry can be used to follow up on any fluctuations identified as well as being used to establish the assumptions used by management when preparing the forecast.

Inspection may be used where items included in the forecast are already established and in progress, for example:

- Inspection of existing loan or lease agreements to agree the repayments included in the forecast.
- Inspection of quotations or price lists to agree forecast costs for new asset.
- Inspection of recent utility bills to assess the reasonableness of forecast utility costs.

Written representations

The practitioner should obtain written representations from management regarding:

- the intended use of the PFI
- the completeness of significant management assumptions
- management's acceptance of its responsibility for the PFI.

It is not appropriate for the practitioner to rely solely on such representations. The practitioner must appropriately plan, perform and review a range of procedures to enable them to obtain sufficient appropriate evidence for the purposes of offering assurance.

PFI procedures: Specific examples

The specific procedures performed on an engagement will depend on the information requirements of the users and the report under scrutiny. However, examples of general procedures include:

- Comparison of forecast amounts to historic performance to ensure consistency. Whilst future results will not always follow previous trends historical patterns give an indication of the capacity of the business. It is also important to consider that rapid growth is unlikely and potentially damaging to a business (overtrading!!).

- Comparison of forecast amounts to actual results. It is likely that by the time that a PFI review is actually conducted some of that period may have elapsed. Internally produced management accounts may therefore be available to use to assess actual performance for the first few months of the forecast period.
- Forecasts for previous periods may also be assessed in comparison to actual results to assess how accurately management have forecast in the past.
- Reasonably certain incomes and costs (such as loan interest) may be verified by comparison of forecast amounts to documents such as orders, contracts, loan agreements, lease contracts etc.
- Comparison of accounting policies/estimates used in forecasts in comparison to financial statements, e.g. depreciation rates.
- Inspection of the non-current asset note to identify if assets are approaching the end of their useful lives and require replacement.
- Comparisons of working capital amounts/liquidity to assess whether liabilities can be met and the company can finance its short term resourcing requirements.
- Comparison of the relationships between the reported figures, for example is a significant increase in revenue supported by increased production costs, advertising costs and distribution costs?
- Calculation of key ratios such as:
  - Gross profit margin
  - Net margin
  - Receivables days
  - Payables days
  - Inventory days
- Typical enquiries may include:
  - When do loan agreements expire?
  - Whether further forms of finance are being sought?
  - Whether any new customer/supplier contracts have been agreed since the year-end?
  - Have any new capital purchases been agreed?
  - Has the company invested in any product research/development and if so what are the results?
  - Has the company conducted any market research and again what are the results?
  - Have there been any new competitors/products in the market place.

This list is by no way exhaustive and is very general in nature. The purpose of the examples is that they all consider events or circumstances that will have an impact on the business in the future. Note that none of the enquiries are vague, such as "how do you forecast sales?" They try and identify issues that will directly impact management's forecasts.

In the exam you will be required to suggest procedures that are relevant to the scenario.

5 Final report

The key elements of the assurance report are summarised below:

- Title and addressee.
- Identification of the subject matter i.e. the forecast information.
- Reference to any applicable laws or standards (e.g. ISAE 3400).
- A statement that it is management's responsibility to prepare the PFI.
- Reporting accountant's responsibilities and basis of opinion.
- A reference to the purpose and restricted distribution of the PFI.
- A statement of negative assurance as to whether the assumptions provide a reasonable basis for the PFI.
- An opinion on whether the PFI is properly prepared on the basis of the assumptions and is presented in accordance with the relevant financial reporting framework.
- Appropriate caveats about the achievability of the results given the nature of assumptions and inherent limitations in the forecasting process.
- Reporting accountant's signature and address.
- Date of the report.

PFI report wording

Based on our examination of the evidence supporting the assumptions, nothing has come to our attention which causes us to believe that these assumptions do not provide a reasonable basis for the forecast. Further, in our opinion, the forecast is properly prepared on the basis of the assumptions and is presented in accordance with...

Actual results are likely to be different from the forecast since anticipated events frequently do not occur as expected and the variation may be material.

Approach to PFI exam questions

Read the requirement carefully to make sure you are clear on whether you are examining a profit forecast or a cash flow forecast.

- A profit forecast should be based on an accruals assumption i.e. the level of revenue and expenses expected to be earned and incurred during the forecast period.
- A cash flow forecast should be based on a cash basis i.e. the cash inflows and outflows expected during the forecast period.
- In particular, non-cash expenses such as depreciation will not be relevant for a cash flow forecast but will be relevant for a profit forecast.

One way to approach an answer is to assume that the client's starting point for preparing the forecast is the prior year actual results. From here they will:

- Remove items which will not be relevant going forward e.g. if they are discontinuing an activity the costs and revenues/receipts and payments for this activity should not be included in the forecast once it has ceased. Remember to consider one-off costs as a result of the discontinued activity such as profit/loss on disposal of assets or proceeds from the disposal of assets. Redundancy costs should also be included if staff are to be made redundant rather than redeployed within the organisation.
- Add in any new costs or revenues e.g. if they are expanding the business there may be more assets acquired and people employed. Within a profit forecast you would expect to see increased depreciation and payroll costs. Within a cash flow forecast you would expect to see payments to acquire assets and increased payments to employees.
- Adjust revenues and expenses/receipts and payments for inflation/growth for items that are expected to continue.

The assurance provider's procedures will focus on whether the figures included in the forecast look reasonable.

- For new items this might be achieved by inspecting quotations or market research data.
- For items to be excluded, review the forecast to ensure they are no longer included.
- For items of a continuing nature, comparison with prior year management accounts can be performed.

Test your understanding 1 – Imperiol

Imperiol, a limited liability company, manufactures and distributes electrical and telecommunications accessories, household durables (e.g. sink and shower units) and building systems (e.g. air-conditioning, solar heating, security systems). The company has undergone several business restructurings in recent years. Finance is to be sought from both a bank and a venture capitalist in order to implement the board's latest restructuring proposals.

You are a manager at Hal Falcon, a firm of Chartered Certified Accountants. You have been approached by Paulo Gandalf, the chief finance officer of Imperiol, to provide a report on the company's business plan for the year to 31 December 20X5.

From a brief telephone conversation with Paulo Gandalf you have ascertained that the proposed restructuring will involve discontinuing all operations except for building systems, where the greatest opportunity for increasing product innovation is believed to lie. Imperiol's strategy is to become the market leader in providing 'total building system solutions' using new fibre optic technology to link building systems. A major benefit of the restructuring is expected to be a lower ongoing cost base. As part of the restructuring it is likely that the accounting functions, including internal audit, will be outsourced.

You have obtained a copy of Imperiol's Interim Report for the six months to 30 June 20X4 on which the company's auditors, Discorpio, provide a conclusion giving negative assurance. The following information has been extracted from the Interim Financial Report:

(1) **Chairman's statement**

The economic climate is less certain than it was a few months ago and performance has been affected by a severe decline in the electrical accessories market. Management's response will be to gain market share and reduce the cost base.

(2) **Statement of financial position**

	30 June 20X4 (unaudited)	31 December 20X3
	$m	$m
Intangible assets	83.5	72.6
Non-current assets	69.6	63.8
Inventory	25.2	20.8
Trade receivables	59.9	50.2
Cash	8.3	23.8
Total assets	246.5	231.2
Non-current liabilities – borrowing	65.4	45.7
Current liabilities	55.6	57.0
Equity and liabilities:		
Share capital	30.4	30.4
Reserves	6.0	9.1
Accumulated profit	89.1	89.0
	246.5	231.2

(3) **Continuing and discontinuing operations**

	Six months to 30 June 20X4 (unaudited)	Year to 31 December 20X3
	$m	$m
Revenue		
Continuing operations		
Electrical and telecommunication accessories	55.3	118.9
Household durables	37.9	77.0
Building systems	53.7	94.9
Total continuing	146.9	290.8
Discontinued	–	65.3
Total revenue	146.9	356.1
Operating profit before interest and taxation – continuing operations	13.4	32.2

Required:

(a) Identify and explain the matters Hal Falcon should consider before accepting the engagement to report on Imperiol's prospective financial information.

(8 marks)

(b) Describe the procedures that a professional accountant should undertake in order to provide an assurance report on the prospective financial information of Imperiol for the year to 31 December 20X5.

(10 marks)

(Total: 18 marks)

6 Chapter summary

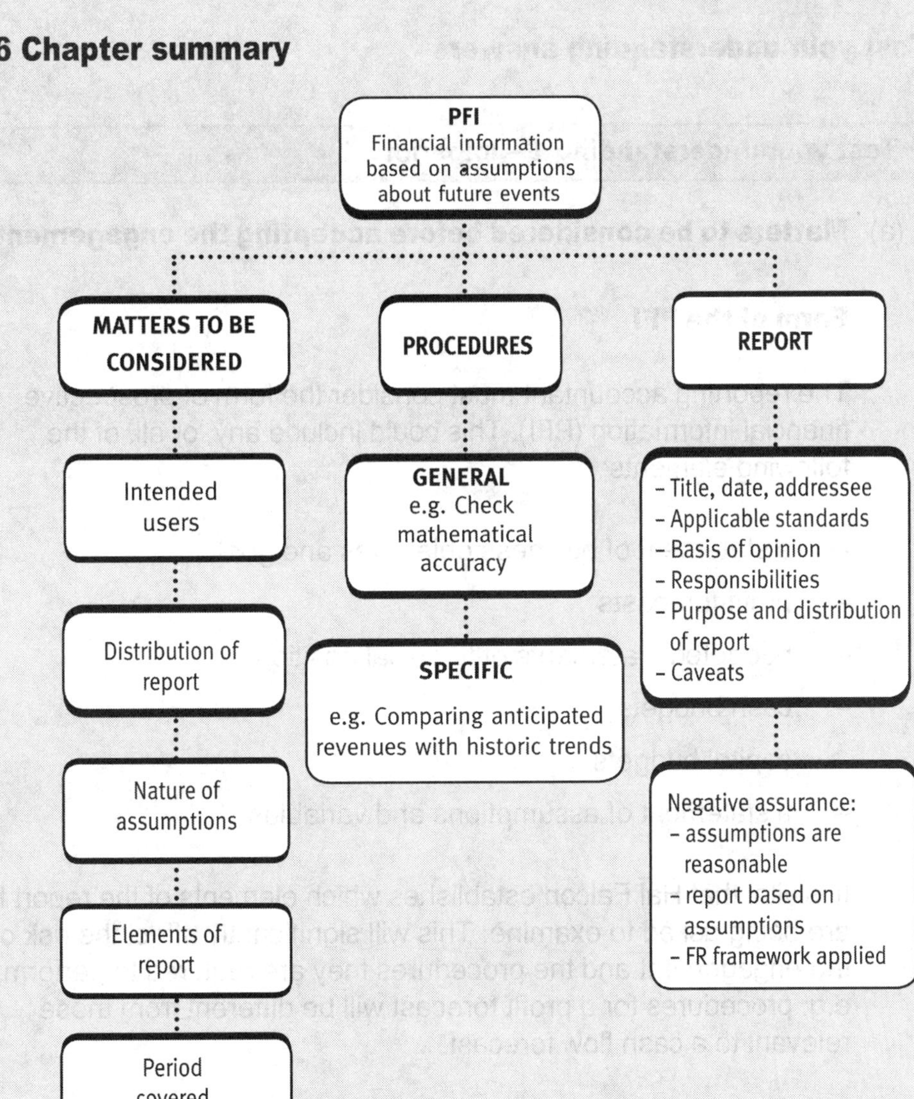

Test your understanding answers

Test your understanding 1 – Imperiol

(a) **Matters to be considered before accepting the engagement**

Form of the PFI

The reporting accountant must consider the form of prospective financial information (PFI). This could include any, or all, of the following elements:

- a statement of business objectives and goals
- profit forecasts
- budgeted statements of financial position
- cash budgets
- capital budgets
- a statement of assumptions and variables.

It is vital that Hal Falcon establishes which elements of the report they are being asked to examine. This will significantly affect the risk of the engagement and the procedures they are required to perform, e.g. procedures for a profit forecast will be different from those relevant to a cash flow forecast.

Level of assurance

It is also vital to establish what sort of report Imperiol requires. It is likely that they will want some form of assurance engagement. If so, it must be clarified that only limited assurance can be offered due to the uncertainty of forecasts. The conclusion will be worded negatively, i.e. that the subject matter is 'plausible' and that nothing has come to light during testing to suggest otherwise.

The conclusion is focused on whether:

- the assumptions are reasonable and consistent with the purpose of the information
- the PFI is properly prepared on the basis of the assumptions
- the PFI is prepared on a consistent basis with historical financial statements, using appropriate accounting principles.

Access to information

To enable this to be performed efficiently, Imperiol must ensure that access to all relevant information and staff is made available. Any restrictions would lead to a breach of engagement terms and a potential disclaimer of opinion.

Permission to communicate with auditors

When an accountant is asked to perform additional work for a client, they should be granted permission to speak to any other accountants or auditors that the company uses in order to obtain relevant information. Hal Falcon should also request permission to communicate with Discorpio, in the form of a professional etiquette letter. If this is not given, the engagement should be declined.

Consider why the auditors, Discorpio, have not been used

To provide a report on the reasonableness of the forecast, a good understanding of the company is required. The auditor is usually the party with the most understanding. The use of a different firm poses a risk as Imperiol may be hoping that a different firm will not identify that the assumptions are not reasonable.

Period covered by the examination

Paulo Gandalf has requested a review of the forecasts to 31 December 20X5. This does not appear to be particularly extensive and it is likely that a provider of significant finance would seek a longer forecast period. Before accepting the engagement Hal Falcon should confirm in the engagement letter that the only period being examined (and requested by the financiers) is to 31 December 20X5.

Reliance on the report by third parties

The report is likely to be used to raise some form of finance. Hal Falcon must agree the distribution of the report prior to accepting. The greater the number of parties that place reliance on the report, the greater the risk involved. Therefore Hal Falcon must seek to reduce this risk by reducing distribution to specific parties and by writing appropriate caveats/disclaimers in the final report.

Authority of Paulo Gandalf to request the work

Hal Falcon should also establish what authority Paulo Gandalf has to appoint them. He may not be empowered by the board and if he is responsible for the preparation of the PFI it may appear to impair Hal Falcon's objectivity if Paulo makes the appointment.

Competence/knowledge of Imperiol

Having never audited Imperiol Hal Falcon should consider whether they have the competence and experience to successfully review the PFI. If they have little knowledge of the building system's industry they would have to seriously question their ability to assess the assumptions about future performance. In particular, if the reporting deadlines are tight there will be little room for extensive planning and knowledge gathering. Under those circumstances the existing auditor may be better placed to assign a team.

Risk

It appears as though Imperiol have undertaken a number of restructuring initiatives. They discontinued some businesses in 20X3 and it appears in the future they will continue to strip away operations until they are left with nothing but building systems. This may suggest that Imperiol is unstable, which increases the risk that forecasts will be inappropriate.

Independence

As Hal Falcon are not the auditors, independence cannot be assumed. The firm needs to ensure there are no threats to objectivity that would prevent them from accepting the engagement. If the firm is not independent, any user of the report may not trust it to be reliable.

Other matters

Hal Falcon could also consider the following before deciding whether to proceed or not:

- The nature of assumptions underlying the preparation of the PFI: i.e. best-estimate or hypothetical.
- Whether there may be an opportunity to offer other services to Imperiol, e.g. internal audit.
- Fees and whether the fee will be appropriate for the level of risk of the engagement.
- Integrity of the preparer of the forecast.

(b) **Procedures to be performed**

General procedures

- Compare the forecast for 20X3 to the results achieved in 20X3 to assess management's competence at preparing PFI.
- Compare the forecast to previous performance to identify if they are in keeping with historical trends. Any significant distortions from historical trends would require explanation.
- Compare accounting policies used in the forecast to the historical accounts to ensure consistency.
- Obtain written representation from management that they acknowledge their responsibility for the forecasts, that they believe the assumptions used in the forecast are reasonable and confirmation of the intended use of the forecast.
- Recalculate the forecast to verify the arithmetic accuracy.

Specific procedures

Discontinued operations

- Enquire of management how soon the remainder of the operations to be discontinued will be wound down or sold and ensure this timescale is reflected in the forecast.
- Review the forecast costs for impairment charges in respect of the intangible assets. Intangible assets for those activities which are discontinuing may be significantly impaired.
- Enquire of management whether the non-current assets relating to discontinued activities will be sold, scrapped or used elsewhere in the business.
- Inspect second hand prices or correspondence from buyers to consider the reasonableness of disposal proceeds (in the cash forecast) and the consistency of gains/losses on disposals in the profit forecast. There may already be sale agreements in place.
- Recalculate the forecast profits/losses on disposal using the proceeds verified above to confirm accuracy.
- Enquire of management whether any of the inventory held relates to discontinued operations. If so, review the valuation to ensure that any write downs have been made if it cannot be sold.

New structure

- Review the forecast to ensure the new forms of finance have been included e.g. interest charges.
- Enquire whether any amounts or rates have been discussed. If there is documentary evidence (for example, an agreement that is contingent upon the PFI) review this to ensure it is accurately reflected in the PFI.
- Review the forecast to ensure the expected increase in fibre optic products has been reflected in the forecast purchases of inventory.
- Compare the forecasts to actual performance in 20X3 and 20X4. The PFI should reflect a reduction in staff costs and an increase in professional fees due to the outsourcing of accounts.
- Enquire of the directors what they believe the extent of the benefit will be from outsourcing accounting functions.
- Compare the forecast outsourcing fees to any quotes received from professional firms.
- Obtain details of salaries for the staff to be made redundant and the redundancy terms, and calculate the expected redundancy cost. Compare with the forecast figure to ensure it is reasonable.

Changing performance

- Enquire of management what they consider to be the key variables which underpin building systems revenue growth. Therefore any assumptions of growth for building systems will require close scrutiny as this is to be the only revenue stream.
- Compare forecast sales in the PFI with any internal management accounts or marketing based forecasts to ensure that the amounts are consistent with the key assumptions of future profitability.
- Enquire of management what their sales terms are. The receivables days at the end of June 20X4 are 74 days. This is considerably higher than 20X3 (51 days) and the effect of this should be discussed with management. In particular, the cash flow forecast should be reviewed to ensure that it is consistent with the deterioration in credit control.

– Discuss what might happen if Imperiol only manages to raise part of the finance. They may not have sufficient resources to develop the newer fibre optic technology, which could lead to reservations about going concern.

chapter

17

Audit of social, environmental and integrated reporting

Chapter learning objectives

This chapter covers syllabus areas:

- G3 – The audit of social, environmental and integrated reporting

Detailed syllabus objectives are provided in the introduction section of the text book.

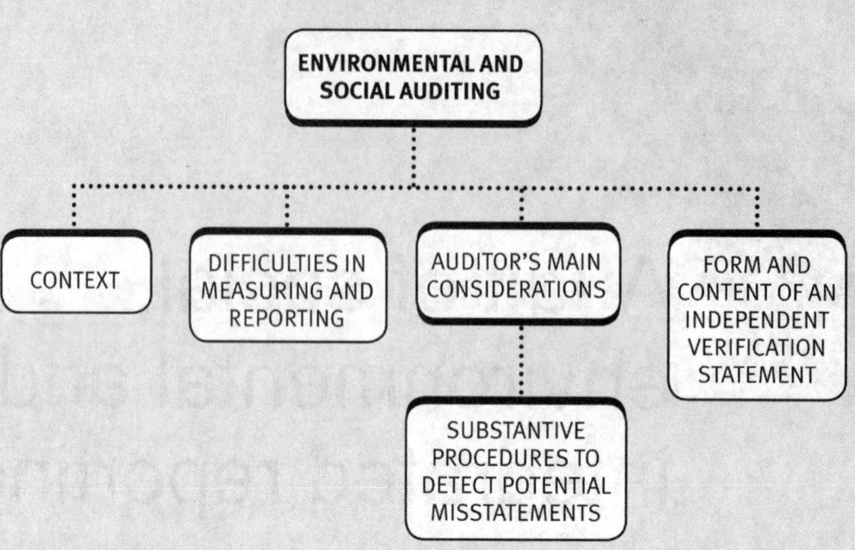

Exam focus

Social and environmental reporting has been examined on several past exams. Any part of the engagement process could be examined from acceptance through to reporting. You may also be asked to identify performance measures for a company.

1 The need for social and environmental reporting and assurance

The need for social and environmental reporting

Many companies develop and maintain social, ethical and environmental policies that can vary from highly generalised statements of ethical intention to more detailed corporate guidelines.

Today's heightened interest in the role of businesses in society has been promoted by increased sensitivity to, and awareness of environmental and ethical issues. In addition, businesses are now expected to account for their impact on the social and natural environment.

Integrated reporting is now common where other performance measures are included such as targets in relation to corporate and social responsibility matters.

Performance in this area is often a factor affecting the decision of employees, customers, and suppliers to engage with an organisation.

Key performance indicators (KPIs)

KPIs or business performance measures are financial and non-financial statistical measures that are chosen and monitored to determine the strategic performance of an organisation, including those factors of performance that are critical for the continued success of the organisation.

Monitoring of KPIs enables performance to be evaluated in comparison to benchmark performance criteria or progress to be compared to the results of competitors.

To generate KPIs for the company, management need to:

- Identify the goals of the organisation in relation to social and environmental matters e.g. reduction of electricity and water usage.
- Measure the performance e.g. taking meter readings of electricity and water usage.
- Assess whether the goal has been achieved e.g. compare usage to the prior year to see if it has reduced.

In the exam you may be asked to suggest KPIs for a company. Make sure your suggestions are measurable, whether this is in:

- $ (e.g. $ spent on charitable activities).
- % (e.g. % of waste that is recycled).
- Number (e.g. number of serious accidents in the workplace).
- Hours/days (e.g. hours/days given to volunteering).

You may also be asked how the assurance provider can verify the validity of the KPI i.e. what evidence would be obtained.

The need for assurance reports on social and environmental reports

- Many companies now publish social and environmental reports within their annual report.
- Auditors may be engaged to report on the fairness and validity of KPIs.
- This independent review will add credibility to the social and environmental data published and give assurance to external users that the progress claimed by a company's management is in fact real progress.
- This type of review is an example of an attestation engagement and is often referred to as an environmental audit.

Common accreditations

Fair Trade Foundation

Fairtrade products include coffee, tea, bananas, sugar, cotton, flowers and gold. Consumers of fairtrade products can be assured that products have been acquired from producers who have been paid a fair price, or where workers have been provided with fair pay and conditions.

Carbon Trust

A company issued with the Carbon Trust Standard must have demonstrated improvements in reducing carbon emissions, water usage or waste. Accreditation can be awarded individually or for all three aspects.

Forest Stewardship Council (FSC)

Promotes responsible management of forests. Consumers purchasing timber or paper products containing the FSC ecolabel can be assured that the trees used have come from sustainable sources, as well as other ethical considerations.

The need for social and environmental reporting

Sometimes there is a marked difference between a company's code of ethics and their actual practices, giving rise to the opinion that such policies may be more of a marketing tool than a serious statement of intent.

In addition, environmental and social reporting is normally voluntary although stakeholder pressure demands it in many industries and organisations in some industries are required to report on specific targets by law, therefore the extent and selection of reporting measures varies significantly from company to company.

Each company is likely to have differing views on what to measure and how to measure it, making comparisons very difficult. For these reasons environmental and social reporting can be a controversial area.

Generally an organisation will set an overall goal with specific targets to meet in relation to that goal. Sustainability indicators are devised to measure performance against each target. They may also report on compliance or variances between the sustainability indicator and target, including narrative explaining measures taken to achieve or improve their performance.

There is obviously a great deal of skill and experience required to derive measures for social and environmental responsibility.

Two possible approaches can be used (which are not mutually exclusive):

- comply with an externally defined set of standards, and/or
- define one's own set of relevant targets and indicators and monitor progress towards achieving these.

Many companies adopt a benchmarking approach where they work with a market leader in order to derive performance standards that will lead to improvement.

The importance of social and environmental policies

- Issues like environmental damage, improper treatment of workers, and faulty production that inconveniences or endangers customers or staff are highlighted in the media.
- In some countries, government regulation regarding environmental and social issues has increased.
- Some investors and investment fund managers have begun to take account of a corporation's social and environmental policies in making investment decisions.
- Some consumers have become increasingly sensitive to the social and environmental performance of the companies from which they buy their goods and services.
- These trends have contributed to the pressure on companies to operate in an economically, socially, and environmentally sustainable way.

McDonald's Environmental reporting

McDonald's is a large international chain of fast food restaurants, established in 1940.

In 1990 McDonald's established a Global Environmental Commitment. McDonald's has three core goals in relation to its environmental commitment:

- Energy conservation – to increase energy efficiency in order to reduce costs and reduce its impact on the environment.
- Sustainable packaging and waste management – to reduce the impact on the environment of its packaging and customer waste.

- Green building design – to increase the use of environmentally efficient measures in the design and construction of its restaurants.

McDonald's has set targets for each goal. For example, in relation to the second goal of sustainable packaging, the targets set include maximising the use of recycled materials.

Sustainability indicators for these targets are then reported. For example McDonald's reports that around 30% of its consumer packaging is made from recycled materials.

However, it is not always possible to identify appropriate sustainability indicators. For example, in relation to McDonald's third goal of green building design, one target is to promote natural lighting in the design and construction of new restaurants. It would be very difficult to quantify the promotion of natural lighting.

John Lewis Partnership example

The John Lewis partnership is the largest employee owned organisation in the UK, i.e. not owned by shareholders. The John Lewis partnership includes Waitrose supermarkets as well as John Lewis department stores.

" The Partnership's ultimate purpose is the happiness of all its members, through their worthwhile and satisfying employment in a successful business. Because the Partnership is owned in trust for its members, they share the responsibilities of ownership as well as its rewards – profit, knowledge and power."

The organisation publishes an annual sustainability report. Some of the measures reported on include:

- Volunteer hours given
- Number of apprentices
- Net new jobs created
- Value donated to good causes
- % of pre-tax profits given to charitable and community activities
- CO_2 emissions
- Refrigeration and cooling direct emissions
- Food packaging reduction
- Transport emissions
- Waste diverted from landfill
- Distribution mileage

- Sustainable products:
  - responsible sourcing of fish from wild capture fisheries
  - soya from certified sustainable sources
  - wooden products from recycled or certified sustainable sources
  - own brand paper products from recycled or certified sustainable sources
  - cotton from sustainable sources.

In addition to measuring these targets internally, the organisation looks to achieve third party accreditation where possible.

2 Planning an engagement

There are a number of issues that should be considered when planning an engagement to provide assurance over an entity's business performance measures and sustainability indicators. These include:

- Understanding and agreeing the scope of the engagement, i.e. is assurance to be provided on the outcome and measurement of the KPIs only, or on the fairness and validity of the entire KPI benchmarking exercise (e.g. including the appropriateness and completeness of the measures chosen).
- Obtaining an understanding of the entity.
- Considering the appropriateness of the KPIs chosen in the light of this understanding, ensuring the KPIs chosen represent the priorities of the company.
- Evaluating the KPIs to ensure that each measure is quantifiable and to ensure that evidence will be readily available to support the stated KPI.
- Reviewing and agreeing the KPIs over which assurance is to be provided, flagging any KPIs that are not specific enough to measure accurately, and over which assurance can therefore not be provided.
- Identifying the evidence that should be available in relation to each KPI in order to provide an assurance conclusion.
- Considering the potential for manipulation of each KPI, to achieve the desired result, i.e. identifying those KPIs which present the highest engagement risk.

3 Procedures

The same principles for gathering evidence apply for any type of assignment. The assurance provider should obtain sufficient appropriate evidence to be able to form a conclusion on the subject matter. Procedures will include:

- Enquiry of management and experts.
- Recalculation of figures to verify arithmetical accuracy
- Inspection of supporting documentation.
- External confirmation from third party certification providers.

McDonald's procedures

Audit procedures

In order to test McDonald's assertion that it has used 30% recycled materials in its packaging, the steps that the assurance provider would take might include:

- Inspect a copy of McDonald's Global Environmental Commitment policy to confirm the target set.
- Obtain an understanding of how the 30% outcome was calculated through enquiries with management including how the outcome was quantified e.g. is it by weight, value, or volume.
- Re-perform the calculation to ensure mathematical accuracy.
- Obtain an understanding of how the underlying data was compiled through enquiries with management.
- Test a sample of the underlying data compiled to the original source, and vice versa, to ensure its completeness and accuracy.
- Obtain an understanding of how materials used in packaging are categorised as recycled and non-recycled through enquiries with management.
- Test a sample of the underlying data to ensure the correct categorisation of materials as recycled/non-recycled.
- Obtain an understanding of how McDonald's obtains assurance that the materials used are recycled (or not).

4 Problems

Measurement problems

- KPIs may not be specific enough to measure accurately. Take, for example: 'To increase the monetary value of charitable donations by 10% over the next 12 months.'

  Although this appears easy enough to assess in principle, what would happen if the company chose to donate goods or time? How would you value donated goods (cost vs. sales price) and how would you value the time of volunteers (wage cost vs. value of skills contributed)? This becomes much more difficult to measure in practice.

- The concepts involved may lack precise definition.

  Consider the concepts of 'sustainability,' 'being green,' 'customer satisfaction,' and 'serious workplace accidents.' All of these are common terms for KPIs but none of them have a standard definition and for that reason may lack credibility.

- The potential for manipulation to achieve the desired result.

Problems auditing social and environmental reports

Due to the complex and often subjective nature of social and environmental performance reporting on these matters is a difficult task.

- Accountants lack the specific skills and experience needed to assess many environmental/social matters. For example, it appears unlikely that an auditor would be able to measure carbon emissions or energy consumption.
- There is a significant amount of subjectivity with regard to social and environmental reports, for example, the use of the term 'environmentally friendly.'
- There are relatively few formally agreed and globally mandatory standards of reporting on such matters, which means directors can be selective in the reports they make.
- Evidence may not be sufficient or appropriate for the purposes of providing assurance. It is unlikely that companies will establish sophisticated measuring and recording systems to gather the data used for all KPIs.

  For example: if a company donates goods to charity it is unlikely that there will be invoices, orders, goods despatched notes, remittances, cash transactions etc. In this case how does the auditor determine the quantity and value of goods donated?

Despite these concerns accountants can still provide a relevant service.

5 Reporting

Independent verification statements

Where a review is carried out by an independent third party into the environmental matters of an organisation, an **independent verification statement** may be issued.

- Some companies conduct an internal audit on environmental matters and have the internal audit verified by external assessors.
- Some companies may contract for a third party independent review of their environmental matters.

Regardless of the type of review undertaken, the report will have some common features:

- the methodology is stated
- the matters reviewed are spelled out precisely
- reference is made to other documents where applicable
- a conclusion is given.

The integrated report of the company will usually refer to the social and environmental performance indicators the company measures. Where an independent third party verifies this data, a statement will be included in the integrated report to this effect to enhance the credibility of such information.

Illustration of an independent verification statement

Below is an example of a report by an external assessor who might be a Registered Environmental Impact Assessor and/or a member of the Institute of Environmental Assessment or other recognised bodies.

External verification statement

AB & Company has conducted a formal independent verification of the internal audit undertaken by CD Construction plc.

Method and scope of the verification

The verification was conducted by reviewing the internal audit report and by interviewing the senior staff responsible for the audit. The verification examined the audit findings against 50 of the 64 targets in detail. The targets selected were those that had been awarded a maximum score for target achievement (10/10).

Internal audit's role related to auditing progress against targets reported by CD Construction plc's businesses and internal audit's findings are included in the section on Environmental Performance Targets (we have not verified other sections of this report).

Opinion

We are satisfied that the internal audit was conducted against an appropriate methodology. We have reviewed the statements made about progress against targets and confirm that they accurately reflect the audit findings.

Signed

AB & Company

Wolverhampton

March 3 20X4.

Impact of environmental matters on the audit

Certain types of organisation are high risk in terms of social and environmental reporting. Typical examples are companies engaged in oil and gas exploration, shipping and nuclear waste reprocessing.

A company's social and environmental obligations may lead to liabilities that must be recognised in the financial statements.

When an auditor realises that his client may have environmental issues that could impact the financial statements, additional procedures should be designed and carried out to detect any potential misstatements.

Possible areas that might lead to the risk of material misstatements include the following:

- Provisions, e.g. for site restoration costs.
- Contingent liabilities, e.g. arising from pending legal action.
- Impairment of asset values, e.g. non-current assets or inventories that may be subject to environmental concern or contamination.
- Accounting for capital or revenue expenditure on cleaning up the production process or to meet legal or other standards.
- Product redesign costs.
- Product viability/going concern considerations.

The following substantive procedures might be appropriate to detect potential misstatements in respect of social-environmental matters:

- Obtain an appropriate understanding of the company, its operations, and, in particular, its environmental issues.
- Enquire of management as to any systems or controls that are in place to identify risk, evaluate control, and account for environmental matters.
- Seek corroborative evidence of any statements made by management on environmental matters and obtain written representations.
- Obtain evidence from environmental experts where possible.
- Use professional judgment to consider whether the evidence in relation to environmental matters is sufficiently persuasive.
- Review available documentation (board minutes, expert's reports, correspondence with authorities or lawyers etc).
- Review all assets for impairment.
- Review liabilities and provisions to ensure all have been included and contingencies to ensure adequate disclosure.
- Include environmental issues in the review of the appropriateness of going concern.

Current issue: Investor demand for ESG disclosures

In February 2012, IFAC published a report on *Investor Demand for Environmental, Social and Governance (ESG) Disclosures*.

The report made five recommendations, which are summarised below:

- The performance measures communicated should **reflect the information needs of investors.**

  Professional accountants should work with their clients to ensure that investors are engaged in the process to determine the appropriate ESG disclosures.

- Performance in relation to **ESG measures should be embedded in the reporting process** of organisations.

  Professional accountants should work with their clients to ensure that management information and systems incorporate ESG reporting.

- **Financial performance and sustainability are directly linked.**

  Professional accountants should work with their clients to **increase** their **understanding** of the link between financial and non-financial drivers of performance and value.

- ESG reporting should be **useful and transparent**.

  Professional accountants should work with their clients to **ensure material, timely, consistent and comparable information** is reported.

- Integrated reporting will enable organisations to deliver the above recommendations.

  Professional accountants should work with their clients to ensure greater **collaboration** between internal client functions and third parties (e.g. suppliers) **when managing and reporting ESG information**.

Test your understanding 1

You are the manager responsible for the audit of The National Literary Museum (NLM), a museum focusing on famous literary works. Entry to the museum is free for all visitors and many visitors make repeat visits to the museum.

NLM receives funding from government departments for culture and education, as well as several large charitable donations. The amount of funding received is dependent on three key performance indicator (KPI) targets being met annually. All three targets must be met in order to secure the government funding.

Extracts from NLM's operating and financial review are as follows:

	KPI target	Draft KPI	Prior year actual
Number of annual visitors:	100,000	102,659	103,752
Proportion of total visitors of school age:	25%	29%	27%
Number of educational programmes run:	4	4	4

Your firm is engaged to provide an assurance report on the KPIs disclosed in NLMs operating and financial review.

Required:

Discuss the difficulties that may be encountered when providing assurance over the stated key performance indicators.

Test your understanding 2

Shire Oil Co ('Shire'), a listed company, is primarily an oil producer with interests in the North Sea, West Africa and South Asia. Shire's latest interim report shows:

	30 June 20X4	30 June 20X3	31 December 20X3
	Unaudited	Audited	Unaudited
	$000	$000	$000
Revenue	22,000	18,300	37,500
Profit before tax	5,500	4,200	7,500
Total assets	95,900	92,300	88,400
Earnings per share (basic)	$1.82	$2.07	$3.53

In April 20X4, the company was awarded a new five-year licence, by the central government, to explore for oil in a remote region. The licence was granted at no cost to Shire. However, Shire's management has decided to recognise the licence at an estimated fair value of $3 million.

The most significant of Shire's tangible non-current assets are its 17 oil rigs (20X3: 15). Each rig is composed of numerous items including a platform, buildings thereon and drilling equipment. The useful life of each platform is assessed annually on factors such as weather conditions and the period over which it is estimated that oil will be extracted. Platforms are depreciated on a straight line basis over 15 to 40 years.

A provision for the present value of the expected cost of decommissioning an oil rig is recognised in full at the commencement of oil production. One of the rigs in South Asia sustained severe cyclone damage in October 20X4. Shire's management believes the rig is beyond economic recovery and that there will be no alternative but to abandon it where it is. This suggestion has brought angry protests from conservationists.

In July 20X4, Shire entered into an agreement to share in the future economic benefits of an extensive oil pipeline.

You are the manager responsible for the audit of Shire. Last year your firm modified its auditor's report due to a lack of evidence to support management's schedule of proven and probable oil reserves to be recoverable from known reserves.

Required:

(a) Using the information provided, identify and explain the audit risks to be addressed when planning the final audit of Shire Oil Co for the year ending 31 December 20X4.

(12 marks)

(b) Describe the principal procedures to be performed in respect of the useful lives of Shire Oil Co's rig platforms.

(5 marks)

You have just been advised of management's intention to publish its yearly marketing report in the annual report that will contain the financial statements for the year ending 31 December 20X4. Extracts from the marketing report include the following:

'Shire Oil Co sponsors national school sports championships and the 'Shire Ward' at the national teaching hospital. The company's vision is to continue its investment in health and safety and the environment.

'Our health and safety, security and environmental policies are of the highest standard in the energy sector. We aim to operate under principles of no-harm to people and the environment.

'Shire Oil Co's main contribution to sustainable development comes from providing extra energy in a cleaner and more socially responsible way. This means improving the environmental and social performance of our operations. Regrettably, five employees lost their lives at work during the year.'

Required:

(c) Suggest performance indicators that could reflect the extent to which Shire Oil Co's social and environmental responsibilities are being met, and the evidence that should be available to provide assurance on their accuracy.

(8 marks)

(Total: 25 marks)

6 Chapter summary

SOCIAL AND ENVIRONMENTAL AUDITING

- Socio-environmental policy
- Measuring performance
- Reporting performance
- Problems

Test your understanding answers

Test your understanding 1

The main reason why it may not be possible to provide a high level of assurance are:

- The museum's entry system may not record the total number of visitors each day and, given that entry is free, it may be difficult to identify relevant data from any accounting or financial systems of the museum.
- However, if the museum has a turnstile entrance or issues a ticket to visitors even though they are not paid for, then evidence will be easier to obtain.
- It is unclear whether multiple visits by one person should be counted as separate visitors.
- The museum's entry system is unlikely to identify the age of all visitors.
- However, it is likely that school parties must book their visits in advance and therefore some record of school age would be maintained. Also, if there is a ticketing system, it is possible that adults and children are recorded separately.
- The KPI relating to educational programmes is poorly defined – what constitutes an educational programme? How long does it have to run? How many users have to benefit from it running?
- If however, an educational programme means an exhibition or event that covers a national curriculum area, it may be easier to verify this KPI.

Tutorial note: When given a requirement of 'discuss', it is advisable to gives reasons both for and against the argument being stated.

Test your understanding 2

(a) **Audit risks**

Licence – initial recognition

A five-year licence has been granted to Shire at no cost. Shire has recognised this at an estimated fair value of $3m.

A licence may be valued at either cost or fair value. However, valuation other than at cost ($nil) is inherently risky as fair value has been estimated by management.

The licence may be unique (being for five years in a remote region) and in the absence of an active market, or recent transactions for which prices can be observed, it seems unlikely that any estimate of fair value made by management can be substantiated.

There is a risk of overvaluation of the licence.

Licence – amortisation

Assuming the recognition of the licence at fair value is deemed appropriate, it should be accounted for under IAS 38 *Intangible Assets* which requires the asset to be amortised over its useful life.

There is a risk that the licence is overstated if it has not been amortised over the five year period of the licence.

Research and development

Research and development costs (may also be described as exploration and evaluation costs or discovery and assessment) must be expensed unless/until Shire has a legal right to explore the area in which they are incurred.

In respect of the remote region, Shire can only capitalise costs incurred from April.

There is a risk of overstatement of intangible assets if research costs are capitalised incorrectly.

Property, plant and equipment

Item replacements (e.g. of drilling equipment) should be recognised as items of property, plant and equipment (and the replaced items as disposals) in accordance with IAS 16 *Property, Plant and Equipment*.

Constituent items of each rig should be depreciated over their useful lives. Management should reassess the useful life of each rig annually to ensure they are being depreciated appropriately.

Assets will be misstated if not depreciated over an appropriate period.

Decommissioning provision

One of the company's oil rigs sustained severe damage in October and management have decided to abandon it. A decommissioning provision is recognised in full in respect of the oil rig.

A provision should only be recognised if there is a present obligation as a result of a past event that is probable to lead to an outflow of economic benefits and can be measured reliably (IAS 37 *Provisions, Contingent Liabilities and Contingent Assets*).

As management intend to abandon the rig, this would imply that there will be no dismantling of the rig and therefore no costs incurred.

There is a risk that the decommissioning provision is overstated if the company intends to abandon the rig and there is no obligation to take it down.

Abandoned rig – value

The cost of the rig includes the cost of decommissioning the rig at the end of its life. The rig is likely to have a value of $nil as there is no value in use and the rig is to be abandoned rather than decommissioned.

As the rig is no longer in use, depreciation should cease and an impairment review performed.

There is a risk the abandoned rig is overvalued in the financial statements as it is now impaired.

Abandonment of rig – liabilities

Further liabilities may result from the abandonment of the rig. This could include provision for redundancy of rig workers, fines/penalties as a result of abandoning the rig (IAS 37).

There is a risk that adequate disclosure is not made of the contingent liabilities and a risk that provisions are understated if not recognised in accordance with IAS 37.

Pipeline agreement

The oil pipeline is a jointly controlled asset that should be accounted for to reflect its economic substance in accordance with IAS 28 *Investments in Associates and Joint Ventures*.

Shire must recognise its share of the asset, liabilities and expenditure incurred and any income from the sale of its share of the oil output (as well as its own liabilities and expenses separately incurred).

There is a risk that appropriate disclosure of the joint venture is not made.

Previous year's auditor's report

The prior year auditor's report was modified due to a lack of sufficient appropriate evidence over the oil reserves.

If there is a similar lack of evidence in the current year the opinion should be similarly qualified.

Even if the correct position at 31 December 20X4 is determinable, the auditor's opinion at that date should be modified in respect of the impact, if any, on the opening position and comparative information (unless the opening oil reserves position has since been ascertained and can be corrected with a prior period adjustment).

Manipulation

As Shire is a listed company there will be pressures on its management to meet the expectations of users, in particular shareholders and analysts.

The fall in basic EPS (as compared with the first six months of the previous half year) may increase management bias to overstate performance in the second half year (to 31 December 20X4).

There is a risk of manipulation of the financial statements in order to impress the shareholders.

Operating segments

As a listed company, Shire is required to comply with the extensive disclosure requirements of IFRS 8 *Operating Segments*.

There is a risk that this disclosure has not been made or has not been made adequately.

Going concern

The oil industry is exposed to a volatile market. Shire operates in different regions with exposure to economic instability, currency devaluation and high inflation.

In addition, the company can only operate if they have a licence. Licences may be withdrawn if, for example, the company does not comply with environmental legislation.

There is a risk of inadequate disclosure of going concern issues.

(b) **Principal audit work – useful life of rig platforms**

- Review management's annual assessment of the useful life of each rig at 31 December 20X4 and corroborate any information that has led to a change in previous estimates. For example, for the abandoned rig where useful life has been assessed to be at an end, obtain:
  - weather reports
  - incident report supported by photographs
  - insurance claim, etc.
- Consider management's past experience and expertise in estimating useful lives. For example, if all lives that are initially assessed as short (c. 15 years) are subsequently lengthened (or long lives consistently shortened) this would suggest that management is being over (or under) prudent in its initial estimates.
- Review the useful lives used by other oil companies as published in their annual reports to assess reasonableness of Shire's depreciation rates.
- Compare actual maintenance costs against budget to confirm that the investment needed to achieve the expected life expectancy is being made.

- Compare actual output (oil extracted) to budget. If actual output is less than budgeted the economic life of the platform may be:
  - shorter (e.g. because there is less oil to be extracted than originally surveyed)
  - longer (e.g. because the rate of extraction is less than budgeted).
- Review the results of management's impairment testing of each rig to assess reasonableness.
- Recalculate the cash flow projections (based on reasonable and supportable assumptions) discounted at a suitable pre-tax rate.
- Review of working papers of geologist/quantity surveyor(s) employed by Shire supporting estimations of reserves used in the determination of useful lives of rigs.

(c) **Performance indicators**

Performance indicator	**Evidence**
Absolute ($) level of investment in sports sponsorship, and funding to the Shire Ward	• Cash book to verify actual level of investment ($)
Number of sporting events/medals/trophies sponsored	• Correspondence with event organisers to confirm sponsorship of events/medals/trophies • Press articles covering sponsored events • Copies of advertisements showing sponsorship by Shire Oil
Number of patients treated successfully during the year	Reports from the hospital regarding the Shire Ward occupancy
Average bed occupancy	• Reports from the hospital regarding the Shire Ward occupancy
Number of oil spills	• Correspondence with industry regulator regarding non-compliance • Press articles covering publicised breaches • Board minutes

Number of breaches of health and safety regulations and environmental regulations	• Correspondence with industry regulator regarding breaches • Press articles covering publicised breaches • Board minutes
Number of accidents and employee fatalities	• Accident book • Correspondence with insurance company relating to claims made • Board minutes • Press articles
Number of insurance claims	• Cash book to verify amounts settled on insurance claims. • Correspondence with insurance company relating to claims made.
Staff turnover	• HR records
Average number of days absent per person per annum.	• HR records

chapter

18

Forensic audits

Chapter learning objectives

This chapter covers syllabus areas:

- E3 – Forensic audits

Detailed syllabus objectives are provided in the introduction section of the text book.

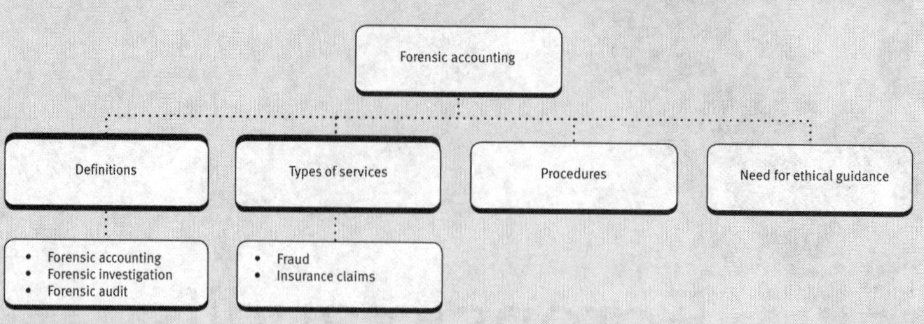

Exam focus

Forensic engagements require a much broader range of skills than other typical non-audit engagements that feature in the P7 exam. However, it is the application of traditional auditing skills and techniques that will be examined in detail from this chapter. It could appear as a question in its own right or as a small part of a question.

Two articles have been published on this syllabus area by the P7 examining team: 'Forensic Auditing' (September 2008) and 'Massaging the Figures' (April 2009). These can be downloaded from the P7 section of the ACCA website.

The field of forensic accounting is a specialist branch of the profession carried out by forensic accountants encompassing forensic auditing and investigation.

1 What is 'forensic accounting'?

Definitions

Forensic accounting

- Uses accounting, auditing, and investigative skills to conduct an examination into a company's financial affairs.
- The aim is to provide accounting analysis that is potentially suitable for use in court.
- It is an umbrella term encompassing both forensic investigations and forensic audits.

Forensic investigations

- This refers to the practical steps that the forensic accountant takes in order to gather evidence that could be used in legal proceedings.
- Such investigations involve planning, gathering evidence, quality control reviews and production of a report.

Forensic audit

- This refers to the specific procedures within a forensic investigation in order to obtain evidence, usually to quantify a financial loss.
- This could include the use of traditional financial auditing techniques such as analytical procedures and substantive procedures for example to quantify the extent of a fraud or to determine the amount of an insurance claim.

2 Types of forensic services

Some of the major applications of forensic auditing are shown below:

Application	Examples	Type of work performed
Fraud investigations	Theft of company funds, tax evasion, insider dealing.	Funds tracing, asset identification and recovery, forensic intelligence gathering, due diligence reviews, interviews, detailed review of documentary evidence.
Insurance claims	Business interruptions, property losses, motor vehicle incidents, personal liability claims, cases of medical malpractice, wrongful dismissal.	Detailed review of the policy from either an insured or insurer's perspective to investigate coverage issues, identification of appropriate method of calculating the loss, quantification of losses.
Professional negligence	Loss suffered as a result of placing reliance on professional adviser.	Advising on merits of a case in regards to liability, quantifying losses.
Shareholder, partnership and matrimonial disputes	Determination of funds to be included in settlements, as benefits or distributions.	Detailed analysis of numerous years accounting records to quantify the issues in dispute, tracing, locating and evaluation of assets.

As part of the assignment a forensic accountant will:

- Communicate their findings in the form of reports, exhibits and collections of documents.
- Assist in legal proceedings, including testifying in court as an expert witness and preparing visual aids to support trial evidence.

The forensic accountant may be used as an expert witness where:

- It is relevant to a matter that is in dispute between the parties.
- It is a reasonable requirement to resolve proceedings.
- They have the expertise relevant to the issue on which an opinion is sought.
- They have experience, expertise, and training appropriate to the value, complexity, and importance of the case.

Examples

Tesco

In 2014, Tesco, Britain's biggest retailer, revealed that it had overstated estimated profits by £263m by overestimating revenues paid to it by suppliers. Tesco was struggling to maintain market share due to pressure from competitors Aldi and Lidl.

Toshiba

In 2015, the electronics company Toshiba admitted that it had overstated its earnings by nearly $2 billion over seven years. An independent investigation found that "Toshiba had a corporate culture in which management decisions could not be challenged" and "Employees were pressured into inappropriate accounting by postponing loss reports or moving certain costs into later years.

Sainsbury's

In June 2012, three men were jailed after defrauding the supermarket Sainsbury's. 2 directors at potato supplier, Greenvale, were found to have overcharged Sainsbury's £8.7m in agreement with Sainsbury's potato buyer, John Maylam. £4.9m was paid to Maylam as his share and he also received excessive gifts and hospitality. The Sainsbury's contract was worth £40m to Greenvale and the directors did not want to risk losing that amount of business and hence bribed Maylam to ensure the contract remained in place.

3 Planning and performing forensic audits

Forensic engagements are generally conducted as 'agreed upon procedures' assignments and cover a variety of scenarios. The procedures are therefore dependent upon the requirements of the client. However, the auditor can select from the procedures used in traditional audits including:

- Enquiries/interviews of key staff.
- Detailed inspections and analysis of documentary evidence.
- Tests of control.
- Analytical procedures to compare trends over time or between business segments.
- Computer assisted audit techniques.

Planning stage

- Hold a meeting to clarify:
  - The objective of the investigation.
  - The actions taken so far e.g. contact with the police and the result of any investigations carried out by them / contact with the insurance company.
  - The planned deadline for the report.
- Confirm that the investigation team will have full access to the information required, and are able to discuss the matter with the police without fear of breaching confidentiality.
- Confirm the output of the investigation and to whom the report will be addressed. It should be clarified that the report is not to be distributed to any other parties.
- The firm should confirm whether they would be required to act as an expert witness in the event of a prosecution.
- Consider the resources and skills that will be needed to conduct the work. If the firm has a forensic accounting department it is likely they will have staff with relevant skills, but the specific type of investigation must be considered as each will be different.
- For fraud investigations:
  - Determine the type of fraud that has taken place.
  - Consider how the fraud could have taken place.

- For insurance claim verification:
  - Inspect the insurance policy to clarify the exact terms of the insurance. The period of the insurance cover should be checked to ensure that the client is covered for any claim they intend to make.
  - Inspect bank statements to confirm payments to the insurance company are up to date to ensure the cover has not lapsed.

Fraud investigation

Examples include fictitious employees being set up on a payroll system or fictitious suppliers being set up on a purchases system.

With most fraud investigations, the basic objectives of a forensic engagement include:

- Identification of:
  - the type of fraud that has occurred
  - how long it has been occurring for
  - how the fraud was concealed
  - the main suspects.
- Quantification of the financial losses.
- Gathering of evidence to support legal action/recovery of losses.
- Providing advice to prevent fraud.

Specific procedures

- Inspect payments for evidence of authorisation.
- Using CAATs, trace all payments made to a particular bank account number.
- Using CAATs, identify employees who have not taken any annual leave entitlement or sick leave.
- Inspect reports detailing changes of standing data to identify whether these changes were authorised.
- Use analytical procedures to identify any trends that may indicate when the fraud commenced and the extent of the fraud.
- Interview the suspect to obtain an explanation of what has happened or to obtain a confession.
- Inspect supporting documentation (e.g. contracts of employment, GRNs, invoices) for expenditure to identify whether the expenditure is legitimate or fraudulent.

- Inspect the company's insurance policy to identify whether fraud is covered. If so, the loss to the company will be limited to the extent of any excess on the insurance policy or any limit imposed by the insurance company.

Insurance claim verification

Examples include insurance claims for theft of assets or claims for business interruption if the business has been affected by a flood or fire.

Specific procedures

- For assets being claimed, inspect the asset register or invoices to verify the value of the asset.
- Where insurance replaces on a new for old basis, inspect price lists to identify the current price of an asset.
- For business interruption insurance, analyse the level of business generated in previous years' and any growth achieved in the current year to date to quantify the level of business lost during the relevant period.
- Perform a reconciliation of records to physical items to quantify the number of goods lost or destroyed for which insurance can be claimed.
- Discuss with the police whether any items being claimed for have since been recovered.

4 The report

Once a forensic investigation is complete, the forensic accountant will write and submit a report of their findings.

As an agreed upon procedure the most important factor of a forensic report is that the practitioner adequately addresses the requirements of the client, as established in the engagement letter.

A basic report will include:

- a summary of the procedures performed
- a summary of the results of procedures
- any limitations in the scope of the engagement
- a conclusion.

5 Fundamental ethical principles

Implications for forensic assignments

Integrity

Given the nature of their work, forensic professionals are likely to deal frequently with individuals who lack integrity or may be involved in criminal behaviour. It is imperative that the investigator recognises this, and does nothing to damage their own reputation, such as accepting bribes or giving in to other forms of coercion/intimidation.

Objectivity

The professional accountant must always be, and be perceived to be, entirely neutral.

This is particularly important if the forensic report is going to be submitted to a court of law. Any threat to objectivity could undermine the credibility of the evidence provided. To assess independence, the expert should consider whether the opinion would be the same if they were engaged by the opposing party.

In particular the accountant must safeguard against self-review and advocacy threats.

- An advocacy threat arises because the firm may feel pressured into promoting the interests and point of view of their fee paying client, which breaches the concept of objectivity in court proceedings. In particular, the forensic expert has a duty to provide evidence to the court which overrides any obligation to the client paying them. The auditor must communicate this duty to the client to prevent any misunderstanding.
- A self-review threat arises when an auditor also becomes involved in some form of forensic work because the investigation is likely to involve fraud or potential misstatement within the financial statements. Separate teams must be used for the different engagements.

Professional competence and due care

Forensic investigations involve very specialist skills, including:

- Detailed knowledge of the relevant legal framework.
- An understanding of how to gather specialist evidence.
- Skills in the safe custody of evidence, including maintaining a clear chain of evidence.

- Strong personal skills: interview techniques, presentation of material in court.

Confidentiality

During legal proceedings the court will require the investigator to reveal information discovered during the investigation. There is an overriding requirement for the investigator to disclose all of the information deemed necessary by the court.

Outside of the court, the investigator must maintain confidentiality, especially because much of the information they have access to will be highly sensitive.

Professional behaviour

Fraud investigations can become a matter of public interest, and much media attention is often focused on the work of the forensic investigator. A highly professional attitude must be displayed at all times in order to avoid damage to the reputation of the firm, and of the profession. Any lapse in professional behaviour could undermine the credibility of the investigator, especially when acting in the capacity of an expert witness.

Test your understanding 1

Your firm performs the audit of Jarvis Co, a company which installs windows. The company's year-end is 31 July 20X2. Jarvis Co uses sales representatives to make direct sales to customers. The sales representatives earn a small salary, and also earn a sales commission of 20% of the sales they generate.

Jarvis Co's sales manager has discovered that one of the sales representatives has been operating a fraud, in which he was submitting false claims for sales commission based on non-existent sales. The sales representative started to work at Jarvis Co in January 20X2. The forensic investigation department of your firm has been engaged to quantify the amount of the fraud.

Required:

Recommend the procedures that should be used in the forensic investigation to quantify the amount of the fraud.

Test your understanding 2

(a) Define the following:

(i) Forensic accounting

(ii) Forensic investigations

(iii) Forensic audit

(3 marks)

(b) You have been asked by the management of The Marvellous Manufacturing Company to carry out an investigation into a suspected expenses fraud within the marketing department.

During a routine annual spend review, management noticed that the expenses budget of $300,000 had been exceeded by nearly $30,000, with no known increase in activity.

Required:

(i) Set out the matters you would consider and procedures you would carry out in planning such an audit.

(10 marks)

(ii) Identify the procedures to be performed to determine whether or not an expenses fraud has taken place.

(7 marks)

(Total: 20 marks)

6 Chapter summary

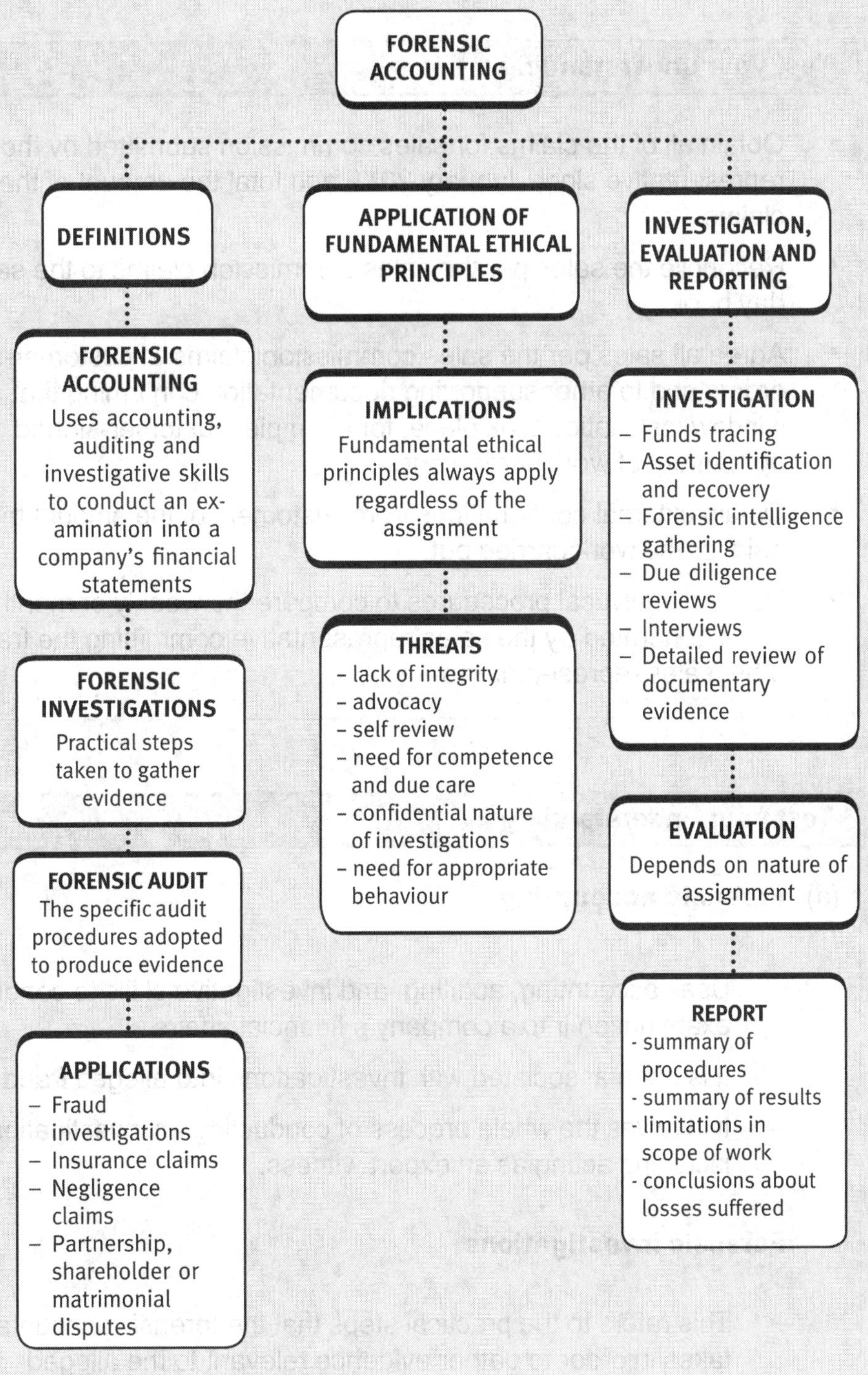

FORENSIC ACCOUNTING

DEFINITIONS

FORENSIC ACCOUNTING
Uses accounting, auditing and investigative skills to conduct an examination into a company's financial statements

FORENSIC INVESTIGATIONS
Practical steps taken to gather evidence

FORENSIC AUDIT
The specific audit procedures adopted to produce evidence

APPLICATIONS
- Fraud investigations
- Insurance claims
- Negligence claims
- Partnership, shareholder or matrimonial disputes

APPLICATION OF FUNDAMENTAL ETHICAL PRINCIPLES

IMPLICATIONS
Fundamental ethical principles always apply regardless of the assignment

THREATS
- lack of integrity
- advocacy
- self review
- need for competence and due care
- confidential nature of investigations
- need for appropriate behaviour

INVESTIGATION, EVALUATION AND REPORTING

INVESTIGATION
- Funds tracing
- Asset identification and recovery
- Forensic intelligence gathering
- Due diligence reviews
- Interviews
- Detailed review of documentary evidence

EVALUATION
Depends on nature of assignment

REPORT
- summary of procedures
- summary of results
- limitations in scope of work
- conclusions about losses suffered

Test your understanding answers

Test your understanding 1

- Obtain all of the claims for sales commission submitted by the sales representative since January 20X2 and total the amount of these claims.
- Reconcile the sales per the sales commission claims to the sales day book.
- Agree all sales per the sales commission claims to customer-signed orders and to other supporting documentation confirming that window installation took place, for example, customer-signed agreement of work carried out.
- Obtain external confirmations from customers of the amount they paid for the work carried out.
- Perform analytical procedures to compare the weekly or monthly sales generated by the sales representative committing the fraud to other sales representatives.

Test your understanding 2

(a) **Forensic accounting**

- Uses accounting, auditing, and investigative skills to conduct an examination into a company's financial affairs.
- It is often associated with investigations into alleged fraud.
- It involves the whole process of conducting an investigation, including acting as an expert witness.

Forensic investigations

- This refers to the practical steps that the forensic accountant takes in order to gather evidence relevant to the alleged fraudulent activity.
- Such investigations involve a planning phase, a phase of gathering evidence, a review phase and a report to the client.

Forensic audit

- This refers to the specific procedures adopted in order to produce evidence.
- From an accountancy perspective, this usually requires the adoption of traditional financial auditing skills and techniques.

(b) **Matters to consider when planning a forensic audit**

- Consider the scope and depth of the investigation and therefore the nature, timing and extent of procedures.
- Determine which staff to include on the assignment ensuring the appropriate skills are included on the team.
- Consider the availability of the staff and whether any other work needs to be rescheduled and whether this is possible.
- Prepare the budget for the assignment of hours, grades of staff and costs.
- Calculate the fee for the assignment based on the budget.
- Discuss with management why they believe the overspend is through fraudulent behaviour.
- Consider who the intended users of the report will be as this will affect risk and liability levels and therefore the amount of work undertaken.
- Develop an engagement plan that focuses on the areas where fraud could have taken place.
- Ensure the team are fully briefed on the client and the assignment.
- Enquire whether the expert will be required to be an expert witness if it is found to be fraud and the suspect it taken to court.
- Obtain confirmation from management that the expert will have full access to information needed to perform the investigation.

Procedures

- Identify risk areas that would provide opportunities for fraud to take place e.g. lack of segregation of duties, poor control environment, etc.
- Obtain management accounts and perform analytical procedures to see if any other significant variances have occurred.
- Speak with the marketing director to identify if there have been more trips required this year that could explain the reason for the increase.

- Enquire if any new customers/contracts have been won in the year that might explain an increase in marketing expenses e.g. entertaining to win new business.
- Enquire with the marketing director whether expenses are authorised and what the authority limits are.
- Enquire if there has been any change in expenses policy that might explain the increase e.g. an increase in the standard of hotels used, meal allowances, etc.
- Enquire when the spending increase was first identified and what measures were taken by the client to find reasons why.
- Analyse expense claims by individual to try to identify who might be the culprit.
- Analyse expenses by type to identify which category of expenses has seen the biggest rise. For example, an increase in fuel costs might be due to fuel prices increasing rather than fraud.

chapter

19

Outsourcing and internal audit

Chapter learning objectives

This chapter covers syllabus areas:

- E4 – Internal audit
- E5 – Outsourcing

Detailed syllabus objectives are provided in the introduction section of the text book.

Exam focus

Outsourcing could feature as a requirement in its own right, within a scenario for a risk assessment requirement, or a requirement relating to gathering audit evidence. Typical requirements include advantages and disadvantages of outsourcing and what is the impact on the audit if the client outsources part of their business.

1 What is 'outsourcing'?

Outsourcing is the practice of contracting out business functions or processes to an external service provider.

Insourcing is where a business performs functions and processes internally. This allows the company to maintain control of the function which is important if it is a core area of the business. The employment of subcontractors may be used to deal with variations in demand/workload.

2 Examples of outsourced functions

Common examples of outsourcing arrangements include:

- Data processing
  - A service organisation may operate a transaction processing system on the company's behalf, raising invoices, etc.
  - This can be more cost effective than employing staff to perform relatively low risk work which is not a core element of the business.
- Pensions
  - Many businesses offer a pension scheme to their employees.
  - Rather than employ pension specialists in a human resources department, many companies will select an external pension scheme provider.
  - Due to the legal complexities of pensions it is advantageous for a company to outsource this function to ensure compliance with laws and regulations.
- Information technology
  - As an extension of outsourcing the transaction processing, a company could outsource the entire IT function.
  - This would allow the company access to all the latest technological advances without having to buy the hardware or software itself.
  - This would also provide expertise to deal with one-off projects, such as systems implementation or software upgrades.

- Internal auditing
  - Rather than setting up its own internal audit department, a company could buy in the service from an external provider such as a firm of accountants.
- Due diligence work
  - A Stock Exchange will typically require listed companies to obtain due diligence (special investigations undertaken by professional firms) assurance when they are considering large transactions, e.g. buying another company.
  - This is specialist work where the necessary high level of expertise can be bought in from an external provider.
  - Additional benefits are increased independence and objectivity, increased credibility and indemnity for negligence.
- Tax management
  - Enables a company to obtain the expertise required without having to pay the ongoing employment costs for such an individual.

Benefits and limitations

Benefits of outsourcing

- Access to skills that might be difficult to obtain otherwise. Services should be provided by suitably competent professionals who specialise in those services.
- Cost effectiveness. It may be cheaper to outsource than employ permanent staff if there is not a need for a full time function. The cost of wastage (idle time) becomes a cost to the service provider.
- It can help transfer risk to another party (e.g. the risk of non-compliance with laws and regulations or risk of fraud).
- It helps organisations manage the peaks and troughs of working cycles.
- It will lead to a fixed fee, thus helping cash flow management.
- Frees up internal resources and management for other activities.

Problems with outsourcing

- The cost involved in changing to an outsourced provider (information transfer, redundancy, teething problems).
- The loss of control of a business process/function.
- The potential for conflict with the service provider should the quality of service not match expectations.
- Contractual problems arising from inflexibility of contracts with service providers or lack of detailed contract specification and issues with service levels.
- The need (potentially) for new systems to be implemented to ensure appropriate information is transferred to the service provider on a timely basis.
- Confidentiality issues as intellectual property is given to the service provider.

3 Outsourcing internal audit

Many companies now outsource their internal audit work to professional firms, whose experience of different company systems and procedures provides added benefit to the client.

The advantages of outsourcing internal audit

- Professional firms follow an ethical code of conduct and should therefore be independent of the client and their management.
- Professional firms should have qualified, competent staff who receive regular development and have a broader range of expertise.
- Overcome a skills shortage as an outsourcing firm will have specialist skills readily available.
- Professional firms can be employed on a flexible basis, i.e. on an individual engagement basis rather than full time employment which may prove more cost effective.
- Costs of employing permanent staff are avoided.
- The risk of staff turnover is passed to the outsourcing firm.
- Professional firms are responsible for their activities and hold insurance.
- Greater focus on cost and efficiency of the internal audit work as this will affect profitability.
- Access to new market place technologies, e.g. audit methodology software without associated costs.
- Reduced management time in administering an in-house department.

The disadvantages of outsourcing internal audit

- Professional firms lack the intimate knowledge and understanding of the organisation that employees have.
- Engagements with professional firms are constrained by contractual terms. Flexibility and availability may not be as high as with an in-house function.
- Professional fees tend to be high. The decision may be based on cost with the effectiveness of the function being reduced.
- Possible conflict of interest if provided by the external auditors. In some jurisdictions – e.g. the ACCA Code of Ethics, prohibits external auditors of a listed company from providing internal audit services for the same client where the service relates to internal controls over financial reporting.
- Pressure on the independence of the outsourced function, for example, if management threaten not to renew contract.
- Lack of control over the standard of service.

Case study: KMPG and Rentokil

In 2009 KPMG in the UK became the external auditor to a company called Rentokil Initial, a FTSE 250 (and sometime 100) pest control and delivery company. This in itself is not unusual, the audit market is extremely competitive and high profile client wins are becoming increasingly common. However, the circumstances of the contract "win" have caused concern to be raised within the auditing profession and by a number of corporate governance commentators. Some of the reasons include:

- The deal with KPMG has allowed Rentokil Initial to reduce their audit fees by a massive 30%.
- KPMG are to provide external audit services and to provide internal audit services alongside Rentokil's own internal audit function.

This creates two significant ethical threats:

- Self-review
- Management.

If the auditor were to rely on its own internal audit work as part of the audit it would undoubtedly scrutinise its own work. Given the costs savings identified it is likely that KPMG will use this relationship to streamline the audit process and avoid duplication of procedures.

There is also a significant management threat for one simple reason: external auditors work on behalf of investors and internal auditors work for management. Therefore KPMG would be contributing to the management process it is supposed to be scrutinising.

Developments in the profession, post Enron, have attempted to reduce the non-audit services provided by auditors of listed clients. The relationship KPMG has with Rentokil is actually not permitted in the US and a handful of other nations.

Test your understanding 1

You are a partner of Finbar & Sons, a firm of accountants. You have been approached by a potential client, Thomas Trends. They recently notified you of their intention to outsource their internal audit function. The company operates a small, high street based, chain of clothes outlets.

They set up the internal audit department some years ago based on advice given them by their external auditors, Suckit & Sea. However, given that most employees use internal audit as a springboard to management positions, the staff turnover is high and the FD believes it may be more effective to use an external provider of this service.

They are interested in some form of evaluation of organisational risks, financial compliance, IT systems and fraud risks. He has asked you if you would be interested in offering this service and, with this in mind, has set up a meeting with you to discuss the role.

Required:

(a) Briefly describe the advantages and disadvantages of Thomas Trends outsourcing its internal audit function.

(6 marks)

(b) Describe the principal matters relating to the assignment to be discussed during your meeting with the FD of Thomas Trends.

(8 marks)

(Total: 14 marks)

4 Chapter summary

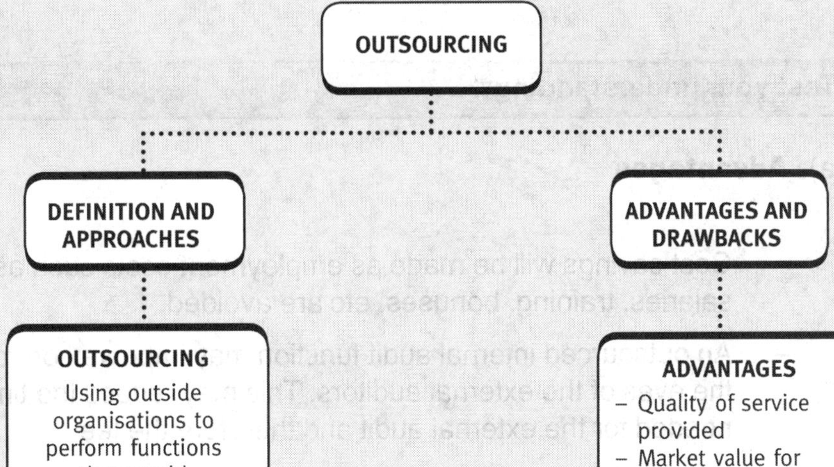

OUTSOURCING

Using outside organisations to perform functions that would otherwise be performed 'in-house'

INSOURCING

Where a business performs a service in-house

REASONS FOR OUTSOURCING

- Internal resources are freed for more productive activities
- Reduces time top management spend on housekeeping functions
- Service organisations keep up to date on equipment and expertise
- Expertise not available in-house
- More flexible and adaptive to business circumstances and change
- May be more cost effective

ADVANTAGES

- Quality of service provided
- Market value for services
- Overcoming a skill shortage
- No waste
- Risk transfer
- Disposal of a non-core activity

DRAWBACKS

- No guarantee of quality
- The captive customer
- Conflicts of interest
- Impact on morale
- Cost control

Test your understanding answers

Test your understanding 1

(a) **Advantages**

- Cost savings will be made as employment costs such as salaries, training, bonuses, etc are avoided.
- An outsourced internal audit function may improve controls in the eyes of the external auditors. This may reduce the time needed for the external audit and therefore the fee.
- Reduced turnover of staff for Thomas Trends should improve continuity, and perhaps morale, of human resources.
- An external provider will have a wider range of industry knowledge. Given the range of evaluation required, it is unlikely the current internal audit function has this range of experience.
- They will also provide an independent perspective. This should lead to recommendations that improve internal procedures.
- Outsourcing should provide more flexibility in terms of access to experienced staff at all times throughout the year, even busy periods.
- The outsourced firm will be technically up to date.
- Management will be able to focus on core competencies.

Disadvantages

- Loss of a training ground for junior managers trying to work their way up to more senior managerial positions. Future managers will have to be identified and trained in other ways.
- Over time the outsourced function may increase their charges if they perceive the company is becoming reliant on their expertise.
- Whilst the outsourced company may have relevant industry knowledge they will lack understanding of Thomas Trends' internal processes and policies. This issue will be further exaggerated if the audit team used by the outsourced company changes each year.
- The outsourced audit staff will not have any allegiance to the Thomas Trends. Therefore the management of Thomas Trends may not buy into any suggestions made as readily.

(b) **Principal matters to be discussed**

- Introduction to your firm, including details of the functions undertaken, the office locations and the experience of the internal audit department and its partners. You would discuss which office would be responsible for providing the services and who the main points of contact would be.
- Discussion of how Finbar & Sons services relate to the specific functions requested, namely: organisational risk analysis; financial compliance; IT systems analysis; and fraud risk analysis.
- Finbar & Sons' approach to assessing the needs for audit and the approach involved.
- The tools/methods adopted for internal audit tasks. including the use of any computer aided audit techniques, e.g. embedded audit software.
- The installation of embedded audit software could require some training for the staff/management of Thomas Trends. You would discuss the provision of any training services offered.
- Any insurance taken out covering, for example, public liability and professional indemnity.
- How your firm ensures quality, namely through the use of the standards you follow (such as the Institute of Internal Auditors).
- Sample report templates to help Thomas Trends understand the nature of the reports they will receive in return. Examples might include: risk analysis reports and reports to the audit committee.
- A list of current clients who you provide internal audit services to so that Thomas Trends can take up references if they so wish.
- Although not an audit client, discuss any potential conflicts of interest. An important area would be identifying any possible competitors to Thomas Trends that are also clients.
- Fee levels including charge out rates for different levels of staff and the firm's policy with regard to recharging travel and others expenses.
- Invoicing/credit terms offered, e.g. payable on demand or 30 days credit.
- Performance targets to be met, such as deadlines for completing fieldwork and submission dates for the various reports.

chapter

20

UK syllabus only: Auditing aspects of insolvency

Chapter learning objectives

This chapter covers syllabus areas:

- E6 – Auditing aspects of insolvency (and similar procedures)

Detailed syllabus objectives are provided in the introduction section of the text book.

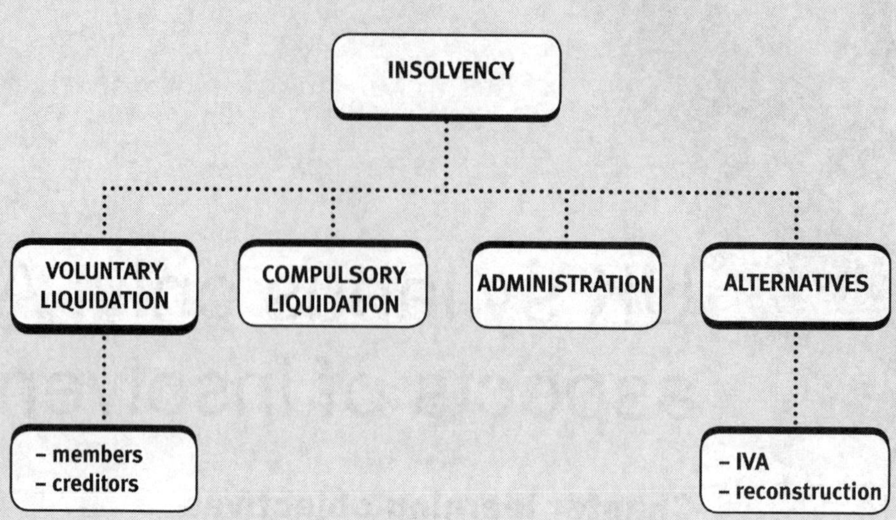

Exam focus

This chapter is relevant to students taking the UK variant of the exam only. Insolvency will not appear in every exam. It is a non-audit area of the syllabus similar in weighting to a topic such as forensic accounting.

Insolvency

There are two tests for insolvency defined in the Insolvency Act 1986.

(1) if assets are exceeded by liabilities, or

(2) if a company is failing to discharge its debts as and when they fall due.

If a company meets either criteria then it is technically insolvent.

1 Voluntary liquidation

Introduction

Liquidation is the process of terminating a company, thus ending its life. The assets of the company are physically liquidated, i.e. they are sold, so that cash can be used to pay off company creditors and equity holders.

There are two forms of voluntary liquidation (Insolvency Act 1986):

- members' voluntary liquidation
- creditors' voluntary liquidation.

Members' voluntary liquidation

This form of liquidation is used when a company is solvent (i.e. has assets greater than its liabilities). In order to facilitate this the members must pass one of two resolutions:

- an ordinary resolution, where the articles provide for liquidation on the expiry of a fixed date or a specific event, or
- a special resolution, for any other reason.

Once this has been passed the directors must make a **declaration of solvency** stating that they are of the opinion that the company will be able to pay its debts within twelve months. A false declaration would constitute a criminal offence.

The company will then appoint a named insolvency practitioner to act as the liquidator. They will realise the company's assets and distribute the proceeds accordingly.

Once the liquidation process is complete the liquidator presents a report at the final meeting of the members, which is then submitted to the registrar of companies. The company will be dissolved three months later.

Creditor's voluntary liquidation

This form of liquidation is used if a company intends to liquidate voluntarily but is insolvent. Once again a resolution of members must be passed (as with a members' voluntary liquidation). However, no declaration of solvency can be made.

Instead a meeting of creditors must be held within fourteen days of passing the resolution. At least seven days written notice must be given for this meeting. During the meeting the directors must present a full statement of the company's affairs and a list of all creditors and amounts owed to them.

Both the members and the creditors are entitled to appoint a liquidator. However, the creditors' choice must prevail over the members' choice. In addition the creditors may appoint up to five people to sit on a liquidation committee.

The liquidator will realise the company's assets and distribute the proceeds accordingly. Once the liquidation process is complete the liquidator presents a report at the final meeting of the members, which is then submitted to the registrar of companies. The company will then be dissolved.

2 Compulsory liquidation

Introduction

Companies may be obliged to liquidate if a winding up order is presented to a court, usually by a creditor or member. Such a petition may be made for a number of reasons, which include (Insolvency Act 1986):

- the company being unable to pay its debts
- it is just and equitable to wind up the company.

If a member petitions on the latter basis this will only be considered if the company is solvent and the member has been a registered shareholder for at least six of the prior eighteen months.

Consequences

If successful, the court will appoint an official receiver (an officer of the courts) as liquidator. They may be replaced by a practitioner at a later date. The receiver investigates the company's affairs and the cause of its failure. The petition also has the following effects:

- all actions for the recovery of debt against the company are stopped
- any floating charges crystallise
- all legal proceedings against the company are halted and none may start unless the courts grant permission
- the company must cease trading activity, unless it is necessary to complete the liquidation, e.g. completing work-in-progress
- the directors relinquish power and authority to the liquidator, although they may remain in office
- employees are automatically made redundant. The liquidator may choose to re-employ them to help complete the liquidation process.

Procedures

Within twelve weeks of being appointed the official receiver will call a meeting of creditors in order to agree the appointment of a licensed insolvency practitioner and to appoint a liquidation committee.

The liquidator will realise the company's assets and distribute the proceeds accordingly. Once the liquidation process is complete the liquidator presents a report at the final meeting of the members, which is then submitted to the registrar of companies. The company will then be dissolved.

3 Allocation of company assets

Liquidators in a compulsory liquidation must pay debts in the following order:

- fixed charge holders
- expenses of liquidation, including liquidator's remuneration
- preferential creditors, including employee's wages and accrued holiday pay
- prescribed part set aside for unsecured creditors *
- floating charge holders
- unsecured creditors (ranked equally)
- preference shareholders
- members.

It is likely that liquidators will also adhere to these principles in a voluntary liquidation as well.

***Prescribed part**

The prescribed part is an amount set aside to give unsecured creditors some protection. In many liquidations, if the prescribed part was not in place, the unsecured creditors would be unlikely to receive anything as it is likely that fixed charge holders, liquidation fees, preferential creditors and floating charge holders would receive any monies crystallised.

The calculation is based on the 'net property' of the company. This is the amount of assets remaining after paying fixed charge holders, liquidator's fees and preferential creditors.

If the net property is less than £10,000, the prescribed part won't apply and any remaining monies will be paid to the floating charge holders.

To calculate the prescribed part:

(1) 50% of the first £10,000 of the net property figure

(2) 20% of £2,985,000 less £10,000

(3) Subject to a maximum of £600,000

If net property is less than £2,985,000 the calculation at step 2 should use the figure of net property remaining.

Example - prescribed part

Assets	£6,000,000
Fixed charge creditors	£2,500,000
Floating charge creditors	£750,000
Preferential creditors	£650,000
Unsecured creditors	£8,000,000
Ordinary share capital	£20,000,000
Liquidators costs	£200,000

Net property calculation:

Assets	6,000,000
Less fixed charge creditors	(2,500,000)
Less liquidator's costs	(200,000)
Less preferential creditors	(650,000)
Net property	2,650,000

Prescribed part calculation (applicable as net property > £10,000)

50% × £10,000	5,000
20% × (2,650,000 – 10,000)	528,000
Prescribed part	533,000

4 Administration

Introduction

Administration is the process whereby an insolvency practitioner is appointed to manage the affairs of a business (Enterprise Act 2002). It is often used as an alternative to liquidation with a view to:

- rescuing a company in financial difficulty
- achieving better results for creditors than could be achieved through liquidation
- realising property to pay off secured creditors.

Appointment

Administrators can be appointed by any one of the following:

- the courts, in response to a petition
- the holder of a qualifying floating charge over company assets
- members or directors, providing that liquidation has not already begun.

Courts will only appoint an administrator if the company is, or is likely to become, unable to pay its debts and if it feels that administration will help meet the objectives listed above.

Consequences

The administrator takes over control of the management of the company. They must follow any proposals approved at any meeting of creditors or dictated by the courts. However, particular powers include:

- removal or appointment of directors
- calling meetings of creditors and/or members
- making payments to secured or preferential creditors
- making payments to unsecured creditors, if it is felt that this will assist the objectives of the administration
- presenting or defending a petition for liquidating the company.

Upon appointing an administrator certain protections are afforded to the company, namely:

- the rights of creditors to enforce security over the company's assets are suspended
- petitions for liquidation are dismissed
- no resolutions to wind up the company may be passed
- the directors continue in office, although their powers are suspended.

Advantages of administration over liquidation

- Administration provides time to develop an alternative plan for survival. Liquidation results in the cessation of the company and therefore any future benefits that might have been generated will be lost.
- Members are less likely to lose their investment.
- Creditors are more likely to be paid. In a liquidation, unsecured creditors are likely to receive nothing.
- Creditors will still be able to trade with the company if the administration is successful. If the company is liquidated, the creditor loses a customer.

5 Alternatives to winding up

Introduction

Often businesses have no alternative but to face up to administration or, in the worst case scenario, liquidation. However, there are alternatives that exist to help both incorporated and unincorporated businesses survive, namely:

- individual voluntary arrangements
- reconstructions.

Individual Voluntary Arrangements (IVAs)

- An IVA is an arrangement available to individuals, sole traders and partnerships to help them reach a compromise with creditors with the aim of avoiding the closure of their business and, perhaps, bankruptcy.
- Such an arrangement usually facilitates lower payments of debt over an extended period, usually five years.
- Once an individual (or their insolvency practitioner) submits a proposal to the courts for an interim order creditors may no longer take action against the individual (referred to as a moratorium on actions). A creditors meeting must be held within fourteen days of the order to include the proposals made by the individual with regard to their debt. The creditors may accept the proposals with a 75% majority (by value of creditors present) vote.
- The main benefit is obviously that the individual may continue in business and work towards the payment of their debt in a more flexible manner.
- They are also not penalised by bankruptcy laws, such as restrictions on becoming a director.
- Creditors also benefit as it is likely that they will receive more under the terms of an IVA than they would if liquidation was enforced upon a company that is potentially insolvent anyway.

Reconstructions

It may be possible for companies facing problems to survive by taking up new contracts or exploiting market opportunities. However, such ventures usually require cash injections and when faced with liquidity problems this can pose a problem, not least because such businesses may not appear attractive to external investment.

Typical traits of such companies include:

- accumulated losses
- debenture interest arrears
- cumulative preference shares dividend arrears
- no payment of ordinary dividends
- share price below nominal value
- share price decline.

To become more attractive to investment the company could reorganise or reconstruct.

Permitted reconstructions

Capital structures protect stakeholders' interests. Therefore changes to these structures are restricted by company law. However, under various mechanisms of the Companies Act 2006 companies are able to:

- write off unpaid share capital
- write off share capital which is not represented by available assets
- write off paid up share capital which is in excess of requirements
- write off debenture interest arrears
- replace existing debentures with a lower interest debenture
- write off preference dividend arrears
- write off amounts owing to trade creditors.

By altering the capital structure of the business and by removing some of the debt of the business, companies may be able to reduce their accumulated losses to the point that they have profits available to begin paying debts and dividends in the future. The reduction in the debt burden also frees up resources for investment in future opportunities and new growth.

To do this the company must ask its stakeholders to surrender some or all of their existing rights and amounts due. They do this in exchange for new rights under a new or reformed company and a share of the benefits that could arise due to future investment. This may be more appealing than the alternatives, which include:

- to remain as they are, with the prospect of no return from their investment and no growth in their investment, or
- to accept whatever return they could be given in a liquidation.

6 Wrongful and fraudulent trading

Fraudulent trading

Fraudulent trading is where a company carries on a business with the **intention of defrauding creditors** or for any other fraudulent purposes. This would include a situation where the director(s) of a company continue to trade whilst insolvent, and enter into debts knowing that the company will not be in a position to repay those debts.

The Insolvency Act 1986 (s.213) governs situations where, in the course of a winding up, it appears that the business has been carried on with the intent to defraud creditors, or for any other fraudulent purpose.

Fraudulent trading is also a criminal offence under the Companies Act 2006.

Wrongful trading

Wrongful trading (s214 1a of the Insolvency Act 1986) is when the director(s) of a company have **continued to trade** when they: "knew, or ought to have concluded that there was **no reasonable prospect of avoiding insolvent liquidation**".

A director can defend an action of wrongful trading if they can prove that they have taken sufficient steps to minimise the potential loss to creditors.

Wrongful trading is an action that can be taken only by a company's liquidator, once it has gone into insolvent liquidation (either voluntary or compulsory liquidation).

Wrongful trading needs no finding of 'intent to defraud', unlike fraudulent trading.

Wrongful trading is a civil offence (fraudulent trading is a criminal offence), it only needs to be proven "on the balance of probabilities" (i.e. it is more likely than not that the director(s) are guilty of wrongful trading).

Fraudulent trading needs to be proven "beyond reasonable doubt" (i.e. it is almost certain that the director(s) are guilty of fraudulent trading).

For these reasons, wrongful trading is more common than fraudulent trading.

Penalties

Fraudulent trading

- directors can be made **personally liable** for the debts of the company (a civil liability under the Insolvency Act);
- **disqualified** as a director for between two and 15 years
- **imprisoned** for up to ten years.

Wrongful trading

- directors can be made **personally liable** for the debts of the company
- **disqualified** as a director for between two and 15 years.

Test your understanding 1

(a) Explain the procedures involved in placing a company into compulsory liquidation.

(b) Explain the consequences of compulsory liquidation for a company's creditors, employees and shareholders.

(Real exam June 2011)

Test your understanding 2

Tommy Co is in compulsory liquidation. The insolvency practitioner has liquidated the company's assets and has £1.125m available for distribution. The following points are relevant:

- the company has an issued share capital of 2.5m £1 shares.
- the directors declared, but have not paid, a dividend of 10 pence per share six months ago.
- the insolvency practitioner's costs total £50,000.
- Tommy Co's bank have a floating charge over the company's stock, which has now crystallised. The value is £400,000.
- the company's employees have been paid, with the exception of £275,000 of accrued holiday pay.
- unsecured creditors total £500,000.

Required:

Identify and explain how the available funds will be distributed to the stakeholders of Tommy Co by the insolvency practitioner.

Test your understanding 3

Compare and contrast the characteristics of a members' voluntary winding up and a creditors' voluntary winding up.

Test your understanding 4

Poppy and Rosie registered their pet food business as a private limited company, Wag Ltd, in January 20W9. They injected £1,000 of share capital of £1,000 into Wag Ltd, and appointed themselves as directors of Wag Ltd.

Wag Ltd made a small profit in its first few years of trading, after the salaries paid to Poppy and Rosie. However, following difficult economic conditions, Wag Ltd made a loss of £15,000 in the year ended 31 December 20X2.

In early 20X3, Poppy said she thought the company should cease trading and be wound up. Rosie, however, insisted that the company would be profitable in the long-term so they agreed to carry on the business. Poppy was no longer involved in the day-to-day running of the business and stopped drawing a salary (although she retained her position as company director).

During 20X3 and 20X4, Rosie falsified Wag Ltd's accounts to disguise the fact that the company had continued to suffer losses, until it became obvious that they could no longer hide the company's debts and that it would have to go into insolvent liquidation, with debts of £75,000.

Required:

Advise Poppy and Rosie as to any potential liability they might face as regards:

- fraudulent trading, under both criminal and civil law; and
- wrongful trading under s.214 of the Insolvency Act 1986.

7 Chapter summary

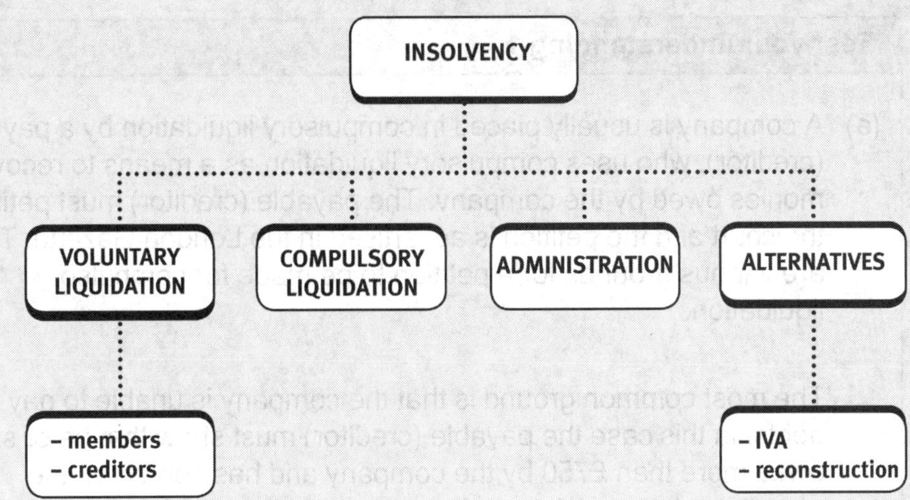

Test your understanding answers

Test your understanding 1

(a) A company is usually placed in compulsory liquidation by a payable (creditor), who uses compulsory liquidation as a means to recover monies owed by the company. The payable (creditor) must petition the court and the petition is advertised in the London Gazette. There are various grounds for a petition to be made for compulsory liquidation.

The most common ground is that the company is unable to pay its debts. In this case the payable (creditor) must show that he or she is owed more than £750 by the company and has served on the company at its registered office a written demand for payment. This is called a statutory demand. If the company fails to pay the statutory demand in 21 days and does not dispute the debt, then the payable (creditor) may present a winding up petition at court.

The application for a winding up order will be granted at a court hearing where it can be proven to the court's satisfaction that the debt is undisputed, attempts to recover have been undertaken and the company has neglected to pay the amount owed.

On a compulsory winding up the court will appoint an Official Receiver, who is an officer of the court. Within a few days of the winding up order being granted by the court, the Official Receiver must inform the company directors of the situation. The court order is also advertised in the London Gazette.

The Official Receiver takes over the control of the company and usually begins to close it down. The company's directors are asked to prepare a statement of affairs. The Official Receiver must also investigate the causes of the failure of the company.

The liquidation is deemed to have started at the date of the presentation of the winding up petition.

At the end of the winding up of the company, a final meeting with payables (creditors) is held, and a final return is filed with the court and the Registrar. At this point the company is dissolved.

Tutorial note: Credit will be awarded to candidates who explain other, less common, means by which a company may face a compulsory liquidation:

A shareholder may serve a petition for compulsory liquidation. The grounds for doing so would normally be based on the fact that that the shareholder is dissatisfied with the management of the company, and that it is therefore just and equitable to wind up the company. This action by the shareholder is only allowed if the company is solvent and if the shareholder has been a shareholder for at least six months prior to the petition.

Very occasionally, if the Crown believes that a company is contravening legislation such as the Trading Standards legislation or is acting against the public or government interest, it is possible for the company to be liquidated compulsorily. This is very serious action to take and is not used very regularly.

(b) **Payables (creditors)** – The role of the Official Receiver (or Insolvency Practitioner, if appointed), is to realise the company's assets, and to distribute the proceeds in a prescribed order. Depending on the amount of cash available for distribution, and whether the debt is secured or unsecured, payables (creditors) may receive some, all, or none of the amount owed to them.

Employees – All employees of the company are automatically dismissed. A prescribed amount of unpaid employee's wages, accrued holiday pay, and contributions to an occupational pension fund rank as preferential debts, and will be paid before payables (creditors) of the company.

Shareholders – Any surplus that remains after the payment of all other amounts owed by the company is distributed to the shareholders. In most liquidations the shareholders receive nothing.

Test your understanding 2

In accordance with the Insolvency Act 1986 the stakeholders of Tommy Co will be paid in the following order:

(1) Liquidator's costs of £50,000.

(2) Preferential creditors: i.e. the employee's accrued holiday pay of £275,000.

(3) Floating charge holders i.e. the bank's debt of £400,000.

(4) Unsecured creditors of £400,000.

At this point, £1.125m is fully allocated. The unsecured creditors who must forfeit the other £100,000 owed to them.

The members' declared but not paid dividends rank below the above stakeholders and will therefore not be paid. Likewise there will be no residual assets left to distribute to the members, who will receive nothing at all upon the liquidation of Tommy Co.

Test your understanding 3

A voluntary winding up takes place when the company resolves by special resolution to be wound up for any cause whatsoever, or by ordinary resolution where the articles provide for liquidation on the expiry of a fixed date or a specific event.

In the case of a members' voluntary winding up, the directors make a declaration of solvency stating that after full inquiry into the company's affairs they are of the opinion that the company will be able to pay its debts within twelve months of the commencement of the winding up.

In a creditors' voluntary winding up, such a declaration is not possible owing to the circumstances leading to the winding up.

In a members' voluntary winding up, the liquidator is appointed by the members and is accountable to them.

In a creditors' voluntary winding up, both members and creditors have the right to nominate a liquidator and, in the event of dispute, subject to the right of appeal to the courts, the creditors' nominee prevails. Here the liquidator is primarily accountable to the creditors.

In a creditors' voluntary winding up, the resolution is followed by a creditors' meeting where it is possible for a liquidation committee to be appointed. Such meetings form no part of a members' voluntary winding up.

Test your understanding 4

The Insolvency Act 1986 governs situations where, in the course of a winding up, it appears that the business of a company has been carried on with intent to defraud creditors, or for any fraudulent purpose.

In such cases, the court, may declare that any persons who were knowingly parties to such carrying on of the business are liable to make such contributions (if any) to the company's assets as the court thinks proper. There is a high burden of proof involved in proving dishonesty on the part of the person against whom it is alleged.

It should be noted that there is a criminal offence of fraudulent trading under the Companies Act 2006, which applies to anyone who has been party to the carrying on of the business of a company with intent to defraud creditors or any other person, or for any other fraudulent purpose.

Given that it is stated that Rosie hid the fact that Wag Ltd was insolvent it is possible that she might be liable under the fraudulent trading provisions both civil and criminal. As a consequence she may well be liable for a maximum prison sentence of 10 years and may have to contribute to the assets of the company to cover any loss sustained by creditors as a result of her actions.

There is no evidence to support either action against Poppy.

Wrongful trading does not involve dishonesty but it still makes particular individuals potentially liable for the debts of their companies. Where a company is being wound up and it appears that, at some time before the start of the winding up, a director knew, or ought to have known, that there was no reasonable chance of the company avoiding insolvent liquidation, they would be guilty of wrongful trading.

In such circumstances, then, unless the directors took every reasonable step to minimise the potential loss to the company's creditors, they may be liable to contribute such money to the assets of the company as the court thinks proper.

It is clearly apparent that Rosie will be personally liable under s.214 for the increase in Wag Ltd's debts from £15,000 to £75,000. However, as a director of the company Poppy will also be liable to contribute to the assets of the company under s.214.

The Insolvency Act 1986 governs situations where, in the course of a winding up, it appears that the business of a company has been carried on with intent to defraud creditors, or for any fraudulent purpose.

In such cases, the court may declare that any persons who were knowingly parties to such carrying on of the business are liable to make such contributions (if any) to the company's assets as the court thinks proper. There is a high burden of proof involved in proving dishonesty on the part of the person against whom it is alleged.

It should be noted that there is a criminal offence of fraudulent trading under the Companies Act 2006, which applies to anyone who has been party to the carrying on of the business of a company with intent to defraud creditors of any other person, or for any other fraudulent purpose.

Given that it is stated that Rosie knew of the fact that Wego Ltd was insolvent it is possible that she might be liable under the fraudulent trading provisions both civil and criminal. As a consequence she may well be liable for a maximum prison sentence of 10 years and may have to contribute to the assets of the company to cover any loss sustained by creditors as a result of her actions.

There is no evidence to support either action against Poppy.

Wrongful trading does not involve dishonesty but it still makes particular individuals potentially liable for the debts of their companies. Where a company is being wound up and it appears that, at some time before the start of the winding up, a director knew, or ought to have known that there was no reasonable chance of the company avoiding insolvent liquidation, they would be guilty of wrongful trading.

In such circumstances, then unless the directors took every reasonable step to minimise the potential loss to the company's creditors, they may be liable to contribute such money to the assets of the company as the court thinks proper.

It is clearly apparent that Rosie will be personally liable under s214 for the increase in Wego Ltd's debts from £10,000 to £75,000. However, as a director of the company Poppy will also be liable to contribute to the assets of the company under s214.

chapter

21

INT syllabus only: Audit of performance information in the public sector

Chapter learning objectives

This chapter covers syllabus areas:

- E6 – The audit of performance information (pre-determined objectives) in the public sector

Detailed syllabus objectives are provided in the introduction section of the text book.

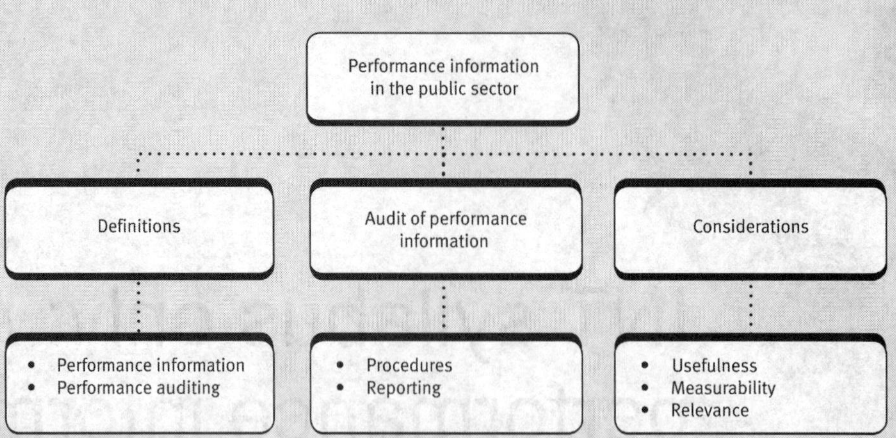

Exam focus

This syllabus area was introduced in 2014. Students are encouraged to read any published technical articles on this topic.

Public sector audit requirements

Public sector organisations are subject to greater regulation and reporting requirements than profit making organisations due to the fact that they are funded by taxpayer money.

There are 2 types of audit that must be performed for public sector organisations:

(1) Financial statement audit

(2) Performance audit.

1 Performance audit

Performance audits aim to provide management with assurance and advice regarding the effective functioning of its operational activities.

A performance audit uses auditing skills (planning & risk assessment, gathering sufficient appropriate evidence, reporting) and applying them to activities of the organisation that an external auditor of the financial statements wouldn't normally consider.

Performance audits may include

(1) Performance information

(2) Value for money – economy, efficiency and effectiveness of operations

(3) Operational audits

2 Performance information

Performance information is information published by public sector bodies regarding their objectives and the achievement of those objectives.

This information should have the same qualitative characteristics of general purpose financial reports such as relevance, completeness, reliability, neutrality, understandability, timeliness, validity and accuracy.

The external auditor may have a responsibility to report on this information to the users of such information.

Performance measures for public sector bodies

Police Performance Measures

- Reduce number of priority crimes e.g. burglary, theft of cars by 18%
- Increase serious violence detection rates by 68%
- Reduce number of anti-social behaviour incidents by 40%
- Reduce reoffending rates by 50%
- Increase public satisfaction to 80%

Hospital Performance Measures

- Reduce number of medical errors
- Reduce number of cases of MRSA (a bacterium responsible for causing infections particularly prevalent in hospitals)
- Reduce waiting times for operations
- Improve satisfaction with hospital food
- Decrease mortality rates

Local Council Performance Indicators

- % of streets that have unacceptable levels of litter on them to be 7% or less
- % residents satisfied with the local environment to be 79% or above
- At least 200 dwellings improved by the actions of the council
- To have no more than 45 households living in temporary accommodation
- At least 57% of bids for external finance/grant applications to be approved

Performance measures such as these are important to various stakeholder groups for example:

- The government who want to see that the money they provide to the relevant departments is being used effectively.
- The users of the services to assess how well their police force/hospital/council is performing in comparison with others.
- Potential users of the services e.g. where there is a choice of hospital to use, the patient may look at this information to decide which hospital at which to have their treatment.

3 Planning an audit of performance information

At the planning stage the auditor will:

- Obtain an understanding of the information to be reported on including how it is collected, aggregated, reporting processes, systems and controls.
- Make enquiries with management and staff to obtain an understanding of the data and how it is processed and reported.
- Establish materiality (see below).
- Examine the processes, systems and controls in place to collect, aggregate and report the performance information.

Materiality for non-financial information

Materiality for non-financial information is just as important as for financial information. For example if the entity is reporting that a target has been met when it hasn't this will affect the penalties faced.

For performance information such as mortality rates for a hospital, the indicator is highly sensitive and therefore material.

Setting materiality for non-financial information is more difficult to apply as compared with financial information and there is a risk that different assurance providers would reach different conclusions. As a result, this will undermine the credibility of the report.

One way of overcoming this issue is to disclose the materiality level used in the assurance report. Where performance measures apply across a variety of public bodies, a consistent approach should be adopted.

4 Procedures

Procedures to gather evidence will be the same as for a normal audit:

- Inspection of the supporting documentation for the information.
- Enquiry of management and other personnel within the organisation.
- Perform analytical procedures on the information such as comparison with prior year or other organisations of a similar size.
- Obtain written representation from management regarding the accuracy and completeness of the information.
- Recalculation of amounts included in the performance information.

Audit procedures

Following on from the illustration above, below are some procedures that could be performed to obtain evidence over the hospital performance measures.

Hospital performance measure	Procedures
Reduce number of medical errors	Enquire of hospital management what the definition of a medical error is. Inspect Department of Health publication to confirm management's understanding of the definition. Inspect hospital records and board minutes to confirm the number of medical errors.
Reduce number of cases of MRSA and C-Diff	Inspect hospital records of the number of cases of MRSA/C-Diff. Compare with prior year's and re-calculate the % change.

Improve satisfaction with hospital food	Review patient feedback questionnaires regarding hospital food.
	Recalculate the average 'score' generated from the feedback and compare with prior year's.
Decrease mortality rates	Inspect hospital records of the number of deaths.
	Review board minutes for evidence of any unrecorded deaths.
	Compare with prior year and re-calculate the % change.

5 Reporting

Reports on performance information may be in the form of reasonable assurance or limited assurance.

A reasonable assurance report would express the conclusion positively e.g. 'In our opinion the number of deaths reported by the hospital is fairly stated'.

A limited assurance report would express the conclusion negatively e.g. 'Nothing has come to our attention that causes us to believe that the number of deaths reported by the hospital is not fairly stated.

The assurance report will contain the usual elements of an assurance report:

- Title
- Addressee
- Introductory paragraph identifying the subject matter – the performance information being reported on
- Scope including the applicable standards and guidance followed e.g. ISAE 3000 *Assurance Engagements other than Audits or Reviews of Historical Financial Statements*
- Respective responsibilities of management and the assurance provider
- Inherent limitations of the report
- Summary of the work performed
- Conclusion based on the work performed
- Signature of the assurance provider
- Date

6 Usefulness, measurability and reliability

Usefulness

Performance information is now more commonplace with the introduction of government targets, league tables and measures for public sector organisations to demonstrate accountability to the taxpayer.

This information is reported to the relevant regulatory authority but may also be published on the organisation's website and included in their annual report.

Users can use this information to assess the performance of government departments or to help make choices such as which hospital to choose for treatment.

Measurability

Some measures may be subjective in terms of definition and as a result may be easily manipulated by management in order to ensure they are being seen to achieve the target.

This may lead the way for some organisations to include measures which are not relevant to their main strategic aims but which have been included to make it appear as though the organisation has achieved something.

There is a risk that organisations are deliberately vague when composing performance measures so that they can claim to have met their target.

For these reasons, measurement of the target may be difficult and therefore difficult for the auditor to prove or disprove.

Whilst there are national performance measures in place which all organisations of a particular type will need to report, each organisation can also determine their own performance objectives they wish to measure. This inconsistency means comparisons cannot be drawn between different entities and may cause confusion for users of the performance information who see that different criteria are being used to assess the same information.

Reliability

It is important that detailed criteria are developed to avoid different entities and assurance providers interpreting them differently. These criteria should be referred to in the assurance report, either via a link to the website detailing the criteria or as an appendix to the report.

Quality assurance processes within the public sector compare the assurance providers work and results to ensure that a level of consistency exists between the different firms and give comfort to users that the conclusions drawn would be the same irrespective of which assurance firm performed the work.

These pre-determined standards and quality assurance processes should improve reliability of the performance information.

Test your understanding 1

Suggest 3 performance measures for a government treasury department and list the audit procedures that an auditor of the performance information could perform to obtain evidence to support the figures reported.

Test your understanding 2

Explain the difference between a performance audit and an audit of performance information.

7 Chapter summary

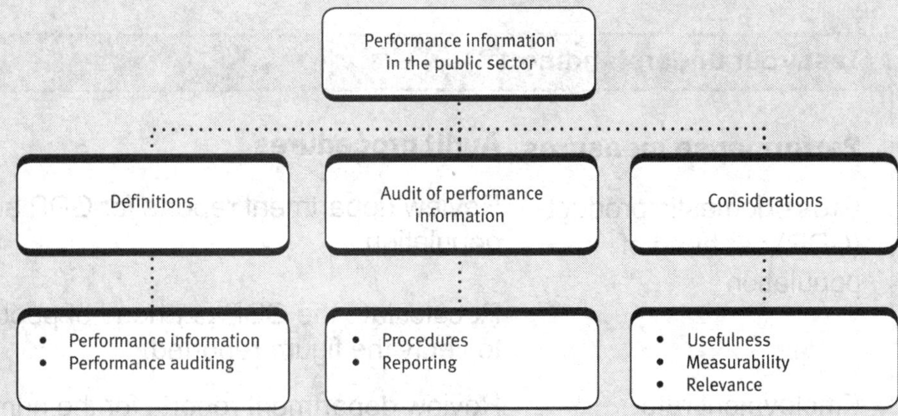

Test your understanding answers

Test your understanding 1

Performance measures	Audit procedures
Gross domestic product (GDP) per head of population	Review department reports for GDP and population.
	Recalculate the GDP per head of population to verify the figure reported.
Employment rate	Review department reports for the number of people in employment and calculate this as a % of the working population.
Public sector net debt as a % of GDP	Review the department report for the level of debt and calculate this as a % of GDP.

These are procedures assuming a limited assurance engagement. If a reasonable assurance engagement was being performed, tests of controls could be performed to evaluate the systems and processes used to collect the information.

Test your understanding 2

Performance audit

A performance audit is an audit of the operational activities of an organisation, typically with a view of assessing value for money.

Value for money is concerned with the 3 Es – economy, efficiency and effectiveness.

- Economy – obtaining the lowest cost for the required level of quality.
- Efficiency – achieving the maximum output for the minimum input.
- Effectiveness – achieving the objectives set.

In the context of a public sector organisation, value for money is concerned with stewardship of the public pound i.e. not wasting taxpayer money.

Performance information audit

Public sector organisations have targets set by the government which must be reported to assess the organisation's performance. This is referred to as 'performance information'.

An audit of the performance information will be concerned with obtaining evidence that the results reported by the organisation against such targets are:

- Accurate – data is recorded correctly.
- Valid – data has been produced in compliance with relevant requirements.
- Reliable – data has been collected using a stable process in a consistent manner over a period of time.
- Complete – all relevant information has been included.

chapter

22

P7 Financial reporting revision

Chapter learning objectives

This chapter is designed to assist you with revision of key financial reporting topics. Given the inter-relationship between financial reporting and auditing it is inevitable that the auditing exam will encompass many aspects of financial reporting that you have encountered in previous studies.

For further clarification with regard to the importance of financial reporting standards please refer to the technical article entitled "The Importance of Financial Reporting Standards to Auditors" (Nov 2008).

This can be found on the P7 section of the ACCA website.

IAS 1 Presentation of Financial Statements

This standard provides standard formats for the statement of profit or loss and other comprehensive income, statement of financial position, statement of cash flows and statement of changes in equity as well as setting out six overall accounting principles that should be applied:

- going concern
- accruals
- consistency of presentation
- materiality and aggregation
- offsetting
- comparative information.

Accounting policies should be selected so that the financial statements comply with all international standards and interpretations.

An entity must make a statement that the financial statements comply with the financial reporting framework.

IAS 1 also requires classification of items of other comprehensive income between those which:

- will not be reclassified to profit or loss; and
- which may be reclassified to profit or loss in future reporting periods.

IAS 2 Inventories

Inventories should be valued **'at the lower of cost and net realisable value'** (IAS 2, para 9).

IAS 2 says that the cost of inventory includes:

- purchase price including import duties, transport and handling costs
- any other directly attributable costs
- direct production costs e.g. direct labour
- direct expenses and subcontracted work
- production overheads (based on the normal levels of activity)
- other overheads, if attributable to bringing the product or service to its present location and condition.

IAS 2 specifies that cost excludes:

- abnormal waste
- storage costs
- indirect administrative overheads
- selling costs.

Some entities can identify individual units of inventory (e.g. vehicles can be identified by a chassis number). Those that cannot should keep track of costs using either the first in, first out (FIFO) or the weighted average cost (AVCO) assumption.

Some entities may use standard costing for valuing inventory. Standard costs may be used for convenience if it is a close approximation to actual cost, and is regularly reviewed and revised.

IAS 7 Statement of Cash Flows

The statement of cash flows provides an important insight into the ways in which the entity has created and applied cash during the period. The fact that a business generated profit during a period means that it has created wealth, but wealth is not necessarily reflected by cash. The fact that a business is liquid according to the statement of financial position at the year-end does not explain the cash movements that occurred during the year.

IAS 7 requires a cash flow statement to show cash flows generated from operating, investing and financing activities.

IAS 8 Accounting Policies, Changes in ....

.... accounting estimates and errors.

IAS 8 is an important standard because it clarifies the accounting treatment of a variety of accounting issues, including:

- selection of accounting policies
- changes in accounting policies
- changes in accounting estimates
- correction of prior period errors.

Accounting policies

Accounting policies are the **'principles, bases, conventions, rules and practices applied by an entity in preparing and presenting financial statements'** (IAS 8, para 5).

Changes in accounting policies

Changes in accounting policies are rare. However, on occasions changes in policy are enforced due to changes/updates to financial reporting standards or if it results in the financial statements providing reliable and more relevant information. It can be difficult to introduce these into a question. Take care not to treat a simple change in an estimate as a rather more complicated change in accounting policy.

Accounting policies should remain the same from period to period in order to allow for consistency of treatment.

In order to preserve the appearance of consistency, IAS 8 says that a change in accounting policy is dealt with as follows: the new policy will be applied retrospectively, with the opening balance on retained earnings recalculated on the basis that the new policy had always been in force. The resulting change in the retained earnings brought forward will be shown as a prior period adjustment in the statement of changes in equity and comparatives will be restated as if the new policy had been in force during the previous period.

The change and its effects must be described in the notes to the accounts.

Accounting estimates

Many of the figures in the financial statements rely on estimates.

Inevitably, some estimates will be revised in the light of unfolding events and new information. For example, a change in the method of charging depreciation, e.g. from reducing balance to straight line method is a change of estimate.

Changes in accounting estimates are recognised in the statement of profit or loss in the same period as the change occurs and included under the same classification as for the original asset. If the change is material then it should be disclosed in the notes to the financial statements.

Prior period errors

Prior period errors are **'omissions from, and misstatements in, the financial statements for one or more prior periods arising from a failure to use, or misuse of, reliable information'** (IAS 8, para 5).

IAS 8 requires that prior period errors are dealt with by:

- restating the opening balance of assets, liabilities and equity as if the error had never occurred, and presenting the necessary adjustment to the opening balance of retained earnings in the statement of changes in equity
- restating the comparative figures presented, as if the error had never occurred.

These adjustments should be disclosed in full in the notes to the accounts.

IAS 10 Events After the Reporting Period

- Events after the reporting period are 'those events, favourable and unfavourable, that occur between the statement of financial position date and the date when the financial statements are authorised for issue' (IAS 10, para 3).
- Adjusting events after the reporting period are those that **'provide evidence of conditions that existed at the reporting date'** (IAS 10, para 3a).
- Non-adjusting events after the reporting period are **'those that are indicative of conditions that arose after the reporting period'** (IAS 10, para 3b).

Accounting treatment

- Adjusting events affect the amounts stated in the financial statements so they must be adjusted.
- Non-adjusting events do not concern the position at the statement of financial position date so the accounts are not adjusted. If the event is material then the nature and its financial effect must be disclosed.

IAS 12 Income Taxes

- IAS 12 covers both current and deferred tax, but deferred tax is the most examinable and will be reviewed here.
- Temporary differences are **'differences between the carrying amount of an asset or liability in the statement of financial position and its tax base'** (IAS 12, para 5).
- Tax base is the **'amount attributed to an asset or liability for tax purposes'** (IAS 12, para 5).

Temporary differences can be either:

(i) Taxable temporary differences. This is when the carrying amount of an asset exceeds its tax base, giving rise to a deferred tax liability.

(ii) Deductible temporary differences. This is when the tax base of an asset exceeds the carrying amount of that asset, giving rise to a deferred tax asset.

Sources of taxable temporary differences.

- Depreciation of an asset is accelerated for tax purposes.
- Development costs that were capitalised and amortised in the accounts, but deducted as incurred for tax purposes.
- A revaluation surplus on non-current assets as the carrying amount of the asset increases but the tax base of the asset does not change. Deferred tax is provided on the revaluation.
- Interest revenue received in arrears, which is accounted for on an accruals basis in the statement of profit or loss but taxable on a cash basis.
- Temporary differences can arise on a business combination if assets or liabilities are increased to fair value but the tax base remains at cost. Deferred tax is recognised on these differences and is included as part of net assets acquired.

Sources of deductible temporary differences

- Losses in the statement of profit or loss where tax relief is only available against future profits.
- Intra-group profits in inventory that are unrealised for consolidation purposes but taxable in the individual company that made the unrealised profit.
- Accumulated depreciation of an asset in the statement of financial position is greater than the cumulative depreciation for tax purposes.

- Pension liabilities that are recognised in the financial statements but only allowable for tax when the contributions are made to the scheme in the future.
- Research expenses are recognised as an expense in determining accounting profit but not deductible for tax until a later period.
- Income is deferred in the statement of financial position but has already been included in taxable profit.

Accounting treatment

- Deferred tax assets can be recognised for all deductible temporary differences to the extent it is probable that taxable profits will be available for these differences to be utilised.
- IAS 12 does not permit the discounting of deferred tax liabilities.
- The charge for deferred tax is recognised in the statement of profit or loss unless it relates to a gain or loss that has been recognised in other comprehensive income e.g. revaluations, in which case the related deferred tax is also recognised in other comprehensive income.
- Deferred tax should be measured at the rates expected to be in force when the temporary differences reverse, although usually the current tax rate is used.

IAS 16 Property Plant and Equipment

Cost and depreciation of an asset

IAS 16 says that property, plant and equipment is initially recognised at cost.

An asset's cost is its purchase price, less any trade discounts or rebates, plus any further costs directly attributable to bringing it into working condition for its intended use.

- Subsequent expenditure on non current assets is capitalised if it:
  - enhances the economic benefits of the asset e.g. adding an new wing to a building
  - replaces part of an asset that has been separately depreciated and has been fully depreciated; e.g. furnace that requires new linings periodically
  - replaces economic benefits previously consumed, e.g. a major inspection of aircraft.

- The aim of depreciation is to spread the cost of the asset over its life in the business.
  - IAS 16 requires that the depreciation method and useful life of an asset should be reviewed at the end of each year and revised where necessary. This is not a change in accounting policy, but a change of accounting estimate.
  - If an asset has parts with different lives, (e.g. a building with a flat roof), the component parts of the asset should be capitalised and depreciated separately.

Revaluation of property, plant and equipment

- Revaluation of PPE is optional. However, if one asset is revalued, all assets in that class must be revalued, i.e. no cherry-picking.
- Valuations should be kept up to date to ensure that the carrying amount does not differ materially from the fair value at each statement of financial position date.
- Revaluation gains are credited to other comprehensive income unless the gain reverses a previous revaluation loss of the same asset previously recognised in the statement of profit or loss.
- Revaluation losses are debited to the statement of profit or loss unless the loss relates to a previous revaluation surplus, in which case the decrease should be debited to other comprehensive income to the extent of any credit balance existing in the revaluation surplus relating to that asset.

Accounting for revaluations

(1) Restate asset from cost to valuation amount: Dr Non-current asset (valuation – cost)

(2) Remove any existing depreciation: Dr Accumulated depreciation

(3) Include increase in other comprehensive income: Cr Revaluation gain within other comprehensive income (valuation – old carrying value).

Depreciation is charged on the revalued amount less residual value (if any) over the **remaining useful life** of the asset.

An entity may choose to make an annual transfer of excess depreciation from revaluation reserve to retained earnings. If this is done, it should be applied consistently each year.

IAS 19 Employee Benefits (revised)

IAS 19 (revised) deals with accounting for pensions and other employee benefits in the employer's accounts.

- The accounting issues lie with defined benefit schemes where an employer guarantees that an employee will have a specific pension on retirement, usually a percentage of final salary.
- To estimate the fund required, an actuary will have to calculate the contributions required to ensure the scheme has enough funds to pay out its liabilities.
- This involves estimating what may happen in the future, such as the age profile of employees, retirement age, etc.
- A pension scheme consists of a pool of assets (cash, investments, shares etc) and a liability for pensions owed to employees when they are at retirement age. The assets are used to pay out the pensions.

Measurement and recognition of defined benefit schemes

Profit or loss	Other comprehensive income	Statement of Financial Position
Service cost components: current and past service costs, including any gains or losses arising on curtailments and settlements	Remeasurement component	Net scheme asset or liability, where assets are measured at fair value and liabilities measured at present value
Net interest component	Remeasurement component: actuarial gains and losses on scheme assets and liabilities, plus any income, gains etc. not taken to profit or loss as part of the net interest component	

Definitions

- **Current service cost** is the increase in the actuarial liability (present value of the defined benefit obligation) resulting from employee service in the current period. This is part of the service cost component.
- **Past service cost** is the increase in the actuarial liability relating to employee service in previous periods but only arising in the current period. Past service costs usually arise because there has been an improvement in the benefits to be provided under the plan. They are part of the service cost component and are recognised when the plan amendments occur.
- A **curtailment** occurs when an entity is demonstrably committed to making a material reduction in the number of employees covered by a plan, or amends the terms of a plan such that a material element of future service by current employees will qualify for no or reduced benefits. This may occur, for example if an entity closes a plant and makes those employees redundant. Any gain or loss on curtailment is part of the service cost component.
- **A settlement** occurs when an entity enters into a transaction to eliminate the obligation for part or all of the benefits under a plan. For example, an employee may leave the entity for a new job elsewhere, and a payment is made from that pension plan to the to the pension plan operated by the new employer. Any gain or loss on settlement is part of the service cost component.
- **Net interest** is computed by applying the discount rate to the net liability (or asset) at the start of the reporting period. This is a separate component included in profit or loss for the year. Net interest expense (or income) is determined by applying the discount rate used to measure the defined benefit obligation, irrespective of whether the is a net interest expense or net interest income.
- **Remeasurement component** comprises actuarial gains and losses arising during the reporting period, including the actual returns on plan assets less any amount taken to profit or loss as part of the net interest component. Actuarial gains and losses are increases and decreases in the pension asset or liability that occur either because the actuarial assumptions have changed or because of differences between the previous actuarial assumptions and what has actually happened (experience adjustments). This component is recognised in Other Comprehensive Income for the year and is not recycled to profit or loss.

IAS 20 Accounting for Government Grants and Disclosure of ....

Government grants are **'assistance by government in the form of transfers of resources to an entity in return for past or future compliance with certain conditions'** (IAS 20, para 3).

Government assistance is **'action by government designed to provide economic benefit to a specific entity'** (IAS 20, para 3).

Accounting treatment

- IAS 20 says that grants are not be recognised until there is reasonable assurance that:
  - the conditions attached to the grant will be complied with, and
  - the grant will be received.
- Grants shall be recognised in the statement of profit or loss so as to match them with the expenditure towards which they are intended to contribute.
  - Income grants given to subsidise expenditure should be matched to the related costs.
  - Income grants given to help achieve a non-financial goal (such as job creation) should be matched to the costs incurred to meet that goal.
- Grants which contribute towards past expenditure, with no related future costs, shall be recognised immediately in the period in which they are received.
- Grants related to income should be presented separately in the statement of profit or loss, or under a general heading, or alternatively deducted from the related expense.
- Grants for purchases of non-current assets should be recognised over the expected useful lives of the related assets.

There are two acceptable accounting treatments for grants related to non-current assets:

- Deduct the grant from the cost of the asset and depreciate the net cost, or
- Treat the grant as deferred income and release it to the statement of profit or loss over the life of the asset. This is the method most commonly used.

Grants that become repayable

A government grant that becomes repayable shall be accounted for as a change in accounting estimate.

Disclosure

The following matters should be disclosed:

- Accounting policy adopted.
- Nature and extent of government grants recognised.
- Unfulfilled conditions attaching to government grants.

IAS 21 The Effects of Changes in Foreign Exchange Rates

IAS 21 provides the accounting guidance on foreign currency transactions.

The main points are summarised below:

Functional and presentation currencies

A company must determine both its functional and presentation currency.

Functional currency is **'the currency of the primary economic environment in which the entity operates'** (IAS 21, para 8).

IAS 21 says that presentation currency is the currency in which the entity presents its financial statements.

In determining **functional currency**, IAS 21 specifies that an entity should consider the following:

- The currency that influences its sales prices for its goods and services.
- The currency that influences the costs associated with providing its goods and services.

If the company is a foreign-owned subsidiary then it will have the same functional currency as its parent if it operates with little autonomy.

Once determined, functional currency should not be changed.

Presentation currency can be any currency and can be different from functional currency.

This is particularly the case if the company is foreign-controlled as the presentation currency may be that of the parent. If the presentation currency is different from the functional currency, then the financial statements must be translated into the presentation currency.

Individual transactions in foreign currency

If a company enters into **foreign currency transactions** the results of these transactions should be translated and recorded in the accounting records in the functional currency:

- at the rate on the date the transaction occurred, or
- using an average rate over a period of time providing the exchange rate has not fluctuated significantly.

At subsequent statement of financial position dates, the following process must be applied.

- Foreign currency monetary items (receivables, payables, cash, loans) must be translated using the closing rate. The closing rate is the exchange rate at the statement of financial position date.
- Foreign currency non-monetary items (non-current assets, investments, inventory) are not retranslated. They are left at the exchange rate that was used at the date of the transaction (called the historic rate).
- Exchange differences on settlement of monetary items or on retranslating monetary items are recognised in the statement of profit or loss.

Foreign subsidiaries

If a company has foreign subsidiaries whose functional currency is their local currency, their financial statements must be translated into the parent's presentation currency.

- All assets and liabilities are translated into the parent's presentation currency at the closing rate at the statement of financial position date.
- Goodwill is calculated in the functional currency of the subsidiary, and translated at each reporting date at the closing rate into the presentation currency of the parent.
- Income and expenses in the statement of profit or loss must be translated at the average rate for the period.

- Exchange differences arising on consolidation are recognised in other comprehensive income until disposal of the subsidiary when they are part of the gain or loss on disposal reported in profit or loss for the year.
- Exchange differences arise from:
  – the retranslation of the opening net assets using the closing rate.
  – retranslation of the profit for the year from the average rate (used in the statement of profit or loss) to the closing rate (for inclusion in the statement of financial position).

IAS 23 Borrowing Costs

IAS 23 requires finance costs to be capitalised providing they are directly attributable to the asset being constructed. Capitalisation commences when construction expenditure is being incurred and ceases when the asset is ready for use.

Capitalised borrowing costs are those actually incurred, although this may be estimated if the entity is financing the cost out of general borrowings.

Borrowing costs incurred after the asset has been completed or while work is suspended must be expensed in the statement of profit or loss.

The disclosures required by IAS 23 are:

- the accounting policy adopted for borrowing costs
- the amount of borrowing costs capitalised during the period
- the capitalisation rate used.

IAS 24 Related Party Disclosures

A related party is a person or entity that is related to the entity that is preparing its financial statements. IAS 24 gives the following rules which should be used to determine the existence of related party relationships:

(a) **'A person or a close member of that person's family is related to a reporting entity if that person:**
  (i) **has control or joint control of the reporting entity.**
  (ii) **has significant influence over the reporting entity.**
  (iii) **is a member of the key management personnel of the reporting entity or of a parent of the reporting entity.**

(b) **An entity is related to a reporting entity if any of the following conditions apply:**

(i) **The entity and the reporting entity are members of the same group (which means that each parent, subsidiary and fellow subsidiary is related to the others).**

(ii) **One entity is an associate or joint venture of the other entity (or an associate or joint venture of a member of a group of which the other entity is a member).**

(iii) **Both entities are joint ventures of the same third party.**

(iv) **One entity is a joint venture of a third entity and the other entity is an associate of the third entity.**

(v) **The entity is a post-employment benefit plan for the benefit of employees of either the reporting entity or an entity related to the reporting entity. If the reporting entity is itself such a plan, the sponsoring employers are also related to the reporting entity.**

(vi) **The entity is controlled or jointly controlled by a person identified in (a).**

(vii) **A person identified in (a)(i) has significant influence over the entity or is a member of the key management personnel of the entity (or of a parent of the entity).**

(viii) **The entity, or any member of a group of which it is a part, provides key management personnel services to the reporting entity or to the parent of the reporting entity'** (IAS 24, para 9).

A related party transaction is **'the transfer of resources, services or obligations between related parties regardless of whether a price is charged'** (IAS 24, para 9).

Disclosures

- Relationships between parents and subsidiaries irrespective of whether there have been transactions between the parties.
- The name of the parent and the ultimate controlling party (if different).
- Key management personnel compensation in total and for each short term employee benefits, post employment benefits, other long term benefits, termination benefits and share based payment.
- For related party transactions that have occurred, the nature of the relationship and detail of the transactions and outstanding balances.
- The disclosure should be made for each category of related parties stated above and include:
  (a) the amount of the transactions.
  (b) the amount of outstanding balances and their terms.

(c) allowances for doubtful debts relating to the outstanding balances.

(d) the expense recognised in the period in respect of irrecoverable or doubtful debts due from related parties.

IAS 27 Separate Financial Statements

This standard applies when an entity has interests in subsidiaries, joint ventures or associates and either elects to, or is required to, prepare separate **non-consolidated financial statements**.

If separate financial statements are produced, investments in subsidiaries, associates or joint ventures can be measured:

- at cost
- using the equity method
- in accordance with IFRS 9 *Financial Instruments*.

IAS 28 Investments in Associates and Joint Ventures

A **joint venture** is a **'joint arrangement whereby the parties that have joint control of the arrangement have rights to the net assets of the arrangement'** (IAS 28, para 3). This will normally be established in the form of a separate entity to conduct the joint venture activities.

An **associate** is defined as an entity **'over which the investor has significant influence'** (IAS 28, para 3).

Significant influence is the **'power to participate in the financial and operating policy decisions of the investee but is not control or joint control over those policies'** (IAS 28, para 3).

It is normally assumed that significant influence exists if the holding company has a shareholding of 20% to 50%.

Equity accounting

In the consolidated financial statements of a group:

- Acquisition accounting is used to account for subsidiaries.
- Equity accounting is used to account for associates and joint ventures.

Unlike acquisition accounting, which combined the holding company's figures with those of the subsidiary or subsidiaries, equity accounting involves single figure adjustments to the consolidated statement of profit or loss and the consolidated statement of financial position.

An interest in an associate or joint venture should be accounted for in the separate financial statements of an entity.

Statement of profit or loss

The consolidated statement of profit or loss and other comprehensive income includes the **investor's share** of the associate or joint venture's results.

Statement of financial position

In the consolidated statement of financial position, the associate or joint venture is initially shown at cost and then increased by the investor's share of the post-acquisition reserve movement.

Balances with the associate

The associate or joint venture is considered to be outside the group. Therefore balances between group companies and the associate or joint venture will remain in the consolidated statement of financial position. If a group company trades with the associate or joint venture, the resulting payables and receivables will remain in the consolidated statement of financial position.

Sales to and from associates

Sales between group members and associates or joint ventures are left in the consolidated statement of profit or loss.

Unrealised profit in inventory

The group share of unrealised profit in closing inventory arising from sales between group members and associates or joint ventures should still be cancelled.

Dividends from associates

Dividends from associates and joint ventures are not included in the consolidated statement of profit or loss. This is because the dividend is effectively being paid out of the group's share of the associate or joint venture's profit, which has already been recognised in the group accounts.

IAS 32 Financial instruments: Presentation

IAS 32 Financial Instruments: Presentation classifies financial instruments as debt or equity according to the substance of the contractual arrangement.

It does not matter whether a financial instrument is called a 'share' or 'equity'. IAS 32 might still classify it as a liability if it has the characteristics of debt.

IAS 32 says that a financial instrument is classified as **debt** if the issuer has a contractual obligation either to deliver cash or another financial asset to the holder or to exchange another financial asset/liability with the holder under conditions that are potentially unfavourable to the issuer.

A financial instrument is classified as **equity** if it does not give rise to such a contractual obligation.

For example, preference shares:

- are classified as equity if they are irredeemable
- are classified as debt if they are redeemable.

Compound instruments

A compound instrument is one which has both a liability and an equity component.

For example, a convertible bond pays interest for the first part of its life, until it is redeemed or converted into ordinary share capital. The interest paid during the debt phase is usually lower than the rate offered on equivalent debt capital that does not carry conversion rights.

Compound instruments must be broken down between their liability element and equity element and each is shown in the appropriate part of the statement of financial position. The liability is calculated as the present value of the repayments. The difference between the proceeds and the liability element is the equity element.

IAS 33 Earnings Per Share

- Earnings per share is an important ratio that is used as a comparison for company performance and forms part of the Price / Earnings ratio.
- IAS 33 applies to all listed companies. Private companies must follow the standard if they disclose an EPS figure.

Basic earnings per share is:

$$\frac{\text{Profit or loss for the period attributable to the equity shareholders}}{\text{Weighted average number of equity shares outstanding in the period}}$$

- Basic earnings are profit after tax less non-controlling investment and preference dividends.
- The weighted average number of equity shares must take into account when the shares were issued in the year.

Diluted earnings per share

- IAS 33 requires diluted earnings per share to be disclosed as well as basic EPS.
- Diluted EPS shows the effect on the current EPS if all the potential equity shares had been issued under the greatest possible dilution.
- Potential equity shares consist of:
  - convertible loan stock
  - convertible preference shares
  - share warrants and options
  - partly paid shares
  - rights granted under employee share schemes
  - rights to equity shares that are conditional.

Disclosure of EPS

- Basic and diluted earnings per share for continuing operations should be presented on the face of the statement of profit or loss for each class of equity share.
- Basic and diluted earnings per share for discontinued operations should be presented on the face of the statement of profit or loss or in the notes to the accounts for each class of equity share.
- If a company discloses an EPS using a different earnings figure, the alternative calculation must show basic and diluted EPS with equal prominence.

These alternative calculations must be presented in the notes to the financial statements, not on the face of the statement of profit or loss.

IAS 36 Impairment of Assets

- Impairment is measured by comparing the carrying value of an asset or cash generating unit with its recoverable amount.
- If the carrying value exceeds the recoverable amount, the asset is impaired and must be written down.

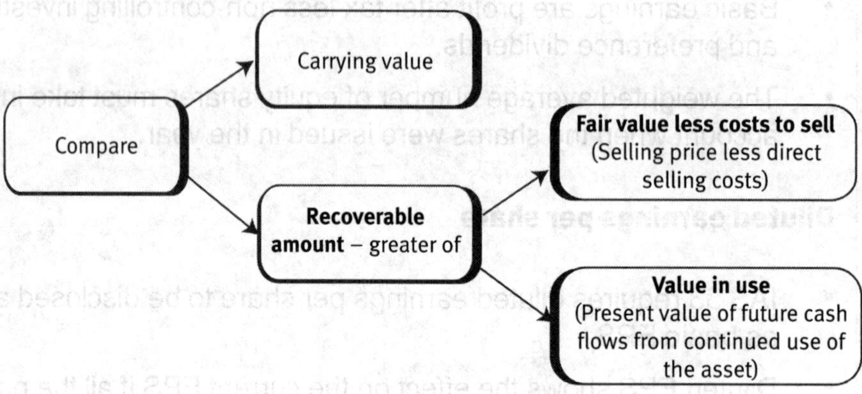

Indicators of impairment

Unless an impairment review is required by another standard (e.g. IAS 38 *Intangible Assets* or IFRS 3 Business Combinations), then impairment reviews are required where there is an indicator of impairment.

Examples of impairment indicators

Internal

- Physical damage to the asset.
- Management committed to reorganisation of the business.
- Obsolete assets.
- Idle assets.
- Major loss of key employees.
- Operating losses in the business where the assets are used.

External

- Competitor actions.
- Increasing interest rates (affect value in use).
- Market values of assets falling.
- Change in the business or market where assets are used (e.g. govt action).

Cash-generating units (CGU)

A **cash-generating unit**, per IAS 36, is the smallest identifiable group of assets that generates external cash inflows.

- It will not always be possible to base the impairment review on individual assets as an individual asset may not generate a distinguishable cash flow. In this case the impairment calculations should be based on a CGU.
- The impairment calculation is performed by comparing the carrying value of the CGU to the recoverable amount of the CGU. This is achieved by allocating an entity's assets including goodwill, to CGUs.
- Impairment losses are allocated to assets with specific impairments first, then allocated in the following order:

  (1) goodwill

  (2) remaining assets on a pro rata basis. Assets cannot be written down below the higher of fair value less costs to sell, value in use and zero.

Recognition of impairment losses

Assets held at cost: The amount of the impairment is charged to the statement of profit or loss for the period in which the impairment occurs.

Revalued assets: The impairment is charged first to OCI to reverse any previous surplus on that asset in the same way as a downward revaluation. Any further impairment is charged to the statement of profit or loss.

IAS 37 Provisions, Contingent Liabilities and Contingent Assets

IAS 37 provides the following definitions:

- A provision is **'a liability of uncertain timing or amount'** (IAS 37, para 10).
- A contingent liability is a possible obligation arising from past events whose existence will only be confirmed by an uncertain future event outside of the entity's control.
- A contingent asset is a possible asset that arises from past events and whose existence will only be confirmed by an uncertain future event outside of the entity's control.

Provisions

Recognition

Recognise when:

- an entity has a present obligation (legal or constructive) as a result of a past event,
- It is probable that an outflow of resources embodying economic benefits will be required to settle the obligation, and
- a reliable estimate can be made of the amount of the obligation.

Measurement

- The amount recognised as a provision should be the best estimate of the expenditure required to settle the present obligation at the SFP date
- Where the time value of money is material, the provision should be discounted to present value.

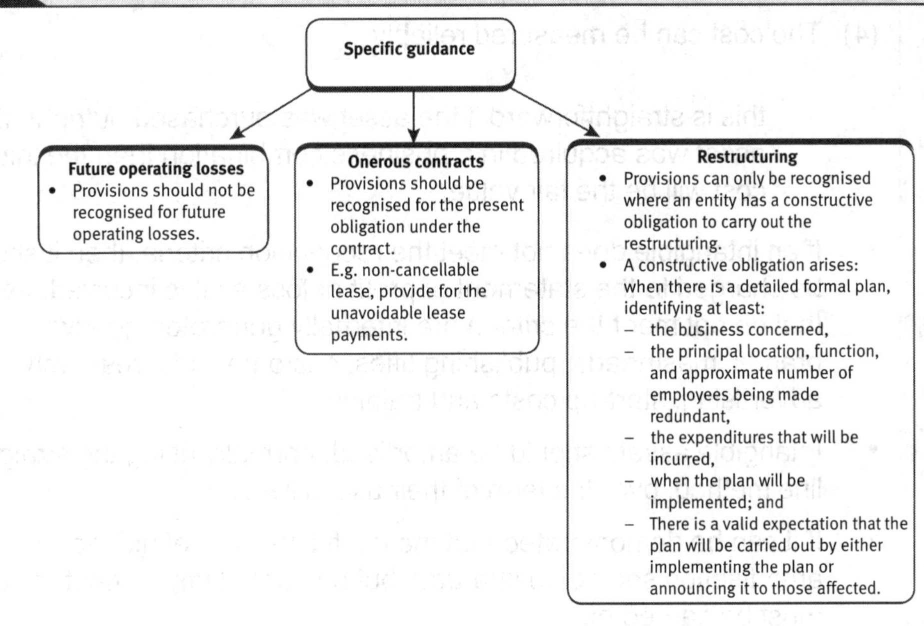

Contingent liabilities should not be recognised. They should be disclosed unless the possibility of a transfer of economic benefits is remote.

Contingent assets should not be recognised. If the possibility of an inflow of economic benefits is probable they should be disclosed.

IAS 38 Intangible Assets

An **intangible asset** is **'an identifiable non-monetary asset without physical substance'** (IAS 38, para 8).

Accounting treatment

IAS 38 says that an intangible asset is initially recognised at cost if all of the following criteria are met.

(1) It is identifiable – it could be disposed of without disposing of the business at the same time.

(2) It is controlled by the entity
   – the entity has the power to obtain economic benefits from it, for example patents and copyrights give legal rights to future economic benefits.

(3) It will generate probable future economic benefits for the entity
   – this could be by a reduction in costs or increasing revenues.

(4) The cost can be measured reliably

– this is straightforward if the asset was purchased outright. If the asset was acquired in a business combination then the initial cost will be the fair value.

- If an intangible does not meet the recognition criteria, then it should be charged to the statement of profit or loss as it is incurred. Items that do not meet the criteria are internally generated goodwill, brands, mastheads, publishing titles, customer lists, research, advertising, start-up costs and training.
- Intangible assets should be amortised, normally using the straight line method, over the term of their useful lives.
- If it can be demonstrated that the useful life is indefinite no amortisation should be charged, but an annual impairment review must be carried out.
- Intangible assets can be revalued but fair values must be determined with reference to an active market. IAS 38 says that this will have homogenous products, willing buyers and sellers at all times and published prices. In practical terms, most intangible assets are likely to be valued using the cost model.
- The recognition of internally generated intangible assets is split into a research phase and a development phase. Costs incurred in the research phase must be charged to the statement of profit or loss as they are incurred. IAS 38 says that costs incurred in the development phase should be recognised as an intangible asset if they meet the following criteria:

  (a) the project is technically feasible

  (b) the asset will be completed then used or sold

  (c) the entity is able to use or sell the asset

  (d) the asset will generate future economic benefits (either by internal use or there is a market for it)

  (e) the entity has adequate technical, financial and other resources to complete the project

  (f) the expenditure on the project can be reliably measured.
- Amortisation of development costs will occur over the period that benefits are expected.

IAS 40 Investment Property

IAS 40 defines **investment property** as property or land held to earn rentals or for capital appreciation or both.

Investment property is not:

- property held for use in the production or supply of goods or services or for administrative purposes.
- owner occupied property (dealt with under IAS 16 *Property, Plant and Equipment*).
- property held for sale in the normal course of business (dealt with under IAS 2 *Inventories*).
- property being constructed for third parties (dealt with under IFRS 15 *Revenue from Contracts with Customers*).
- property leased to another entity under a finance lease.

Accounting treatment

- An entity can choose either the cost model or the fair value model.
- The cost model in IAS 40 is the same as the cost model in IAS 16.
- The fair value model recognises investment properties in the statement of financial position at fair value.
- Gains and losses on revaluation when using the fair value model are recognised in the statement of profit or loss.

IAS 41 Agriculture

A biological asset is **'a living plant or animal'** (IAS 41, para 5). (Agricultural land is accounted for under IAS 16 PPE).

Agricultural produce is **'the harvested product of the entity's biological assets'** (IAS 41, para 5).

Biological assets should be valued at fair value less estimated costs to sell and revalued each year-end. Any changes in fair value should be recognised in the statement of profit or loss.

At the date of harvest, agricultural produce should be recognised and measured at fair value less estimated costs to sell. It is then accounted for under IAS 2 Inventories.

IFRS 1 First-time Adoption of International Reporting Standards

IFRS 1 sets out the procedures to follow when an entity adopts IFRS Standards in its published financial statements for the first time.

The **date of transition** is **'the beginning of the earliest period for which an entity presents full comparative information under IFRS Standards in its first IFRS financial statements**' (IFRS 1, App A).

IFRS 1 requires entities to prepare an opening IFRS statement of financial position at the date of transition. This statement must:

- recognise all assets and liabilities required by IFRS Standards.
- not recognise assets and liabilities not permitted by IFRS Standards.
- reclassify all assets, liabilities and equity components in accordance with IFRS Standards.
- measure all assets and liabilities in accordance with IFRS Standards.

Any gains or losses arising on the adoption of IFRS Standards are recognised in retained earnings.

IFRS 2 Share Based Payments

A **share based payment** transaction is one where an entity obtains goods or services from other parties with payment taking the form of shares or share options issued by the entity.

There are two types of share based payment transactions:

(1) equity-settled share based payment transactions where an entity receives goods or services in exchange for equity instruments (e.g. shares or share options).

(2) cash-settled share based payment transactions, where an entity receives goods and services in exchange for a cash amount paid based on its share price.

Accounting

- If an entity issues share options (e.g. to employees), the fair value of the option at the grant date should be used as the cost of the services received.

- For cash settled share based payments, the fair value of goods and services is measured and a liability recognised. The liability is re-measured at each statement of financial position date until it is settled with changes in value being taken to the statement of profit or loss.
- The expense in relation to the share based transaction must be recognised over the period in which the services are rendered or goods are received (vesting period).

Grant date: the date a share based-payment transaction is entered into.

Vesting date: the date on which the cash or equity instruments can be received by the other party to the agreement.

Example:

A company grants share options of 5000 shares due to vest in 5 year's time. The fair value of the option at the grant date is $3.

Assuming that 5000 shares are expected to vest, the cost to the company will be 5000 × $3 = $15,000 which is spread over the vesting period. Therefore $3,000 is charged to the statement of profit and loss.

Each year the cost should be remeasured and any adjustment taken through the SPL with a corresponding credit to equity. If it is expected that only 4000 shares are expected to vest, the cost would be 4000 × $3 = $12,000 with a cost per year of $2,400. Therefore, at the end of year 2 a total cost of $4,800 needs to be recognised. As $3,000 was charged in year 1, the charge for year 2 needs to be $1,800.

Assuming no further changes in the number of shares expected to vest, $2,400 will be charged to the SPL in year's 3 to 5.

IFRS 3 Business Combinations

On acquisition, both the cost of investment and the net assets acquired are recorded at their fair value. Assets and liabilities must be recognised if they are separately identifiable and can be reliably measured. The future intentions of the acquirer are not taken into account when calculating fair values.

Fair value is **'the price that would be received to sell an asset or paid to transfer a liability in an orderly transaction between market participants at the measurement date'** (IFRS 13, para 9).

Fair value of the cost of acquisition

The cost of acquisition is:

(a) the amount of cash paid, plus

(b) the fair value of other purchase consideration given by the acquirer.

Note:

- If payment of cash is deferred it should be discounted to present value using a rate at which the acquirer could obtain similar borrowing.
- If the acquirer issues shares, fair value is normally the market price at the date of acquisition.
- The acquirer must recognise the fair value of contingent consideration as part of the consideration.

Goodwill and the non-controlling interest

The standard allows the acquirer (parent) to measure any non-controlling interest (NCI) in one of two ways:

- at fair value – this measures goodwill for the entity as a whole, or
- at the NCI's proportionate share of the acquiree's (subsidiary's) identifiable net assets.

Negative goodwill

If the net assets acquired exceed the fair value of consideration, then negative goodwill arises.

After checking that the calculations have been done correctly, negative goodwill is credited to the statement of profit or loss and other comprehensive income immediately.

Other adjustments

Other consolidation adjustments need to be made, including:

- dividends declared by the subsidiary or associate and not accounted for by the parent.
- interest on inter-company loans that has not been accounted for by the receiving party.
- inter-company management charges that have not been accounted for by the receiving party.
- inter-company sales, purchases and unrealised profit in inventory.
- inter-company transfer of non-current assets and unrealised profit on transfer.
- inter-company receivables, payables and loans that need eliminating.

IFRS 5 Non-current Assets Held for Sale & Discontinued

A **discontinued operation** is a **'component of an entity that either has been disposed of, or is classified as held for sale; and**

- **represents a separate major line of business or geographical area of operations.**
- **is part of a single coordinated plan to dispose of a separate major line of business or geographical area of operations.**
- **is a subsidiary acquired exclusively with a view to resale'** (IFRS 5, App A).

IFRS 5 says that a non-current asset or a disposal group is classified as held for sale if its carrying amount will be recovered primarily through a sale rather than continued use in the business.

A **disposal group** is a group of assets, and associated liabilities, that will be sold together in a single transaction.

Assets can only be classified as held for sale (and therefore a discontinued operation) if they meet all of the criteria below:

- management commits itself to a plan to sell.
- the asset (or disposal group) is available for immediate sale in its present condition.
- sale is highly probable and is expected to be completed within a year from date of classification.

- the asset (or disposal group) is being actively marketed for sale at a reasonable price compared to its fair value.
- it is unlikely that significant changes will be made to the plan or it will be withdrawn.

If the criteria are met after the statement of financial position date but before the accounts are authorised for issue, the assets should **not** be classed as held for sale but the information should be disclosed.

Measurement

- A non-current asset (or disposal group) classified as held for sale should be measured at the lower of its carrying value and fair value less costs to sell.
- Assets classified as held for sale should not be depreciated, regardless of whether they are still in use by the reporting entity.

Presentation

IFRS 5 says that information about discontinued operations should be presented on the face of the statement of profit or loss as a single amount. This comprises:

- the profit or loss from the discontinued operations.
- the gain or loss on the measurement to fair value less costs to sell or on the disposal of the discontinued operation.

IFRS 7 Financial Instruments: Disclosures

IFRS 7 requires two main categories of disclosures in relation to financial instruments:

(1) information about the significance of financial instruments

(2) information about the nature and extent of risks arising from financial instruments.

Qualitative disclosures must describe:

- risk exposures for each type of financial instrument.
- management's objectives, policies, and processes for managing those risks.
- changes from the prior period.

Quantitative disclosures include:

- summary quantitative data about exposure to each risk at the reporting date.
- disclosures about credit risk, liquidity risk, and market risk.
- concentrations of risk.

IFRS 8 Operating Segments

IFRS 8 requires an entity to disclose information about each of its operating segments.

An **operating segment** is defined as a component of an entity:

- that engages in business activities from which it may earn revenues and incur expenses.
- whose results are reviewed by the entity's chief operating decision maker(s)
- for which financial information is available.

Reporting thresholds

IFRS 8 requires that an entity separately reports information about any operating segment that meets one of the following quantitative thresholds:

- sales are 10 per cent or more of the combined revenues of all operating segments, both international and external sales revenues.
- its reported profit or loss is 10 per cent or more of the greater, in absolute amount, of:
  - the combined reported profit of all operating segments that did not report a loss and
  - the combined reported loss of all operating segments that reported a loss.
- Its assets are 10 per cent or more of the combined assets of all operating segments.

At least 75% of the entity's **external revenue** should be included in reportable segments. If the quantitative test results in segmental disclosure of less than this, other reportable segments should be identified until this 75% is reached.

Disclosures

For each reportable segment IFRS 8 requires an entity to disclose:

- a measure of profit or loss
- a measure of total assets
- a measure of total liabilities (if such an amount is regularly used in decision making).

IFRS 9 Financial Instruments

Financial assets

Investments in equity

Investments in equity instruments (such as an investment in the ordinary shares of another entity) are normally measured at fair value through profit or loss. It is possible to designate an equity instrument as fair value through other comprehensive income, provided that the following conditions are complied with:

- the equity instrument must not be held for trading, and
- there must have been an irrevocable choice for this designation upon initial recognition of the asset.

Investments in debt

IFRS 9 requires that financial assets that are debt instruments are measured in one of three ways:

(1) **Amortised cost**

An investment in a debt instrument is measured at amortised cost if:

- The financial asset is held within a business model whose aim is to collect the contractual cash flows.
- The contractual terms of the financial asset give rise on specified dates to cash flows that are solely payments of principal and interest on the principal amount outstanding.

(2) **Fair value through other comprehensive income**

An investment in a debt instrument is measured at fair value through other comprehensive income if:

- The financial asset is held within a business model whose objective is achieved by both collecting contractual cash flows and selling financial assets.
- The contractual terms of the financial asset give rise on specified dates to cash flows that are solely payments of principal and interest on the principal amount outstanding.

(3) **Fair value through profit or loss**

An investment in a debt instrument that is not measured at amortised cost or fair value through other comprehensive income will be measured at fair value through profit or loss.

Financial liabilities

Normally, financial liabilities will be measured at amortised cost. Liabilities held for trading are measured at fair value through profit or loss.

IFRS 9 also retains the option for some liabilities to be measured at fair value if, in doing so, it eliminates or reduces an accounting mismatch. Where this is the case, to the extent that part of the change in fair value of the financial liability is due to a change on own credit risk, this must be taken to other comprehensive income in the year, with the balance of any change in fair value taken to profit or loss.

Impairments of financial assets

Definitions

Credit loss: The difference between the contractual cash flows and the cash flows that the entity expects to receive (i.e. all cash shortfalls), discounted at the original effective interest rate.

Lifetime expected credit losses: The expected credit losses that result from all possible default events over the expected life of a financial instrument.

12 month expected credit losses: The expected credit losses that result from default events possible within 12 months of the reporting date.

Loss allowances

Loss allowances must be recognised for financial assets that are debt instruments and which are measured at amortised cost or at fair value through other comprehensive income:

- If the credit risk on the financial asset has not increased significantly since initial recognition, the loss allowance should be equal to 12-month expected credit losses.
- If the credit risk on the financial asset has increased significantly since initial recognition then the loss allowance should be equal to the lifetime expected credit losses.

Adjustments to the loss allowance are charged (or credited) to the statement of profit or loss.

Measuring expected losses

An entity's estimate of expected credit losses must be:

- unbiased and probability-weighted
- discounted to present value
- based on information about past events, current conditions and forecasts of future economic conditions.

Receivables

The loss allowance should always be measured at an amount equal to lifetime credit losses for trade receivables and contract assets (recognised in accordance with IFRS 15 *Revenue from Contracts with Customers*) if they do not have a significant financing component.

Derivatives

IFRS 9 defines a derivative as a financial instrument with all three of the following characteristics:

(1) Its value changes in response to the change in a specified interest rate, security price, commodity price, foreign exchange rate or similar variable.

(2) It requires little or no initial investment.

(3) It is settled at a future date.

Derivatives include:

- Options
- Forward contracts
- Futures
- Swaps.

Derivatives which are not part of a hedging arrangement are classified to be measured as fair value through profit or loss.

Hedge accounting

Hedge accounting is the accounting treatment where the gains or losses on the **hedging instruments** are recognised in the same performance statement and in the same period as the offsetting gains or losses on the **hedged items**.

A hedging relationship exists when a company can define three elements.

(1) A hedged item – the asset/liability or transaction on which risks need to be reduced.

(2) A hedging instrument – the instrument (usually a derivative) used to offset the risks on the hedged item.

(3) The hedged risks – the specific risk (currency, interest rate, etc) that is being hedged.

In order to follow the hedge accounting rules in IFRS 9 the following criteria need to be met:

- The hedging relationship consists only of eligible hedging instruments and hedged items.
- At the inception of the hedge there must be formal documentation identifying the hedged item and the hedging instrument.
- The hedging relationship is effective.
- If the hedged item is a forecast transaction, then the transaction must be highly probable.

Accounting treatment of a fair value hedge

At the reporting date:

- The hedging instrument will be remeasured to fair value.
- The carrying amount of the hedged item will be adjusted for the change in fair value since the inception of the hedge.

The gain (or loss) on the hedging instrument and the loss (or gain) on the hedged item will be recorded:

- in profit or loss in most cases, but
- in other comprehensive income if the hedged item is an investment in equity that is measured at fair value through other comprehensive income.

Accounting treatment of a cash flow hedge

For cash flow hedges, the hedging instrument will be remeasured to fair value at the reporting date. The gain or loss is recognised in other comprehensive income.

However, if the gain or loss on the hedging instrument since the inception of the hedge is greater than the loss or gain on the hedged item then the excess gain or loss on the instrument must be recognised in profit or loss.

IFRS 10 Consolidated Financial Statements

IFRS 10 says that a subsidiary must be consolidated if it is controlled by another entity.

Control, according to IFRS 10, consists of three components:

(1) **Power** over the investee: this is normally exercised through the **majority of voting rights**, but could also arise through other contractual arrangements.

(2) **Exposure** or rights to variable returns (positive and/or negative), and

(3) The **ability to use power** to affect the investor's returns. The ability to use power over an investee to affect returns is regarded as a crucial determinant in deciding whether or not control is exercised.

Whether or not control exists should be reassessed at each reporting date.

IFRS 11 Joint Arrangements

A joint arrangement is a contractual arrangement whereby two or more parties undertake an economic activity that is subject to joint control.

IFRS 11 says that joint arrangements may take one of two forms:

- **Joint operations:** the parties that have joint control have rights to the assets and obligations for the liabilities. Normally, there will not be a separate entity established to conduct joint operations.
- **Joint ventures:** the parties that have joint control of the arrangement have rights to the net assets of the arrangement. This will normally be established in the form of a separate entity to conduct the joint venture activities.

IFRS 11 requires that:

- **Joint operators** recognise their share of assets, liabilities, revenues and expenses of the joint operation.
- **Joint ventures** are accounted for using the equity method.

IFRS 12 Disclosure of Interests in Other Entities

IFRS 12 details **disclosure** requirements for entities that have an interest in subsidiaries, joint arrangements and associates, i.e. where there is control, joint control or significant influence. The accounting treatments are dealt with under IFRS 3, IFRS 10, IFRS 11 and IAS 28 respectively.

IFRS 9 details accounting requirements where control, joint control or significant influence does not apply as the investment is a financial instrument.

IFRS 12 is designed to provide relevant information to users of financial statements. It requires disclosure of:

- details relating to the composition of the group
- details of non-controlling interests within the group
- identification and evaluation of risks associated with any interests held in other entities which give rise to control, joint control or significant influence.

IFRS 13 Fair Value Measurement

The objective of IFRS 13 is to provide a single source of guidance for fair value measurement.

Note that IFRS 13 does not apply to IFRS 2 *Share-based Payment* and IFRS 16 *Leases*.

Fair value is defined as **'the price that would be received to sell an asset or paid to transfer a liability in an orderly transaction between market participants at the measurement date'** (IFRS 13, para 9).

In order to increase comparability between entities, IFRS 13 states that an entity should maximise the use of observable inputs when determining fair value.

To aid with the application of the above, IFRS 13 establishes a hierarchy that categorises the inputs to valuation techniques used to measure fair value:

- **Level 1** inputs comprise quoted prices ('observable') in active markets for identical assets and liabilities at the measurement date. This is regarded as providing the most reliable evidence of fair value and is likely to be used without adjustment.
- **Level 2** inputs are observable inputs, other than those included within Level 1. Level 2 inputs include quoted prices for similar (not identical) asset or liabilities in active markets, or prices for identical assets and liabilities in inactive markets. Typically, they are likely to require some degree of adjustment to arrive at a fair value measurement
- **Level 3** inputs are unobservable inputs for an asset or liability. This may include use of the entity's own data.

IFRS 13 gives priority to level 1 inputs.

IFRS 15 Revenue from Contracts with Customers

IFRS 15 outlines a five step process for revenue recognition.

(1) Identify the contract

A contract is an agreement between two or more parties that creates rights and obligations.

(2) Identify the separate performance obligations within a contract

Performance obligations are, essentially, promises made to a customer.

(3) Determine the transaction price

The transaction price is the amount the entity expects to be entitled in exchange for satisfying all performance obligations. Amounts collected on behalf of third parties (such as sales tax) are excluded.

(4) Allocate the transaction price to the performance obligations in the contract

The total transaction price should be allocated to each performance obligation in proportion to stand-alone selling prices.

(5) Recognise revenue when (or as) a performance obligation is satisfied.

For each performance obligation an entity must determine whether it satisfies the performance obligation over time or at a point in time.

An entity satisfies a performance obligation over time if one of the following criteria is met:

(a) **'the customer simultaneously receives and consumes the benefits provided by the entity's performance as the entity performs.**

(b) **the entity's performance creates or enhances an asset (for example, work in progress) that the customer controls as the asset is created or enhanced, or**

(c) **the entity's performance does not create an asset with an alternative use to the entity and the entity has an enforceable right to payment for performance completed to date'** (IFRS 15, para 35).

For a performance obligation satisfied over time, an entity recognises revenue based on progress towards satisfaction of that performance obligation.

If a performance obligation is not satisfied over time then it is satisfied at a point in time. The entity must determine the point in time at which a customer obtains control of the promised asset.

IFRS 16 Leases

Identifying a lease

Lessees are required to recognise an asset and a liability for all leases, unless they are short-term or of a minimal value. As such, it is vital to assess whether a contract contains a lease, or whether it is simply a contract for a service.

A contract contains a lease if it **'conveys the right to control the use of an identified asset for a period of time in exchange for consideration'** (IFRS 16, para 9).

Lessee accounting

If the lease is short-term (less than 12 months at the inception date) or of a low value the lessee can choose to recognise the lease payments in profit or loss on a straight line basis.

In all other cases, IFRS 16 requires that the lessee recognises a lease liability and a right-of-use asset at the commencement of the lease:

- The right-of-use asset is initially recognised at cost. This will be the initial value of the lease liability, plus any lease payments made at or before the commencement of the lease, as well as any direct costs.
- The right-of-use asset is subsequently measured at cost less accumulated depreciation and impairment losses (unless another measurement model is chosen).
- The lease liability is initially measured at the present value of the lease payments that have not yet been paid.
- The carrying amount of the lease liability is increased by the interest charge. This interest is also recorded in the statement of profit or loss.
- The carrying amount of the lease liability is reduced by cash repayments.

Lessor accounting

The lessor must assess whether the lease is a finance lease or an operating lease. A finance lease is a lease where the risks and rewards of ownership substantially transfer to the lessee. Key indicators of a finance lease, according to IFRS 16, are:

- Ownership of the asset transfers to the lessee at the end of the lease term.
- The lessee has the option to purchase the asset at the end of the lease term, or to continue to lease it, for less than fair value.

- The lease term is for the major part of the asset's economic life.
- The present value of the lease payments amounts to substantially all of the asset's fair value.

If the lease is a finance lease then the lessor will:

- Derecognise the asset.
- Recognise a lease receivable equal to the net investment in the lease (the present value of the payments).
- Interest income arising on the lease receivable is recorded in profit or loss.

If the lease is an operating lease then the lessor recognises the lease income in profit or loss on a straight line basis over the lease term.

Sale and leaseback

The treatment of a sale and leaseback depends on whether the 'sale' represents the satisfaction of a performance obligation (as per IFRS 15 Revenue from Contracts with Customers).

	Transfer is not a sale	**Transfer is a sale**
Seller – lessee	Continue to recognise asset. Recognise a financial liability equal to proceeds received.	Derecognise the asset. Recognise a right-of-use asset as the proportion of the asset's previous carrying amount that relates to the rights retained. Recognise a lease liability. A profit or loss on disposal will arise.
Buyer – lessor	Do not recognise the asset. Recognise a financial asset equal to transfer proceeds.	Account for the asset purchase. Account for the lease by applying lessor accounting requirements.

- The lease term is for the major part of the asset's economic life.
- The present value of the lease payments amounts to substantially all of the asset's fair value.

If the lease is a finance lease then the lessor will:

- Derecognise the asset
- Recognise a lease receivable equal to the net investment in the lease (the present value of the payments).
- Interest income arising on the lease receivable is recorded in profit or loss.

If the lease is an operating lease then the lessor recognises the lease income in profit or loss on a straight line basis over the lease term.

Sale and leaseback

The treatment of a sale and leaseback depends on whether the sale represents the satisfaction of a performance obligation (as per IFRS 15 Revenue from Contracts with Customers).

	Transfer is not a sale	Transfer is a sale
Seller-lessee	Continue to recognise the asset. Recognise a financial liability equal to proceeds received.	Derecognise the asset. Recognise a right-of-use asset at the proportion of the asset's previous carrying amount that relates to the rights retained. Recognise a lease liability. A profit or loss on disposal will arise.
Buyer-lessor	Do not recognise the asset. Recognise a financial asset equal to transfer proceeds.	Account for the asset purchase. Account for the lease by applying lessor accounting requirements.

chapter

23

Additional practice questions

Test your understanding 1

Hydrasports, a limited liability company and national leisure group, has sixteen centres around the country and a head office. Facilities at each centre are of a standard design which incorporates a heated swimming pool, sauna, air-conditioned gym and fitness studio with supervised childcare. Each centre is managed on a day-to-day basis, by a centre manager, in accordance with company policies. The centre manager is also responsible for preparing and submitting monthly accounting returns to head office.

Each centre is required to have a licence from the local authority to operate. Licences are granted for periods between two and five years and are renewable subject to satisfactory reports from local authority inspectors. The average annual cost of a licence is $900.

Members pay a $100 joining fee, plus either $50 per month for 'peak' membership or $30 per month for 'off-peak', payable quarterly in advance. All fees are stated to be non-refundable.

The centre at Verne was closed from July to September after a chemical spill in the sauna caused a serious accident. Although the centre was reopened, Hydrasports has recommended to all centre managers that sauna facilities be suspended until further notice.

In response to complaints to the local authorities about its childcare facilities, Hydrasports has issued centre managers with revised guidelines for minimum levels of supervision. Centre managers are finding it difficult to meet the new guidelines and have suggested that childcare facilities should be withdrawn.

Staff lateness is a recurring problem and a major cause of 'early bird' customer dissatisfaction with sessions which are scheduled to start at 07.00. New employees are generally attracted to the industry in the short-term for its non-cash benefits, including free use of the facilities – but leave when they require increased financial rewards. Training staff to be qualified lifeguards is costly and time-consuming and retention rates are poor. Turnover of centre managers is also high, due to the constraints imposed on them by company policy.

Three of the centres are expected to have run at a loss for the year to 31 December due to falling membership. Hydrasports has invested heavily in a hydrotherapy pool at one of these centres, with the aim of attracting retired members with more leisure time. The building contractor has already billed twice as much and taken three times as long as budgeted for the work. The pool is now expected to open 2 months after the year-end.

Cash flow difficulties in the current year have put back the planned replacement of gym equipment for most of the centres.

Insurance premiums for liability to employees and the public have increased by nearly 45%. Hydrasports has met the additional expense by reducing its insurance cover on its plant and equipment from a replacement cost basis to a net realisable value basis.

Required:

(a) (i) Evaluate the business risks faced by Hydrasports.

(8 marks)

(ii) Evaluate the risks of material misstatement to be considered when planning the audit of Hydrasports.

(8 marks)

(b) Describe the principal audit work to be performed in respect of the carrying amount of the following items in the statement of financial position of Hydrasports as at 31 December:

(i) deferred income, and

(3 marks)

(ii) hydrotherapy pool.

(3 marks)

(c) Suggest performance indicators that could be set to increase the centre managers' awareness of Hydrasports' social and environmental responsibilities and the evidence which should be available to provide assurance on their accuracy.

(8 marks)

(Total: 30 marks)

Test your understanding 2

Cerise, a limited liability company, manufactures computer controlled equipment for production-line industries such as cars, washing machines, cookers, etc. On 1 September 20X4 the shareholder-managers decided, unanimously, to accept a lucrative offer from a multinational corporation to buy the company's patented technology and manufacturing equipment.

By 10 September 20X4 management had notified all the employees, suppliers and customers that Cerise would cease all manufacturing activities on 31 October 20X4. The 200-strong factory workforce and the majority of the accounts department and support staff were made redundant with effect from that date, when the sale was duly completed.

The marketing, human resources and production managers will cease to be employed by the company at 31 December 20X4. However, the chief executive, sales manager, finance manager, accountant and a small number of accounting and other support staff expect to be employed until the company is wound down completely.

Cerise's operations extend to fourteen premises, nine of which were put on the market on 1 November 20X4. Cerise accounts for all tangible, non-current assets under the cost model (i.e. at depreciated cost). Four premises are held on leases that expire in the next two to seven years and cannot be sold or sub-let under the lease terms. The small head office premises will continue to be occupied until the lease expires in 20X7. No new lease agreements were entered into during 20X4.

All Cerise's computer controlled products carry a one-year warranty. Extended warranties of three and five years, previously available at the time of purchase, have not been offered on sales of remaining inventory from 1 November onwards.

Cerise has three-year agreements with its national and international distributors for the sale of equipment. It also has annual contracts with its major suppliers for the purchase of components. So far, none of these parties have lodged any legal claim against Cerise. However, the distributors are withholding payment of their account balances pending settlement of the significant penalties which are now due to them.

Required:

You are required to answer the following in the context of the final audit of the financial statements of Cerise for the year ending 31 December 20X4:

(a) Using the information provided, identify and explain the audit risks to be considered when planning the audit.

(16 marks)

(b) Explain how the extent of the reliance to be placed on:

(i) analytical procedures, and

(4 marks)

(ii) written representations

(4 marks)

should compare with that for the prior year audit.

(c) Describe the principal audit work to be performed in respect of the carrying amount of the following items in the statement of financial position:

(i) amounts due from distributors

(3 marks)

(ii) lease liabilities.

(3 marks)

(Total: 30 marks)

Test your understanding 3

Geno Vesa Farm (GVF), a limited liability company, is a cheese manufacturer. Its principal activity is the production of a traditional 'Farmhouse' cheese that is retailed around the world to exclusive shops, through mail order and web sales. Other activities include the sale of locally produced foods through a farm shop and cheese-making demonstrations and tours.

The farm's herd of 700 goats is used primarily for the production of milk. Kids (i.e. goat offspring), which are a secondary product, are selected for herd replacement or otherwise sold. Animals held for sale are not usually retained beyond the time they reach optimal size or weight because their value usually does not increase thereafter.

There are two main variations of the traditional farmhouse cheese: 'Rabida Red' and 'Bachas Blue'. The red cheese is coloured using Innittu, which is extracted from berries found only in South American rain forests. The cost of Innittu has risen sharply over the last year as the collection of berries by local village workers has come under the scrutiny of an international action group. The group is lobbying the South American government to ban the export of Innittu, claiming that the workers are being exploited and that sustaining the forest is seriously under threat.

Demand for Bachas Blue, which is made from unpasteurised milk, fell considerably in 20X2 following the publication of a research report that suggested a link between unpasteurised milk products and a skin disorder. The financial statements for the year ended 30 September 20X3 recognised a material impairment loss attributable to the equipment used exclusively for the manufacture of Bachas Blue. However, as the adverse publicity is gradually being forgotten, sales of Bachas Blue are now showing a steady increase and are currently expected to return to their former level by the end of September 20X4.

Cheese is matured to three strengths – mild, medium and strong – depending on the period of time it is left to ripen, which is six, 12 and 18 months respectively. When produced, the cheese is sold to a financial institution, Abingdon Bank, at cost. Under the terms of sale, GVF has the option to buy the cheese on its maturity at cost plus 7% for every six months which has elapsed.

All cheese is stored to maturity on wooden boards in GVF's cool and airy sheds. However, recently enacted health and safety legislation requires that the wooden boards be replaced with stainless steel shelves with effect from 1 July 20X4. The management of GVF has petitioned the government health department that to comply with the legislation would interfere with the maturing process and the production of medium and strong cheeses would have to cease.

In 20X3, GVF applied for and received a substantial regional development grant for the promotion of tourism in the area. GVF's management has deferred its plan to convert a disused barn into holiday accommodation from 20X4 until at least 20X6.

Required:

(a) Identify and explain the principal audit risks to be considered when planning the final audit of GVF for the year ending 30 September 20X4.

(15 marks)

(b) Describe the audit work to be performed in respect of the carrying amount of the following items in the statement of financial position of GVF as at 30 September 20X4:

(i) goat herd

(5 marks)

(ii) equipment used in the manufacture of Bachas Blue

(5 marks)

(iii) cheese.

(5 marks)

(Total: 30 marks)

Test your understanding 4

Bellatrix is a carpet manufacturer and an audit client of your firm. Bellatrix has identified a company in the same business, Scorpio, as a target for acquisition in the current year.

As audit manager to Bellatrix and its subsidiaries for the year ended 31 December 20X4, you have been asked to examine Scorpio's management accounts and budget forecasts. The chief executive of Bellatrix, Sirius Deneb, believes that despite its current cash flow difficulties, Scorpio's current trading performance is satisfactory and future prospects are good. The chief executive of Scorpio is Ursula Minor.

The findings of your examination are as follows:

Budget forecasts for Scorpio, for the current accounting year to 31 December 20X4 and for the following year, reflect a rising profit trend.

Scorpio's results for the first half year to 30 June 20X4 reflect $800,000 profit from the sale of a warehouse that had been carried in the books at historical cost. There are plans to sell two similar properties later in the year and outsource warehousing.

About 10% of Scorpio's sales are to Andromeda, a limited liability company. Two members of the management board of Scorpio hold minority interests in Andromeda. Selling prices negotiated between Scorpio and Andromeda appear to be on an arm's length basis.

Scorpio's management accounts for the six months to 30 June 20X4 have been used to support an application to the bank for an additional loan facility to refurbish the executive and administration offices. These management accounts show inventory and trade receivables' balances that exceed the figures in the accounting records by $150,000. This excess has also been reflected in the first half year's profit. Upon enquiry, you have established that allowances, to reduce inventory and trade receivables' to estimated realisable values, have been reduced to assist with the loan application.

Although there has been a recent downturn in trading, Ursula Minor has stated that she is very confident that the negotiations with the bank will be successful as Scorpio has met its budgeted profit for the first six months. Ursula believes that increased demand for carpets and rugs in the winter months will enable results to exceed budget.

Required:

(a) Identify and comment on the implications of your findings for Bellatrix's plan to proceed with the acquisition of Scorpio.

(10 marks)

(b) Explain what impact the acquisition will have on the conduct of your audit of Bellatrix and its subsidiaries for the year to 31 December 20X4.

(15 marks)

(Total: 25 marks)

Test your understanding 5

You are the manager responsible for the audit of Volcan, a long-established limited liability company. Volcan operates a national supermarket chain of 23 stores, five of which are in the capital city, Urvina. All the stores are managed in the same way with purchases being made through Volcan's central buying department and product pricing, marketing, advertising and human resources policies being decided centrally. The draft financial statements for the year ended 31 March 20X4 show revenue of $303 million (20X3 – $282 million), profit before taxation of $9.5 million (20X3 – $7.3 million) and total assets of $178 million (20X3 – $173 million).

The following issues arising during the final audit have been noted on a schedule of points for your attention:

(a) On 1 May 20X4, Volcan announced its intention to downsize one of the stores in Urvina from a supermarket to a 'City Metro' in response to a significant decline in the demand for supermarket-style shopping in the capital. The store will be closed throughout June, re-opening on 1 July 20X4. Goodwill of $5.5 million was recognised three years ago when this store, together with two others, was bought from a national competitor. 60% of the goodwill has been written off due to impairment.

(7 marks)

(b) On 1 April 20X3 Volcan introduced a reward scheme for its customers. The main elements of the reward scheme include the awarding of a points to customers' loyalty cards for every $1 spent, with extra points being given for the purchase of each week's special offers. Customers who hold a loyalty card can convert their points into cash discounts against future purchases on the basis of $1 per 100 points.

(6 marks)

(c) In October 20X3, Volcan commenced the development of a site in a valley of outstanding natural beauty on which to build a retail 'megastore' and warehouse in late 20X4. Local government planning permission for the development, which was received in April 20X4, requires that three 100-year-old trees within the valley be preserved and the surrounding valley be restored in 20X5. Additions to property, plant and equipment during the year include $4.4 million for the estimated cost of site restoration. This estimate includes a provision of $0.4 million for the relocation of the 100 year-old trees.

In March 20X4 the trees were chopped down to make way for a car park. A fine of $20,000 per tree was paid to the local government in May 20X4.

(7 marks)

Required:

For each of the above issues:

(i) comment on the matters that you should consider; and

(ii) state the audit evidence that you should expect to find,

in undertaking your review of the audit working papers and financial statements of Volcan for the year ended 31 March 20X4.

Note: The mark allocation is shown against each of the three issues.

(Total: 20 marks)

Test your understanding 6

You are the manager responsible for the audit of Albreda Co, a limited liability company, and its subsidiaries. The group mainly operates a chain of national restaurants and provides vending and other catering services to corporate clients. All restaurants offer eat-in, take-away and home delivery services. The draft consolidated financial statements for the year ended 30 September 20X4 show revenue of $42.2 million (20X3 – $41.8 million), profit before taxation of $1.8 million (20X3 – $2.2 million) and total assets of $30.7 million (20X3 – $23.4 million).

The following issues arising during the final audit have been noted on a schedule of points for your attention:

(a) In September 20X4 the management board announced plans to cease offering home delivery services from the end of the month. These sales amounted to $0.6 million for the year to 30 September 20X4 (20X3 – $0.8 million). A provision of $0.2 million has been made as at 30 September 20X4 for the compensation of redundant employees (mainly drivers). Delivery vehicles have been classified as non-current assets held for sale as at 30 September 20X4 and measured at fair value less costs to sell, $0.8 million (carrying amount, $0.5 million).

(8 marks)

(b) Historically, all owned premises have been measured at cost depreciated over 10 to 50 years. The management board has decided to revalue these premises for the year ended 30 September 20X4. At the statement of financial position date two properties had been revalued by a total of $1.7 million. Another 15 properties have since been revalued by $5.4 million and there remain a further three properties which are expected to be revalued during 20X5. A revaluation surplus of $7.1 million has been credited to equity.

(7 marks)

(c) During the year Albreda paid $0.1 million (20X3 – $0.3 million) in fines and penalties relating to breaches of health and safety regulations. These amounts have not been separately disclosed but included in cost of sales.

(5 marks)

Required:

For each of the above issues:

(i) comment on the matters that you should consider, and

(ii) state the audit evidence that you should expect to find

In undertaking your review of the audit working papers and financial statements of Albreda Co for the year ended 30 September 20X4.

Note: The mark allocation is shown against each of the three issues.

(Total: 20 marks)

Test your understanding 7

You are the manager responsible for the audit of Visean, a limited liability company, which manufactures health and beauty products and distributes them through a chain of 72 retail pharmacies. The draft accounts for the year ended 31 December 20X3 show profit before taxation of $1.83m (20X2: $1.24m) and total assets $18.4m (20X2: $12.7m).

The following issues are outstanding and have been left for your attention:

(a) Visean owns nine brand names of fragrances used for ranges of products (e.g. perfumes, bath oils, soaps, etc), four of which were purchased and five internally generated. Purchased brands are recognised as an intangible asset at cost amounting to $589,000 and amortised on a straight-line basis over 10 years. The costs of generating self-created brands and maintaining existing ones are recognised as an expense when incurred. Demand for products of one of the purchased fragrances, 'Ulexite', fell significantly in January 20X4 after a marketing campaign in December caused offence to customers.

(8 marks)

(b) In December 20X3 the directors announced plans to discontinue the range of medical consumables supplied to hospital pharmacies. The plant manufacturing these products closed in January 20X4. A provision of $800,000 has been made as at 31 December 20X3 for the compensation of redundant employees and a further $450,000 for the three years' unexpired lease term on the plant premises.

(7 marks)

(c) Historically the company's statement of cash flows has reported net cash flows from operating activities under the 'indirect method'. However, the statement of cash flows for the year ended 31 December 20X3 reports net cash flows under the 'direct method' and the corresponding figures have been restated.

(5 marks)

Required:

For each of the above issues:

(i) comment on the matters that you should consider; and

(ii) state the audit evidence that you should expect to find, in undertaking your review of the audit working papers and financial statements of Visean.

(Total: 20 marks)

Test your understanding 8

(a) Explain the importance of the role of objectivity to the auditor-client relationship.

(5 marks)

(a) You are the audit partner in a firm which provides a variety of accountancy-related services to a large portfolio of clients. The firm's gross practice income is $1 million. The firm has a particularly successful tax department, which carries out a great deal of recurring and special tax work for both audit and non-audit clients. The tax manager has recently involved you in discussions with a major tax client who is considering changing its auditors. The client, Rainbow, would expect audit fees of around $100,000 (which is a reasonable fee for the audit). Your adult daughter has been working as an administrative assistant in the sales department of Rainbow for a year, after being introduced by the tax manager. She has just joined an employee share benefit scheme.

The client is keen to use the firm to provide audit services as he is pleased with the taxation services they provide. The managing director and major shareholder, Mr Parkes, has therefore offered an incentive to the audit fee of an additional 1% of profits in excess of $20 million, annually where relevant. The current recurring taxation fees from Rainbow are $35,000, and last year special tax work amounted to $25,000. Last year's fees remain outstanding.

The managing director has suggested that you give consideration to the matter while staying for the weekend at his villa in Tenerife. He has arranged flights for both you and your spouse.

Required:

Comment on the matters that you should consider in deciding whether or not your audit firm can accept appointment as auditors of Rainbow.

(10 marks)

(Total: 15 marks)

Test your understanding 9

You are an audit manager in Sepia, a firm of Chartered Certified Accountants. Your specific responsibilities include advising the senior audit partner on the acceptance of new assignments. The following matters have arisen in connection with three prospective client companies:

(a) Your firm has been nominated to act as auditor to Squid, a private limited company. You have been waiting for a response to your letter of professional enquiry to Squid's auditor, Krill & Co, for several weeks. Your recent attempts to call the current engagement partner, Anton Fargues, in Krill & Co have been met with the response from Anton's personal assistant that 'Mr Fargues is not available'.

(5 marks)

(b) Sepia has been approached by the management of Hatchet, a company listed on a recognised stock exchange, to advise on a takeover bid which they propose to make. The target company, Vitronella, is an audit client of your firm. However, Hatchet is not.

(5 marks)

(c) A former colleague in Sepia, Edwin Stenuit, is now employed by another audit firm, Keratin. Sepia and Keratin and three other firms have recently tendered for the audit of Benthos, a limited liability company. Benthos is expected to announce the successful firm next week. Yesterday, at a social gathering, Edwin confided to you that Keratin lowballed on their tender for the audit as they expect to be able to provide Benthos with lucrative other services.

(5 marks)

Required:

Comment on the ethical and professional issues raised by each of the above matters and the steps, if any, that Sepia should now take.

Note: The mark allocation is shown against each of the three issues.

(Total: 15 marks)

Test your understanding 10

(a) Explain why quality control may be difficult to implement in a smaller audit firm and illustrate how such difficulties may be overcome.

(5 marks)

(a) Kite Associates is an association of small accounting practices. One of the benefits of membership is improved quality control through a peer review system. Whilst reviewing a sample of auditor's reports issued by Rook & Co, a firm only recently admitted to Kite Associates, you come across the following modified opinion on the financial statements of Lammergeier Group:

Qualified opinion arising from material misstatement accounting treatment relating to the non-adoption of IAS 7

The management has not prepared a group statement of cash flows and its associated notes. In the opinion of the management it is not practical to prepare a group statement of cash flows due to the complexity involved. In our opinion the reasons for the departure from IAS 7 are sound and acceptable and adequate disclosure has been made concerning the departure from IAS 7. The departure in our opinion does not impact on the truth and fairness of the financial statements.

'In our opinion, except for the non-preparation of the group statement of cash flows and associated notes, the financial statements give a true and fair view of the financial position of the Company as at 31 December 20X3 and of the profit of the group for the year then ended, and have been properly prepared in accordance with …'

Your review of the prior year auditor's report has revealed that the 20X2 audit opinion was identical.

Required:

Critically appraise the appropriateness of the audit opinion given by Rook & Co on the financial statements of Lammergeier Group for the years ended 31 December 20X3 and 20X2.

(10 marks)

(Total: 15 marks)

Test your understanding 11

(a) Explain the auditor's responsibilities for other information in documents containing audited financial statements.

(5 marks)

(b) You are an audit manager with specific responsibility for reviewing other information in documents containing audited financial statements before your firm's auditor's report is signed. The financial statements of Hegas, a privately owned civil engineering company, show total assets of $120 million, revenue of $261 million, and profit before tax of $9.2 million for the year ended 31 March 20X5. Your review of the annual report has revealed the following:

(i) The statement of changes in equity includes $4.5 million under a separate heading of 'miscellaneous item' which is described as 'other difference not recognised in income'. There is no further reference to this amount or 'other difference' elsewhere in the financial statements. However, the directors' report, which is required by statute, is not audited. It discloses that 'changes in shareholders' equity not recognised in income includes $4.5 million arising on the revaluation of investment properties'.

The notes to the financial statements state that the company has implemented IAS 40 *Investment Property* for the first time in the year to 31 March 20X5 and also that 'the adoption of this standard did not have a significant impact on Hegas' financial position or its results of operations during 20X5'.

(ii) The chairman's statement asserts 'Hegas has now achieved a position as one of the world's largest generators of hydro-electricity, with a dedicated commitment to accountable ethical professionalism'. Audit working papers show that 14% of revenue was derived from hydro-electricity (20X4: 12%). Publicly available information shows that there are seven international suppliers of hydro-electricity in Africa alone, which are all at least three times the size of Hegas in terms of both annual revenue and population supplied.

Required

Identify and comment on the implications of the above matters for the auditor's report on the financial statements of Hegas for the year ended 31 March 20X5.

(10 marks)

(Total: 15 marks)

Test your understanding answers

Test your understanding 1

(a) **Business risks**

Customer dissatisfaction

Sauna facilities are currently not available for members to use. Childcare facilities are considering being withdrawn due to complaints about levels of supervision. Hydrasports' inability to retain lifeguards increases the risk that pools cannot open due to health and safety regulations. In addition, gym equipment is obsolete and therefore will not reflect the most up to date technology.

These issues are likely to lead to customer dissatisfaction. Additional expenditure will need to be incurred to resolve any problems. Members may ask for a partial refund on their membership fees as they do not have use of all of the facilities for which they are paying which will reduce future revenue.

Health and safety

Hydrasports could be sued if a member suffers injury as a result of unsafe equipment or due to a lack of qualified lifeguards. This will result in legal costs and may result in compensation payments.

Serious accidents may prompt investigation by local authority resulting in penalties, fines and / or withdrawal of licence to operate.

Licence

Hydrasports cannot operate a centre if a licence is suspended, withdrawn or not renewed (e.g. through failing a local authority inspection or failing to apply for renewal). Revenue will fall as a result.

Advance payments

Membership fees are received in advance. If cash flow is not managed properly, Hydrasports may not be able to meet future liabilities.

Monthly accounting returns

Centre managers prepare monthly accounting returns. The managers may not have sufficient knowledge to do this accurately or efficiently. This could result in submission of inaccurate returns and incorrect management information being used for decision making. Centre managers may not have enough time to fulfil their day-to-day responsibilities (e.g. relating to customer satisfaction, human resources, health and safety) if the management information to be reported takes up too much of their time.

Centralised control

Centralised control through company policy is resulting in inefficient and ineffective operations as managers cannot respond on a timely basis to local needs. This may lead to poor decision making and customer dissatisfaction.

Insurance cover

The reduction in insurance cover reduces the recoverable amount of assets in the event of loss. Due to Hydrasports' cash flow issues, they may not have adequate resources to replace any assets not covered by insurance. This will impact the facilities that can be offered to members limiting the amount of revenue that can be earned.

High staff turnover

High staff turnover will lead to higher recruitment and training costs. Employees will not be fully productive until they are familiar with Hydrasports' working practices. This will reduce profitability.

Going concern

Due to the issues mentioned above, members may cancel their subscriptions and find alternative facilities. This will result in a permanent loss of revenue and increases the risk that Hydrasports will not be able to continue as a going concern.

Risks of material misstatement

Non-compliance with health and safety regulations

There are several potential health and safety issues present in Hydrasports:

- childcare facilities are not adequately supervised
- obsolete equipment may be unsafe to use

- accidents may occur due to pools being operated without a qualified lifeguard on duty.

Breaches of regulations could lead to fines and penalties.

Liabilities may be understated if adequate provision for fines / penalties imposed by the local authority has not been made.

Overstatement of assets

There are several indicators of impairment:

- The saunas are no longer in use.
- Childcare facilities may be withdrawn.
- Pools may need to close if there are no qualified lifeguards to supervise.
- The continued construction of the hydrotherapy pool may be threatened by cash flow problems. This may mean it does not get completed.
- Gym equipment needs to be replaced. Assets which are obsolete but not fully depreciated will be overstated if an impairment review is not performed.

The carrying amount of non-current assets may be overstated if an impairment review is not performed.

Provision for refunds

Although fees are non-refundable, suspension of a facility (e.g. sauna) may result in customers asking for partial refund. In particular Hydrasports may have an obligation to refund fees paid in advance when centres are closed (e.g. the Verne centre from July–September).

Liabilities may be understated if provisions for refunds are not adequately made.

Revenue

Revenue may be overstated if accurate cut-off is not achieved. If Hydrasports' revenue recognition policy does not comply with IFRS 15 *Revenue from contracts with customers*, revenue and deferred revenue will be misstated.

Licences

Licences may not have been amortised over the licence period. Licences may not have been reviewed for impairment.

Intangible assets may be overstated as a result.

Going concern disclosure

Due to the problems mentioned above which are likely to lead to a loss of future revenue, in addition to the cash flow problems already being experienced, Hydrasports may have difficulty continuing as a going concern.

Going concern uncertainties may not be adequately disclosed in the financial statements.

Monthly accounting returns

Accounting information flowing into the financial statements may not be properly captured, input, processed or output by the centre managers resulting in misstatements in the financial statements.

Centralised control

Management circumvention or override of control procedures laid down by head office may result in system deficiencies.

If errors arising are not detected and corrected the risk of misstatement in the financial statements is increased.

(b) **Principal audit work**

(i) **Deferred income**

- Trace a sample of peak / off-peak membership fees and joining fees to member contracts to verify the income that should be deferred.
- Reconcile membership income to fees paid. If customers can renew their membership without payment there should be no deferral of income (unless the debt for unpaid fees is also recognised).
- Inspect correspondence from members to identify any disputes which may mean membership fees should be refunded.
- Recalculate the deferred income element of fees received in the three months before the statement of financial position date to verify arithmetical accuracy.

– Compare the year-end balance with prior year and investigate any significant variance.

(ii) **Hydrotherapy pool**

– Inspect the contract with the builder, contractors billings and stage payments to confirm the cost of the asset.

– Review the expert's assessment of stage of completion as at the statement of financial position date, estimated costs to completion, etc. Hydrasports is likely to be advised by its own expert (a quantity surveyor) on how the contract is progressing.

– Physically inspect the construction at the year-end to confirm work to date and assess the reasonableness of stage of completion.

– Agree borrowing costs associated with the construction to the loan agreement to confirm finance terms and payments.

– Recalculate the borrowing costs capitalised to confirm arithmetical accuracy.

– Confirm that the basis of capitalisation complies with IAS 23 *Borrowing Costs* (e.g. interest accruing during any suspension of building work should not be capitalised).

– Critically evaluate management's assessment of possible impairment (of the hydrotherapy pool and the centre). As the construction has already cost twice as much as budgeted, its value in use (when brought into use) may be less than cost.

(c) **Performance indicators**

Member satisfaction

– Number of people on membership waiting lists (if any).

– Number of referrals/recommendations to club membership by existing members.

– Proportion of renewed memberships.

– Actual members: 100% capacity membership (sub-analysed between 'peak' and 'off-peak').

Membership dissatisfaction

– Proportion of members requesting refunds per month/quarter.

– Proportion of memberships 'lapsing' (i.e. not renewed).

Staff

– Average number of staff employed per month.
– Number of starters/leavers per month.
– Staff turnover/average duration of employment.
– Number of training courses for lifeguards per annum.

Predictability

– Number of late openings (say more than 5, 15 and 30 minutes after advertised opening times).
– Number of days closure per month/year of each facility (i.e. pool, crèche, sauna, gym) and centre.

Safety

– Incidents reports documenting the date, time and nature of each incident, the extent of damage and/or personal injury, and action taken.
– Number of accident free days.

Other society

– Local community involvement (e.g. facilities offered to schools and clubs at discount rates during 'off-peak' times).
– Range of facilities offered specifically to pensioners, mothers and babies, disabled patrons, etc.
– Participation in the wider community (e.g. providing facilities to support sponsored charity events).

Environment

– Number of instances of non-compliance with legislation/regulations (e.g. on chemical spills).
– Energy efficiency (e.g. in maintaining pool at a given temperature throughout the year).
– Incentives for environmental friendliness such as discouraging use of cars/promoting use of bicycles (e.g. by providing secure lock-ups for cycles and restricted car parking facilities).

Evidence

- Membership registers clearly distinguishing between new and renewed members, also showing lapsed memberships.
- Pool/gym timetables – showing sessions set aside for 'over 60s', 'ladies only', schools, clubs, special events, etc.
- Staff training courses and costs.
- Staff timesheets – showing arrival/departure times and adherence to staff rotas.
- Documents supporting additions to/deletions from payroll standing data (e.g. new joiner/leaver notifications).
- Engineer's inspection reports – confirming gym equipment, etc is in satisfactory working order.
- Engineer and safety check manuals and the maintenance program.
- Levels of expenditure on repairs and maintenance.
- Energy saving equipment/measures (e.g. insulated pool covering).
- Safety drill reports (e.g. alarm tests, pool evacuations).
- Accident report register – showing date, nature of incident, personal injury sustained (if any), action taken (e.g. emergency services called in).
- Any penalties/fines imposed by the local authorities and the reasons for them.
- Copies of reports of local authority investigations.
- The frequency and nature of insurance claims (e.g. to settle claims of injury to members and/or staff).

Test your understanding 2

(a) **Risks of material misstatement**

Computer controlled equipment for production-line industries

- Cerise is ceasing manufacturing two months prior to the year-end. Any items remaining in inventory at the year-end will need to be written down to the lower of cost and NRV in accordance with IAS 2 *Inventories*.
- There is a risk that inventory is overstated if sufficient allowance is not made for items that will not be sold.

Cessation of trade

- Cerise ceased to trade during the year. The financial statements therefore not be prepared on a going concern basis, but on a 'break-up' or other 'realisable' basis.
- This has implications for:
  - the reclassification of assets and liabilities (from non-current to current).
  - the carrying amount of assets (at recoverable amount).
  - the completeness of recorded liabilities.
- There is a risk that the basis of preparation used is inappropriate.

Redundant workforce

- Although statutory redundancy pay, holiday pay, accrued overtime etc may have been settled before the year-end, there may be additional liabilities in respect of former employees e.g. pension obligations.
- Liabilities may be understated if there are claims arising from the redundant workers if their statutory or contractual rights have been breached.

Sale of patented technology and manufacturing equipment

- All assets sold should be derecognised and the profit on disposal disclosed as an exceptional item arising from the discontinuance of operations.
- Plant and equipment will be overstated if:
  - manufacturing equipment that has been sold is still included in the financial statements.
  - assets that were not part of the sale are not tested for impairment (in accordance with IAS 36 *Impairment of Assets*).
- There is also a risk that the profit or loss on disposal has not been calculated correctly.

Accounts department

- Fewer staff will be employed in the accounts department until the company is wound down completely. This may increase the risk of errors arising as staff assume wider areas of responsibility. Staff may also not take as much care with their work as they know they will not be working for the company in the near future.
- The risk of errors arising not being detected by the control system is also likely to increase as levels of supervision and segregation of duties may be reduced.
- There is a greater risk of misstatement in the financial statements as a result.

Premises

- If the unsold properties meet all the criteria of IFRS 5 *Non-current Assets Held for Sale and Discontinued Operations* at the statement of financial position date they should be:
  - separately classified as held for sale.
  - carried at the lower of carrying amount (i.e. depreciated cost) and fair value less estimated costs to sell.
- Any after-date losses on disposal would provide evidence of impairment.
- The financial statements will be materially misstated if non-current assets held for sale are not separately disclosed in accordance with IFRS 5.

Onerous contracts

- Four of Cerise's premises are leased and cannot be sold or sub-let under the lease terms. These leases are onerous leases and the future payments which cannot be avoided should be recognised as a liability.
- There is a risk that provisions are understated if lease obligations under onerous contracts are not recognised.

Product warranties

- Cerise's products have been sold with either a one, three or five year warranty. Adequate provision must be made for warranties of:
  - one year (sales in the year to 31 December 20X4)
  - up to three years (sales between 1 January 20X2 and 31 October 20X4) and
  - up to five years (sales between 1 January 20X0 and 31 October 20X4).
- As Cerise can no longer undertake the warranty work itself, arrangements will have to be made to honour the warranty obligations, e.g. by outsourcing it to another company which may be more expensive than performing the work in-house.
- There is a risk that the warranty provision is understated if the basis of its calculation is no longer appropriate.

Breach of agreements/contracts

- Since Cerise no longer has the means of fulfilling contracts with distributors, provision should be made for any compensation or penalties arising. Where the penalties due to distributors for breach of supply agreements exceed the amounts due from them, the receivables should be written down.
- Adequate provision should be made for breaches of contracts with suppliers. If suppliers do not exercise their rights to invoke penalty clauses, disclosure of the contingent liability may be more appropriate than a provision.
- There is a risk that provisions are understated or contingent liabilities are not adequately disclosed.

(b) **Reliance on audit work**

(i) Analytical procedures

- Overall the extent of reliance on analytical procedures is likely to be less than that for the prior year audit as the scale and nature of Cerise's activities will differ from the prior year.
- There are a number of individually material transactions in the current year which will require detailed substantive testing (e.g. sale of patented technology and manufacturing equipment and sale of premises).
- Budgetary information used for analytical procedures in prior periods (e.g. budgeted production/sales) will have less relevance in the current year as the cessation of trade is unlikely to have been forecast.
- Information will only be comparable with the prior year for 10 months (January to October). Costs incurred in November and December will relate to winding down operations rather than operational activities therefore cannot be compared with the prior year.
- The impact of the one-off circumstances on carrying amounts is more likely to be assessed through detailed substantive testing (e.g. after-date realisation) than reliance on ratios and past history.
- For example, analytical procedures on an aged trade receivables analysis and calculation of average collection period used in prior years will not be relevant to assessing the adequacy of the write-down now needed. Similarly, inventory turnover ratios will no longer be comparable when inventory is no longer being replenished.
- Some reliance will still be placed on certain analytical procedures. For example, in substantiating charges to the statement of profit or loss for the 10 months of operations.

(ii) Written representations

- Overall the extent of reliance on written representations is likely to be increased as compared with the prior year audit.
- The magnitude of matters of judgment and opinion is greater than in prior years. For example, inventory and trade receivable write-downs, impairment losses and numerous provisions.
- The auditor will seek to obtain as much corroborative evidence as is available. However, where amounts of assets have still to be recovered and liabilities settled, management will be asked to make representations on the adequacy of write-downs, provisions, and the completeness of disclosures for claims and other contingent liabilities.
- Where negotiations are under discussion but not yet formalised (e.g. with a prospective buyer for premises), management may be the only source of evidence (e.g. for the best estimate of sale proceeds). However, the extent to which reliance can be placed on representations depends on the extent to which those making the representation can be expected to be well-informed on the particular matters. Therefore, as the human resources and production directors will not be available after the statement of financial position date particular thought should be given to obtaining representations on matters pertaining to areas of judgment, for example, employee obligations and product warranties.

(c) **Principal audit work – carrying amount**

(i) Amounts due from distributors

- Review after-date cash to assess whether payments have been received post year-end.
- Review of agreements with distributors to confirm the unexpired period (up to three years) and the penalties stipulated.
- Recalculate amounts due to distributors for the early termination of the agreements with them.
- Review correspondence with distributors offering financial settlement, and the responses received.

(ii) Lease liabilities

- Review Cerise's correspondence with the lessors requesting terms for an early exit from the lease period to confirm contracts as onerous and justify full provision.
- Visit premises to confirm that Cerise is not receiving any economic benefit from them (i.e. they are not still occupied or sub-let).
- Agree/reconcile the amounts provided for liabilities under onerous contracts to the present value of the future minimum lease payments under non-cancellable leases.
- Agree/reconcile the future minimum lease payments used in the calculation of the provision to those disclosed in the financial statements to 31 December 20X4 as 1 - 5 years and later than five years.

Test your understanding 3

(a) **Principal audit risks**

Goat herd

The goat herd will consist of:

- mature goats held for use in the production of milk (i.e. accounted for as depreciable non-current tangible assets – IAS 16 *Property Plant and Equipment*).
- kids which are held for replacement purposes (accounted for as biological assets under IAS 41 *Agriculture*), and
- kids which are to be sold (held as inventory under IAS 2 *Inventories*).

There is a risk that due to the complexities of the various accounting standards, the non-current assets, biological assets and inventories are misstated.

There is a risk that the carrying amount of the production animals will be misstated if, for example:

- useful lives/depreciation rates are unreasonable.
- estimates of residual values are not kept under review.

Animals raised during the year should be recognised initially and at each statement of financial position date at fair value less estimated point-of-sale costs. Such biological assets will be understated in the statement of financial position if they are not recorded on birth.

The net realisable value of animals held for sale may fall below cost if they are not sold soon after reaching optimal size and weight.

Unrecorded revenue

Raised (bred) animals are not purchased and, in the absence of documentation supporting their origination, could be sold for cash and the revenue unrecorded.

Although the controls over retailing around the world are likely to be strong, there are other sources of income – the shop and other activities at the farm.

There is a risk that revenue could go unrecorded due to lack of effective controls.

Skin disorder

If 'Bachas Blue' has been specifically cited as a cause of a skin disorder then GVF could face compensation for pending litigation.

If it is probable that GVF would have to make payments, a provision should be recognised. If it is possible, a contingent liability should be disclosed.

There is a risk that provisions are understated or contingent liabilities have not been disclosed in respect of any claims.

Maturing cheese

The substance of the sale and repurchase of cheese is that of a loan secured on the inventory. Therefore revenue should not be recognised on 'sale' to Abingdon Bank. The principal terms of the secured borrowings should be disclosed, including the carrying amount of the inventory to which it applies.

Borrowing costs should be capitalised in accordance with IAS 23 *Borrowing Costs* since the cost of maturing cheese includes interest at 7% per six months and the borrowings are specific. The cost of inventories should include all costs incurred in bringing them to their present location and condition of maturity.

There is a risk that, if the age of maturing cheeses is not accurately determined, the cost of cheese will be misstated.

Health and safety legislation – non-compliance

New legislation came into effect on 1 July which required wooden boards to be replaced with stainless steel shelves. At 30 September 20X4 the legislation will have been in effect for three months.

If GVF's management has not replaced the shelves, fines/penalties may be payable due to non-compliance.

There is a risk that liabilities are understated if any fines/penalties have not been accrued.

Health and safety legislation – impairment of assets

If the legislation is complied with the wooden boards previously used will be impaired and should be written down.

GVF are concerned that the new process will interfere with the maturing process and production of medium and strong cheeses will have to cease. This will also indicate impairment of equipment.

There is a risk of overstatement of plant and equipment if they are impaired as a result of the impact of the new legislation.

Grant

GVF received a substantial regional development grant in 20X3 but has deferred its plans to use this grant until 20X6.

If the terms of the grant required the money to be used within a specified timeframe the grant may have become repayable as the terms have not been complied with. In this case the grant should be presented as a payable in the statement of financial position.

There is a risk of understatement of liabilities if GVF will have to repay the grant money.

Going concern

The cost of an ingredient which is essential to the manufacturing process has increased significantly. If the cost is passed on to the customers, demand may fall and supplies of the ingredient, Innittu, may be restricted increasing uncertainty over going concern.

There is a risk that disclosure of going concern issues is not made adequately.

(b) **Audit work on carrying amounts**

(i) Goat herd

- Physically inspect the number and condition of animals in the herd and confirming, on a test basis, that they are tagged (or otherwise 'branded' as being owned by GVF).
- Perform tests of controls on management's system of identifying and distinguishing held-for-sale animals (inventory) from the production herd (depreciable non-current assets).
- Compare GVF's depreciation policies (including useful lives, depreciation methods and residual values) with those used by other farming entities to assess reasonableness.
- Perform a proof in total of the depreciation charge for the herd for the year.
- Observe test counts of animals held for sale.
- Inspect market values of kids, according to their weight and age, as at 30 September 20X4 – for both held-for-sale and held-for-replacement animals.
- For held-for-sale animals only, vouch (on a sample basis) management's schedule of point-of-sale costs (e.g. market dealers' commissions).

(ii) Equipment used in the manufacture of Bachas Blue

- Agree cost less accumulated depreciation and impairment losses at the beginning of the year to prior year working papers (and/or last year's published financial statements).
- Recalculate the current year depreciation charge based on the carrying amount (as reduced by the impairment loss).
- Calculate the carrying amount of the equipment as at 30 September 20X4 without deduction of the impairment loss.
- Agree management's schedule of future cash flows estimated to be attributable to the equipment for a period of up to five years (unless a longer period can be justified) to approved budgets and forecasts.

- Recalculate the cash flows included in the forecast and GVF's weighted average cost of capital.
- Compare production records and sales orders with the prior period to confirm a steady increase.
- Compare sales volume at 30 September 20X4 with the pre-'scare' level to assess how much of the previously recognised impairment loss it would be prudent to write back (if any).
- Scrutinise sales orders post year-end. Sales of such produce can be very volatile and another 'incident' could reduce sales again in which case the impairment loss should not be reversed.

(iii) Cheese

- Examine the terms of sales to Abingdon Bank to confirm the bank's legal title (e.g. if GVF were to cease to trade and so could not exercise buy-back option).
- Obtain a direct confirmation from the bank of the cost of inventory sold by GVF to Abingdon Bank and the amount repurchased as at 30 September 20X4 (the net amount being the outstanding loan).
- Inspect the cheese as at 30 September 20X4 (e.g. during the physical inventory count) paying particular attention to the factors which indicate the age (and strength) of the cheese (e.g. its location or physical appearance).
- Observe how the cheese is stored. If on steel shelves discuss with GVF's management whether its net realisable value has been reduced below cost.
- Inspect, on a sample basis, the costing records supporting the cost of batches of cheese.
- Confirm that the cost of inventory sold to the bank is included in inventory as at 30 September 20X4 and the nature of the bank security adequately disclosed.
- Agree the repurchase of cheese which has reached maturity at cost plus 7% per six months to purchase invoices (or equivalent contracts) and cash book payments.
- Inspect GVF's aged inventory records to production records. Confirm the carrying amount of inventory as at 30 September 20X4 that will not be sold until after 30 September 20X5, and agree to the amount disclosed in the notes to inventory as a 'non-current' portion.

Test your understanding 4

Tutorial note:

The first part of this question is essentially a due diligence question. You have been asked to examine the management accounts and forecasts of a target company that your client is interested in acquiring.

(a) **Implications of findings**

$800,000 profit on sale of property

Although the profit on sale of the property arises from ordinary activities, it needs to be separately identified (IAS 1) so that Scorpio's current trading performance can be assessed (by Bellatrix and the bank). It should be excluded from any trading results that are being extrapolated to provide figures for profit forecasts. To include it would result in a distortion of sustainable profits.

Scorpio's properties are being valued at historical cost in its financial statements (IAS 16). Bellatrix should obtain an independent valuation of the properties before finalising a purchase price for the acquisition of Scorpio.

The property sale could have been made to realise cash and so mitigate current cash flow difficulties. The proposed sale of two more properties and outsourcing of warehousing may further improve the cash flow situation in the short-term. However, outsourcing warehousing could place a further burden on cash flow if an agreement is entered into and no buyer can subsequently be found for the properties.

Scorpio's management is seeking (or negotiating with) a suitable organisation to provide warehousing. However, one of the synergies to be obtained from acquiring Scorpio may be utilising Bellatrix's spare warehousing capacity. Bellatrix should therefore obtain warranties and indemnities in the purchase contract in respect of any contingent liabilities that could arise. For example, penalties may be incurred if an agreement to outsource warehousing is entered into and subsequently cancelled.

Sales to Andromeda

The two members of the management board of Scorpio will be related parties (IAS 24) if they are key management personnel (i.e. having authority and responsibility for planning, directing and controlling the activities of Scorpio).

Andromeda will be a related party if the management board members have the ability to exercise influence over Andromeda's financial and operating policy decisions. This seems likely, as 10% of Scorpio's sales constitutes material inter-company transactions. (Control of Andromeda is not an issue as the two members have only a minority interest.)

Sales to Andromeda appear to be related party transactions which should be disclosed in Scorpio's financial statements for the year to 31 December 20X4.

Although prices appear to be on an arm's length basis, the transactions may not be at arm's length if other trading terms (e.g. delivery or payment terms) are more or less favourable than transactions with unrelated parties. If credit terms are not 'normal commercial' these sales could be contributing to Scorpio's current cash flow difficulties.

The sales to Andromeda are material to Scorpio and may be lost after the acquisition (e.g. if the two minority shareholders do not continue to hold positions on the management board of Scorpio). A proportional (i.e. 10%) reduction in gross profit would also be expected (assuming margins on sales to Andromeda are not dissimilar to those on other sales).

Bank loan application

The $150,000 discrepancy between the current asset values per the management accounts and the balances per the accounting records appears to be an irregularity that could constitute a fraud against the bank. It casts serious doubts on the integrity of Scorpio's management. Revising the accounting estimates for allowances against asset values downwards is clearly inappropriate as it is most likely that they should be increased (as inventory levels increase with falling demand and receivables are more likely to be bad or doubtful debts).

Refurbishing the offices is unlikely to constitute essential expenditure when the company is experiencing cash flow difficulties. Also it is possible that refurbishment may not be required when Bellatrix acquires Scorpio because the functions of the executive and administration offices may be relocated elsewhere within the Bellatrix group of companies.

Although current trading performance is clearly below budget (after deducting the profit on disposal and reinstating the allowances for inventory and receivables), the loan finance is not being sought for a purpose that would increase the company's revenue-earning opportunities. This may cast doubt on the business acumen of Scorpio's management. It is possible that the loan finance would not be forthcoming if the bank were aware of Scorpio's true position.

Bellatrix should seek to have the negotiations with the bank suspended until after the acquisition, when the need for loan finance can be reassessed. Bellatrix should obtain guarantees from Scorpio's executives in the event that they pursue the loan application (which may possibly create charges over Scorpio's assets).

Budget forecast

The profit estimates made by the management of Scorpio appear to be unduly optimistic because the first six month's budget has only been 'met' by the inclusion, in the reported results of:

- a non-sustainable profit on disposal of a warehouse.
- unwarranted reversals of allowances against asset values.

Perhaps it is more likely that the forecast 'rising profit trend' will be achieved (and the annual budget exceeded) through profits arising on the disposals of two more properties rather than increased demand.

Budgeted profits should therefore be disregarded in the determination of the purchase price.

(b) **Impact of acquisition on audit**

Tutorial notes:

(1) The acquisition will be completed before 31 December 20X4 (see 1st para 'acquisition in current year').

(2) Accounting year-ends will be coterminous ('first half year to 30 June 20X4').

(3) You will be appointed as auditor to Scorpio ('as audit manager to Bellatrix and its subsidiaries').

(4) 'Conduct of your audit' must not be confined to the 'audit testing' phase but requires consideration of the whole audit process.

Practice management

It is possible that audit objectivity may appear to be impaired (e.g. due to a closer relationship between Bellatrix's management and the audit team having developed during the acquisition assignment). A second partner review may therefore be required as an appropriate safeguard.

Bellatrix's individual company accounts

The acquisition will constitute an addition, at cost, to investments in subsidiaries in Bellatrix's own financial statements. The purchase consideration paid (or contingently payable) should also be disclosed.

The cost of acquisition should be verified to the sale agreement. Cash consideration must be agreed to entries in the cash book and bank statements. Company minutes and entries in the share register will evidence consideration in shares.

Bellatrix's consolidated accounts

Statement of financial position

Scorpio's assets and liabilities, at fair value to the group, will be combined on a line-by-line basis and any goodwill arising recognised.

The fair value of such assets as the properties (assuming that they have not yet been sold) may be material to the consolidated statement of financial position. Assuming that the properties were independently valued prior to the acquisition, it will be appropriate to seek to place reliance on the work of the expert valuer.

The calculation of the goodwill arising on acquisition must be recalculated and the component figures agreed. Goodwill must be reviewed for impairment by Bellatrix's management. The auditor will need to assess this impairment review for appropriateness to ensure the asset is not overstated.

Statement of profit or loss

As Scorpio will be acquired quite late on in the year (certainly the second half of the year) it is possible that its post-acquisition results are not material to the consolidated statement of profit or loss.

Unless accounting adjustments are required (e.g. to bring any accounting policies of Scorpio into line with Bellatrix) the addition of one more subsidiary into the consolidation working papers is unlikely to have a significant impact.

Other subsidiaries

The materiality of other subsidiaries, in the group context, should be reassessed in terms of the enlarged group. The existence of another company (Scorpio) in the same business within the group may extend the scope of analytical procedures available. This could have the effect of increasing audit efficiency.

Scorpio's financial statements

Planning

Much of the collection of background information associated with planning the conduct of a new audit assignment will have already been obtained as a result of the pre-acquisition work.

Materiality assessment

Material matters requiring attention will include:

- sales to Andromeda
- property valuations
- inventory valuations (raw materials, WIP and finished carpets)
- trade receivables balances
- liabilities (including bank loans).

The management accounts for the six months to 30 June should provide information sufficient to make an initial evaluation of materiality. However, as the reliability of certain management information is in doubt, this should be reassessed before detailed work commences.

The materiality of these items should also be assessed in the context of monetary amounts in the consolidated financial statements.

Risk assessment

Specific areas of audit risk have already been identified, thereby reducing the time required to assess the risk of misstatement at the planning stage.

In particular:

- inherent risk is high due to Scorpio's management overstating profit (even if the management board has since been replaced)
- inventory may be overstated/allowances understated due to inventory having increased (due to a fall in demand)
- trade receivables may be overstated/allowances for bad and doubtful debts understated due to Scorpio's management having manipulated these figures to achieve their profit estimates.

Ascertaining the systems and internal controls

Some systems review work may have already been undertaken (e.g. when considering the source of information used in the preparation of Scorpio budgetary information).

The relevance of Scorpio's current accounting systems and internal controls will depend on Bellatrix's plans for change. For example, a Bellatrix office may account for Scorpio's transactions. If significant changes are proposed it may be more appropriate to adopt a substantive approach to the first audit of Scorpio.

Audit evidence

Some audit evidence should have been obtained for the due diligence file e.g. concerning the sales to Andromeda and the sale of property. This should be copied and referenced to the audit working papers to ensure that work is not unnecessarily re-performed.

As Scorpio is in the same business as Bellatrix, ratio analysis and other substantive analytical procedures should provide a more cost-effective approach to obtaining audit evidence than tests of detail.

Review

The relationship between the two members of Scorpio's management board and Andromeda after the date of acquisition must be established and the extent of transactions between them, if any. For example, these non-controlling interests of Andromeda may no longer hold board positions, and/or sales to Andromeda may have ceased.

The proportion of sales should be disclosed (e.g. 10%) along with factual information concerning the pricing policy. Audit tests must verify, for example, that price is determined based on a published price list.

Test your understanding 5

(a) **Store impairment**

(i) Matters

The cost of goodwill represents 3.1% of total assets and is therefore material.

After three years the carrying value of goodwill ($2.2m) represents 1.2% of total assets and 23% of PBT, and is also material.

The announcement is after the statement of financial position date and is therefore a non-adjusting event insofar as no provision for restructuring (for example) can be made.

The event provides evidence of a possible impairment of the cash-generating unit which is this store and, in particular, the value of goodwill assigned to it.

If more than 22% of goodwill is attributable to the City Metro store, then its write-off would be material to PBT (22% × $2.2m ÷ $9.5m = 5%).

Management should have considered whether the other four stores in Urvina (and elsewhere) are similarly impaired.

There is a risk that assets including goodwill are overstated in the financial statements if an appropriate impairment review has not been undertaken.

(ii) Audit evidence

- Board minutes approving the store's refurbishment and documenting the need to address the fall in demand for it as a supermarket.
- Recalculation of the carrying amount of goodwill (2/5 × $5.5m = $2.2m).
- A schedule identifying all assets that relate to the store under review and the carrying amounts agreed to the underlying accounting records (e.g. non-current asset register).
- Recalculation of value in use and/or net selling price of the cash-generating unit that is to become the City Metro as at 31 March 20X4.

- Agreement of cash flow projections (e.g. to approved budgets/forecast revenues and costs for a maximum of five years, unless a longer period can be justified).
- Written representation from management relating to the assumptions used in the preparation of financial budgets.
- Agreement that the pre-tax discount rate used reflects current market assessments of the time value of money (and the risks specific to the store) and is reasonable. For example, by comparison with Volcan's weighted average cost of capital.
- Inspection of the store (if this is the month it is closed for refurbishment).
- Actual after-date sales by store compared with budget.
- Revenue budgets and cash flow projections for:
  - the two stores purchased at the same time
  - the other stores in Urvina
  - the stores elsewhere.

(b) **Reward scheme**

(i) Matters

If the entire year's revenue ($303m) attracted loyalty points then the cost of the reward scheme in the year is at most $3.03m. This represents 1% of revenue and 31.9% of profit before tax which is material.

To the extent that points have been awarded but not redeemed at 31 March 20X4, Volcan will have a liability at the statement of financial position date.

In accordance with the accruals concept, the expense and liability of the reward scheme should be recognised as revenue is earned.

The calculation of the expense and liability will need to take into consideration

- Any restrictions on the terms for converting points (e.g. whether they expire if not used within a specified time).
- The proportion of reward points awarded which are not expected to be claimed (e.g. the 'take up' of points awarded may be only 80%, say).
- The proportion of customers who register for loyalty cards and the percentage of revenue (and profit) which they represent (which may vary from store to store depending on customer profile).

There is a risk that liabilities and expenses in relation to the reward scheme are understated.

(ii) Audit evidence

- New/updated systems documentation explaining how:
  - loyalty cards (and numbers) are issued to customers
  - points earned are recorded at the point of sale
  - points are later redeemed on subsequent purchases.
- Reconciliation of the total balance due to customers at the year-end under the reward scheme to the sum of the points on individual customer reward cards.
- Documentation of walk-through tests (e.g. on registering customer applications and issuing loyalty cards, awarding of points on special offer items).
- Results of tests of controls supporting the extent to which audit reliance is placed on the accounting and internal control system. In particular, how points are extracted from the electronic tills (cash registers) and summarised into the weekly/monthly financial data for each store which underlies the financial statements.
- Analytical procedures on the value of points awarded by store per month with explanations of variations. For example, similar proportions (not exceeding 1% of revenue) of points in each month might be expected by stores, possibly increasing following any promotion of the loyalty scheme.
- Results of tests of detail on a sample of transactions with customers undertaken at store visits. For example, for a sample of copy till receipts:
  - check the arithmetic accuracy of points awarded (1 per $1 spent + special offers).
  - agree points awarded for special offers to that week's special offers.
  - for cash discounts taken confirm the conversion of points is against the opening balance of points awarded (not against purchases just made).

(c) **Site restoration**

(i) Matters

The provision for site restoration represents nearly 2.5% of total assets and is therefore material.

The estimated cost of restoring the site is a cost directly attributable to the initial measurement of the tangible non-current asset to the extent that it is recognised as a provision under IAS 37 *Provisions, Contingent Liabilities and Contingent Assets* (IAS 16 *Property, Plant and Equipment*).

A provision should only be recognised for site restoration if there is a present obligation as a result of a past event that can be measured reliably and is probable to result in a transfer of economic benefits (IAS 37).

The provision is overstated by nearly $0.34m since Volcan is not obliged to relocate the trees and only has an obligation of $60,000 as at 31 March 20X4 (being the penalty for having felled them). When considered in isolation, this overstatement is immaterial (representing only 0.2% of total assets and 3.6% of PBT).

It seems that even if there are local government regulations calling for site restoration there is no obligation unless the penalties for non-compliance are prohibitive (unlike the fines for the trees).

It is unlikely that commencement of site development has given rise to a constructive obligation, since past actions (disregarding the preservation of the trees) must dispel any expectation that Volcan will honour any pledge to restore the valley.

Consideration should also be given to whether commencing development of the site and destroying the trees conflicts with any statement of environmental responsibility in the annual report.

There is a risk that provisions are overstated and profit understated if this provision does not meet the criteria of IAS 37.

(i) Audit evidence

- Payment of $60,000 to local government in May 20X4 agreed to the bank statement.
- The present value calculation of the future cash expenditure making up the $4.0m provision.
- Agreement that the pre-tax discount rate used reflects current market assessments of the time value of money (as for (a)).
- Asset inspection at the site as at 31 March 20X4.
- Any contracts entered into which might confirm or dispute management's intentions to restore the site. For example, whether plant hire (bulldozers, etc) covers only the period over which the warehouse will be constructed, or whether it extends to the period in which the valley would be 'made good'.
- A copy of the planning application and permission granted setting out the penalties for non-compliance.

Test your understanding 6

(a) **Cessation of home delivery service**

(i) Matters

$0.6 million represents 1.4% of reported revenue (prior year 1.9%) and is therefore material.

The home delivery service is not a component of Albreda and its cessation does not classify as a discontinued operation in accordance with IFRS 5 *Non-current Assets Held for Sale and Discontinued Operations* because:

- It is not a cash-generating unit because home delivery revenues are not independent of other revenues generated by the restaurant kitchens.
- 1.4% of revenue is not a major line of business.
- Home delivery does not cover a separate geographical area (but many areas around the numerous restaurants).

The redundancy provision of $0.2 million represents 11.1% of profit before tax (10% before allowing for the provision) and is therefore material. However, it represents only 0.6% of total assets and is therefore immaterial to the statement of financial position.

As the announcement was made before the year-end, there is a present obligation and a probable outflow of economic benefits in respect of the redundancies therefore the provision is appropriate.

The delivery vehicles should be classified as held for sale if their carrying amount will be recovered principally through a sale transaction rather than through continuing use. For this to be the case the following IFRS 5 criteria must be met:

- the vehicles must be available for immediate sale in their present condition, and
- their sale must be highly probable.

However, even if the classification as held for sale is appropriate, the measurement basis is incorrect. Non-current assets classified as held for sale should be carried at the lower of carrying amount and fair value less costs to sell.

It is incorrect that the vehicles are being measured at fair value less costs to sell which is $0.3 million in excess of the carrying amount. This amounts to a revaluation and should be reversed. $0.3 million represents just less than 1% of assets and 16.7% of profit which is material.

Comparison of fair value less costs to sell against carrying amount should have been made on an item by item basis (and not on their totals).

There is a risk that the delivery vehicles held for sale are overstated.

(ii) Audit evidence

- Copy of board minute documenting management's decision to cease home deliveries (and any press releases/internal memoranda to staff).
- An analysis of revenue (e.g. extracted from management accounts) showing the amount attributed to home delivery sales.
- Redundancy terms for drivers as set out in their contracts of employment to assess adequacy of the redundancy provision.
- A proof in total for the reasonableness/completeness of the redundancy provision (e.g. number of drivers × sum of years employed × payment per year of service).
- A schedule of depreciated cost of delivery vehicles extracted from the non-current asset register to confirm carrying value of assets held for sale.
- Second hand market prices as published/advertised in used vehicle guides to verify fair value.
- After-date net sale proceeds from sale of vehicles and comparison of proceeds against estimated fair values to confirm fair value.
- Physical inspection of condition of unsold vehicles to assess whether they are likely to be sold for the estimated fair value in their current condition.
- Draft financial statements to assess the appropriateness of the disclosure of assets held for sale on the face of the statement of financial position or in the notes, and shown in the reconciliation of carrying amount at the beginning and end of the period.

(b) **Revaluation of owned premises**

(i) Matters

The revaluations are material as $1.7 million, $5.4 million and $7.1 million represent 5.5%, 17.6% and 23.1% of total assets, respectively.

The change in accounting policy, from a cost model to a revaluation model, should be accounted for in accordance with IAS 16 *Property, Plant and Equipment* (i.e. as a revaluation).

Independence, qualifications and expertise of valuer(s) should be considered to determine the reliability of the valuations.

IAS 16 does not permit the selective revaluation of assets thus the whole class of premises should have been revalued.

The valuations of properties after the year-end are adjusting events (i.e. providing additional evidence of conditions existing at the year-end) per IAS 10 *Events after the reporting date*.

The revaluation exercise is incomplete. If the revaluations on the remaining three properties are expected to be material and cannot be reasonably estimated for inclusion in the financial statements perhaps the change in policy should be deferred for a year.

There is a risk that property is overstated as the revaluations do not comply with the requirements of IAS 16.

(ii) Audit evidence

- A schedule of depreciated cost of owned premises extracted from the non-current asset register.
- Calculation of the difference between valuation and depreciated cost by property to assess materiality.
- Copy of valuation certificate for each property to confirm the valuation amount.
- Physical inspection of properties with the largest surpluses (including the two valued before the year-end) to confirm condition.
- Extracts from local property guides/magazines indicating a range of values of similarly styled/sized properties.
- Financial statements to confirm adequacy of the IAS 16 disclosures in the notes including:
  - the effective date of revaluation.
  - whether an independent valuer was involved.
  - the methods and significant assumptions applied in estimating fair values.
  - the carrying amount that would have been recognised under the cost model.
  - reconciliation of carrying amount at the beginning and end of the period.
  - revaluation surpluses in the statement of changes in equity.

(c) **Fines and penalties**

(i) Matters

$0.1 million represents 5.6% of profit before tax and is therefore material.

The payments may be regarded as material by nature as they are payments related to non-compliance with regulations. However, separate disclosure may not be necessary if, for example, there are no external shareholders.

The accounting treatment (inclusion in cost of sales) should be consistent with prior year.

The reason for the fall in expense should be investigated. This may due to an improvement in meeting health and safety regulations or due to incomplete recording of liabilities (understatement).

There is a risk of inadequate disclosure of the fines and penalties and a risk of understatement of fines and penalties if they have not been completely recorded.

(ii) Audit evidence

- Cash book and bank statements confirming payment of fines.
- Review/comparison of current year schedule against prior year for any apparent omissions.
- After-date cash book and bank statements for payments made in respect of liabilities incurred before 30 September 20X4.
- Correspondence with relevant health and safety regulators (e.g. local authorities) for notification of liabilities incurred before 30 September 20X4.
- Notes in the prior year financial statements confirming consistency, or otherwise, of the lack of separate disclosure.
- Written representation from management that there are no fines/penalties other than those which have been reflected in the financial statements.

Test your understanding 7

(a) **Brand names**

(i) Matters

The cost of the purchased brands represents 3.2% of total assets and 32% of profit before tax (carrying value will be less). Annual amortisation amounts to 3.2% of profit before tax. Brands as a whole are therefore material.

Ulexite is a purchased brand and therefore has a carrying value in the statement of financial position. If the carrying value of Ulexite at the year-end is greater than $91,500 (i.e. 5% PBT) its total write-off due to impairment is likely to be regarded as material.

The fall in demand in January 20X4 as a result of the marketing campaign is an adjusting event (IAS 10 *Events After the Reporting Period*) providing evidence about the valuation of assets as at 31 December 20X3.

There is a risk that the value of intangible assets (brands) and profits are overstated if an impairment charge has not been recognised.

There is also a risk the net realisable value of inventory of Ulexite products may be less than cost and inventory is overstated.

There could be a loss of customer goodwill to Visean as a whole if customers boycott Visean's other products by the association of Ulexite with Visean. This could result in overstatement of the other purchased brands.

(ii) Audit evidence

- Cost/carrying value of Ulexite agreed to prior year working papers, less current year's amortisation charge.
- Comparison of actual after-date sales (and/or inventory turnover) against budget, month on month, and by fragrance to identify:
  - the significance of the fall in demand of Ulexite.
  - whether other fragrances have been similarly affected.
  - if demand is picking up again (in February to June).
- Monthly sales analysis returns received from retail pharmacies.
- The advert, promotional literature or slogan relating to Ulexite which caused the offence.
- Media reports, if any, arising from bad publicity.

- Board minutes reflecting any decisions taken by management e.g. to discontinue the fragrance.
- Schedule of expenses incurred since April (reflected in the cash book and/or after-date invoices) to rectify the damage done (e.g. a new marketing campaign).
- Copy of correspondence and notes concerning any pending legal action and possible quantified outcomes.

(b) **Discontinued operation**

(i) Matters

The provisions have reduced profit before tax by 40% (i.e. 1.25 ÷ [1.83 + 1.25]) and now represent 68% of profit before tax and are therefore considered to be material.

The plan to close the plant facility is likely to result in a discontinued operation if hospital medical consumables are a separate line of business which can be distinguished operationally and for financial reporting purposes (IFRS 5 *Non-current Assets Held for Sale and Discontinued Operations*).

If hospital medical consumables were reported as a business segment in the notes to the financial statements for the prior year (IFRS 8 *Operating Segments*) this will satisfy the separate line of business criteria.

The initial disclosure event will be the earlier of:

- the directors' announcement in December (that the factory closed in January strongly suggests that a formal detailed plan existed and was approved before it was announced).
- a binding sale agreement for substantially all the related assets (i.e. equipment and inventory – not the plant itself, as it is leased).

Tutorial note: The announcement is the more likely in the context of the given scenario.

The disposal of any assets (e.g. equipment) arising from the plant closure in January is a non-adjusting event (IAS 10) which will require disclosure in the financial statements if material.

No provision should be made for the loss on sale of related assets after the year-end unless a binding sale agreement was entered into before the year-end. However:

- plant assets (plant and equipment) should be reviewed for impairment (IAS 36 *Impairment of Assets*), and

- inventory of hospital consumables should be measured at the lower of cost and net realisable value (IAS 2 *Inventories*).

Assuming that the announcement in December raised valid expectations that a detailed formal restructuring plan would be carried out, a constructive obligation to restructure arises (IAS 37 *Provisions, Contingent Liabilities and Contingent Assets*). The provision made should include:

- Redundancy costs (but not any costs of retraining or relocating continuing staff).
- Present obligations under onerous contracts (e.g. for the unexpired lease term on the factory premises).
- Further provision may be necessary for onerous contracts with customers (and possibly suppliers). For example, hospitals (as public sector bodies) are likely to have contracts with Visean containing penalty clauses for non-performance, breach of contract, etc.

(ii) Audit evidence

- Segmental information in the prior year financial statements showing hospital medical consumables to be a business segment (e.g. if this activity accounted for 10% or more of Visean's revenue, profit or assets).
- Initial disclosure of:
  - carrying amounts of assets being disposed of (if any), and
  - revenue, expenses, pre-tax profit or loss and income tax expense attributable to the discontinuing of medical consumable supplies.
- Agreement of initial disclosure to underlying financial ledger accounts, management reports, etc.
- Comparison of separate disclosure with budgeted amounts and prior year.
- Board minutes approving the formal plan to discontinue the product range, close the factory and make staff redundant.
- Copies of announcements e.g. press releases and letters to customers and employees.
- The binding sale agreement (if any) for plant, equipment and inventory.
- The contractual terms of the factory lease and correspondence with the lessor to notify them of the surrender of the lease.
- Contracts with hospitals and suppliers to identify penalty clauses, if any.
- Calculations of the provisions and assumptions made.

- Redundancy terms for employees (both contractual and statutory) to enable verification of any redundancy provision calculation.
- Past redundancy settlements (as compared with statutory and contractual obligations).
- After-date sales of hospital medical consumables.

(c) **Statement of cash flows**

(i) Matters

Matters affecting disclosure are material by nature.

The statement of cash flows should be prepared in accordance with IAS 7 *Statement of Cash Flows* i.e. reporting cash flows classified under the standard headings (including operating activities, returns on investments, taxation, capital expenditure, etc). IAS 1 *Presentation of Financial Statements* requires comparative figures for all items in the primary statements (and therefore for the statement of cash flows).

Cash flows from operating activities may be reported using either:

- the 'direct' method (i.e. showing relevant constituent cash flows) or
- the 'indirect' method (i.e. calculating operating cash flows by adjustment to the operating profit reported in the profit and loss account).

IAS 7 the permits a change from the indirect to the direct method. It is appropriate, in the interest of comparability that the corresponding figures have been restated. The reason for reclassification should be disclosed.

The auditor's responsibility for corresponding figures (ISA 710 *Comparative Information - Corresponding Figures and Comparative Financial Statements*) is to obtain sufficient appropriate audit evidence that they have been correctly reported and appropriately classified.

There is a risk of material misstatement if the corresponding figures have not been restated appropriately or if disclosure of the restatement has not been made adequately.

(ii) Audit evidence

– Agreement of corresponding amounts for 'Net cash from operating activities' downwards to the prior year statement of cash flows.

– For the prior year, agreement (or reconciliation) of profit before tax adjusted for non-cash items (e.g. depreciation) and working capital changes to cash receipts from customers less cash paid to suppliers and employees.

– Schedules of cash receipts (per analysis of cash book receipts) agreed to the receivables ledger control account.

– Schedules of cash payments to suppliers and employees (per analysis of cash book payments) agreed to the payables ledger and payroll control accounts respectively.

– Analytical procedures such as the comparison of trade receivables (and payables) days (i.e. average credit periods given to customers and received from suppliers) with prior year.

Test your understanding 8

(a) Objectivity is one of the fundamental principles for a member of ACCA. It is defined as being 'The state of mind which has regard to all considerations relevant to the task in hand and no other. It presupposes intellectual honesty'.

Objectivity is particularly important to an auditor, whose role it is to provide an independent opinion on financial statements. Objectivity can only be assured if the member is independent.

The ACCA provides detailed guidance on how auditors should maintain their objectivity and independence. The guidance covers issues such as dependence on an audit client (fee-related issues), close relationships with the client, provision of other accountancy or other services to the client, and accepting goods and services.

The auditor must always strive to maintain his objectivity in all his dealings with the client.

(b) **Audit engagement**

There are a number of matters to be considered in relation to accepting the audit of Rainbow.

Undue dependence

Accepting the work of Rainbow may lead to the firm having an undue dependence on the client creating a self-interest threat. The firm may be reluctant to raise issues with the client for fear of losing the work.

The audit fee discussed is substantial and, in connection with the tax work, may affect the objectivity of the firm. ACCA suggest that recurring fees from one client should not exceed INT: 15% / UK: 10% of gross practice income.

Consideration should be given to the regularity of special work undertaken by the firm on behalf of the client. It may be arguable that this work is in some sense recurring and this would mean objectivity was impaired.

An engagement quality control review should be carried out to ensure the outcome of the audit has not been affected.

Contingency fee

Linking the audit fee to the success of the client's business creates a self-interest threat. The firm may not request audit adjustments that should be made but would lead to a reduction in profit and as this would reduce the audit fee.

This type of fee arrangement is not acceptable and the firm should not accept these terms.

Unpaid fees

Overdue fees can be construed as a loan to the client, which would create a self-interest threat. The firm may be reluctant to raise issues with the client in case the fees remain unpaid.

The auditor should consider whether the unpaid fees are overdue, or whether it is normal practice for the firm to have such outstanding fees. The amount outstanding should be considered to see if the threat is significant. The length of time that the fees have been overdue would also affect the significance of the threat.

The firm should discuss the outstanding fees with the client and make arrangements for payment. If the fees are significant, an independent review partner should be assigned to the audit.

Relationships

The audit partner is related to a member of the client's staff which creates a familiarity threat. The partner may be too trusting of the client and not apply sufficient scepticism when conducting the audit. The staff member appears to be junior in the organisation, and is an adult daughter and therefore not dependent on the auditor.

However, as the relationship is with the audit partner it may be advisable to change the partner to be seen as demonstrating appropriate consideration of the ethical issue.

Shareholding

As the daughter is not a dependant of the auditor, her shareholding should not affect his objectivity towards this audit. Again, as it is the partner with the connection, it would be advisable to remove him from the audit to remove any threat.

Other services

Provision of other services to an audit client can create a self-review threat. If an auditor is responsible for auditing work they were responsible for preparing, they are unlikely to be critical of it and errors may remain uncorrected.

It appears that different staff would be involved in tax and audit work so (other than the fee issue above) this should not pose any issues in relation to objectivity.

Hospitality

Auditors should not accept excessive gifts as this can create self-interest and familiarity threats. The offer of hospitality may be seen as a bribe for an unmodified opinion.

The weekend in Tenerife appears to be excessive and should not be accepted.

The auditor should consider whether the offer of the free holiday casts significant doubt on the integrity of the director, and whether this would affect his decision to accept the audit work.

Test your understanding 9

(a) **Professional enquiry**

Krill has a professional duty of confidentiality to its client, Squid. If Krill's lack of response is due to Squid not having given them permission to respond, Sepia should not accept the appointment. However, in this case, Anton Fargues should have:

– notified Squid's management of the communication received from Sepia.

– written to Sepia to decline to give information and state his reasons.

Krill should not have simply failed to respond.

Krill may have suspicions of some unlawful act (e.g. defrauding the taxation authority), but no proof, which they do not wish to convey to Sepia in a written communication. However, Krill has had the opportunity of oral discussion with Sepia to convey a matter which may provide grounds for the nomination being declined by Sepia.

Steps by Sepia

Obtain written representation from Squid's management, that Krill & Co has been given Squid's written permission to respond to Sepia's communication.

Send a further letter to Krill by a recorded delivery service (i.e. requiring a signature) which states that if a reply is not received in the next seven days, Sepia will assume that there are no matters of which they should be aware and so proceed to accept the appointment. Advise also that unless a response is received, a written complaint will be made to the relevant professional body.

Make a written complaint to the disciplinary committee of the professional body of which Anton Fargues is a member so that his unprofessional conduct can be investigated.

(b) **Takeover bid**

Sepia has a professional duty of confidentiality to its existing audit client, Vitronella.

Vitronella may ask Sepia to give corporate finance advice on Hatchet's takeover bid which would be incidental to the audit relationship. Providing Sepia can maintain and demonstrate integrity and objectivity throughout, there would be no objection to Sepia providing such an additional service, to advance their existing client's case.

It is often in a company's best interests to have financial advice provided by their auditors, and there is nothing ethically improper in this. So it seems unusual that Hatchet should have approached Sepia, rather than their current auditors.

ACCA's Code of Ethics and Conduct consider that it would not be improper for an audit firm to audit two parties, even if the takeover is contested, and that to cease to act could damage the client's interests. However, the situation is different here in that Sepia is not Hatchet's auditor.

Sepia should take all reasonable steps to avoid conflicts of interest arising from new engagements and the possession of confidential information. Sepia cannot therefore resign from Vitronella in order to undertake the advisory role for Hatchet. (A relationship which has ended only in the last two years is still likely to constitute a conflict.)

Steps by Sepia

As it is clear that a material conflict of interest exists, Sepia should decline to act as adviser to Hatchet.

Advise Vitronella's management that Hatchet's approach has been declined.

(c) **Lowballing**

Lowballing is a practice in which auditors compete for clients by reducing their fees for statutory audits. Lower audit fees are compensated by the auditor carrying out more lucrative non-audit work (e.g. consultancy and tax advice).

The fact that Keratin has quoted a lower fee than the other tendering firms (if that is the case) is not improper providing that the prospective client, Benthos, is not misled about:

- the precise range of services that the quoted fee is intended to cover, and
- the likely level of fees for any other work undertaken.

Although an admission to lowballing may sound improper, it does not breach current ethical guidance providing Benthos understands the situation. For example, Keratin could offer Benthos a free first-year audit, providing Benthos understands that future audits will be chargeable and what the cost will be.

The risk is that if the non-audit work does not materialise, Keratin may be under pressure to cut corners or resort to irregular practices (e.g. the falsification of audit working papers) in order to keep within budget. If a situation of negligence was then to arise, Keratin could be found guilty of failing to exercise professional competence and due care.

Provided the auditor performs the audit to the required level of quality and issues an appropriate opinion, the level of the fee is not an issue.

Keratin may not just be lowballing on the first year audit fee, but in the longer term, perhaps indicating that future increases might only be in line with inflation. If Keratin was to later increase Benthos' audit fees substantially, a fee dispute could arise. In this event Benthos could refuse to pay the higher fee. It might be difficult then for Keratin to take the matter to arbitration if Benthos was misled.

Steps by Sepia

There are no steps which Sepia can take to prevent Benthos from awarding the tender to whichever firm it chooses.

If Keratin is successful in being awarded the tender, Sepia should consider its own policy on pricing in future competitive tendering situations.

Test your understanding 10

(a) **Quality control in a smaller audit firm**

Why difficult to implement

Audit quality depends on the quality of the people. Smaller firms may lack resources and specialist expertise. In particular, small firms may not be able to offer the same reward structures to attract and retain staff as larger firms.

Larger firms can afford to recruit staff in sufficient numbers to allow for subsequent leavers and provide for their training needs. Smaller firms may not be able to offer the same training opportunities. Prospective trainees may perceive a smaller firm's client base to be less attractive than that of a larger firm.

Smaller practices may have less scope to provide staff with internal and on-the-job training due to their smaller client base.

The cost of external training may be prohibitive for smaller firms and also fail to provide the hands-on experience necessary for professional development.

Audit committees play an oversight role which contributes to quality control in larger firms (e.g. on matters of client acceptance/retention, independence issues, etc). When the client base is largely of owner-managed businesses, as for many smaller audit firms, there are no non-executive directors to support the auditor when difficult issues arise.

Quality control requires leadership within the firm. In a larger firm, one senior partner may have responsibility for establishing quality control policies and procedures and a different partner may have responsibility for monitoring work performed. Splitting these roles may not be practical for a smaller firm and is impossible for sole practitioners.

Small firms operate in a highly competitive environment for audit work, are often busy with non-audit work, and may be under-resourced. Technical updating on audit matters may not be as regular as desirable and audit practice may become inefficient.

How overcome

Quality control procedures in a smaller firm can be distributed between the reporting partners.

Smaller firms may draw on the expertise of suitably qualified external consultants (e.g. on technical matters). Small firms and sole practitioners have the same access to a wide range of technical and ethical advisory services provided by ACCA (and other professional bodies) and should take advantage of these.

Small firms may work together as a network to share training opportunities and sometimes staff. For example, an association of small firms may adopt the same methodology and meet periodically for technical updates.

(b) **Lammergeier Group – auditor's report**

The report is clearly headed 'Qualified opinion arising from material misstatement …' yet the reasons for departure from IAS 7 are 'sound and acceptable'. This is confusing.

The heading is a statement of disagreement with the application of a standard, the latter a statement of concurrence. If the auditor concurs with a departure, the opinion should not be modified.

The title of IAS 7 should be stated in full, i.e. 'International Accounting Standard 7 *Statement of Cash Flows*. The full title of the accounting standard not being complied with should be stated in the basis for qualified opinion paragraph.

The opinion paragraph itself should simply be titled 'Qualified opinion'.

The auditor should not be expressing an opinion of Lammergeier's management in their report. This is not professional.

Management's justification should be set out in a note to the financial statements (e.g. in the accounting policies section). The auditor's report should clearly state that there is non-compliance with IAS 7.

It cannot be true that the departure 'does not impact on the truth and fairness …'. The requirement to prepare a statement of cash flows (and its associated notes) stems from the need to provide users of financial statements with information about changes in financial resources. If this information is omitted the financial statements cannot show a true and fair view.

'Except for [the non-preparation of the group statements of cash flows and associated notes] ….' is a modified auditor's opinion. This contradicts Rook & Co's assertion that the matter 'does not impact on the truth and fairness …'.

The grounds for non-compliance is 'the complexity involved', which does not seem likely. IAS 7 offers no exemption on these, or any other grounds.

A statement of cash flows is required by IAS 7 and as a result the failure to include one will means the financial statements are not true and fair. This will require an adverse opinion.

A basis for adverse opinion will explain the reason for the adverse opinion. This section should be distinguishable from the opinion section by including a title 'Basis for Adverse Opinion'.

The fact that the audit opinion was similarly modified in the prior year shows that the matter has not been resolved. It is possible that the auditor thought it was an easy option to do the same again rather than draft a more appropriate opinion for the current year.

The 20X3 opinion makes no reference to the fact that the matter is not new and that the opinion was similarly modified in the prior year.

Test your understanding 11

(a) **Auditor's responsibilities for 'other information'**

The auditor has a professional responsibility to read other information to identify material inconsistencies with the audited financial statements (ISA 720 *The Auditor's Responsibilities Relating to Other Information in Documents Containing Audited Financial Statements*).

A material inconsistency arises when other information contradicts that which is contained in the audited financial statements or which contradicts information obtained by the auditor about the entity. It may give rise to doubts about:

– the auditor's conclusions drawn from the audit evidence
– the basis for the auditor's opinion on the financial statements.

In certain circumstances, the auditor may have a statutory obligation under national legislation to report on other information.

Even where there is no such obligation e.g. the chairman's statement, the auditor should read it for consistency, as the credibility of the financial statements may be undermined by any inconsistency.

If an inconsistency is identified, the auditor should determine whether it is the audited financial statements or the other information which needs amending.

If an amendment to the audited financial statements is required but not made, there will be misstatement. This may result in a qualified or adverse opinion.

Where an amendment to the other information is necessary but refused, the 'Other Information' section of the auditor's report should include a description of the inconsistency.

(b) **Implications for the auditor's report**

Management report

$4.5 million represents 3.75% of total assets, 1.7% of revenue and 48.9% profit before tax. This is material and the specific disclosure requirements need to be met.

The directors' report discloses the amount and the reason for a material change in equity. The financial statements do not show the reason for the change and suggest that it is immaterial. As the increase in equity attributable to this adjustment is nearly half as much as that attributable to PBT there is a material inconsistency between the directors' report and the audited financial statements.

Amendment to the financial statements is required because the disclosure is:

- incorrect – on first adoption of IAS 40 *Investment Property*, the fair value adjustment should be against the opening balance of retained earnings, and
- inadequate – because it is being supplemented by additional disclosure in a document which is not within the scope of the audit of financial statements.

Whilst it is true that the adoption of IAS 40 did not have a significant impact on results of operations, Hegas' financial position has increased by nearly 4% in respect of the revaluation to fair value of just one asset category (investment properties). As this is significant, the statement in the notes should be redrafted.

The matter is material but not pervasive, therefore if the financial statements are not amended, the auditor's opinion should be qualified 'except for' due to material misstatement caused by non-compliance with IAS 40.

The basis for qualified opinion should explain the reason for the qualified opinion and should quantify the effect of the material misstatement.

Chairman's statement

The assertion in the chairman's statement claims two things:

– the company is 'one of the world's largest generators of hydro-electricity', and

– the company has 'a dedicated commitment to accountable ethical professionalism'.

The first statement presents a misleading impression of the company's size. In misleading a user of the financial statements with this statement, the second statement is not true as it is not ethical or professional to mislead the reader and potentially undermine the credibility of the financial statements.

The first statement is materially inconsistent with the auditor's understanding of the entity because:

– the company is privately-owned, and publicly-owned international/multi-nationals are larger.

– the company's main activity is civil engineering not electricity generation (only 14% of revenue is derived from HEP).

– as the company ranks at best eighth against African companies alone it ranks much lower globally.

Hegas should be asked to remove these assertions from the chairman's statement.

If the statement is not changed there will be no grounds for modification of the opinion on the audited financial statements as the Chairman's statement does not form part of the financial statements.

The auditor's report however should be modified.

The 'Other Information' section will explain the inconsistency between the Chairman's statement and the auditor's understanding of the company.

chapter

24

References

Chapter learning objectives

References

The Board (2016) *IAS 1 Presentation of Financial Statements*. London: IFRS Foundation.

The Board (2016) *IAS 2 Inventories*. London: IFRS Foundation.

The Board (2016) *IAS 7 Statement of Cash Flows*. London: IFRS Foundation.

The Board (2016) *IAS 8 Accounting Policies, Changes in Accounting Estimates and Errors*. London: IFRS Foundation.

The Board (2016) *IAS 10 Events after the Reporting Period*. London: IFRS Foundation.

The Board (2016) *IAS 12 Income Taxes*. London: IFRS Foundation.

The Board (2016) *IAS 16 Property, Plant and Equipment*. London: IFRS Foundation.

The Board (2016) *IAS 19 Employee Benefits*. London: IFRS Foundation.

The Board (2016) *IAS 20 Accounting for Government Grants and Disclosure of Government Assistance*. London: IFRS Foundation.

The Board (2016) *IAS 21 The Effects of Changes in Foreign Exchange Rates*. London: IFRS Foundation.

The Board (2016) *IAS 23 Borrowing Costs*. London: IFRS Foundation.

The Board (2016) *IAS 24 Related Party Disclosures*. London: IFRS Foundation.

The Board (2016) *IAS 27 Separate Financial Statements*. London: IFRS Foundation.

The Board (2016) *IAS 28 Investments in Associates and Joint Ventures*. London: IFRS Foundation.

The Board (2016) *IAS 32 Financial Instruments: Presentation*. London: IFRS Foundation.

The Board (2016) *IAS 33 Earnings per Share*. London: IFRS Foundation.

The Board (2016) *IAS 36 Impairment of Assets*. London: IFRS Foundation.

The Board (2016) *IAS 37 Provisions, Contingent Liabilities and Contingent Assets*. London: IFRS Foundation.

The Board (2016) *IAS 38 Intangible Assets*. London: IFRS Foundation.

The Board (2016) *IAS 40 Investment Property*. London: IFRS Foundation.

The Board (2016) *IAS 41 Agriculture*. London: IFRS Foundation.

The Board (2016) *IFRS 1 First-time Adoption of International Financial Reporting Standards*. London: IFRS Foundation.

The Board (2016) *IFRS 2 Share-based Payment*. London: IFRS Foundation.

The Board (2016) *IFRS 3 Business Combinations*. London: IFRS Foundation.

The Board (2016) *IFRS 5 Non-current Assets Held for Sale and Discontinued Operations*. London: IFRS Foundation.

The Board (2016) *IFRS 7 Financial Instruments: Disclosure*. London: IFRS Foundation.

The Board (2016) *IFRS 8 Operating Segments*. London: IFRS Foundation.

The Board (2016) *IFRS 9 Financial Instruments*. London: IFRS Foundation.

The Board (2016) *IFRS 10 Consolidated Financial Statements*. London: IFRS Foundation.

The Board (2016) *IFRS 11 Joint Arrangements*. London: IFRS Foundation.

The Board (2016) *IFRS 12 Disclosure of Interests in Other Entities*. London: IFRS Foundation.

References

The Board (2016) *IFRS 13 Fair Value Measurement*. London: IFRS Foundation.

The Board (2016) *IFRS 15 Revenue from Contracts with Customers*. London: IFRS Foundation.

The Board (2016) *IFRS 16 Leases*. London: IFRS Foundation.

Index

A

ACCA Logo.....119

Accepting a new client or engagement.....78, 260, 465

Administration.....536

Adverse opinion.....343, 392, 394, 397

Advertising.....118

Advocacy threat.....36, 47

Allocation of assets (liquidation).....535

Analytical procedures.....203, 204, 292, 293, 348, 439, 468, 511

Anti-money laundering program.....146

Appointment as auditor.....17, 18, 71, 84

Approach to exam questions
  Auditor's reports.....404
  Completion.....354
  Due diligence.....447
  PFI.....471
  Risk assessment.....220

Assurance services.....2, 432

Attestation.....436, 485

Audit committees.....13

Audit procedures.....291, 317

Audit related services.....432

Auditor's reports.....367, 370, 374

Audit risk.....210, 267

Audit strategy.....200, 262

B

Bannerman.....173

Basis for paragraph.....370, 378, 393

Big data.....214

Business relationships.....40

Business risk.....210

C

Changing auditors.....134

Code of ethics.....31

Cold reviews.....96

Comparatives and corresponding figures.....352

Component auditor.....260

Compulsory liquidation.....534

Computer assisted audit techniques.....214, 319

Conceptual framework.....33

Confidentiality.....35, 54, 515

Conflicts of interest.....56

Consolidated financial statements.....258

Contingent fees.....41, 121

Corporate governance.....7

Creditor's voluntary liquidation.....533

Criminal liability.....171

Customer identification procedures.....147

D

Data analytics.....214

Direct engagement.....436

Disclaimer of opinion.....79, 261, 391, 392, 398

Documentation.....101, 316

Due diligence.....443

Duty of care.....170

E

Elements of an assurance engagement.....433

Emphasis of matter paragraph.....339, 343, 352, 383

Engagement letter.....81

Engagement performance (QC).....93

Engagement quality control review.....94

Enron.....12

Estimates and fair values.....311, 313

Ethical threats.....35

Etiquette letter.....79

Evaluation of misstatements.....349

Evidence.....290

Expectation gap.....175, 380

Experts.....298

External confirmations.....294

F

Familiarity threat.....36, 41

Fee dependency.....38

Final analytical procedures.....347

Financial interests.....39

Financial reporting revision.....561

Financial statement assertions.....291

Forecast.....465

Forensic audits.....507

Fraud and error.....163

Fraudulent trading.....540

Fundamental principles.....33, 514

G

Global regulation.....3, 4

Globalisation.....4, 273

Going concern.....340

Index

Group audits.....257
- Acceptance.....260
- Audit procedures.....269
- Audit risks.....267
- Completion.....270
- Component auditor.....261, 263, 265
- Consolidation schedule.....269
- Engagement letter.....83
- Materiality.....263
- Non-coterminous year ends.....268
- Planning.....262
- Reporting.....271
- Review of work.....270
- Risk assessment.....267
- Significant component.....262
- Understanding the client.....262

H

Hospitality.....39

Hot reviews.....94

Human resources (QC).....92

I

IAASB.....2

IFAC.....3, 4, 5

Independent verification statements.....492

Individual voluntary arrangements.....538

Informed management.....37

Initial engagement planning.....201

Initial engagements – opening balances.....351

Insolvency.....532

Integrated reporting.....483

Integrity.....34, 514

Internal audit.....300

Internal control.....205

Intimidation threat.....36, 47

ISA 200.....157, 203, 206, 315

ISA 210.....82

ISA 220.....91, 101

ISA 230.....316

ISA 240.....163

ISA 250.....156

ISA 260.....315, 422

ISA 265.....425

ISA 300.....262, 315

ISA 315.....201, 203, 223, 315, 389

ISA 320.....206, 315

ISA 330.....202, 316, 320

ISA 402.....305

ISA 450.....163, 349

ISA 500.....290

ISA 501.....314

ISA 505.....294

ISA 510.....201, 351

ISA 530.....295

ISA 540.....311

ISA 550.....310

ISA 560.....336

ISA 570.....340

ISA 580.....296, 391

ISA 600.....224, 260

ISA 610.....300

ISA 620.....298

ISA 700.....368

ISA 701.....388

ISA 705.....296, 382

ISA 706.....382

ISA 710.....352

ISA 720.....382

ISAE 3000.....448, 554

ISAE 3400.....464

ISAE 3402.....307

ISAE 3420.....453

ISQC 1.....91

ISRE 2400.....437

ISRE 2410.....438

J

Joint audits.....272

K

Key audit matters.....388, 424

Key performance indicators.....485

L

Laws and regulations.....156

Leadership (QC).....92

Legal liability.....170

Letters of support.....271

Limited assurance.....434, 436

Limiting liability.....175

Liquidation.....532

Litigation.....41

Loans.....40

Long association.....42

Lowballing.....121